ALFRED H. BARR JR.
MISSIONARY
for the MODERN

ALFRED H. BARR JR.

MISSIONARY for the MODERN

Alice Goldfarb Marquis

CB
CONTEMPORARY
BOOKS
CHICAGO · NEW YORK

Library of Congress Cataloging-in-Publication Data

Marquis, Alice Goldfarb.
    Alfred H. Barr, Jr. : missionary for the modern / Alice Goldfarb
Marquis.
        p.   cm.
    Bibliography: p.
    Includes index.
    ISBN 0-8092-4404-7 : $21.95
    1. Barr. Alfred Hamilton, 1902–1981.   2. Art directors—United
States—Biography.   3. Museum of Modern Art (New York, N.Y.)—
History.   I. Title.
N620.M9M37   1989
709'.2'4—dc19
[B]   88-34261
                                                                                              CIP

Published by Contemporary Books, Inc.
180 North Michigan Avenue, Chicago, Illinois 60601
Manufactured in the United States of America
Library of Congress Catalog Card Number: 88-34261
International Standard Book Number: 0-8092-4404-7

Published simultaneously in Canada by Beaverbooks, Ltd.
195 Allstate Parkway, Valleywood Business Park
Markham, Ontario L3R 4T8 Canada

To my sister, Suzanne Atkins,
who has heard it all

Contents

ACKNOWLEDGMENTS

W riting a biography of a near-contemporary figure calls for the cooperation of an extraordinary array of individuals—the friends, colleagues, and associates of the subject. In this regard, I was honored to engage the help of more than sixty people who were close to Alfred H. Barr, Jr., both professionally and personally. They gave generously of their time and insights, several of them on more than one occasion, and are named both in the text and in the footnotes.

Many libraries and archives were helpful, including the Museum of Modern Art Library, the Archives of American Art in Washington and Detroit, and the Huntington Library in San Marino, California. The Central University Library of the University of California at San Diego was, as always, my nearest and dearest resource, especially chief librarian Dorothy Gregor and reference librarian Sue Galloway. The reference department of the San Diego Public Library, particularly Eileen J. Reynolds and Jessiemay Faith, encouraged my presence for some three years and expedited the busy traffic in microfilm between San Diego and the Detroit branch of the Archives of American Art.

The Department of History at the University of California shaped me as a historian and continues to encourage my efforts. I still write with my mentor, H. Stuart Hughes, in mind. Allan Mitchell and David Luft sponsored me as a visiting scholar in the department and have consistently encouraged me as an independent scholar. Most helpful also was my "surrogate department," San Diego Independent Scholars, many of whose members shared the insights of disciplines other than mine for the benefit of this work.

This book would have looked different and taken far longer without the computer wizardry generously given by my son, John Blankfort. And when a new word processor became unavoidable, the professionals at Byte & Floppy Computers in San Diego provided lightning service to keep the manuscript flowing.

Two magnificent friends devoted many hours to listening to my obsession and weeks to close reading of the manuscript, always providing many valuable suggestions for improvement. Reva Greenburg carted all 600 pages on a European trip in order to meet the deadline. Ariss Treat-Sedgwick took weeks out of a vacation in Italy to read, correct, and comment. When these two skeptical readers as well as devoted friends had questions, I was forced to clarify, amend, and rethink. My editor at Contemporary Books, Bernard Shir-Cliff, read the manuscript with uncommon care and insight, giving constructive and specific suggestions in the spirit of a friend and colleague. I appreciate the eagle eyes and sharp mind of copy editor Karin Horgan.

During my many research trips to New York, I was pampered with the affection and intelligence of Freda and James Polak, Suzanne and Richard Atkins, and Steven Watson, who was always generous in sharing his research in a neighboring field.

Among the host of friends who shared my agonies and languors and joys during the four-year gestation of this book—and who aided me physically and spiritually—were Joseph Abrahams, Kimberley and James Barter, James Bubar, Jody and Dave Chambless, Jane Ford, Gerson Greenburg, Dorothy and David Hewes, Gerry and Robert Horwitz, Paul and Luisa Larson, Betty and Sol Lubin, Tiffany Modell, Peter and Maryanne Powell, Marion Steinberg, Norma Sullivan, John Treat-Sedgwick, and Tom Trunnell. Julie

Castiglia and Bill Gladstone are not just my agents but also my friends.

The help without which no book would have materialized came generously, kindly, and wisely; errors or omissions are my own fault.

Alice Goldfarb Marquis
La Jolla, California

ALFRED H. BARR JR. MISSIONARY for the MODERN

1

GENESIS

When Alfred H. Barr, Jr., opened the Museum of Modern Art in late November 1929, only a small coterie of wealthy collectors had ever heard of modern art and few of them had any notion of what kind of art was "modern," or why, or where it came from. As for the general public, art of any kind seemed a remote and fussy occupation of maiden ladies and effete keepers of museums. Nevertheless, most people believed that looking at art was good for you, a worthwhile way to fill a rainy afternoon, an attenuated brush with genius. For schoolchildren, a visit to an art museum was widely believed to be a tonic. Led by their teachers on an annual field trip through awesomely still halls, they gazed hopefully at cows peacefully grazing under Dutch clouds or giggled over naked ladies reclining on red plush. These were the masterpieces of the past, their guide would tell them, and the children wondered when it would be time to eat their sack lunches outside in the park.

Among newspaper and magazine editors, staunchly philistine gatekeepers of American culture, art was good for an occasional feature story, especially that strange phenomenon, modern art,

1

whose practitioners did bizarre things. There was that French fellow who abandoned his family and painted savages in Tahiti and the Dutchman who cut off his ear. More recently, there had been a black-eyed Spaniard who painted freakish-looking fat ladies and daubed angular lines on a canvas, claiming that this was a portrait of a girl with a mandolin.

In 1913 quite a few people in New York, Boston, and Chicago had trooped through an exhibition where these affronts to the eye were actually on display. Former president Theodore Roosevelt had gazed at one canvas there and declared that it looked like an explosion in a shingle factory. Cartoonists had rushed to lampoon this work, Marcel Duchamp's *Nude Descending a Staircase*, with depictions of a subway mob titled "The Rude Descending the Staircase" and of mobile cherries and melons titled "Food Descending the Staircase."

Fortunately, Americans had been able to beat back the artistic outrages displayed at the 1913 Armory Show. Or so it seemed to the native guardians of traditional art. Word occasionally filtered into print that certain madmen in Europe were creating even more bizarre visual phenomena—blue horses, green faces, little drips and squirts of color that refused to divulge even by their titles the answer to: "What is it?"

But Americans were largely spared exposure to such baffling works of art. They listened to jazz and felt no need to ask, "What does it mean?" They took Sunday drives in their new automobiles without inquiring into the significance of such an aimless activity. They built skyscrapers designed to look like Gothic cathedrals, snug in the belief that they were importing Old World culture. They bought radios that looked like Louis XVI cabinets and were sure that their cultivation would impress the Joneses.

Alfred Barr charged into this smug atmosphere with all the missionary zeal of a tent revivalist. A young man of twenty-seven, he was determined to rattle the foundations of American provincialism. An unlikely looking reformer, a tall and stooping bean pole with severe wire-rimmed spectacles on his nose, he told people that some factory buildings were beautiful architecture and that they could find art at the movies. He sent them out to the dime store in search of handsome cereal bowls and made them study advertisements for the quality of their typographical design.

Most important of all, he created a museum that introduced Americans to the art of their own time. It was not hushed and somnolent, nor did it intimidate visitors with lofty vaulting or unexplained gatherings of "masterpieces." In Barr's museum, wall labels, booklets, handbills, and catalogs attempted to explain what people were seeing, why the artists were doing these peculiar things, and what was important, interesting, and enjoyable about them.

A minister's son from Baltimore, Barr knew his Bible and had no qualms about preaching a revolutionary doctrine. In his baggy tweed jacket, he charged across the American cultural landscape, jabbing at the cobwebs of old-fashioned aesthetics and musty design. A quintessential American, he briskly, relentlessly prodded and shamed and proselytized his countrymen into embracing his vision of modern art. Wrathful as an Old Testament prophet, he did battle with the ever-present philistines and harried them even as they fled.

This book is the story of his life. It is also the story of a fascinating passage in American history, of an adventuresome odyssey in which the American people traveled from the periphery to the heartland of Western culture. The day came when they stood in line for hours in the cold to glimpse the pictures the crazy Dutchman had painted, and eagerly paid scalpers' prices to view the Spaniard's ingenious fantasies. Art became an essential part of their lives.

Alfred Barr forever changed American taste as he changed the look and atmosphere and content of art museums around the world. His books, exhibition catalogs, and articles gave modern art a language, a literature, and a history. The collection he amassed for the Museum of Modern Art remains the definitive statement of the visual arts in the twentieth century. Righteously, zealously, stubbornly, Alfred Barr hewed the pillars which continue to frame for us the art of our time.

2
A LONG LINE
OF PREACHERS

L ong before anyone anywhere could imagine that a soup can could be a meaningful work of art, the skyline of the city of Baltimore was dominated by a giant icon of American inventiveness and ultimate kitsch. In the heart of downtown, Capt. Isaac Emerson constructed a 357-foot tower, a monument not only to the pluck and resiliency of a city whose entire commercial area had been devastated by fire in 1904 but also to the brash ingenuity and merchandising skill of early twentieth-century America. The fire had destroyed eighty-six blocks in the heart of the city, 140 acres, the worst urban blaze in America since the great Chicago fire of 1871. Captain Emerson's tower symbolized Baltimoreans' defiance of adversity and their determination to build more grandly on the ashes. Its rusticated stone and Italianate arches added up to a vaguely Florentine Renaissance ensemble, a fine example of the flamboyant borrowings from the cookbook of historic styles so beloved by American architects of the day.

Planted at the summit of its complex arches, pediments, and pilasters derived from the European past was a gigantic emblem of the American present, a loving replica of a bottle of Bromo-

Seltzer. A headache powder concocted to cure his wife's migraine when he was a poor drug clerk in Annapolis, it had made Captain Emerson one of Baltimore's richest men. The model of the bright blue bottle which had made Captain Emerson's fortune was a million times larger than the original ten-cent item. It weighed seventeen tons and glowed in the nighttime Baltimore sky with the lights from 596 electric bulbs inside it.

In 1911, Captain Emerson built an elaborate town house on Eutaw Place, Baltimore's most exclusive street. Around the house he installed spacious Italian gardens. To shelter all this opulence from the crowds of plain Baltimore folks passing by on Sundays on their way to Druid Hill Park, the captain ordered construction of a high stone wall, studded at the top with sparkling glass shards of a blue familiar to all—broken Bromo-Seltzer bottles.

To the end of his days, Alfred Barr would fulminate against the kind of provincial bad taste so blatantly displayed in Baltimore, the city where he grew up. He detested the excesses of commercial zeal to which Americans were prone and the poor design which often resulted. He was infuriated by architecture mindlessly replicating the great buildings of the past. He inveighed sternly against those who were uninterested in or even mocked the art of their own time, people who echoed the favorite song of Baltimore's Hamilton Street Men's Club: "In art I pull no highbrow stuff, I know what I like and that's enough."

Baltimore in the first two decades of the twentieth century was an unlikely place to nourish a youngster who would grow up to revolutionize American taste. A city of brick, brownstone, or whitestone row houses with distinctive white stoops, its considerable black population was tucked into crowded pockets of shanties, all but invisible to the casual visitor. A busy port and manufacturing center, the city nevertheless cultivated the genteel airs of the South, and grew large in the shadow of Washington, D.C.

In 1911, when the Barr family moved to Baltimore from Detroit with their two sons, seven-year-old Andrew and nine-year-old Alfred, Baltimore citizens took great pride that peaches began arriving at the outdoor markets as early as June and strawberries were to be had as late as October. "The moderately circumstanced can eat soft-shell crabs by the dozen, and the really impoverished buy oysters by the barrel." The ubiquitous white stoops were not simply an architectural feature of the city but a moral symbol, "the outward and visible sign of thrift, neatness, a kind of guarantee that within, too, there are cleanliness and all the domestic virtues. . . . It will be an evil day for Baltimore," wrote a contemporary observer, "when she gives up this emblem of her civilization."

The year Barr's father was called to Baltimore's First Presbyterian Church, the city was festively honoring its outstanding religious figure: James Cardinal Gibbons was celebrating his fiftieth anniversary as a priest and his twenty-fifth anniversary as cardinal. A month after the Reverend Barr preached his first sermon, he was among the many clergymen of all denominations who attended the cardinal's majestic rites, which also drew Pres. William Howard Taft and former president Theodore Roosevelt.

The cardinal's importance in the life of the city bespoke the large and long-standing role of Catholics in Baltimore. The city's outstanding architectural landmark was its neoclassical cathedral, designed by Benjamin Latrobe, the chief architect of the Capitol in Washington. In the late nineteenth and early twentieth centuries, the long-established, largely German, Catholic community swelled with the arrival of waves of immigrants who came to work in the city's industrial outskirts, to labor on its busy docks, to fish in Chesapeake Bay, and to enliven the city's colorful outdoor markets. Catholics joined with severe southern-style Protestants to maintain Baltimore's strict blue laws. To appease this vocal minority, the city council in February 1914 rejected a proposal to permit Sunday baseball.

Baltimore also took extremely seriously its position as the birthplace of "The Star-Spangled Banner." In July 1916, in a burst of patriotism only partly caused by the war in Europe, the city council made it a misdemeanor to fail to stand during the singing of "The Star-Spangled Banner." In November 1917, some six months after the United States entered the First World War, a Boston Symphony concert was actually canceled in Baltimore because of a controversy over how and when the national anthem would be played. Barr's lifelong suspicion of mindless patriotism probably was a reaction against such misguided zeal. Baltimore's patriotic excesses in 1916 and 1917 were symptoms of a nationwide

wave of chauvinism as the country hovered on the brink of entering
the First World War, but the city's chauvinistic fever may also have
been aggravated by excessive local pride; the city council had just
appropriated $6,000 for establishing its own symphony orchestra,
had authorized planning for an art museum, and encouraged the
founding of the Vagabond Players, America's oldest Little Theater.

This cultural surge was built upon unprecedented prosperity in
Baltimore, as both sides in the European war poured orders into
American factories and ports like Baltimore burgeoned with piers
and ships. Caribbean oil fields and mines fed refineries and a steel
mill nearby, contributing to record growth in 1915 and 1916 and
even faster growth after the United States entered the war. By
1927, the city was producing 800 million tin cans for New Jersey
packers, while canning more tomatoes and producing more fertil-
izer than any other city in the country. It also manufactured
enough straw hats to cover the head of every adult male in New
York, Chicago, Philadelphia, and Detroit and enough umbrellas to
shelter at least half of those hats. Baltimore also led the world in
production of overalls, pajamas, middy blouses, and bottle
stoppers. A visitor was aghast at the ugliness such sprawling
industry had brought; Baltimore "had studied ugliness and raised
it to a fine art," wrote Gerald W. Johnson mockingly, "so that in the
end it has become a work of genius more fascinating than spick-
and-span tidiness could ever be."

Among those who allowed the city to descend into such notable
urban disarray was a remarkably frivolous elite, its money derived
from old shipping and railroads or new industries, its status rein-
forced by the city's pretensions to southern society. The petty
diversions of Baltimore's idle rich attained a climax on May 18 and
19, 1914, when George Howell Parr set a world's record for rolling.
Trained by his two brothers, garbed in football pants, his hands
bandaged and pads affixed to his elbows, knees, and "other vulnerable spots," the young man rolled his body over a 15,580-foot
course. He did not smoke or eat during his ordeal, but the record is
silent on whether (or what) he drank. The feat took fifteen hours,
ten minutes, including a few brief rests on a mattress dragged
along by his brother. After a bath and a brief rest, George appeared at the Pimlico Race Track to collect his bets.

This was exactly the sort of dissolute excess that parishioners of the Reverend Barr's church would deplore. Though second to none in the staunchness of their faith, Baltimore's Presbyterians were conservatively middle class. The city's elite, more than 36 percent of the business elite and 62 percent of those in the Social Register, belonged to the Protestant Episcopal Church. The Presbyterians attracted only 21 percent of the business elite and 13 percent in the Social Register.

Most members of the First Presbyterian Church were middling people, sober shopkeepers, modest professionals, managers of smaller enterprises, many of them of Scottish or Irish Protestant background. The oldest Presbyterian church in the city, it had been founded in 1761 and in its early years included among its members some of Baltimore's wealthiest merchants; its first minister, the Reverend Dr. Patrick Allison had been a friend of George Washington and a champion of religious freedom. The church the Reverend Barr took over in 1911 had been built in the 1870s during the forty-year tenure (1836–1875) of John Chester Backus. The location for the dignified Victorian Gothic edifice, at the intersection of Park and Madison avenues, was then considered "the centre of fashion." Under the Reverend Backus's leadership and with the financial support of generous parishioners, the church had founded eighteen other Presbyterian churches in the city of Baltimore.

During the thirty years before the Reverend Barr arrived on the scene, however, many apartment houses had been built in the neighborhood, and more substantial residents were moving into new single-family houses to the north and west of the church. In 1910, the year before the Barrs arrived, only one among ten elders and only five among twelve trustees had been baptized in the church. Where previously the Sunday school's pupils were mostly children of church members, by 1910 they were gathered largely from outside the congregation.

To halt this decline in the church's prestige may well have been the reason church elders called the Reverend Alfred Hamilton Barr to Baltimore in 1911. He held bachelor and master of divinity degrees from Princeton Theological Seminary, the oldest and most prestigious Presbyterian seminary in America. It must have appealed to the middling trustees of the Baltimore church, mostly

self-made men, that the new pastor was a serious scholar; he had
supported himself at Princeton by teaching Greek at a nearby
boarding school. Faced with a dwindling congregation of substantial people, the trustees would also have been impressed that, for
the previous fifteen years, as pastor of the Jefferson Avenue Presbyterian Church in Detroit, the Reverend Barr had concentrated
on missionary work among the ethnic immigrants attracted to the
steady, relatively well-paid work in the fledgling automobile plants
around the city. Baltimore too offered a fertile missionary field
among newly arrived immigrants.

In an era when many upwardly mobile young men would move to
churches that matched their ambitions, the Reverend Barr also had
an impeccably Presbyterian background. His father, the Reverend
John Campbell Barr was a Presbyterian minister in Geneseo,
Illinois, when his son was born in 1868. A year after arriving in
Detroit, the Reverend Barr had married Annie Elizabeth Wilson,
whose father was minister of the First Presbyterian Church in
Indiana, Pennsylvania. Her brother was also a Presbyterian minister, educated at Princeton, where he stayed on for three decades as
professor of Semitic languages. While laboring in Detroit, the
Reverend Barr had continued his education as well, receiving a
degree of doctor of divinity from Alma College in Michigan in
1910.

The move to Baltimore also confirmed the Reverend Barr's
rising prestige within the councils of the Presbyterian church. In
that year, he became a director of the Princeton Theological Seminary and took an active role in the Presbyterian church's governing
body, serving on the general assembly's committee on Christian
life and work, the general board of education, the committee on
evangelism, and a committee which organized the Presbyterian
Brotherhood, a nationwide men's club which could offer ambitious
members a useful network of contacts while strengthening male
membership in individual churches. This was the model for Alfred
Barr's perpetual drive to join a multitude of organizations, stretching the time he could devote to them far beyond the breaking point.

The Presbyterian church at the turn of the century was at the
crest of a missionary wave. Church magazines and books were
filled with accounts of how nine hundred churches in Fiji had

weaned the heathen from cannibalism and other "atrocious customs," that "Arabia is promised for Christ," and that, indeed, "the
evangelization of the world" was at hand. To speed this millen-
nium, ministers were advised to preach a missionary sermon
whenever their congregations became lax in contributions; parishioners were to be "kept in an habitual and alarming sense of the . . .
wretched, terrible state of the heathen."

Whatever his sermon topic might be, his parishioners were
grateful that the Reverend Barr "relied less upon rhetorical methods than upon direct exposition of Christian teachings." The author
of the First Presbyterian Church's official history recalled his
talent for interpreting scriptures "in relation to people and their
needs, rather than in abstract philosophical terms." The Reverend
Barr also paid close heed to the church's financial health. When he
arrived in Baltimore, a drive to raise a $100,000 endowment had
been languishing since 1905, with only $67,300 subscribed. Some
$25,000 of this amount was contingent on obtaining an additional
$75,000 before January 1, 1912. By some miracles of persuasion,
perhaps making his move to the church contingent upon additional
pledges, the Reverend Barr raised the full $75,000 before the end
of his first month in Baltimore.

Alfred Barr, Jr., learned the art of extracting large and small
contributions from the wealthy—and supporters of modest
means—while growing up in Baltimore. Like a pastor, he was able
to keep his eyes focused firmly upon the spiritual, while constantly
reminding his followers of their material obligations. Building
funds, endowments, anniversary gifts, bequests, pledges—the
whole panoply of fund-raising techniques familiar in a religious
context eventually found their way into the Museum of Modern
Art's operations.

In May 1911, the Barrs moved from Detroit into a spacious,
simplified Victorian house, then called the Backus House and now
renamed the Patrick Allison Mission House. Solidly built of red
brick with brownstone trim, it was at 808 Park Avenue, adjacent to
the church. Alfred Hamilton (after his grandmother and father),
born on January 28, 1902, was nine years old; his brother, Andrew
Wilson (after his mother), was two years younger. The interior was
by no means somber, Barr's childhood friend Edward S. King

recalled; it was "homelike and comfortable." An important part of the household was Reverend Barr's copious library, books which he frequently consulted, opening a volume "readily to the page in mind" and then reading a section "with a kind of affection." He was "a connoisseur of literature and ideas," King recalled, and also a spellbinding storyteller. For the boys who sought him out in his study, he would relate "with great drama," for example, his own version of Conan Doyle's *Hound of the Baskervilles*.

Barr's mother was an enthusiastic, energetic lady who was also pious and replete with old-fashioned virtue. She had attended Vassar College for two years, from 1887 to 1889, rare for a woman in her day. According to one of her son's close associates later in his life, she was "a difficult taskmaster, very strict and stern." Like a typical minister's wife at the time, she participated fully in her husband's duties, calling on parishioners, teaching a Bible class, taking a leading role in the various women's groups, offering hospitality to various church groups meeting in her home. To a successful minister, his wife's total, unquestioning identification with his career was essential. For her son, Mrs. Barr was a model of what he would expect in a wife.

The Reverend Barr seems to have been an expansive, gregarious man who enjoyed the casual socializing that the ministry entails. He was a Democrat and outspoken in his liberal views. Edward King recalled once bursting into the reverend's study during a conference with another minister and indulgently being permitted to hold forth on his current enthusiasm: phrenology. After listening to King at some length, both men docilely submitted to having their heads measured. Barr's mother, by contrast, seemed to be one of those parents who worry that their children will become spoiled by experiencing too much success. When she learned of one of Alfred's childhood triumphs, she tartly reminded him, "Don't get a swelled head."

Nevertheless, Barr's parents had wide interests and involved their children in them. During a summer vacation in the Poconos in 1903, eighteen-month-old prodigy Alfred delighted mother and father, both avid bird-watchers, by crawling under a spruce tree and discovering a whippoorwill's nest. In pursuit of bird-watching, then a newly discovered pastime, the Barrs also spent two summers at Magnetawan in the Canadian wilderness, some two hundred miles north of Toronto, when Barr was around ten years old, to "collect" seldom-seen birds.

In 1915, when Barr was thirteen, the family began spending summers in Greensboro, Vermont, where they built a modest cottage. This was a vacation colony in the Green Mountains near the Canadian border. The advent of the automobile made it accessible for families to spend summer months there, away from the oppressive heat in eastern cities. Like many such communities at that time, Greensboro enforced rigid restrictive covenants against sales of property to blacks or Jews. However, the undemocratic discrimination spelled out in the fine print in property deeds was so common that it went totally unnoticed among the professionals, academics (especially from Princeton), writers, and Protestant clergymen who settled in the forest around the frigid mountain lake.

Despite his gangling unathletic frame and bookish bent, Barr enthusiastically reveled in the icy waters of Greensboro's lake and in the hearty outdoor pleasures the area offered. In 1917, a gang of young people from Baltimore stayed with the Barrs at their summer home. Very early one morning, they marched off on a twenty-five-mile hike to Mount Mansfield. As they straggled wearily back, Barr kept the company from dwelling on its aching legs by whistling tunes from all the operas he knew by heart.

His mother may have worried about his getting a swelled head, but her son's precocious childhood achievements must have been a source of pride. A studious boy not given to pranks, he roamed Baltimore with his friend Edward King, hunting for butterflies, which they both collected. "I only knew their common names," King recalled, "but Alfred knew all the scientific names too." On Saturday mornings they would head for the Enoch Pratt Free Library to select their weekly ration of volumes by H. G. Wells and, their favorite, Arthur Conan Doyle. Barr also collected stamps and maintained lists of birds he had seen, hobbies he would pursue for the rest of his life. He used tin soldiers to recreate famous battles, such as Gettysburg and Waterloo, developing a fascination with military history which also continued all his life. At the weekly meetings of the Boy Scout troop his father had founded at the

church, Barr would frequently hold forth about another of his
interests, prehistoric animals, while King sketched them on the
chalkboard.

King's father was the kind of successful middling entrepreneur
who formed the backbone of the First Presbyterian Church's congregation. He had founded a small bank and a storage company,
which flourished until the Great Depression. Like most children of
his station, King was raised by a black nanny, an upright lady who
wore high-necked black taffeta dresses even in the cruel heat and
humidity of summer. If he didn't eat up, she would warn him, the
Bad Man would come. Cowed, little Edward invariably cleaned his
plate. When King was a schoolboy, his father's vans were as yet
unmotorized. At the beginning of each summer, his father would
buy an extra horse from the livery stable for the boys to ride during
vacation. Along with Barr, King was sent to Boys' Latin School, the
best among several private schools in the city.

There, Barr's phenomenal memory and studious habits brought
him immediate recognition. He knew the names of all the English
rulers by heart, perhaps another side of his penchant for collecting,
and associated each name with what he or she had done. He was the
only boy in the school who studied Greek, coached perhaps by his
father. When occasionally he strayed from what was expected of
the head boy, which he always was, the headmaster would cry,
"Alfred, where's your Greek?" Slender and bespectacled, Barr also
was highly strung and prone to vague illnesses. He played tennis
but did not participate in organized sports, although he was loyal
to the school's teams. Still, King thought him "courageous . . . not
afraid of anything except the dentist . . . he was undaunted."

Barr's own recollections, as he wrote them for the school's newspaper in 1934, began with his initiation into Baltimore's southern
ways as a boy of nine. "I had supposed that the Civil War had been
forgiven and forgotten, save as history," he wrote, but as a Yankee
from Detroit, he had to defend himself with a ruler wrapped in
newspapers and occasionally stayed inside during recess to avoid
attack. Frail even then, he most admired a fellow student, said to
have the finest physique in the school's history and who could swim
two lengths of pool underwater without coming up for breath. He
also recalled a legendary football game in which Boys' Latin

defeated its traditional rivals, Gilman Country School, 84-0. "After this famous victory over Gilman, a legend was revived among the Lower Forms," he wrote, "telling of how twenty years before a Boys' Latin School crew (!) had beaten the Navy at Annapolis and how a Boys' Latin School football team had beaten Princeton 30-3." He contrasted these feats with his own performance as an end on the third team playing against the Institute for the Blind. "We were outweighed twenty or thirty pounds to the man, but fortunately the blind back sometimes ran in the wrong direction."

Barr also reminisced about a Latin teacher who instructed his charges in declensions by twisting their ears and about the headmaster who was reputed to see everything that went on behind his back. "After careful study we discovered that he used his glasses as a mirror." Another Latin teacher brought a toy catapult to school and fired a soap eraser at the worst boy in the class. Describing the Germanii, who confronted Caesar so barbarically, this teacher "would seize a yardstick, brandish it as a spear, and stamp about the room, to our great satisfaction."

In June of 1918, at the age of sixteen, Barr graduated at the head of his class and spoke as valedictorian. The school newspaper, *The Inkwell*, which Barr edited, described him as "a sincere nut of the silent but deadly type." The author of the newspaper's article admired his calm, insight, wide knowledge, and sense of humor, adding that "he shows the human faculty of acquisitiveness in the form of a collector of stamps, butterflies, botanical specimens, and many other oddities. . . . He can't understand how anyone can fill up on sodas, smoke cigarettes, or bet on horses." His Latin and Greek teacher gave Barr a copy of Henry Adams's *Mont St. Michel and Chartres*, which Barr later credited with turning his attention for the first time to the history of art. However, he still was more interested in paleontology and planned to pursue studies in this field when he entered Princeton on a scholarship in the fall.

The First World War was cannonading bloodily toward its conclusion that summer, even as young men all across America schemed and dreamed of going "over there." In Baltimore, where one-third of the population was of German extraction, the war fever may have been a shade muted. Nevertheless, the city experienced its greatest industrial growth immediately after the United States entered the war in 1917. The Reverend Barr felt "a terrible sense of agony" over American involvement in the war, but he did his bit when needed. Late one evening, an entire company of soldiers arrived in the city and had no place to stay. "The cushions of the church pews were reversed," related the church's official history, "and the men had shelter for the night in the sanctuary itself."

As he had been in Detroit, the Reverend Barr was a diligent missionary in Baltimore. The Presbyterian church as a whole was the most active among Protestant proselytizers, both in the United States and abroad. In Detroit, a frequent houseguest of the Barrs had been Henry Luce, the father of the publishing tycoon. He had founded an important university in China as a Presbyterian institution and tirelessly traveled the circuit of American churches to raise money. In Baltimore too the Reverend Barr's congregation contributed generously to missionary work. When the church celebrated its sesquicentennial with eight days of festivities, November 9–16, 1913, the guest of honor was Robert E. Speer, secretary of the Presbyterian Board of Foreign Missions. Within his first five years in Baltimore, the Reverend Barr established the Reid Memorial Mission in a poorer neighborhood, staffed at first by a lay assistant and later by a full minister. In 1916, the church also hired an assistant pastor, partly because the Reverend Barr's health was precarious.

In his fifth-anniversary sermon, an occasion deemed by the church trustees as worthy of a printed booklet, the Reverend Barr stressed the importance of missionary outreach. "A mother church has great privileges. Her members have that soil of tradition and memory into which loyalty strikes deep roots," he told the congregation on Sunday, May 7, 1916. But he also stressed a mother church's obligations "to produce in her own fold a type of layman especially catholic in sympathy, liberal in gifts and outlook, and broadly representative in church matters. A church to which many other churches look as mother owes it to them as well as to herself to keep well housed and nourished and prosperous."

Fourteen-year-old Alfred, listening from his dark-varnished wooden pew on that day, drew precepts from this sermon, one of many in a similar vein, that would reverberate throughout his life. The church's endowment, his father said, was a critical part of its "life and usefulness." He quoted a prominent church leader who had stated that "the argument for the endowed church is the unendowed church," and therefore he was pleased that the First Presbyterian Church endowment, his first accomplishment upon arriving in Baltimore, was continuing to grow. But it was still insufficient, the pastor said, a lack which "may well be considered by members . . . when making their last Will and Testament."

While the son would devote his life to missionary work in a nonreligious realm, he drew again and again on the ideas and methods expounded so eloquently by his father. He, too, would contend with raising funds for an endowment and with rousing adherents into generous bequests. The combination of worthy ideas and the need for money to spread them echoed and reechoed in Barr's later accomplishments.

The building in which his father spoke, and which he had ample time to study during many, many Sunday services, also left a strong impression on the young man. Completed in 1873, the interior was lit by ten windows, Gothic in shape and filled with the style of stained glass most admired in late nineteenth-century America: large panes garishly painted to resemble hand-pieced glass, illustrating Bible scenes in saccharine detail. Everything about the church's interior was reminiscent of something else, somewhere else, some other time, a flamboyant display of late nineteenth-century eclecticism. The elaborate fan vaulting in the ceiling referred to the Henry VII Chapel in Westminster Abbey; the intricate foilage on the ceiling was a plaster replica of Gothic carvings at Winchester Cathedral; the fronts of the balcony and the entrance doors were hand-grained to resemble genuine walnut when, in fact, they were white pine. This was the kind of brazen, derivative fakery that Alfred Barr would ringingly denounce as the worst sin of retrograde American architects.

There was no hint in Barr's early environment of the architectural revolution that was already gathering in Europe or even any echoes of the stylistic innovations being pioneered by Louis Sullivan and Frank Lloyd Wright elsewhere in America. In Baltimore, the 150-odd years from the early nineteenth century to the 1960s were an architectural black hole. In G. E. Kidder-Smith's authoritative three-volume survey of American architecture (published in association with the Museum of Modern Art), no new Baltimore building was considered worthy of discussion after the Latrobe Cathedral of 1821 until Mies van der Rohe's Highfield House apartments of 1965.

In the fine arts, too, Baltimore seemed singularly deprived, for a city of its size, during the years Barr was growing up there. The only significant art collection had been gathered by William Walters and later by his son, Henry. While the Walters Gallery is now one of two major museums in Baltimore, it was in those days more an idiosyncratic accumulation of costly curiosities than a museum; an expensive attic stuffed with sculpture, porcelain, tapestries, armor, precious stones, minerals, and almost a thousand paintings. The nucleus of the collection had been formed during the Civil War, when William Walters, a Confederate sympathizer in a Union city, stayed in Europe. When he returned after the war, he chartered a ship to bring home all his purchases.

Housed in crowded annexes to the Walters home, the collection was open to the public only twenty days per year. A photo of its galleries from the turn of the twentieth century shows a dark-clad bearded visitor crouched upon an upholstered bench to contemplate pictures crammed three-deep on ornately tapestried walls amid heavy, dark wooden cases packed with bibelots and artifacts. Henry Walters gave it all to the city in 1931, along with 25 percent of his estate for maintenance. Alfred Barr's friend from his youth, Edward King, became its director and until his retirement in 1966 labored to prune and shape the unfocused *omnium gatherum* into a meaningful museum.

Baltimore's few art collectors, like most American collectors of that day, favored the undemanding canvases of Corot and Daubigny, if they could afford them, and lesser French and German genre painters, if they could not. Startling exceptions were the Cone sisters: Claribel, who was the first woman to receive a medical degree from Johns Hopkins, and Etta, her shy and shrinking shadow. Assimilated Jews and the only two of their parents' twelve children who did not marry, they disposed of a handsome fortune from their father's southern cotton mills. In 1901, the pair made the first of twenty-eight trips to Europe and were met at the boat in Naples by a voluble young friend, Leo Stein.

They became close friends of Gertrude Stein, whom they had first met when she was a student at Johns Hopkins Medical School from 1897 to 1902. Stein went to live in Paris in 1903, and the Cone sisters were frequent visitors at her bohemian *atelier* at 13 rue de Fleurus. Etta was allowed to type Stein's manuscript for her first book, *Three Lives*, after promising that she would avoid reading it as she typed. Through Stein, they met Pablo Picasso, whom they delighted by bringing him American comic strips and who painted a portrait of Claribel. But their lifelong friendship was with Henri Matisse, who sold them many of his best paintings as well as drawings and sculptures.

Claribel was regularly seen at Lyric concerts in Baltimore, "draped in Oriental shawls, laden down with exotic jewelry, and her coiffure stabbed through by silver skewers." A story went around the city that Kaiser Wilhelm II had once offered her his arm in the lobby of the Munich opera house because he thought she was a duchess. Etta "affected delicate laces" and did the housekeeping in their opulent home in the Marlborough Building on Eutaw Place. Occupying three adjoining apartments draped in red damask and embroidered burgundy velvet, the Cone sisters accumulated Renaissance and Queen Anne tables and chairs, antique chests and armoires, and Oriental carpets. Every inch of wall space, including the bathrooms, was covered with gold-framed paintings which would have baffled and no doubt outraged proper Baltimoreans: Cézannes, van Goghs, Renoirs, Manets, Picassos, and forty-one Matisses.

So retarded was their native city's taste in art that when Claribel died in 1929, she left instructions for Etta that the collection should go elsewhere, "unless the spirit of appreciation of modern art in Baltimore becomes improved." Fortunately, this change of heart on the part of Baltimoreans took place, at least to Etta's satisfaction, and the entire collection, plus $400,000 for a wing to house it, went to the Baltimore Museum of Art in 1949.

During Barr's youth in Baltimore, however, the Museum of Art was nothing more than a gleam in the city fathers' eyes. Like so many American city officials in the first two decades of the twentieth century (and, alas, frequently even today), they were eager to establish a city art museum not for love of beauty or the education of the public, but because such a manifestation of culture might attract industry and commerce. In 1911, a committee to study a municipal art gallery was formed and marched, on leadenly bureaucratic feet, toward incorporation in 1914. Two years later, a tract of land was acquired near Johns Hopkins University, but no museum materialized for many years. In 1922, Dr. M. Carey gave his mansion to house the museum, and in 1926, plans were announced for a new building, completed in 1929.

It seems unlikely, therefore, that Barr visited an art museum while he lived in Baltimore; Edward King could not recall any such visit with Barr. However, Barr's mother did occasionally take him to local galleries where domesticated landscapes and still lifes were sold to bring out the color scheme in cultivated homes. The first modern picture he could recall seeing was Joseph Stella's *Coney Island*, in a gallery on Mt. Vernon Place, to which his mother took him when he was thirteen or fourteen years old. The picture had been exhibited in the San Francisco Exposition of 1915, and mother and son "were deeply impressed" with it; indeed, Barr recalled many decades later, it was "the only picture in the exhibition which I can remember."

It would be the only original modern picture he would see for many years. Nor was he much interested at all in art. When Barr and Edward King boarded the train for Princeton in the fall of 1918, they both expected to study paleontology. Barr's parents may have harbored hopes that exposure to the university where there already were many family ties would eventually persuade their son to follow the family tradition and continue on to the Theological Seminary. In any event, he would be safely educated in a traditional environment. Then, as now, Princeton was a small university and one especially favored by Baltimore's business elite, who chose to send more of their sons to Princeton than to any other Ivy League school.

The campus at which Barr arrived had a proud history, tracing its origins back to the College of New Jersey, established at Princeton in 1756. Its buildings and those of the town nearby included examples of every architectural style fancied by American builders over the past 160 years. The simplicity of the Georgian style could be seen in Stanhope Hall and its twin, Philosophical

Hall, on the opposite side of the campus, built soon after 1802 possibly with the influence of Benjamin Latrobe. Nassau Hall was the center of the Theological Seminary, completed in 1826. Four stories high and sheathed in ivy, its classic Georgian wings enfolded an ungainly slate-roofed cupola derived, at considerable remove in time, space, and fitness, from Christopher Wren's London churches.

One of the most distinguished buildings on the campus was the Presbyterian church, designed by Princeton's most able local architect, Charles Steadman, and completed in 1838. A pure white Greek temple, with two massive Ionic columns supporting a plain pediment, it presents a sober, simple facade even today to the busy traffic in front, on Nassau Street. Its equally classic interior, however, was defaced in 1874 by expansion and addition of that era's particularly sentimental stained-glass windows. But this lapse was minor compared with the massive visual overkill sprouting on the Princeton campus during the later nineteenth century.

Reunion Hall, constructed in 1870, celebrated the reconciliation of two warring Presbyterian factions with a Frenchified mansard roof brooding over a dark stone pile. Stuart Hall, of the Theological Seminary, was completed in 1876 in the clumsiest, heaviest Venetian Gothic mode. Witherspoon Hall was added in 1877, a Victorian evocation of Fontainebleau, laden with turrets, towers, arches, pediments, dormers, and chimneys. Alexander Hall was completed nearby in 1892, an orgy of Tuscan Romanesque, its striped light and dark stone exterior featuring thick rusticated stone arches flanked by squat columns topped with meaninglessly ornamented cushion capitals.

In view of this architectural riot, the Princeton trustees decreed in 1896 that henceforth all new buildings would be designed in the English Gothic style. The chief advocate for this new foray into architectural history was Andrew F. West, a professor of classics, the first dean of the Princeton graduate school, and a tireless fundraiser of whom the seniors sang: "Here's to Andy three million West/At gathering money he is the best." When Woodrow Wilson became president of Princeton in 1902, he declared that permanent adoption of this architectural style had added a thousand years to the university's history by directing each viewer's imagination to

Oxford and Cambridge, the oldest traditions of learning among English speakers.

In a small book of Princeton sketches published a year after Barr arrived on campus, the authors asserted that "the new Princeton is becoming justly famous for several groups of buildings in the collegiate Gothic style of the older colleges of England." To Barr, the insincerity, even fakery, of the buildings around him was unforgettable. To all who would listen or read, he would later fulminate on the evils of collegiate Gothic.

Its architecture aside, Princeton was a paradise for a serious young man like Barr, who loved reading and reveled in scholarship. He wandered often into the natural history museum in Guyot Hall and may have overlooked the ghastly Gothic Tudor pastiche of its architecture in his fascination with the natural history museum it housed. The young man who had lovingly tended his collections of leaves and butterflies in Baltimore returned often to study the neatly labeled specimens arrayed there. On display were fossils brought back by Princeton expeditions to the western United States and Patagonia, examples of almost every mineral and gem in the world, and a wondersome array of animal skeletons: mastodon, saber-toothed tiger, giant pig, three-toed horse. Exhibits like this would attract Barr to natural history museums wherever he happened to travel. Many years later, he recalled seeing Haida and Tlingit Indian objects in Guyot Hall and still found them so fine that he suggested they be added to the Princeton Art Museum.

Barr's interest in paleontology may have been spurred by the doctrinal battles which racked the Presbyterian church during the late nineteenth and early twentieth centuries. Fundamentalists who insisted on a literal reading of the Bible split churches and schools over how to respond to mounting evidence for the great age of the earth and of the Darwinian evolution of the species upon it. The Reverend Barr sided with the modernists who were fighting to reconcile scientific discoveries in geology, paleontology, and biology with religious doctrine. In 1923, he would be called to McCormick Seminary in Chicago to reinforce the liberals on the faculty there.

Barr's interest in studying paleontology, therefore, was a gesture of support for his father's views. His visits to the fossils and skeletons in Guyot Hall went beyond curiosity, comprising a quiet

protest against the religious reactionaries who clung to control of
the Princeton Theological Seminary until 1935. He may have been
further diverted from his plan to study paleontology by the dearth
of teachers at Princeton in that subject. When he arrived on the
campus, the entire biology department consisted of five professors,
who also taught botany and zoology. There was also considerable
ferment in the field, with a biochemistry department established as
a very progressive step in 1920.

In 1918, in any event, there was no need yet to decide on a major;
he reveled in the prospect of two years of general education
courses, including Latin, Greek, German, history, calculus, and
English. He wrote home regularly, maintaining a correspondence
chess game with fourteen-year-old Andrew and showing off his
dubious poetic prowess to his parents after some five months at
college. He volunteered that "the sestet is poor" and modestly titled
his effort "Pome."

> Lo! at my foot I see the butterfly,
> An azure jewel, so delicately wrought,
> So passing small, indeed I long had sought,
> Ere, having searched successfully, I spy
> Thee now, thou tiny gem, so daintily
> Set in a ring of blue forget-me-not;
> As though some flakes of color had been dropt
> By Him, who tinted yon cerulean sky.
> And yet forsooth, men call thee Lycaena
> Pudargiolus Violacia,
> The rarest butterfly of early spring:
> My net is poised; why do I hesitate?
> Shall science bow to sentiment? But fate
> Decides; thou'rt gone upon thy sapphire wing.

The weight of Princeton's long history lies heavily in the class-
rooms where Alfred Barr struggled to create these lines. The
interior of a typical room brazenly mocks the modern architect's
dictum that form follows function. Behind two-inch-thick, Gothic-
arched, and brass-handled wooden doors, rough wooden chairs and
rudimentary blackboards insist that education involves considerable pain and only sober pleasure. Between a dark wooden-

coffered ceiling and a floor of narrow, scuffed planks and surrounded by dark oak paneling, the young men sat up in stiff collars and neckties, absorbing knowledge. Beyond the small panes of bubbled antique glass, a young man whose eyes strayed from the professor's podium could glimpse the dark tracery of the trees which are the glory of the Princeton campus. At least two of them are by tradition called Stamp Act Sycamores, planted to commemorate repeal of the infamous Stamp Act in 1766. The most massive native tree in the eastern United States, the sycamore was used by Indians for making dugout canoes. The specimens on campus "were vigorous saplings when George Washington's troops scattered three British regiments during the Battle of Princeton" on January 3, 1777. The most imposing trees on the campus in Alfred Barr's day, as today, are white ash, planted around 1830.

For a school with fewer than two thousand undergraduates (only about five thousand today), Princeton offered extraordinary amenities. Chief among them was the accessibility of the faculty; about one-third of the tenured professors lived within one-quarter of a mile from Nassau Hall, and none lived much farther away than one mile. Spread out over more than a thousand acres, an expansiveness lacking in more urbanized Ivy League schools, the campus included Carnegie Lake, a three-mile-long body of water for rowing, canoeing, sailing, fishing, and skating; a magnet for birds and waterfowl, it attracted Barr, who was becoming serious about bird-watching. There was an astronomical observatory on campus, its smooth and functional dome a sharp contrast to the collegiate Gothic building supporting it.

There were buildings and fields for every imaginable kind of athletics, including lacrosse, tennis, golf, and, of course, football; the first American intercollegiate contest had taken place between Princeton and Rutgers at New Brunswick in 1869. The head football coach during Barr's years at Princeton was Bill Roper, described by an opposing mentor as "not a coach . . . an evangelist." Barr was impressed enough with the team's performance to write home about it, and he often traveled back to Princeton in later life to cheer the Tigers to victory in Palmer Stadium against traditional opponents, especially their arch-rival, Rutgers.

In scholarly resources, the faculty, library, and museums were tightly intertwined. Many of the professors were wealthy men, as close to an aristocracy as Americans have ever achieved. Typical was the founder and chairman for four decades of the department of art and archaeology, Allan Marquand. His father was a New York banker who was one of the founders of the Metropolitan Museum of Art. In 1883, a year after he had started the department, his uncle endowed his chair, and seventeen years later, Marquand relinquished the chair and served without salary so that another professor could be hired. He augmented the art library from his own collection and bought other supplies from his own pocket. He also founded and financed the Princeton Monographs in Art and Archaeology, one of the earliest and best American scholarly series in art history, and gave the Princeton Art Museum one of its most valuable paintings, *Christ Before Pilate*, by Hieronymus Bosch.

Professor Marquand retired in 1920, the year that Barr decided to major in history of art. Art and archaeology was then one of the largest and most popular departments at Princeton. A staff of thirteen professors taught sixteen courses to some eight hundred undergraduates. Among Barr's contemporaries there were A. Hyatt Mayor, later curator of prints at the Metropolitan Museum of Art, and Millard Meiss, a medievalist at the Princeton Institute for Advanced Study. The department was strong in the history of classical, medieval, and Renaissance art, but almost seventy years after the Impressionists had scandalized Paris with their Salon des Refusés, news of modern art had barely reached Princeton. Barr would recall with great pain that as an undergraduate he had heard only three lectures dealing with modern art: "one [professor] was querulously resentful, a second wittily condescending, the third dismissed painting from Cézanne to 1920 with a glib retelling of the donkey's tail legend. All three knew several times as much about Sano di Pietro as Picasso. About the art of the previous fifty years, they were either complacently superficial or profoundly ignorant."

In the spring semester of 1920, Barr took Charles Rufus Morey's imaginative course in medieval art. It was unique in that students learned about medieval life and culture, as well as about painting, sculpture, and architecture. "I'm sure I shall like it," Barr wrote home, and within two months he was working on a paper about Chartres. The panorama of the Middle Ages unfolding before him, through fine arts as well as obscure paintings on walls and in books, minor crafts, clothing, and ornament, may have influenced Barr's concept for the Museum of Modern Art as a center for study of all the visual arts.

Barr himself acknowledged that Morey's course in medieval art only "confirmed my interest in art history." Frank Jewett Mather, who taught Barr Italian painting and modern painting during his junior year "developed my interest in painting," Barr wrote. Mather, who was a prolific scholarly and popular writer, may have influenced Barr even more than Morey did. "None of my teachers was nearly so open to new ideas and so tolerant of contemporary art they didn't like as you were," Barr wrote to Mather many years later. "Furthermore, I always felt that you had and passed on to your students a real sense of the importance of first-hand contact with a work of art and of qualitative judgement."

Mather was a shrewd observer of the art world's foibles and wrote a witty column in *Scribner's* beginning in about 1907. He attacked dealers with cynical savagery, describing one Vogelstein as paying for old pictures "lavishly, foolishly, counting . . . confidently on the ignorance of his clients." Mather mocked "the relish with which he could . . . impose a false Rembrandt at six figures upon a wavering iron-master." He was equally ferocious about collectors, whom he lampooned as mindless gatherers of wood, ivory, silver, bronze, marble, and plaster "much as a dredge collects marine specimens." In a book of such observations, published in 1912 and almost certainly read by Barr, Mather printed "A Ballade of Art Collectors":

Oh Lord! We are the covetous.
Our Neighbor's goods afflict us sore.
From Frisco to the Bosphorus
All sightly stuff, the less the more
We want it in our hoard and store . . .
. . . Lord! Crave my neighbor's wife! What for?
I much prefer his crystal ball
From Far Cathay. Then, Lord, ignore
Collector folk who're sinners all.

To a young man who would spend a lifetime humoring and courting art collectors, Mather's observations on their foibles must have been impressive. "Morally considered," wrote Mather, "the art collector is tainted with the fourth deadly sin [greed]; pathologically, he is often afflicted by a degree of mania. His distinguished kinsman, the connoisseur, scorns him as a kind of mercenary." But Mather also was merciless to those who abet collectors. "The wealthy gentleman who gives *carte blanche* to his dealers and agents is merely a spoilsport," he wrote. "He makes what should be a matter of adroitness simply an issue of brute force. . . . Not only does he lose the real pleasures of the chase, but he raises up a special clan of sycophants to part him and his money."

A few years after Barr graduated, Mather set down his views on modern art, giving a vivid picture of the skepticism he must have conveyed in the classroom. While acknowledging the importance of Cézanne, Mather also believed that his "generally sound views were largely belied by the eccentricity and the inadequacy of his practice." His "double revolution under the watchwords of liberty and discipline" evoked in his followers "only a liberty at which he would have shuddered and a discipline which he would have utterly renounced." Of Henri Rousseau, Mather wrote that he "merely painted away at his imaginary tropical forests and at his holiday scenes until he got the substance and seriousness of a well-made embroidered sampler." Cubism he described as "a world of slipping and sliding planes . . . one gets a similar vertiginous sensation . . . by standing on a railroad bridge and watching several trains passing each other in different directions." He accused the German Expressionists of hardening "into a dictum, Monet's practice of 'painting as the bird sings.' Even among birds the doctrine is defective. There are birds which sing badly." Matisse's paintings, Mather believed, illustrated "a fine draughtsman gone wrong . . . garish and unsteady, splotched with conventionally sharp colors, like a tomato salad with mayonnaise."

Barr would disagree heartily with all these judgments, but there is something of Mather's style in Barr's later writings. Unlike most writers on art in his day, Mather expressed himself vigorously, clearly, directly, colorfully, and, rare indeed, humorously. He gave specific examples and obviously had carefully studied the works themselves, even though he did not appreciate many of them. When asked in 1931 to review the book in which Mather gathered his views on modern art, Barr diplomatically declined: "Unfortunately I am both a former pupil and a friend of Mr. Mather," he wrote, "while at the same time I find myself in frequent disagreement with his opinions."

While he disputed Mather's derisory conclusions, Barr was developing, even as an undergraduate, his own strongly held opinions. Michelangelo had "a certain cold perfection," he told Edward King, while Conrad Witz, a fifteenth-century German follower of the Flemish Ten Eycks, struck him as "a kind of proto-Cézanne." Of any wide philosophical speculations about art, King, who was Barr's roommate and colleague in art history, remembered none. "We were notably, if not strangely, silent in this regard," he wrote. "We seem to have been satisfied by dealing with the academic problems at hand as well we might, and let it go at that." However, Barr exercised his collecting urge even upon new words and phrases; "Why should the snake otate to bake?" he would often repeat, along with the mellifluous names of ancient monuments, such as Artemis Leucophryne Magnesia.

Ancient monuments and their precise names were the bone and sinew of an art historian's training long after Barr's schooling at Princeton. Having decided to major in art at Morey's behest, Barr found that he enjoyed accumulating the obscure terminology by which novices were initiated into the discipline. In his senior year, having already decided to stay on at Princeton for a master's degree in art history, Barr filled several notebooks with the research for his senior paper on ornament in medieval art. These notebooks contain hundreds of sketches of ornamental details, painstakingly copied out of books, along with the dry, dull observations of other scholars. The real art seems utterly remote from this boring exercise. Later he would complain that while concentrating on four areas of art history during his graduate studies, "never once . . . was I led to examine an original work of art; nor was I aware . . . that my instructors had any direct contact with original works of art except outside their scholarly pursuits. These men loved art and believed profoundly in its importance, but as university art historians they and their students could work for long periods with books and photographs alone."

As an undergraduate, Barr longed for closer communion with real works of art. He devoured what little he could find about contemporary art at Princeton. As a sophomore, in the spring of 1919, he was much impressed with Millard Huntington Wright's description of synchromism, a colorful abstract style of painting developed by his brother, Stanton Macdonald-Wright, and Morgan Russell, two Americans in Paris. As Barr's father espoused contemporary ideas within the Presbyterian church, so Barr began to align himself ideologically with the progressives in art. Later he explained that he had "a strong reaction" to "the general ignorance of or contempt for twentieth century art on the part of most of my teachers."

While dutifully absorbing data about the visual landmarks of Western civilization to the joy of his professors, Barr also began spending many hours with the drawings and photographs of modern works of art in such magazines as *The Dial* and *Vanity Fair*. He saw his first reproduction of a Paul Klee painting in *Vanity Fair* in about 1922, he later recalled. While he would later denigrate both publications as "dilettante, the one highbrow, the other fashionable," he was certain that "both succeeded in awakening in me and many others of my generation an interest in the work of living artists in various media from painting and sculpture to movies and photography." During 1920 and 1921, *The Dial* illustrated sculptures and paintings by many artists whose work Barr would later gather enthusiastically into the Museum of Modern Art: Gaston Lachaise, Jacques Lipchitz, Paul Cézanne, Henri Rousseau, Robert Delaunay, Charles Burchfield. In quite a few instances, the actual piece illustrated ended up in the museum (for example, Matisse's *The Dance* and Lehmbruck's *Kneeling Girl*).

For poor, deprived Americans who had to stay home while the lucky ones were living creatively in Paris, many articles in *The Dial* reported *le dernier cri* abroad. Unquestioningly Francophile, they made it clear that art meant Paris, with a side trip to Berlin or Munich. Henry McBride, who guided two generations of smart young Americans through the cultural minefields of modern art, told *Dial* readers in 1920 that only because he himself was not a bourgeois could he comprehend Marcel Duchamp's most recent gesture, a glass chemist's vial titled *Paris Air*. In America, by contrast, Barr visited a 1921 exhibition at the Metropolitan of 127 Impressionist and Post-Impressionist paintings which stirred up riotous controversy. An anonymous circular charged the exhibition with being part of a worldwide movement aimed at "the breaking down of all law and order and the revolutionary destruction of our entire social system." John Quinn, a New York attorney who owned many of the works on display, called the circular "ku klux criticism . . . rancid with envy" and its authors "degenerates."

This was not the kind of debate that engaged the patient scholars of classical or Renaissance art, but it did resonate with the fiery controversy within the Presbyterian Church which inevitably had engaged Reverend Barr. Near the end of his senior year, young Barr had what Edward King described as "a vision," clearly seeing his future. He would specialize in contemporary art, unifying all the visual arts in the manner Morey had used in elucidating medieval art.

Barr graduated Phi Beta Kappa, with high honors in art and archaeology, in June 1922, twenty-second in a class of 250. After a summer in Greensboro and Baltimore, he returned to Princeton on a fellowship for graduate studies in the fall. Edward King, "Kingibus," was again his roommate. King knew Barr would make "a big splash somehow," but as Barr pushed forward conscientiously with his thesis on Piero di Cosimo—a thesis on a modern topic was unthinkable at the time—the direction that his life would finally take seemed obscure.

The Princeton Graduate College had been dedicated in 1913, the first residential liberal arts graduate college in America. Its dean, Andrew Fleming West, the man who had persuaded the trustees to build only in collegiate Gothic, indulged in a veritable orgy of this style in the design of the quadrangle of residential and dining halls, lounge, and library. Barr may have been relatively unaware of Princeton's architectural peccadillos through much of his undergraduate life there, but a diligent perusal of *The Dial* would by now have shown him the sleekly unornamented designs of Erich Mendelsohn. He may also have been aware of Walter Gropius's progressive plans for the Bauhaus, founded in Weimar, Germany, in 1919.

The environment in which Barr now found himself was dominated by a lofty tower derived from Oxford's Magdalen Tower; "by
moonlight," Dean West raved to Pres. Woodrow Wilson, it was "a
dream in silvery grays and whites." Over the great dining hall
loomed massive hammerhead beams carved with caricatures of
trustees, and its lancet windows displayed the usual simpering
stained glass. The gardens even included ivies gathered abroad,
and in its wall Dean West had actually had embedded genuine
fragments from Oxford and Cambridge. A close study of the
exterior gargoyles and grotesques showed that they were in fact
humorous depictions of student life.

Surrounded by such architectural levity, Barr himself kicked up
his heels. At a mock commencement prepared by all the graduate
students, he played the role of Princeton president John G. Hibben,
while a colleague, Thornton Wilder (whose father was a professor
at Yale), walked at the end of the processions garbed as a "pee-
lady," sweeping up the debris. When a new wing of Dean West's
Gothic fantasy was completed, the students held their own dedication. One recited an ode in the florid forensic poetry style of Prof.
Henry Van Dyke, while another, with a broad southern twang,
imitated Pres. Calvin Coolidge. A third impersonated Dean West,
his Oxford gown mocked by a red bathrobe stretched over a fake
paunch.

Barr received his M.A. in art and archaeology in June of 1923. In
the fall he began teaching at Vassar, where his mother had attended forty years earlier and where the art department comprised only four teachers. One of them had a Ph.D., rare for
teachers of art history at that time. Using black-and-white lantern
slides and typically smudged and dog-eared reproductions, Barr
taught Venetian painting and joined two colleagues to teach "modern painting." Like Princeton's—and catalogs of most art history
departments—Vassar's catalog divided the discipline into narrow
compartments. Barr lived in the home of the Vassar art department's chairman, Prof. Oliver Tonks and maintained apparently
cordial relations, even though Tonks disdained modern art. Concluding a lecture on nineteenth-century art with a single slide of a
Cézanne, Tonks had scoffed: "And this is modern art . . . I ask you?"

While Barr was not yet ready to innovate, he was remembered by at least one of his students as "a fervent teacher." This was Katharine Kuh, who would have a distinguished career as a curator at the Art Institute of Chicago and as a popular writer on art. He was "somewhat emaciated," she wrote, yet passionate. "I never failed to learn from Alfred Barr."

3

PILGRIMAGE

I n the summer of 1924, after a year of teaching art history at Vassar, Alfred Barr finally embarked for Europe, the Promised Land so richly, yet vaguely, described in all his Princeton courses in history of art. Now the lantern slides and the yellowing photographs would give way to firsthand impressions of the museum that is Italy. Guided by Professor Mather's recommendations, Barr drew up an ambitious itinerary and embarked in a tourist third cubby for Genoa, where he would meet his childhood friend and Princeton roommate, the faithful Kingibus. In Italy they voraciously covered thirty places in thirty days, a breathless dash through a list of landmarks King would remember more than sixty years later: Genoa, Naples, Pompeii, Paestum, Rome, Tivoli, Orvieto, Siena, San Gimignano, Florence, Fiesole, Pisa, Pistoia, Perugia, Assisi, Ravenna, Bologna, Modena, Parma, Ferrara, Venice, Lido, Murano, Padua, Milan, Brescia, Bergamo, Verona, Pavia, and Turin. Like two famished urchins turned loose to gorge in a pastry shop, the two young men paused only briefly each day in the late afternoon to plan out, over a sidewalk aperitif, the next day's visual assault. Having consulted their 1903 Baedeker, which King found still "perfectly reliable," they would board the train for tomorrow's objective.

King's entire budget for the summer's adventure was $800; Barr had only $700, scraped together from his family and savings. But such was the strength of the dollar at that time that the pair lodged comfortably at two-star hotels with such fanciful names as Grand Hotel of the Universe and Automobilism and still had a small nest egg for a farewell banquet before sailing home. As he would on many of his travels, Barr kept a diary in a small pocket notebook, listing notable works of art he had seen and often adding the kind of stick-figure sketches that help art history students recall works for examinations. Perhaps inspired by King, who dabbled in painting all his life, Barr was also attempting a few soft pencil drawings that aspired to art. As the ship steamed toward Genoa, he strived to convey the romantic mystery of the first landfall, a calm sea with the distant port cradled beneath undulating hills. Barr's sweet pencil lines concealed the excitement of arriving in Europe at last, though they reveal an extremely amateurish artist. Later at Paestum he sketched the Temple of Ceres and the Basilica. He drew Capri, "from our window," and added an ink sketch with a tiny sailboat and great boiling clouds to set off the island's jagged mass.

To educated young Americans of their generation, the places Barr and King visited were as familiar, yet as legendary, as Camelot. For years they had been studying and writing "learned" papers and actually teaching about objects and sites as famous as they were visually vague. It is hard to imagine today the extreme dearth of graphic materials available to American art historians during Barr's Princeton years. Books were sparsely and sometimes inaccurately illustrated; photographs were rare; engravings and other graphics showing the architecture, sculpture, and painting covered in academic courses gave only a faint hint of what the originals looked like. The fuzzy black-and-white lantern slides professors used to illustrate their lectures often concealed more than they revealed. So faded and distorted were the odd color illustrations that it was probably better to avoid them entirely and rely on verbal descriptions and imagination if one wanted to gain some notion of what the great masterpieces of Western art really looked like.

Since the beginning, Americans knew that all the essential landmarks on the road to cultivation were in Europe. Isolated by an ocean that still took ten days to cross, the United States had remained an abject colonial subject of European culture. "When good Americans die they go to Paris," one of Oscar Wilde's most insufferably snobbish characters sneered in 1893. But Americans themselves had long been self-conscious about their provincialism. Wilde was merely repeating a remark published by Oliver Wendell Holmes in 1858, and Holmes was quoting Thomas Gold Appleton, Boston's first collector of contemporary French art. More than the catty sally of a playwright, more even than the rueful observation of one of America's most sophisticated men, the remark was the simple truth: an American schooled only in his native land was likely to remain an uncultivated boor.

What American universities taught under the general heading "history of art" was European art; American art was not considered a worthy subject for academic attention. Nor did American museums devote much attention to non-European art. As late as 1969, the leading art history textbook, H. W. Janson's 578-page *History of Art*, allotted exactly ten pages, a postscript, to art outside the European tradition.

A year after their first hectic pilgrimage across the Atlantic, Barr and King returned for another massive gulp at the fount of European culture. Although Barr was already fascinated with modern art, Princeton's conservatism still dictated their itinerary. This time they toured France and Holland, together with Walter Haring, who would later become director of education at the Metropolitan Museum of Art. This was a more casual trip, King recalled, although they were still "conscientiously covering all the important things." In Beaune, where they'd gone to see Rogier van der Weyden's *Last Judgment*, they sampled too much of the local red Burgundy and ended up sleeping in the railroad station. In Montmartre, they were having cocktails when they spotted the epic poet of Princeton Presbyterianism, Prof. Henry Van Dyke, emerging from the crypt of Sacre Coeur. Boisterously, they gave him a "locomotive," a particularly raucous Princeton football cheer, but, said King, he was not amused. Perhaps he would have been even less amused had he known that one member of this unseemly chorus, Barr, would in the fall be teaching in the Princeton department of art and archaeology. Before leaving Europe, Barr and King blew the last of their money, five dollars each, for a lavish farewell banquet in Brussels.

Just before embarking for Europe, Barr had passed his preliminary Ph.D. exams, after just a year of full-time work in art history at Harvard, supported by the Thayer Fellowship. His mentor, Paul Sachs, reported to Morey at Princeton that though Barr had "decided suddenly" to take the exam on the previous afternoon, he had "acquitted himself better than any other candidate . . . during the time I have been here." He predicted that Barr would be "a scholar of distinction." This was high praise indeed from Sachs, a dwarfish gnome who exploded frequently into fierce, uncontrollable tantrums. Himself a Harvard man, he had endured working for his father's Goldman Sachs investment banking business for some ten years before escaping to become associate director at the Fogg Museum and a teacher of graduate students.

In 1923 Sachs had originated the first course anywhere in museum management, ferociously guiding students in planning, arranging, and labeling exhibitions and in writing catalogs. Sachs lectured little on art history and a great deal on the suave arts of humoring museum patrons, methods quite similar to the shrewd courtliness so useful to the investment banker in dealing with wealthy clients. "What he really did," said one former student, "was teach you how to make the right noises in front of pictures." Sachs's unique seminar attracted men who would eventually direct many of America's major art museums. One student insisted that the reason paintings in American museums often are hung so low on the wall is that Paul Sachs demanded they be at his eye level.

The first Jew to obtain an appointment in art history at a major American university, Sachs used his family fortune to enrich the Fogg Museum with gifts from his own collection of drawings. He at first struck Julien Levy, who attended his course in 1924, as pompous and willful, but turned out to be gentle, scholarly, and dedicated. "He was a kingmaker without kingly pretensions," Levy concluded. Lacking the appropriate degrees, Sachs was not then a professor and would continually correct students who addressed him as such. In Cambridge, he had bought the residence of Charles

Eliot Norton, whose lectures during the 1880s and 1890s on the history of art were the foundation of art-history scholarship in America.

It was in Sachs's seminar room and at frequent gatherings at the diminutive professor's suburban home, Shady Hill, that Barr first preached the gospel of modern art. During Sachs's year-long seminar on prints, Barr slyly told his colleagues that the hour he had been given to review nineteenth-century graphics was "a task so nearly impossible that I have added thereto a discussion of the twentieth century. In addition, [Sachs] generously gave me an hour to talk about modern woodcuts. . . . I have piled Ossa on Pelion in this foolhardy way because I feel that we who have been retrospective for eight long months can well afford a few minutes' glance at those much neglected people, our contemporaries." Unintimidated by Sachs's blustery temper, Barr dispatched to him a lengthy critique of the course: modern art, he complained, had been slighted. "No one has ever given me such real help in my ten years of teaching," graciously replied Sachs. Of the forty-seven letters which awaited him in Rome after several months' touring, "not one has interested me more," he wrote, "than your perfectly frank letter with its full *constructive* criticism."

To his fellow students, Barr could be "aloof, even haughty," Edward King recalled, "especially to anybody he thought a philistine." He cultivated a veneer of preciousness and appeared absolutely forbidding to a Harvard sophomore who happened to approach him on the first day of a seminar with Prof. Kingsley Porter. "I understand that this will be a hard course," the sophomore timidly said. "The harder, the better," was Barr's chilly reply.

In the fall of 1925, lack of money forced Barr to leave temporarily the cosmopolitan milieu of Harvard and return to Princeton, where he taught art history in the traditional manner still favored there. In the spring he organized his first art exhibition, works borrowed from friends and fellow students. The selection indicates the motley array of modern art then available for exhibition in America: a Marie Laurencin oil; two Eugene Speicher drawings; lithographs by Odilon Redon, George Bellows, and Edgar Degas; a George Luks drawing; a Maurice Vlaminck oil; and two small

bronzes by Aristide Maillol. To his mother, Barr enthusiastically
described his plans for this exhibition. He also asked her to read
Sheldon Cheney's *A Primer of Modern Art*, the only textbook then
available. "I may use parts of it next year and want your opinion—
and father's if he has the time," he wrote.

That summer, Barr dropped in at the New Art Circle, the only
gallery in New York to exhibit recent works by such German
Expressionist artists as Max Pechstein, Max Beckmann, Ernst
Kirchner, and Emil Nolde. Barr was fascinated by the few emotional, brilliantly colored canvases and the many strong graphics
gathered by the gallery's owner, J. B. Neumann, who was a German immigrant only a few years older than Barr, and who maintained close contacts with the German avant-garde. After animated conversation in the gallery, the two adjourned to a nearby
Childs restaurant for lunch, the beginning of a long and friendly
relationship.

Two weeks later he wrote to Neumann, identifying himself as
"the ignorant young man with whom you had lunch a fortnight ago"
and asking to come back for a longer visit. Neumann was one of the
few people in all of Barr's life to whom he seemed able to express
his emotional reaction to a work of art. After seeing an early Corot
in Neumann's bedroom the following November, Barr would write:
"It hurt—it made my throat feel queer and my eyes smart—it is
very beautiful—how you must hate to part with it."

Barr was back in Cambridge by then, enrolled in Sachs's museum course and teaching art at Wellesley. He was also beginning
to share his radical views with whatever public cared about modern art in mid-1920s Cambridge. For a Fogg Museum exhibition of
modern paintings and of "facsimiles reproduced so miraculously
that under glass it is impossible to detect them from originals," he
wrote the earliest of the wall labels which some (Philip Johnson, for
one) consider his most artful writings. In his own notes, Barr called
these labels a "Critical Catalog," their content and style foreshad-
owing the spate of illuminating wall labels and exhibition catalogs
Barr would create in the future. In these early labels, he sharpened
his talent for crystalline, magisterial prose, although he would
later modify many of the judgments he made. A work by Chagall,
for example, he called "partially DADA . . . but there are subtly

sophisticated overtones." Later, he would also revise his dictum that "Camille Pissarro's name is less conspicuous than that of Monet, his fellow impressionist, but his modest art bids fair to outlast that of the latter." But on his dogma that "Picasso is the most inventive intelligence in modern art," he would never waver. Even then, he was already developing a hierarchy of modern artists, naming Gauguin and Matisse as "the most important representatives of another phase of modern art, the emphasis on decorative qualities."

Half a century later, art dealer and collector Julien Levy was still impressed with Barr's energy and ingenuity in arranging this exhibition. Sachs had insisted that it be limited to works Barr could borrow among Harvard students, "a neat problem," Levy wrote, "in local exhibitioning, fund-raising, picture borrowing and cataloging." Levy never did learn how Barr ferreted out his name but was glad to loan a Chagall etching, a Campendonck woodcut, a Schiele drawing, and a Klee color lithograph.

Only a few undergraduates and the odd professor might have wandered in to browse before this exhibition passed into oblivion had not Barr written a provocative news release about it to the *Harvard Crimson*. "Boston Is Modern Art Pauper—Barr," said the headline over his sorrowful assertion that Boston and Cambridge, "places which have a deserved reputation as centers of alert cultivation of the Seven Arts," offered the public no examples of works by the most important living painters, men like Matisse, Bonnard, Picasso, or Derain. Nor could the amateur study in any local galleries the great forerunners of the contemporary tradition, men who had been dead for two decades or more: Cézanne, van Gogh, Seurat, Gauguin. These were "masters who are honored the world over," Barr asserted, "in London, Paris, Berlin, in Italy, Russia, Scandinavia, in the Low Countries, in Chicago and New York and Cleveland—but not in Boston."

Today, such comments pass unnoticed and virtually unread into the footnotes of local history. But so intense were feelings about modernism in 1926 America that the controversy boiled for many a month. The *Boston Herald*'s art critic, F. W. Coburn, devoted a column to pour what Barr later described as "the most libelous, ignorant and even obscene contumely" upon the four long-dead masters Barr had cited. Cézanne he dismissed as "a poor painter with bad eyesight"; van Gogh was "a crazy galoot who painted for years in an insane asylum"; and he assailed Gauguin as "a perpetrator of gross caricatures in the name of art."

The *Boston Globe* and the *Boston Evening Transcript* leaped into the fray. An article in *The Arts* professed shock that "Rembrandt, Turner, Ingres [are] in competition with Matisse, Picasso, Laurencin, Marin and the most extreme of ultra-moderns." But in an editorial in the same magazine, Forbes Watson suggested that Coburn's column, "In the World of Art," should be renamed "In the Depths of Ignorance." Barr shrewdly kept the publicity pot bubbling by sending a correction to the editor of *Art News*. He would never have asserted that an art desert existed in "a city which has the greatest Oriental and Classical collections in America," he wrote, subtly needling Boston's boosters one more time. Interest in art thrived in that city, he conceded, "even though it be a decade behind Cleveland, Chicago, and Worcester, Massachusetts."

By this time, Barr had been teaching traditional art history at Wellesley for about six weeks, but already he was an intriguing figure on the campus. Cosseted by the maiden ladies who were his colleagues, ogled and adored by his students, this twenty-four-year-old whirlwind was devising for the spring semester America's first university course on contemporary art. Armed with what few lantern slides and reproductions he could laboriously gather, bereft of textbooks because none existed, lacking models or precedent, Barr simply invented an umbrella curriculum for modernism and sailed forth into the classroom. Anyone who wished to take his course first had to complete other courses in more traditional history of art. Then he made prospective students pass a quiz so provocative that it was published in *Vanity Fair* the following August, perhaps at Barr's behest. It asked for identification of fifty contributors to "modern artistic expression," among them George Gershwin, Max Reinhardt, Oswald Spengler, James Joyce, Alfred Stieglitz, Le Corbusier, Jean Cocteau, and Roger Fry.

The answers Barr provided were packed with bold assertions in behalf of his pet Modernists. France's avant-garde composers, Les Six, he wrote, "embrace most of the progressive musical talent in France." The advertisements and show windows of New York's

Saks Fifth Avenue department store had accomplished more "to popularize the modern mannerism in pictorial and decorative arts than any two proselytizing critics." Aristide Maillol, eight of whose works Barr would acquire for the Museum of Modern Art, was simply "one of the greatest living sculptors." John Quinn, whose collection had recently been sold at auction, "was the most emancipated among the great American collectors of modern art."

Such names and judgments evoked a delicious frisson of rebellion among Wellesley's elite young ladies—and in a good many of the elite older ladies among the faculty as well. Elsewhere, Marie Stopes was advocating open discussions of sex, Margaret Sanger was campaigning for birth control, and the ideological heiresses of Lucy Stone were recommending trial marriage and, perhaps, free love. Skirts flapped above the knee, bootleg gin fizzed, and wicked diversions, whether rumble seats or anarchism, beckoned as never before to the genteel daughters of genteel families. By comparison with such lurking perils, many parents were relieved that their girls were busy with a harmless lark: forays into modernism offered by the prim and pinched and cadaverous-looking Mr. Barr in his steel-rimmed glasses, the son of a prominent Presbyterian preacher, a Princeton and Harvard gentleman.

An explorer into unknown territory, Barr intrepidly pursued every possible resource of printed or illustrated material as he was planning Art 305. He wrote to J. B. Neumann to inquire about buying a German folio titled *Art of Our Time* and ordered what European books and prints might be had for his "absurdly small" budget of $200. To stretch this amount, Barr suggested that the reproductions could be imported duty free if addressed to Wellesley College. What with its promise of intimate propinquity to "advanced" art and ideas and its elitist winnowing of prospective students via the quiz, the course attracted not so much students as acolytes when it began in January 1927.

Because he had so few traditional teaching materials at hand, the young ladies in Barr's course did not simply listen to lectures, read textbooks, write papers, and take exams. In addition, each student was responsible for reading current periodicals and newspapers to keep up with the latest in such fields as photography, modern dance, drama, and architecture, arbitrarily assigned by

Barr, and for reporting weekly to the class. "To keep abreast of the art work of the moment is the ideal of the course," Barr wrote, "and to acquire familiarity with the names and accomplishments that are prominent not only in art circles but in all currents of life."

He relied a good deal on showing lantern slides he had accumulated, including a wedding announcement designed by Herbert Bayer at the Bauhaus, Marcel Breuer's steel-tubing chair, a bookcase resembling a skyscraper, American Indian masks and fetishes, fashion drawings for Marshall Field's department store, African and Melanesian sculptures, and photographs by Edward Steichen, Lyonel Feininger, and Man Ray. Often, he would display a slide "for an eternity," a student recalled, saying nothing and simply allowing the class to absorb it. For examinations, he would ask students to plan a fifteen-item exhibition and write a catalog to go with it. They called him Mr. Mixed Pants because he avoided wearing a suit to class.

But the slides and examinations were only background for the total immersion in modern art that Barr hoped to provide. To that end, students gazed critically at the factory buildings they passed on the train to Boston, tried to view movies as an art form, searched magazines for modern advertisements, hunted for Victrola records of polyphonic music, and cast a cold critical eye upon industrial design from automobiles to refrigerators. In class Barr sometimes held up an egg, asking, "How does that impress you?" Then he would send the girls rummaging through the dime store for well-designed objects to display in class. The best still life composed of these objects would win a prize, perhaps a papier-mâché dinosaur, it was rumored.

These bohemian doings were described in an unsigned *Boston Evening Transcript* article on April 27, 1927, lauding their stimulating effect in focusing the entire campus on "the study of modern artistic achievement." Students were getting to know the avant-garde in all the arts, but nervous readers, parents perhaps, who might become alarmed by the course's revolutionary content, were reassured that "primary attention is paid to painting, with special study in the nineteenth century of the forerunners of modern painting." Only then were the young ladies exposed to the myster-

ies of the "super-realists" as well as "the psychology of expressionism, the discipline in cubism and constructivism and the importance of the machine." The article concluded that "the course
proves valuable in infusing modernist interpretations of art
through the college." The author of this article remained anonymous until 1986, when a former student attributed it to Barr.

With typical thrift, Barr had used the public print to publicize
not only his path-breaking art course, but also a concurrent exhibition called "Progressive Modern Painting" he had organized in the
college's Farnsworth Gallery. Even then, Barr was keeping track
of collectors and collections of modern art and wrote, with mixed
success, to the few Bostonians on his list for loans to the exhibition.
Robert Treat Paine II replied that he had already loaned one or two
of his treasures that winter and could not bear to "denude my house
further." Gladys Saltonstall, however, offered her whole collection,
a mixed bag including a late Jacques Blanche, three small Léger
watercolors, a Gontcharova oil, and several John Carrolls. Such was
the low status of Americans that she relegated her two Demuth
watercolors to a postscript.

In this exhibition, too, Barr used the wall labels to elucidate the
distorted, truncated images which might shock or baffle the
viewer. To clarify Man Ray's *Still Life*, he explained that "his
painting seems analogous to his photographs in two ways: in each
art, he experiments with abstractions and, more important, ex-
plores and exploits the qualities peculiar to the medium. . . . The
composition is related to later phases of cubism with its bisected
bottle, tilted table plane, painted letter and two-dimensional
space."

Despite the spartan limitations of what he could borrow, the
names of the artists whose work he chose for this exhibition still
read like a roll call of important modern figures: Americans like
Maurice Prendergast, Max Weber, Edward Hopper, Charles
Sheeler, Georgia O'Keeffe, Charles Demuth; Europeans like Camille Pissarro, Claude Monet, Georges Seurat, Henri Rousseau,
Fernand Léger, Juan Gris, Max Beckmann, Mark Chagall. That
Barr was able to discern so long ago who the lasting innovators of
the twentieth century would be is a tribute to his wide-ranging

knowledge and incomparable taste. But even more, it demonstrates his extraordinary power to impose his taste upon his contemporaries and successors.

The course young Barr devised for his young women at Wellesley would become the model for his program at the Museum of Modern Art. The exhibition he organized to accompany the course was his first necessarily incomplete gallery of the giants of Modernism, the prophets chosen by Barr for his solitary devotions. Before he left Wellesley in the spring of 1929, he gave a series of five lectures which further refined his schema of modern art. He began by describing "the ideal of a 'pure' art," which resulted in "the final purification of painting," total abstraction, which he called "the demon of the absolute." He related abstract painting to architecture, theater, films, photography, decorative arts, typography, and commercial art. He also described artists' renewed interest in subject matter, during the 1920s, along with "new adventures in appreciation" of works by children, lunatics, and savages, as well as dream images. Modern art developed, like all art, from the perennial struggle between the two sides of human personality, the thoughtful, orderly Apollonian and the spontaneous, erotic Dionysian; or, as Barr put it in terms more familiar to his audience, "Descartes vs. Rousseau." Treading even further onto unknown terrain Barr devoted one lecture to American painting, tracing the European heritage as it seeped into native ground. Describing the Bauhaus, Barr again noted the creative tension between its director, the precise executive and architect Walter Gropius, and the "expressionist counterpoint" provided by painters like Kandinsky and Klee. Barr had already inscribed the pioneers of modern art into the niches of a precise flow chart, and they would remain there not only for the rest of his life but until the present. Later many others would be added, but not a single one has yet been erased.

The names and the niches they occupy are familiar today to every student who has ever sat through a college survey course of modern art. Millions of museum visitors unconsciously absorb the schema devised by Barr in 1929, never reflecting that there could be any other way to view modern art. In the late twenties, however, the world of modern art was a tiny, informal, and idiosyncratic enclave even in the sophisticated world around Harvard Square.

When a few students decided that the college needed a gallery for modern art, it was indulgently viewed as a youthful intellectual caper. The Harvard Society for Contemporary Art sprang into reality at the instigation of a few wealthy, insouciant young men: Edward Warburg, the adventuresome son of an investment banker; Lincoln Kirstein, an opinionated, indefatigable aesthete; and John Walker, a witty, high-spirited Pittsburgher who would become director of the National Gallery. After a few months of diligent organization, they opened their space in the Harvard Coop. Under a silvered ceiling, in two rooms strewn with steel café chairs and tables with severe, highly polished metal tops were paintings and sculptures freely borrowed from collectors like Chester and Maud Dale and Duncan Phillips. The exhibition attracted 1,100 visitors in two weeks, but more importantly, the Society attracted an influential board of directors, including *Vanity Fair* editor Frank Crowninshield, Paul Sachs, and Mrs. John D. Rockefeller, Jr.

In his memoirs, John Walker captures the casual, irreverent mood among those who orbited around Modernism in those days. Having invited Alexander Calder to exhibit some of his inventions, "Eddie Warburg and I got a truck and went to meet Calder's train. I headed for the express office to pick up the boxes containing the exhibition, and Eddie went to the platform to greet our artist. To my horror no boxes had arrived. I joined Eddy . . . and there was the sculptor with a coil of wire over his arm. He said he intended to make the exhibition in the gallery; forty-eight hours, he stated, was plenty of time." The work that resulted is *Circus*, the object of reverent gazes from the multitudes who daily mill around the lobby of New York's Whitney Museum.

Along with their radical view on art, the embryonic museum directors of the Society for Contemporary Art also cultivated a distinctive personal style. Their education "presupposed a microscopic study of the Old Masters," wrote art critic Forbes Watson, and some "assume the position of rather haughty experts even before they enter upon their professional duties." Barr, for example, had blithely told Watson that he considered Vitruvius's classic ideas about architecture "gray with the dust of still-born pedantry." Watson was surprised that the typical member of the group was "able to talk fluently upon Picasso and Matisse" while traveling in a social circle where such names, if known at all, were viewed with horror. Despite their "bright knowingness" about modern art, Watson wrote, the works they bought for themselves showed "painful susceptibility to names and an occasional tendency to be both precious and snobbish."

Barr amply demonstrated these virtues and flaws in a series of book reviews he published during 1926. He was merciless to anyone who dared write a book on modern art. Frank Rutter's *Evolution in Modern Painting*, he wrote, was "too replete with specious generalizations and too omissive of fundamentals to be trustworthy." Barr reproached the author of a volume about famous painters for omitting El Greco, Poussin, Vermeer, and Renoir, while including John Everett Millais and Rosa Bonheur. But he was scathing about the illustrations. "The half-tones are mediocre, the dozen color plates very bad," he wrote, "so bad that they transform an otherwise innocuous volume into one insufferable for the experienced eye and perversive to the innocent."

When it came to courting people who might be useful, Barr mustered exquisite reserves of tact. Already in the Wellesley quiz he had referred to "the finest collection of modern French pictures in America" owned by the eccentric Dr. Albert Barnes of Merion, Pennsylvania. Reviewing Barnes's *The Art in Painting*, Barr gently disagreed with the doctor's irrational contention that only "plastic values" were important in painting. The subject of a picture also mattered, Barr mildly asserted, and confessed that his intricate classroom analysis of a painting's plastic values sometimes fell apart when "a philistine undergraduate ... ask[ed] why the madonna has such a funny chin."

Within less than a year after publishing these lively brief reviews, Barr himself was facing the long labors of composing his doctoral thesis. To complete his research for it and begin the writing, he was in Europe on a year's traveling fellowship arranged by Paul Sachs. Sailing for London in mid-July of 1927, Barr luxuriated in the prospect that this time he would not pant through thirty places in thirty days, but rather follow a loose itinerary which left room for a grand surprise. He hungrily studied the collections at the Victoria and Albert, the Tate, and the Courtauld Institute but seemed to make little progress on his dissertation. Sachs had urged him to write on nineteenth- or twentieth-century art, in which "the *real* book has yet to be written," but, as befalls so many graduate students, Barr seemed unable to focus on a topic both grand enough to reward the labor of writing it and narrow enough to impress a thesis committee. Instead, he took notes on what he conceived as the wealth of modern art in London galleries and eventually used them to write a diatribe about the backwardness of American art museums for publication in *Arts* in 1928.

When J. B. Neumann failed to join him in London during the summer, Barr decided to forego any trips outside the city because "I hate travelling alone so much." About this time Barr began affecting a chop in addition to or substituting for his signature on letters. A large capital *A* steepled over a smaller *B*, it looked vaguely Oriental, although Edward King believed it was based on the signature frequently used by Albrecht Dürer.

In October, Barr warmly greeted Jere Abbott, his Harvard roommate, who would spend many months with him, gawking in galleries, sharing typical travelers' misadventures, tracking down artists, a staunch Jonathan to Barr's David. Abbott was the son of a Maine textile magnate and had spent a year living in Paris during 1923 and 1924. He had met Gertrude Stein and begun a lifelong friendship with Virgil Thompson while living in a little pension in the rue Jacob, "run by a busty lady with a gold watch the size of an alarm clock pinned over her heart." A sensitive gourmet and a talented pianist with a lively sense of humor, he had delighted in regaling Barr's Wellesley students with stirringly dissonant renditions of works by Stravinsky and Les Six. He never married, and Edward King politely described Abbott as "definitely a recluse where girls were concerned." A classmate of King and Barr at Princeton, Abbott also attended Paul Sachs's museum course at Harvard and shared digs with Barr at 34A Irving Street in Cambridge. When all three men were returning from Europe one time, a niece of the dancer Nazimova was so intrigued with Abbott that she followed him to Princeton. But, King recalled sixty years later, "Abbott rushed out." The warm letters Abbott wrote to Barr indicate that he was emotionally as well as intellectually attracted to Barr, but there is no evidence of sexual involvement. Henry-

Russell Hitchcock, who visited the pair in their apartment on Irving Street, cattily described them to the composer Virgil Thompson as "*cette étrange ménage.*"

Soon after Abbott joined Barr in London, the two young aesthetes moved on to Holland, to visit innovative architect J. J. Oud. As Barr reported to American readers of *Arts* the following January, Oud's buildings were sleekly functional; unlike American structures, they featured "no compromise with dead styles, no revamping of the Beaux Arts." Reminding readers of the clean, geometric rooms depicted by such painters as Vermeer, Barr found that "the spotless foursquare interiors of the cottages at Maarken, the bright new paint of barges and house shutters . . . express[ed] perfectly a nation which perhaps put cleanliness above godliness and whose churches are as cold and white as a Childs restaurant." He also shared his delight at the ubiquity of American movies, especially one featuring Adolphe Menjou who, according to the subtitles, looked with dismay "upon the beshingelt, charleston-trappende, cocktail-beslurpende younger generation."

Along with his lively description, Barr again decried that American museums were "indifferent to modern art," in sternly reproachful tones that a Presbyterian minister might use to regret that American churches were indifferent to God. In Rotterdam, he rejoiced, one could see works by Severini, Maillol, and Archipenko; in The Hague there were paintings by Kokoschka, and at the Kröhler-Müller, Seurat, Picasso, Gris, and Léger were on view. "To Americans, the success with which this policy of showing contemporary advanced work has been carried out is a sad reminder and perhaps a challenge," he preached. A visitor to Dutch museums could study what local artists and other Europeans were doing while "neither is at present possible in American museums."

But it was a visit to the Bauhaus in Dessau, Germany, that Barr most fervently anticipated. He had learned about this progressive school and workshop from J. B. Neumann, who was the only regular resource in America for the lively, innovative art produced in the Weimar republic. The Bauhaus's comprehensive approach to the visual arts, its curriculum which included architecture, industrial design, graphic arts, painting, sculpture, stage design, films, and photography, had provided inspiration for Barr's Wellesley

course, as it would later for his museum plans. As he was planning
his trip through Germany, Barr relied on a list provided by Neumann of progressive artists, critics, and galleries in Cologne,
Mannheim, Frankfurt, Stuttgart, and Berlin. As a dealer struggling to sell modern German works to a largely indifferent public,
Neumann no doubt was delighted to learn of the two young scholars' thrilling four-day sojourn in early December 1927 at the
mother church of the modern movement.

Even forty years later, Barr was still dazzled by his sojourn on
that sacred ground. He had seen photographs of Walter Gropius's
glassy, rectilinear building and had read what few books and
articles were available in America about this pioneering artists'
commune. But it was high adventure to Barr to converse in his
college German with the architect himself, unsmilingly earnest
and wearing English plus fours. Barr and Abbott excitedly dashed
through the building, observing the students at their varied exer-
cises and firing questions at the teachers. László Moholy-Nagy
looked sullen when Barr asked him whether he or El Lissitzky had
first used photomontage. Oskar Schlemmer, Josef Albers, Wassily
Kandinsky, Marcel Breuer, and Herbert Bayer all were quizzed by
the two American visitors.

They called on Paul Klee in his Gropius house, a *machine à
habiter* near the main building. A "smallish man, simple in speech
and gently humorous," Barr reported, Klee showed the two visitors
the drawings in his studio while the sounds of his wife playing a
Mozart sonata drifted up from the room below. In one corner Barr
noted "significant curiosities," a table littered with shells, a skate's
egg, bits of dried moss, a pinecone, a chunk of coral, fragments of
textiles, and two children's drawings. "These served to break the
logical severity of the Gropius interior and Bauhaus furniture,"
Barr wrote, "perhaps also served as catalytics to Klee's creative
activity."

Next door, in another Gropius house, the two visitors spent a
couple of hours with Lyonel Feininger, an American who had been
living in Germany for some forty years. The artist was impressed
that they were Harvard men and found them "charming . . .
enthusiastic about everything." Before they had a chance to call on
him, he had already spotted the pair, wandering around Dessau

and at a church concert the previous evening. Afterward he wrote to a friend: "One of them is a professor, like a boy though twenty-five years old, and intensely interested in my work . . . he is going to write about German art of which nothing has been written in England or America." To Barr, Feininger was one of "a dazzling constellation of artist-teachers such as no art school has ever known before or since." Greeting him in the doorway, Barr saw "one of the most American figures I had ever seen—tall and spare—though with nothing of the tight-lipped, rock-bound Yankee about him. He seemed shy, but his smile melted my own shyness." When he spoke, Barr was startled at Feininger's forty-year-old English; he was using antiquated slang like "bully," and Barr felt "as though we were talking with an American who, through some time-machine miracle, had been preserved unchanged since the 1880's."

Barr was bedazzled by the Bauhaus, its aesthetic daring, its community of artists, its revolutionary sweep across the artistic spectrum, and, perhaps, its idealistic left-wing social tenets as well. But what Feininger called a "Cathedral of Socialism" was more a shrine to the middle class than to the proletariat. Its products were made in capitalistic factories for consumption by the well-to-do. Philip Johnson, who visited there at the end of the 1920s, noticed the all-too-human warts on the face of the future. "Poor Lyonel [Feininger]," he wrote to Barr, "so weighed down by the wife that nothing was to be got from him and apparently they don't get along well with the rest of the colony." Kandinsky he considered "a little fool who is completely dominated by his swell Russian Grande Dame of a wife. He has millions of his sometimes painful abstractions sitting around the house and thinks he is still the leader of a new movement." Architect Erich Mendelsohn, Johnson was pleased to note, had abandoned romantic brick work, but his new plain plaster house cost more than $100,000.

After the delirium of the Bauhaus, Berlin was disappointing. Barr found the Prussians barbarous: "The Jews," he wrote to Neumann, "seem to be the only cultivated and artistic part of Berlin." In planning their trip, the two young scholars had expected to visit the major shrines of Modernism in Europe. But during their London sojourn, the artist and writer Wyndham Lewis had introduced them to an art crowd which included Nina

Hamnett, an enthusiastic pilgrim who had recently returned from the Soviet Union. She had given them a list of her friends there, and in the damp chill of Berlin, Barr and Abbott made a snap decision to head east. They felt as though they "were about to go to the moon," Abbott recalled a half century later, but obtaining the visa took only a week and on Christmas Eve 1927, at 6:52 P.M., they boarded a second-class sleeper at Berlin's Ostbahnhof bound for Moscow.

Barr and Abbott planned to stay three weeks but ended up spending almost three months in the Soviet Union, just during the period when the artistic tumult that surrounded the 1917 revolution was beginning to be throttled by Stalin's iron fist. Adventuresome, impetuous, and insatiably curious and critical, the two young men, neither of whom had ever been west of Chicago or south of Washington, D.C., plunged into the exotic maelstrom of Soviet cultural life. While still in London, Barr had scribbled into his notebook names of people to look up: A. V. Lunacharsky, commissar of education who spoke German and French and was "influential and interested in art"; diplomat Maxim Litvinov, the friend of a friend; Constantin Umanski, manager of Tass and a brilliant writer on modern art; and Vladimir Tatlin, a modern designer. An Irishwoman, May O'Callaghan, would be a willing guide, Barr noted; though temperamental, she "knows ways and means."

The diary Barr kept of their visit is a priceless account of the rich intellectual and artistic life swirling through Moscow and Leningrad at that time. From their $1.50-per-night room at the Hotel Bristol, a cavernous velvet-draped chamber containing two narrow beds—and a multitude of bedbugs—they rushed forth to the theater, to concerts and exhibitions, to churches and museums, and to passionate all-night discussions about art and life with the leaders of the Soviet avant-garde. "We feel as if this were the most important place in the world for us to be," Barr scribbled on his first day in Moscow. "Such abundance, so much to see . . . it is impossible to describe the feeling of exhilaration . . . the extraordinary spirit of forward-looking, the gay hopefulness of the Russians, their awareness that Russia has at least a century of greatness before her, that she will wax, while France and England wane." Before the day was out, Barr and Abbott had been bundled off to see Vsevolod Pudovkin's *The End of St. Petersburg*, a film Barr thought marvelously photographed and directed; its propaganda theme "gave it dignity and punch."

He tried to make sense of the volatile band of artists and writers who called themselves the LEF (for left-front), who despised the word *aesthetic*, abhorred romantic individualism, considered their program "aggressively utilitarian," and, to Barr's chagrin, were "strong in the illusion that men can live by bread alone." A leader among them was Sergei Tretyakov, whose very appearance intrigued the earnest young professor from Wellesley. In his khaki shirt and whipcord riding breeches with leather puttees, his face and head clean shaven, Tretyakov peered owl-like through horn-rimmed spectacles. Bursting with books and periodicals, the "ostentatious efficiency" of his study impressed Barr as a laboratory of the arts.

Tretyakov lived in one of the few Moscow buildings whose style could be considered modern and functional. But "only the superficials are modern," Barr noted, "the plumbing, heating, etc. are technically very crude and cheap, a comedy of the strong modern inclination without any technical tradition to satisfy it." The building had been completed less than two years earlier, ostensibly to house insurance workers, but the Tretyakovs and other favored intellectuals had managed to commandeer spacious apartments in it. Barr found the entire structure disappointingly shabby: "poorly built . . . circulation bad, doors too wide, door fixtures bad, piping crude, taps rusty, garbage chute inconvenient, bath plumbing pathetic." The Lenin Institute, built in 1924, struck Barr as "a huge, gloomy, dark gray mass, unhappy in its proportions and monotonous in its fenestration. One virtue is apparent—there are no offensive attempts at decoration." Naively, Barr believed that the brand-new Moscow Telegraph Building, with its "rusticated basement and Gothic reminiscences," would be "the last monument of the older style."

As the weeks passed, Barr and Abbott repeatedly confronted the central paradox of Soviet life: a rhetoric of scientific progress, modern efficiency, and revolutionary logic and a reality of shoddy work, broken promises, and bureaucratic sloth. After many frustrating days attempting to arrange a visit to the Kremlin, Barr and Abbott were finally admitted only to discover that many of the buildings were closed and others were under repair. Barr, who was recovering from a two-week siege of intestinal distress, was furious that they missed two-thirds of what they had hoped to see, and both men were disappointed in what was open. "To cap the climax," Barr fumed to his diary," we were told that the charge for our visit would be twenty-five rubles," or $6.25. They refused to pay and instead complained, successfully, to Narkomindel (People's Commissariat for Foreign Affairs), the bureaucracy responsible for showing the Soviet Union's best face to foreigners.

On another day, when Barr showed up at the Tretyakov Gallery to pick up a stack of photographs he had ordered, no one had even begun the work and he was given an astronomical price for the job. He was not admitted to see the icons in the gallery because other pictures had been stored in front of them. Barr left in disgust, noting in his diary that it was "a typical Russian day of delays and disappointments and wasted time." In Leningrad, Barr and Abbott were kept waiting for an hour to meet a curator and then were told that the person was not even in the building. "Perhaps we can see him next Tuesday," Barr grumbled, "perhaps—perhaps—time wasted—Russia—Russia."

One evening they took the train to Novgorod, a showplace of medieval Russian architecture considered to be the birthplace of the nation. Routed from their berths before dawn, they piled into a horse-drawn cart to jounce "over an incredibly bumpy road past dark houses," Barr wrote in his notebook. "The stars are out so that we have a marvelous view of the Novgorod Kremlin with the white and gold St. Sofia [church] and the great many arched belfries ghostlike in the night." At an inn, they learned from a man with a candle that two rooms were cheaper than one room with two beds, "curious mathematics but the straw ticks are not uncomfortable." By 7:00 A.M., they were back in bed and slept until the thin winter light woke them at 9:30. For several days, the two travelers gaped at the ancient buildings, sometimes clambering over shaky scaffolding to view recently uncovered frescoes from the fourteenth century.

As a result of his trip to the Soviet Union, Barr developed a lifelong enthusiasm for Russian icons. He stayed in his hotel room for many an evening, studying books on the subject, including Muratov's *Les Icones* which he had borrowed from the Ostroukhov Museum in Moscow. Finishing it, he felt "eager to see and talk icons," he wrote in his diary. "A great new field is opening up. . . . I spent the afternoon in a vain hunt for books." Playfully intellectualizing, he was also earnestly attempting to reconcile the intense spirituality of the icons with the intense materialism of postrevolutionary Russia. "What then is the correct Marxian attitude toward God or, to humanize, toward St. Thomas?" he wondered. "And what is the correct Thomistic attitude toward St. Marx?" Humorously, he added, "Elucidate also the debate between the Sts. Marx and Engels and St. Mark and the Angels."

Back in Moscow, the two Americans reveled in Russia's last cultural flowering before the long Stalinist frost. In the daytime they tracked down artists like El Lissitzky, Alexander Rodchenko, and Vladimir Tatlin, searched out the incomparable early modern art collections the Soviets had confiscated from emigré collectors Serge Shchukine and Ivan Morosov, shopped for posters and books, and goggled at Soviet intellectuals' dramatic garb and bohemian life-styles. In the evenings, they sat entranced through plays lasting as long as five hours, concerts of Scriabin, Prokofiev, and a sensational revolutionary ensemble, the Leaderless Orchestra. "I'm sure they would have played better with Klemperer or Koussevitsky," Barr observed dryly. He was more impressed by a young bass singing some Glazunov songs, not so much by his voice but by his rise from a proletarian background: he had started his career as a mechanic and chauffeur in Odessa before being sent by his union to the Leningrad Conservatory.

In his diary, Barr was impetuously poking his critical scalpels at every feature of Soviet culture. On his ninth day in the Soviet Union, he observed that "Russian music is at present curiously romantic and about ten or fifteen years behind the rest of the world." He was not very impressed with Prokofiev, finding a concert of his works "entertaining . . . witty . . . charming" but less stylish than Ravel. Visiting the leading art school in Moscow, Barr winced at the lack of equipment and organization. There was no printed description of the school at all, not even a list of teachers and classes, and the building itself was a mess. "A good janitor to direct storage and clean up rubbish would be a boon," he noted in his diary.

Often after their long, hectic days, Barr and Abbott would repair to the Dom Gertsena, a smoky, overheated artists' and writers' hangout where, over cheese and beer, raucous arguments over truth and beauty competed with booming jazz from the grand piano. Returning to the Bristol in the wee hours, they girded themselves for nightly battles against bedbugs. "Powder and *baume analgésique* having miserably failed," Barr wrote, "we arranged ourselves in pajamas, four pairs of socks, two for the feet, two for the hands, and a kerchief around the neck. They refuse adamantly and obligingly to come out in the cold so that our ears and faces are safe." Conscientious collector that he was, Barr glued a dead bug to a page of his journal. "This is another species," he noted. "This seems to belong to the tick family."

The most impressive individual Barr met during these hectic weeks was Sergei Eisenstein. In the informal ways of that time and place, Barr and Abbott tracked the revolutionary film director to the set at Russkino. He was "almost a clown in appearance," Barr wrote to Eisenstein's biographer more than two decades later, "based on his general physiognomy, the tipped up nose, the baldish head, the wide mouth, the mobile, expressive face . . . the continuous sense that he was playing a rather self-mocking, humorous role." At the studio, the director looked weary and sardonically told the two Americans that he would probably soon die. They took his remark for exaggerated humor and realized only much later how sharply he was already being buffeted by the ideological winds swirling around the Trotsky expulsion and Stalin's drive for ideological purity.

Perhaps to reassure the lurking censors, Eisenstein told the two Americans that he approached filmmaking much as his education as an engineer and mathematician had trained him to deal with equipping a poultry farm or a water system. But, as Barr pointed out in an article based on his visit with Eisenstein, "one must also speak of his rare seventeenth century books, of his passion for the lithographs of Daumier and of his most conspicuous characteristic, a profound sense of humor." The censorship which had turned *Ten Days That Shook the World* into a crude propaganda piece would not hamper him if the director tried to make any films in America. Instead, Barr predicted, he would encounter "timidity, vulgarity, prudery and other varieties of constraint, as well as a severe temptation to cheapen his art." When Eisenstein did come to the United States some two years later, he became the center of a storm of coarse publicity, including his being asked to pose for photographs with Rin Tin Tin. Paramount Studios rejected his screen adaptation for Theodore Dreiser's novel *An American Tragedy*. Then, faced with a noisy campaign for his deportation as a Communist, the studio hurriedly bought him a return ticket to Moscow and announced his departure to the press.

While the two Americans lingered raptly in his Moscow studio, Eisenstein showed them reel after reel of his two current films, *October* and *The General Line*. Asked whether his films derived their sharp cinematic quality from the cutting rather than the shooting, Eisenstein laughingly quoted critics who insisted that his filming was "always carefully premeditated"; then he chuckled wickedly and repeated, "Always carefully premeditated." Having gorged all afternoon on Eisenstein's films, the pair rushed away to the theater, where a less than typically propagandistic play intrigued them. Meeting Tretyakov there, Barr asked him how soon it would be possible to write altogether objectively about the revolution. "Objectivity is bad," Barr was told.

Swept along by such ideological dogma, perhaps finding in it echoes of a religion keyed to the modern world, Abbott and Barr struggled against the stresses and everyday irritations that they considered but a temporary dislocation, an understandable sidebar to the thrilling construction of a revolutionary society. That the food was abysmal Abbott attributed to the fact that all restaurants had been in the hands of foreigners before the revolution. Yet ten years after the ten days that shook the world, the search for a decent place to eat still took tremendous time and tolerance. Barr's diary occasionally exulted in having discovered "a really good one—with real waiters and clean tablecloths and not expensive." Abbott's diary disclosed typical details of Russia's perennial inefficiency, perhaps only slightly exacerbated by the Bolshevik revolution. Most eating places had no silverware: "We had to eat with kitchenware. The service is very shopworn, nothing seems to have been repaired and the upkeep is practically nil."

Famished and flea-bitten, Barr and Abbott emerged from the Soviet Union in early March 1928. Like most Western travelers to Russia during that time, they were relieved at surviving the journey's discomforts and frustrations and also elated that they had witnessed heroic events. In almost three months, they had met a fascinating cross section of the avant-garde in art, theater, and film. Interestingly, both diaries dwell in detail on important cultural figures while saying not a word about starving peasants whom other travelers described, milling in pitiful desperation at provincial railroad stations, of children orphaned by the civil war who were observed hunting for food in ratlike packs, of political commissars ruling by tyrannical decrees. The worst feature of Soviet life, to read these diaries, was bureaucratic gridlock at the post office; Barr had to repack and repack the books he was shipping home. Like so many open-minded visitors to the Soviet experiment, they were thrilled to have glimpsed the future and chagrined that everyday life, at least, did not work.

Yet Barr remained passionately interested in Russian art and in the Soviet Union for the rest of his life. Much to the amusement and occasional awe of his colleagues and friends, the voluminous thick black overcoat he had bought for this journey became a symbol of his individualism and thrift. For a half century he would swathe his spindly frame in its weather-beaten folds at the first sign of frost. Three decades after this trip, Barr still preferred drinking sugared tea Russian-style, out of a glass. The stuffed mammoth he tracked down in Leningrad's Zoological Museum would appear on countless itineraries he prepared for American acquaintances planning a Russian tour. More significantly, Barr tried to maintain his contacts in the Russian art world, corresponding with Russian art historians and museum people whenever it was possible. Eventually he would make two more trips to the Soviet Union, under more luxurious, but inevitably taxing, circumstances. Years after becoming director of the most exciting museum in the world, Barr still considered his Russian visit "the most wonderful experience of my life."

The end of their glorious rush through the culture of revolution left Barr and Abbott depressed. Their guide, Pyotr Likacher, a squat nineteen-year-old whose growth had been stunted by hunger, waved disconsolately from the railroad platform, while the two

Americans burst into tears. Abbott soon went to Paris to join his parents for a motor trip around Europe, and Barr continued dutifully making the rounds of collectors and museums in Munich, Stuttgart, Frankfurt, Darmstadt, Mannheim, and Basel. He considered his German rather good, but at least one native speaker, the dealer Curt Valentin, later listened to Barr and exclaimed, "My God, and I thought I was a German until now!" Barr then went on to France, where the language would prove a lifelong challenge. However, the adventures of Barr's year abroad were not quite over. In July, his funds all but gone, he boarded the boat-train for Cherbourg and his first—and last—crossing in steerage.

American college men, poor though they might be, did not in those days travel in steerage, and Barr, in his diary, carefully noted that, "I don't refer to tourist cabin with its respectable, nay quasiacademic atmosphere. In the tourist third one experiences all the discomforts of steerage without any of the advantages." The *real* steerage, by contrast, immersed Barr in an atmosphere that promised adventure outside the experiences of a prim young man whose superior schooling encompassed little more than Baltimore's gentility, Princeton's tradition, Harvard's snobbery, and Wellesley's well-bred feminism. On the way to boarding the ship, Barr described with wry relish, his passage "in succession through the atmospheres of prison, military conscription, Russian bureaucracy [crossed out], the plague, exile in Siberia [crossed out], ethnographical exhibition and the tower of Babel."

Arriving in Cherbourg, the prospective passengers, all men, were separated from their luggage and fed a supper of beef broth and hard-boiled eggs at long tables. Then they marched under guard to an upper floor of the Grand Hotel Atlantique. In a vast barracks crammed with double-deckers, Barr had barely picked a sleeping shelf before the lights went out. He listened to the men swear and laugh and to the clunk of their shoes dropping to the floor. "You breathe a prayer to St. Eligio to guard your watch," he wrote, "and to St. Martin to watch your coat. Soon snoring triumphs over talk—snoring contrapuntal, polyglot, a cacophony of Hypnos." While consuming his breakfast, a bowl of coffee and bread, Barr heard a nearby Albanian mutter, "Just like jail in New York."

Barr's proletarian return voyage could not have contrasted more sharply with the crossing made some six months later by Abby Aldrich Rockefeller, whose life was about to intersect with his in a most astonishing manner. Mrs. Rockefeller and her husband, John Jr., the only heir to America's most lavish fortune, were returning in first-class splendor from a winter of touring the ancient monuments of Egypt. The couple had made innumerable trips to Europe, especially Abby, whose father, Nelson Aldrich, had squired his family on countless energetic tours of European museums, libraries, galleries, and cathedrals in order to properly introduce them to "their cultural heritage." When Nelson Aldrich entered the U.S. Senate in 1881, he was worth $50,000, it was said; when he left thirty years later, having served under seven presidents, his fortune was estimated at $30 million. In an era when each senator was said to represent a special interest, wrote an unkind biographer, Aldrich "was reputed to represent them all." An iron-fisted Republican in the Senate, Aldrich liberally indulged his eight children; he encouraged his daughters to buy new dresses, provided they chose happy colors, and liked to have the house overflowing with young people.

Abby Aldrich and her three closest siblings were tutored at home by a sternly affectionate German governess, Asenath Tetlow. In a schoolroom on the top floor of their father's house at 565 Broad Street in Providence, Rhode Island, and later in Washington, D.C., they learned proverbs, read a Bible chapter daily, memorized edifying poems, diagrammed sentences, and read American history. Though strong in mathematics, Abby would to the end of her days be uncertain about spelling; Rubens, writes her biographer, "clearly did not look odd as 'Reubens.'" For her coming-out party at the age of nineteen, Abby appeared in a white satin-and-tulle confection, trimmed with white roses. She received fifty-two bouquets and her engagement books for the next seven years, wrote Mary Ellen Chase, were "little else than a roster of Providence young manhood." Her diaries described a breathless round of teas, calls, sleighing, theater, dancing, card parties, parades, and Sunday evening rarebit feasts, each of them described by her as "the best I have ever tasted in all my life."

Into this frivolous social round came an intensely serious, sternly religious young man, a student at Brown University and the only male offspring of the man Sen. Robert LaFollette called "the greatest criminal of the age." John D. Rockefeller, Jr.'s idea of courtship was to pray fervently to learn what God wanted. Still uncertain after four years, already miserable as a minion in his father's office, Junior (as he would be known throughout his life) turned to his strong-willed mother, Cettie, for advice. "Of course you love Miss Aldrich," this sensible rock of a woman replied. "Why don't you go and get her?" Within forty-eight hours, Junior was in Newport, Rhode Island, asking Senator Aldrich for Abby's hand. The senator chuckled over the young man's detailed recital of his financial prospects and cheerfully gave Abby away on October 9, 1901, at Warwick Neck, a lavish waterfront estate he had recently developed some ten miles south of Providence. The main house overlooked acres of lawn, gently sloping to the water. There, from an immense wood and stone boat house built for entertaining, one could board a dinghy to the senator's handsome steam yacht anchored offshore. "I could bring you no daughter," Junior had written to his mother, "whom you would love and yearn over and be more proud of than Abby. She will add new brightness and honor to the name which I am so proud, so very proud, to give her." Junior could hardly believe his good fortune: "She was so gay and young and so in love with everything," he would say, "that I kept wondering why she had ever consented to marry a man like me."

The shrewdest among the many Rockefeller family biographers observed that Abby Aldrich was "the best thing that ever happened to Junior." When the young couple moved in with the senior Rockefellers, wrote Ferdinand Lundberg, Abby introduced "life itself . . . into what until then was a heavily gloomy, Gothic menage which concentrated on sin, prayers, spoils and stratagems . . . a much-needed ray of sunshine in the encircling terror of hellfire baptism and psychic dissonance." Politely, elegantly, joyfully, resolutely, she pursued her own practical philanthropic goals, beginning with her donation of Junior's generous wedding gift to the Providence YWCA. When she saw to construction of the Grace Dodge Hotel for Women in Washington, D.C., during the 1920s, Abby insisted that it include a beauty parlor, a tea garden, and child-care facilities.

As their family grew, Abby and Junior moved into a rented house at 13 West Fifty-fourth Street, and finally in 1910, when their fourth child, Laurance, was born, they built a grand brownstone town house at 10 West Fifty-fourth Street. Although both Abby and Junior shunned ostentation, it was one of the largest private homes in New York. Its nine floors were furnished in the typical style of that day, dark and somber, with formal mahogany stairways, thick moldings, and many rooms crowded with dark, heavy Victorian furniture. But it also housed a gym, an infirmary for the children, and an open-air roof playground. On the walls hung the darkly varnished, morally uplifting oils so beloved by American millionaires, but elsewhere in the house was scattered evidence that this couple also enjoyed exercising individual taste: Junior had begun collecting Chinese porcelains and Abby bought American folk art. While Junior devoted long hours to the trying responsibilities of giving away his fortune, Abby gave herself to her children, a daughter and five sons, born between 1903 and 1915. She saw to it that they did homework and chores and spent their paltry allowances wisely and protected them from Junior's rigidly puritanical rulings; it was a memorable triumph when he allowed them to play tennis on Sundays. Abby also organized their near-royal progresses to the family estate at Pocantico on weekends or to the summer mansion at Seal Harbor, Maine, and arranged for them to meet stimulating people. In 1928, Charles Lindbergh came to supper on the first anniversary of his electrifying solo flight, and, Abby wrote to her sister, when the family went into the dining room, "there, standing around the table was every maid in the house that could possibly get in."

During the middle twenties, Abby suddenly began buying works by contemporary Americans, a mixed bag selected with the advice of an architect, Duncan Candler, ranging from Regionalist Pop Hart to Abstractionist Georgia O'Keeffe. Junior never would understand this kind of art, but he was nevertheless delighted that his wife, in late middle age, could pursue her new interest so enthusiastically. By the middle twenties, her children flying away, Abby had set up a private museum in an unused playroom on the mansion's eighth floor. There, in an Art Deco gallery designed by Donald Deskey, she would serve forbidden sherry to intimate friends and artists. To her son Nelson, a dyslexic who was then at Dartmouth, she wrote: "It would be a great joy to me if you did find that you have a real love for and interest in beautiful things. We could have such good times going about together and if you start to cultivate your taste and eye so young, you ought to be very good at it by the time you can afford to collect much."

While touring Egyptian antiquities during the winter of 1928–1929, Abby and Junior had encountered Lillie P. Bliss, a mature maiden lady whose apartment was crammed with modern art masterpieces she had been buying ever since the 1913 Armory Show. Bliss was a first-rate pianist who had played with a professional chamber group and spent every afternoon like a dutiful Victorian daughter, reading aloud to her mother. In the family's brownstone on New York's East Thirty-seventh Street, Bliss began accumulating modern pictures, with the advice of a close friend, artist Arthur B. Davies. Because old Mrs. Bliss disapproved of her daughter's pictures, they had to be stored in the basement. When a visitor asked to see them, Lillie Bliss would send for a black porter known only as Richard from the Macbeth Gallery, an easel would be set up in the parlor, and Richard would shuttle up and down in a cramped elevator, bringing out one treasure after another. After Bliss's mother died, Lillie rented the top three floors at 1001 Park Avenue and luxuriated in hanging all her pictures in the open.

When she chatted with Abby Rockefeller among the temples and pyramids in Egypt, the two women shared their dismay that New York had no museum where modern art was welcome, a lack which Bliss had for years been lamenting almost daily over tea with the suave and knowledgeable Davies. Then on the boat home, Abby ran into another New York collector of modern art, Mary Sullivan, who had taught art in New York City schools before marrying a prominent attorney whose clients included the New York Giants. The idea of starting a museum of modern art in New York grew out of these casual conversations. In late May (such was the speed with which thoughts became deeds in those days) Abby had her secretary telephone an invitation to a crusty Buffalo businessman and art collector, A. Conger Goodyear: would he come to lunch with Mrs. Rockefeller and the two other ladies?

So conservative was the prevailing attitude toward modern art in American museums that Goodyear had recently been ousted as president of Buffalo's Albright Art Gallery over his unauthorized purchase of an inoffensive Rose Period Picasso, *La Toilette*. Gruffly military in bearing and speech, he seemed an unlikely patron of the avant-garde. Yet he had been investing some of the profits from the family lumber business in modern works ever since 1895, when he acquired a first-rate Gauguin for less than $150. He had never met Mrs. Rockefeller and later said he accepted her invitation mostly because he was eager to see her house and collection. "As usual I had nothing to wear," he wrote later. "I went out and bought a very dignified gray suit which my friends thereafter always called the Rockefeller suit." In the middle of lunch, Abby said to the two other women, "Shall we ask Mr. Goodyear the question we have in mind?" Though the women were clearly the instigators of the museum, seemliness demanded that a man serve as chairman of a committee to found the new museum. Goodyear asked for a week to think it over but was so excited that he accepted the very next day. "It seems unlikely that any other cultural organization had as brief a germination as the Museum of Modern Art," its official historian Russell Lynes would write, "but it was cultivated by people who were used to seeing their visions become realities, people whose wishes were indeed horses and who, not stinting themselves, expected others to act as quickly and effectively as they did."

To find a director for the proposed museum, the group turned to Paul Sachs, whom Abby had met the previous year through the Harvard Society for Contemporary Art. Although Sachs had long ago abandoned his family's investment banking business to pursue his interest in art, his background lent soundness to his opinions in the eyes of the moneyed group which met during the second week in July of 1929 to plan the new museum. In addition to the three women and Goodyear, this organizing committee included many of the most enthusiastic collectors of modern art in the northeastern United States: *Vanity Fair* publisher Frank Crowninshield; paper heiress Mrs. W. Murray Crane; Art Institute of Chicago trustee Frederick Clay Bartlett; Abby's brother, Boston banker William T. Aldrich; Singer sewing machine heir Stephen C. Clark; art collector Chester Dale; philanthropist Samuel C. Lewisohn; and Pittsburgh steel heir Duncan Phillips, who was building a private museum in his Washington, D.C., mansion.

The group was shocked when Sachs proposed that the fledgling museum's director be paid $12,000 per year, plus $3,000 expenses. Trimmed to $10,000 per year, plus $2,500 expenses, it was still a munificent sum at a time when an associate professor earned $3,000 and the director of the Minneapolis Museum of Art was paid $5,000. But the group was even more shocked when Sachs named the individual to be hired: a callow and often tactlessly outspoken twenty-seven-year-old professor with less than two years' experience in teaching modern art to Wellesley girls.

During July, Alfred Barr made the complicated overnight train trip to The Eyrie at Seal Harbor, Maine, where Abby interviewed him while a parlormaid arranged flowers in Japanese pots. "She never ran out of questions," Barr later recalled. To Goodyear, Abby confided that she "liked Mr. Barr . . . his enthusiasm and knowledge would make up for his not having a more impressive appearance." Certainly his impeccably Presbyterian background weighed in his favor. During August he was summoned once again, this time accompanied by Jere Abbott, whom he insisted on having as his assistant. Barr was delighted, he wrote to Abby, that they agreed "so extemporaneously and completely on almost every question concerning our great enterprise." Abbott, he added, was "overjoyed to learn of your remarkably unconventional and youthful tastes in art." By September, when he received his first paycheck, Abby was already asking Barr for advice on purchases of modern art for her own collection, a role to which he would devote himself for many decades, not only for Abby but also for her sons Nelson, David, and John III.

Meanwhile, Barr and Abbott moved their *étrange ménage* into the Hotel Bristol, just off Fifth Avenue in the Forties. "I was excited, I can tell you," Abbott wrote more than a half century later. "We sweated—there was no air conditioning!—over composing the catalog for the museum's first exhibition." Abbott went shopping with Mary Sullivan for office and gallery fixtures, while Barr arranged for blocking off some windows in the rented quarters to give more hanging space. Mary Sands left her job at the Fogg Museum and moved to New York to become secretary to the new enterprise. Goodyear rushed off to Europe to borrow pictures.

As word seeped out into the art world about plans for the new museum, the opposition was already gathering. Published stories emphasized that the organizers were "well-known collectors" who would lend their own works to exhibitions and no doubt "provoke the social buzz of the cognoscenti." Art was "their exclusive toy," sneered one critic, "with which they ride the crest of the wave on an exclusive beach, where only the rich and idle may disport themselves." But the museum's powerful organizers also mustered support from the heavy artillery among New York's opinion makers. "Nothing has recently stirred more interest in art circles," editorialized the *New York Times* on September 9, 1929, "than the project to establish in this city a modern art museum." On the same day, an editorial in the more conservative *Herald Tribune* said that "even if the exhibitions and acquisitions turn out to be chiefly representative of the left wing, an admirable purpose will be served. It will, after all, put that wing to the acid test." The *New York World* editorialized that "a museum given over to modern pictures ought to do much to wake us up."

Sponsored as it was by "disinterested collectors," art critic Forbes Watson predicted that the new museum could "catch up with and pass the Luxembourg . . . in such a short period that Francomaniacs will be surprised." Barr, stunned and elated by the sudden change in his prospects, wrote to Paul Sachs that the possibility of being "a participant in this great scheme has set my mind teeming with ideas and plans. This is something that I could give my life to—unstintedly."

4
A PULPIT FOR MR. BARR

T he Museum of Modern Art preview reception on the afternoon of November 8, 1929, attracted what seemed like every social luminary in New York. "Dressed to the nines," as Barr's associate Helen Franc remembered, they lined up to sign the guest book and then swarmed through the show, chattering affably and probably seeing little. The trustees, many of whom had lent works to the exhibition, wandered about benevolently viewing what they had so rapidly wrought. Most art dealers and critics were surprised to learn that all but fourteen of the works on display were owned by Americans. Among the guests was famous British dealer Sir Joseph Duveen, who had sold millions of dollars' worth of Old Masters to American collectors. He was not the only one in the crowd pressing through the exhibition who was ignorant of modern works, but he was singled out for a personal tour, with Jere Abbott leading him from canvas to canvas and discreetly mentioning the artist who had painted each one.

The glitter and excitement of the opening may have briefly distracted some of those who attended from the shocking stock market plunge, which had transfixed New York's financial estab-

lishment for more than two weeks. During the fortnight before the
opening, the stock market had lost more than one-quarter of its
total value. Before the dive halted on November 13, it had consumed almost half of what stocks had been worth scarcely two
months earlier. As some of New York's wealthy elite debated over
what to wear to the MOMA opening, there was panic on Wall
Street, although no one yet dreamed that this financial cataclysm
would signal the ten years of the Great Depression.

On the twelfth floor of the Heckscher Building, quite another
sort of pandemonium ruled. In three tiny rooms—the largest measured fifteen by forty feet—the four-person staff of the new museum was frantically assembling and sorting and hanging and
rehanging ninety-eight paintings for its first exhibition. Preview-
ing the show a few days before the opening, *Times* critic Edward
Alden Jewell described the chaos—the catalog would not be ready
for a fortnight—but the pictures were "so superb . . . that those of us
who were prepared . . . to deplore the decision to start off with a
French show face palpable embarrassment. Quality disarms."

The space in which the first show was hung had been located by
Frank Crowninshield and Mary Sullivan after considering ten
alternate locations suggested by the Rockefeller family's real estate
agent, William A. White and Sons. The notion of a museum in
midtown Manhattan was unusual enough at that time, when luxury department and specialty stores were just beginning to move
to upper Fifth Avenue. The Heckscher Building at the southwest
corner of Fifth Avenue and Fifty-seventh Street was a medium-
rise office structure, built during New York's boom of the twenties
with typical beaux arts ornamental touches. Locating a museum
on the twelfth floor, where it occupied only two-thirds of the space,
was another unusual idea. Barr was delighted with the site, however, because it was "in a well-known landmark and . . . the rent is
very low—a little over $2.50 a [square] foot, in comparison with
$3.50 and $4 in nearby buildings." Abby Rockefeller hoped that the
building's owner, August Heckscher, might be persuaded to contribute the $12,000 annual rental to "the work," but nothing came
of this solicitation. Crowninshield meanwhile obtained the free
services of an experienced gallery designer who drew up estimates
for wall partitions, lighting, floor covering, and the light beige

monk's cloth Barr specified for wall coverings.

For months before the opening, the trustees and Barr had sparred over the content of the first exhibition. Abby Rockefeller had first proposed a potpourri typical of the pretty, unfocused connoisseurs' collections she knew—safe, dead Americans like Albert Pinkham Ryder, Winslow Homer, Maurice Prendergast, and Arthur B. Davies alongside almost as safe, dead Europeans such as Seurat, Cézanne, Gauguin, Daumier, and Renoir. A few days later, she suggested "a stunning exhibition" of only the Europeans. While Goodyear toured Europe during the summer to see what could be borrowed, the trustees fussed until finally Paul Sachs suggested that the choice be left to Barr. "If our director is worthy of the place," Sachs wired Abby, "his decisions will be correct." Yet, while Barr favored opening with Ryder, Homer, and Eakins, followed by Seurat, van Gogh, Gauguin, and Cézanne, the four women on the exhibitions committee were solidly opposed and eventually Barr joined "the adamantine ladies."

In the end, Barr and the ladies chose the artists for the MOMA's first exhibition exceedingly shrewdly, not only from the standpoint of art history but also of public relations. Cézanne, Seurat, van Gogh, and Gauguin were unlikely to shock anyone at all familiar with more recent avant-garde painting; all four had been dead for decades while Fauvism, Futurism, Cubism, Constructivism, Dadaism, Surrealism, and a host of other provocative "isms" danced on the grave of traditional art. The Post-Impressionist masters shown in the MOMA opening "were respected by all serious French critics ... not long after 1900," wrote Gerald Reitlinger in his classic study of the art market, *The Economics of Taste*. "After 1920, it was useless to expect undiscovered masterpieces."

The artists shown in the MOMA's first exhibition had for decades been a gilt-edged investment for art collectors, and by 1930, the more radical generation which followed had also become profitable. In 1904, a small group of French speculators had agreed to contribute sixty dollars per year for the purchase of modern paintings into a syndicate called *la peau de l'ours*, the bearskin. When the group auctioned its investment ten years later, its holdings included a Bonnard, ten Matisses, and twelve Picassos. All of the group's members vigorously denied being art speculators, but when the sale was over, they divided among themselves more than $25,000.

By 1929 even the Western world's philistines were no longer mocking the four Old Masters of Modernism featured in the Museum of Modern Art's opening exhibition. But more recent works were still provoking angry discussion and even violence. In October, a gang of anti-Modernist vandals had tarred and feathered a Jacob Epstein sculpture in London's Hyde Park. And in November, American philistines were crowing over a front-page story in the *New York Times* about a prize-winning painting at the National Academy of Design whose composition was so obscure that it appeared in two exhibitions and no one had noticed that it was hung on its side.

Nevertheless, in the very same week the MOMA exhibition opened, a New York lover of modern art could view a far more adventuresome array elsewhere in the city: works by Maurice Utrillo, Giorgio de Chirico, Chaim Soutine, Pablo Picasso, Henri Matisse, and André Derain at the Newhouse Gallery; Arthur B. Davies at the Ferargil Gallery: and Clemente Orozco at the Delphic Studios. Barr called his first exhibition "a declaration of faith in the greatness of these men as artists and in their importance as the nineteenth century ancestors of the progressive art of our own time." But quite a few collectors had long ago declared their faith in those works; most of the paintings in the museum's first show had been admired for years in the collections of Lillie Bliss, Samuel Lewisohn, Duncan Phillips, and Chester Dale.

The art critics in America raised a chorus of boosterish hosannas to the exhibition. "The effect is tremendous, breath-taking, and if the exhibition has a flaw, it is that of too great power," raved the anonymous writer for the *Art News*. "The foundation of the new museum marks the final apotheosis of modernism and its acceptance in respectable society," Lloyd Goodrich jubilated in *The Nation*. Forbes Watson in *Arts* deemed the MOMA opening "the most important event of the 1929-30 art season." The champion of Modernism, Henry McBride, acknowledged that "the cause represented by these masters was won long ago," yet he was awed by how many of "our best people" were "consciously undertaking brain work in an art gallery." Even the *Herald-Tribune*'s Royal

Cortissoz choked back his usual fulminations against Modernism and allowed that among the forty Cézannes on display, there were "some notable landscapes" and two or three exceptional examples of still life. "There can be no question that in assembling evidence for a much discussed school," he wrote with uncharacteristic kindness, the museum "has had extraordinary good fortune."

The day after the opening, the *Times* reported Barr's observation that "several art connoisseurs known for their antipathy to modern painting were converted after seeing the exhibition." He also announced that the museum had already received donations of several sculptures. But more than the thin upper crust of art supported the new museum; Barr and his staff were stunned by the eager crowds of ordinary people who thronged to the exhibition. They overloaded the Heckscher Building's elevators and clogged the sidewalk outside, much to the rage of the building's other tenants. Day after day they crammed the museum's modest rooms so tightly that art classes from Columbia, Princeton, and Barnard had to be admitted in the evenings. On December 7, the show's last day, fifty-three hundred people jammed in, bringing total attendance for the month's run to forty-seven thousand.

The museum's opening preview brought a good deal more than professional recognition to Alfred Barr. In the crush of dignitaries trooping through was a young Italian art historian who had been teaching Italian at Vassar while studying art history at New York University. In the fall of 1929, Margaret Scolari-Fitzmaurice had moved to New York to take up a $2,000 art history fellowship at NYU. Attending the MOMA preview with her college advisor, Walter W. S. Cook, Margaret had eyes not only for the pictures but also for the man who had assembled them so handsomely. Slender, dark-haired, bright, and ambitious, her quick tongue and haughty manner alienated her from the other graduate students. But she was drawn to the reedy, intense young man who bustled nervously about, attempting to avoid having to summon up small talk. More than two years earlier, Henry-Russell Hitchcock, who occasionally lectured at Vassar, had regaled Margaret with excited readings of Barr's letters. Now, in the midst of the babbling multitude, Hitchcock introduced her to the young museum director.

Marga, as she was called, had decided to stay permanently in the

United States and to that end had cultivated a colleague, Helen Franc, whose father was a lawyer dealing with immigration matters. But one day in the spring of 1930, Marga flabbergasted her friend by telling her not to bother any further; she and Alfred Barr were planning to get married. Barr's sudden decision to marry, especially just when he was facing the greatest career challenge of his life, was a surprise to many who knew Barr at that time. While the Vassar and Wellesley girls seem to have adored him, Barr had had no known friendships with eligible women. Philip Johnson described him as a loner, who often turned to Johnson as his only confidante.

Though Barr was cool and aloof and unlikely to reciprocate, both women and men often formed strong emotional attachments to him. Jere Abbott, for example, passed up a chance to establish an art department at Wesleyan University to become associate director at Barr's side. "I would rather work with you on this thing than anything I know," Abbott wired Barr. A day later, he wired again: "Don't care what I'm called, door clerk if necessary so long as I can help." Henry-Russell Hitchcock gossiped to Virgil Thompson that Abbott was "preferring apparently the old liaison to all the intangible *seducteurs*" he might encounter elsewhere.

Margaret, who was also nicknamed Daisy, was more than a year older than Barr. She was the daughter of a Protestant Irish mother and an Italian antique dealer who died in the First World War, when Margaret was fifteen. Raised in Rome, where she graduated from the Liceo Mamiani in 1919, she worked as a bilingual secretary in the American embassy and thereby located an appointment to teach Italian at Vassar. She continued her studies in art history and in 1927 received her M.A. from Vassar. Never one to mince words, she later described the degree as "absolutely a farce." She lacked a faculty adviser and had been permitted to write her thesis in Italian. The college was lenient, apparently because it was paying her a pittance for teaching. From her stipend of $900 per year, she had to send a portion to her mother in Rome.

A young woman who boasted of the crowded social calendar she had juggled during her two years at the American embassy in Rome, Margaret felt excruciatingly shy at Vassar. In Rome, she went on ski trips with young men who had just returned from the war and was out dancing three or four times a week in "a constant atmosphere of flirtation." But when confronted with teaching her first classes at the all-women's college she was terrified. "I walked out of my room, walked off on the road, and missed at least a week's worth of classes," she told an interviewer many years later. "I couldn't face the class; I was too frightened."

In order to stay in the United States on a student visa, she began to take graduate courses at NYU, commuting between Poughkeepsie and New York. Some three months after Daisy and Alfred were introduced, she was offered a job teaching at Smith College, with a promise that the following year she would also become director of the Smith College Museum. In mid-March 1930, she rented an apartment near the campus in Northampton, Massachusetts, large enough to accommodate herself and her mother, whom she expected to bring over from Rome.

The growing intensity of her courtship with Barr, however, ended these plans. Soon after her first visit to the new museum, Barr invited her to the Park and Tilford Tea Room, a sedate parlor on the southeast corner of Fifty-seventh Street and Fifth Avenue. Then they went on to dinner at a nearby restaurant. In December, Alfred and Margaret were on the train to Boston to attend the College Art Association annual meeting. Paging through the program, Barr found her name and playfully erased its last three letters. "Why don't we do this?" he asked gravely, leaving her name as Marga. By January of 1930, she knew that "I was hopelessly in love with Alfred." He, however, had qualms, and agreed to marry only after a visit to Princeton for a weekend of soul-searching with George Rowley, a professor of Sienese and Chinese Art, and his wife, Ethel.

After that, "everything was going a mile a minute," Margaret recalled. "We ate crazy meals in terrible restaurants." In the evenings, Barr and Abbott were out incessantly; in white tie and toppers, they were much sought after as "extra men" for social functions. Nevertheless, in May Barr wrote to his mother, "If you turn to page 145 of Frankie Mather's *History of Italian Painting*, you will see the picture of the girl I want to marry." Mrs. Barr may have been impressed or shocked that the painting depicted not a woman but a swarthy young man wearing a scalloped doublet under elaborate armor and brandishing a sword. However, when she was told of her son's engagement to Margaret, she rushed to New York in horror that the proposed bride might be a Catholic.

The elder Mrs. Barr was only "partly reassured" when she learned that Daisy was Church of England. Because a New York wedding would involve delicate "social conventions," Barr told his mother he would marry in Paris. Having learned that this involved considerable red tape and delay, Marga and Alfred married immediately after his mother had gone back to Chicago. Their surprise wedding took place in extreme privacy on May 8, 1930, at New York's city hall, with Jere Abbott and Cary Ross as witnesses. It is doubtful that Barr's parents were even informed; certainly they did not attend. Later that summer there was a ceremony in the living room of the rectory at the American Church in Paris, attended by Marga's mother, Mary Scolari-Fitzmaurice; Philip Johnson; and Hitchcock. Then, "after not a minute of honeymoon," the Barrs were off on the first of many European ramblings together, "on the warpath," as Marga put it, in search of new art. By early July, Barr and dealer J. B. Neumann were combing Germany and Switzerland for art to be shown in a MOMA exhibition during the following season.

A casual oversight by Barr gives a hint that he was suffering from some ambivalence over his impulsive marriage. The newlyweds spent many days addressing austerely elegant wedding announcements to their many friends in the United States, as well as to MOMA trustees and supporters. Margaret bought stamps and mailed her stack of announcements in a street mailbox. Alfred, however, handed his announcements to the hotel concierge to stamp and mail. Like many another letter given to a hotel clerk to mail, the announcements never arrived, much to the Barrs' embarrassment.

The only overt clue left by Barr that he was thinking about domestic arrangements during this time is in an article he submitted to a home-decorating magazine published by Marshall Field's department store. It was never printed, but in it he wrote critically about the way Americans furnished their houses: "In most American homes, the only honest furniture is to be found in kitchens and bathrooms." He particularly admired refrigerators as "the finest examples of modern furniture—a machine for keeping food cold, but also to the eye a beautiful and perfect object." He blamed women for choosing overdecorated furniture and men for letting them do it. "The aesthetic judgement of the American man is most highly developed in the matter of deciding whether the 1930 Buick is better looking than the 1930 Chrysler." He suggested that couples shop together for furniture: "Let his wife buy the curtains; let him buy the chairs!"

Following his own advice, Barr was adamant in rejecting the furniture Margaret's mother offered to give the couple when they set up their first household in New York. Instead, he wanted only expensive Mies van der Rohe, Breuer, or Le Corbusier copies. For some months, therefore, they made do with two beds, two bridge tables, and four folding chairs in the apartment they leased at 424 East Fifty-second Street. Their flat was in the same building where Philip Johnson had an apartment, furnished with genuine Mies van der Rohe, Breuer, and Le Corbusier. In the Barrs' small bedroom, there were two narrow single beds from Bloomingdale's, with black headboards and footboards, along with two narrow chests of drawers, also painted dead black. It took two years to get the dining-room table, specially ordered from the Herman Miller Company in Zeeland, Michigan.

From the beginning, Marga played the supportive role typical of a minister's wife, while also guarding Barr's precarious health and his precious time. Faced with his scatterbrained indifference to practical matters and his consuming love affair with the museum, she soon took charge of the family finances and all the other quotidian details of life. At considerable cost to her own career— she never pursued the Ph.D. in art history for which she had a fellowship at NYU—Marga thenceforth devoted herself primarily to the care and feeding of Alfred Barr.

She was at his side during almost all his trips to Europe, serving as a translator in many delicate negotiations, while keeping a detailed record of every taxi fare and restaurant tab for reimbursement from the museum. More than forty years later, she still resented that the MOMA did not provide them a per diem expense account. They often crossed the Atlantic in third class and had to eat in "shopkeepers' . . . and truck drivers' restaurants," she com-

plained to an interviewer. Once, they could hear the sounds of
Bastille Day celebrations in the streets outside while "nailed into
our room in the Avenue Matignon" struggling with bookkeeping. "I
would torture myself trying to make up these accounts," Marga
recalled. "Torture myself."

Marga worked late into the night to help her husband assemble
his famous catalogs, saw that his slides were in order when he
lectured, controlled the foods he ate and the liquids he drank,
fished crumpled unpaid bills or undeposited checks out of his
pockets, and sequestered herself behind a frosty hauteur which
chilled almost all those it touched. "The museum was his mistress,"
she would say without rancor after he died, and years later she was
still guarding his sacred flame with fierce, Cerberus-like devotion.
Until she died in December 1987, Marga Barr refused to counte-
nance a full biography of her husband.

The courtship of Marga and Alfred that spring of 1930 and their
subsequent marriage had to occupy the small space left over after
Barr's single-minded labors to establish his modernist chapel. Like
her mother-in-law, Marga had to adapt her wishes and activities to
her husband's work and be ready at all times to help. For a brief
moment, the philistines had been repelled, some even charmed, but
they would soon besiege the museum afresh. As Conger Goodyear
remarked about the reception for the opening show: "For this once
and once only, not a finger of scorn was pointed." When the museum's second exhibition opened, however, the sunshine of critical
approval vanished. "Nineteen Living Americans," which opened on
December 13, 1929, attracted derision from even the MOMA's
friends.

Choosing living artists was always an extremely ticklish matter.
Europeans, at least, were far away and in any event mostly unaware of the tiny new museum in New York. But many of the
Americans lived, literally, within a stone's throw of the museum.
People who were ignored could storm in to complain or have their
friends make trouble for the museum. Barr sidestepped the whole
mess by letting the trustees choose the artists to be shown. From a
ballot which listed one hundred artists' names, each trustee selected fifteen; these votes were then tabulated by an anonymous
committee which named the final nineteen. If this procedure was

designed to protect the museum against the wrath of artists who were left out, it failed. It also guaranteed a motley array of works, with no focus and of mixed quality. Barr had tried to liven up the final exhibition by urging the inclusion of photographs by Tina Modotti and Sherrill Schell, but the trustees could see no artistic value in such work and refused.

In the catalog, he tried to anticipate criticism with uncharacteristic disclaimers: the committee had tried to avoid favoring any school or manner; all the artists chosen were American citizens, even though five were foreign born and three lived permanently abroad. In hanging the pictures, Barr had tried to create visual themes and contrasts, but this had meant scattering works by the same artists in different locations. Understandably, he had trouble finding any unifying relationship among the artists whose only unifying characteristic was their nationality. Nor was the catalog enlightening about how these artists related to the larger world of art or to the past. Barr professed pride that this show was "deliberately eclectic," but he would never have dreamed of presenting such a jumbled mass of works by Europeans.

Now the critics pounced. One said the show had "the mediocre taste of 70-cent roast beef." Another suggested that its title should have been "Some Pictures We Thought Good and Some That Have Been Bought by the Directors." The *Times*'s Jewell grumbled about the foreigners masquerading as Americans, and even kindly Henry McBride was horrified at the unprogressive examples on display; all of them should be relegated to the conservative Metropolitan, he wrote. The crowds did not tax the Heckscher Building's elevators to glimpse these canvases, either; of those who did come, many showed up only to complain about the omission of their friends or of themselves. Indeed, the eccentric way the artists had been chosen eliminated several talented American Modernists, for example Arthur G. Dove, Stuart Davis, and Charles Sheeler.

But the masses returned in greater numbers than ever before for the museum's third exhibition, "Painting in Paris," featuring works by Picasso, Matisse, Derain, Bonnard, Braque, and Rouault. Barr's catalog essay mercilessly shamed visitors about American backwardness in supporting Modernism. He included lists of other museums where the artists' work was shown "to remind visitors of what progress other museums . . . have made in the acquisition of modern paintings." The mobs of visitors returned; on Saturdays more than 3,000 bodies squeezed into the galleries, a blockbuster crush that obstructed the pictures. So dense was the swarm that the show was extended for an extra two weeks, and the final attendance record, always carefully tallied at Barr's insistence, came to 58,575. By contrast, an exhibition of Winslow Homer, Albert Pinkham Ryder, and Thomas Eakins at the end of that season drew only 11,388 viewers. The message was clear: the public was ready for first-rate European painting but not for second-rate contemporary Americans; and it was indifferent even to first-rate American painting from the nineteenth century.

A museum was not a college classroom, Barr was learning. Audiences had to be lured in with all the wiles of showmanship he could devise. Worried about the need to present a steady parade of sensational exhibitions, Barr and Abbott drew up a list of fifty possible shows, many of which never materialized. How much should the MOMA pander to attendance figures? How could he induce people to look at unfamiliar, even shocking, works, not to mention appreciate them? Over the next few years, Barr would hone a strategy for attracting public attention that would impress the most zealous missionary. With controversial exhibitions and lively social events, with enticing catalogs and provocative public statements, with articles and lectures, he pounded home the message that modern art was progressive, interesting, perhaps even slightly wicked, and that the American ideal of fair play demanded that it be given an open, honest, and educated evaluation. Paul Sachs had advised Barr to "follow the line of least resistance in our Board of Trustees to start with," advice typical of an investment banker dealing with wealthy clients. Now Barr decided on a more evangelical tack: he would never again directly involve the trustees in choosing works to exhibit.

He also sedulously cultivated an image of being sympathetic to American art, the more so because of Abby Rockefeller's interest in it. But his actions during the next few years indicated that Barr felt much more comfortable with European art than with American. His orientation developed naturally from his schooling. Like all scholars of his generation, Barr had been trained to look eastward across the Atlantic for the pinnacles of artistic achievement. He had never studied American art for the simple reason that no college gave courses in it. Married to a European, a woman who sniffed aristocratically at American barbarism, Barr himself discussed American painters disdainfully, in European terms: John Singer Sargent was "Manet vulgarized," he told Goodyear; Stuart Davis was "a rather feeble [Raoul] Dufy, plus [Jean] Lurcat"; the odd European critic might be interested in Sheeler or Marin, he believed, but definitely not in Robert Henri, Walt Kuhn, or George Bellows. Asked for advice on buying a modern picture for Wellesley's Farnsworth Gallery, Barr replied that a European picture would be "considerably better in quality . . . unless you wish to spend perhaps twice as much for the American picture."

Despite such contempt, Barr worried about his ignorance of American culture. A few years later, when he was preparing to write the catalog for an exhibition of American works in Paris, he asked a Princeton professor of American history for a reading list to fill in his "scanty knowledge of American civilization."

Answering critics who persistently claimed that the MOMA slighted Americans, Barr would point out that the Whitney Museum was dedicated exclusively to American art, while the Metropolitan had an annual fund for buying works by Americans. His museum, he insisted, had a special responsibility to Modernists of all nationalities; if Europeans dominated its exhibitions, it was simply because European art was more innovative, more interesting, and, without a doubt, more difficult for Americans to encounter. But in all these pronouncements, Barr surely had an eye on attendance figures, and Americans simply did not draw the crowds. Barr's central task was to build an audience for Modernism and attendance was the key to the MOMA's future success. No other museum kept such a close count of every body that crossed its threshold. Nor would a museum at that time have thought to hire a publicist to polish its image.

In the winter of 1930, Barr paid $5,000 given by Abby Rockefeller to public relations pioneer Edward L. Bernays for advice on the museum's first membership and fund-raising drive. But Barr himself was not exactly bereft of ideas for promoting the museum. In June of 1930, the MOMA timed the release of news about its gift of a statue of prizefighter Max Schmeling to capitalize on the excitement over the world championship bout between Schmeling and Jack Sharkey. Barr also was not above using backdoor contacts to obtain more newspaper publicity. In the winter of 1931, he asked Abby Rockefeller to write to a friend who had the ear of *New York Times* publisher C. L. Sulzberger to complain about skimpy coverage of the museum in the newspaper's Sunday rotogravure section. "I noticed two weeks ago, for instance, a whole page devoted to a very mediocre exhibition of photographs," he noted, while the museum's Corot-Daumier exhibition had been ignored. If her friend spoke to Sulzberger mentioning the Rockefeller name, Barr was sure "it would help us a great deal."

During those first crucial years of the museum's existence, it often seemed that not a sparrow fell in the world of modern visual sensibility that escaped Barr's driving curiosity or his contentious opinions. He ordered photos of all Thonet bentwood furniture, with a possible exhibition in mind. He insisted on choosing the style in which *Men* and *Women* were lettered on the museum's toilets. He suggested to Abby Rockefeller that she would find "exciting, witty and clarifying" summer reading in Thorstein Veblen's *Theory of the Leisure Class* and bought her a subscription to *Consumer Reports* because the new publication's "more or less scientific analyses of . . . manufactured goods . . . from radios and motorcars to cosmetics and canned goods . . . [are] . . . extremely entertaining as well as informative." Abby Rockefeller gamely agreed to accept the subscription, but only if Marga would first send her a sample copy. Barr also bought art for her private collection and spent many an afternoon in her penthouse gallery, holding forth on modern art. Like a minister cultivating his wealthiest parishioner, he complimented Abby on her purchase of two watercolors from an indigent artist; Barr hoped that the man's talent would develop "so that your reward may be on earth as well as in heaven!"

Six weeks after the museum opened, he lectured at the College Art Association's annual meeting in Boston on his museum's objectives, one of the earliest papers about modern art ever given before this scholarly group. The rest of the panel conveys the iron grip that medievalists then exerted on art history: Italo-Byzantine ivories, early textiles, a corner of the Caravaggio oeuvre, English Gothic embroidery. Even Margaret Scolari, who was already eyeing Barr romantically and was enchanted by his broad vision of art, gave a traditional paper on "Two Silver Caskets from the Sancta Sanctorum."

Like American scholars, American art critics were mired in a second-hand and second-rate tradition. American publications devoted to art belatedly retailed what was going on in Europe or described the American scene in empty generalities rooted in ignorance. Art writers spun sentences and long, gray essays out of meaningless verbiage. Barr was battling not only the vituperation of those who hated Modernism, but also the woolliness of its defenders. Cézanne and John Marin were both traveling toward "fundamental rhythms," wrote Elizabeth Luther Carey in *The American Magazine of Art*. Of another artist, long forgotten, she noted that he "uses essentials of a style that will belong to the future as it belongs to the present, that imperishable essence that cannot be extinguished by any period fashion." To Barr, whose prose was as free of mannerisms and ambiguity as a Mies van der Rohe chaise and as polished as a steel ball bearing, this sort of lardy tripe was nauseating. He even dealt sternly with the writing of his friends. While he considered Henry-Russell Hitchcock's *Modern Architecture* "a scholarly and critical achievement of the greatest originality and distinction," Barr thought the prose style too Germanically involuted, the spelling too pretentiously French, the illustrations "parsimonious," the margins poorly proportioned, and he even made fun of the author's hyphenated first name. Yet, he remarked, Hitchcock's book was a great improvement over typical American writing on architecture, a body of literature "as provincial, as ill-informed, as complacent, and as reactionary as are most American architects and American schools of architecture."

Barr considered most American art criticism "rotten" and didn't hesitate to say so. Even though he himself had no difficulty in getting his controversial writings published, Barr deplored the low standards of American art magazines. To be acceptable, he wrote to a Harvard friend, articles had to "emphasize gossip, a touch of scandal, personalities and the other tricks of journalism." Asked by a respected dealer, Samuel Kootz, to contribute to a series of deluxe monographs on modern French painters, Barr puritanically declined: "I feel we should have a great many more inexpensive books in English on modern painters before experimenting with de luxe editions." Sent a review copy of *Men of Art*, by Thomas Craven, a respected popularizer of traditional art, Barr pounced on several errors of scholarship and asserted that Craven was "meagerly informed on modern art." Then he lectured the publisher Simon and Schuster on the "grave faults" in the way the illustrations were laid out. The lack of margins left the viewer wondering if the whole picture or only a detail had been reproduced, he argued, while the binding cut half a centimeter off the inner edge of each plate. "I hope that you will not again reproduce paintings," he wrote sternly, "with this unfortunate layout." When the president of the American Federation of Arts asked him to contribute to its publication, Barr snapped that "the *American Magazine of Art* has never interested me because it seemed to carry articles of little scholarly value and to present material of little interest to one concerned with either history of art or more progressive phases of contemporary art." It did not matter to this righteous young whippersnapper barely thirty years old that he was addressing F. A. Whiting, director of the venerable Cleveland Museum of Art.

So consumed was Barr with his missionary task that he even choked back his anxiety, bordering on phobia, at giving public lectures. He still smarted from the trauma of lecturing on religious art at McCormick Seminary in Chicago some years earlier, the trauma sharpened no doubt by the presence in the audience of his father, who was then teaching the art of sermonizing, or homiletics, there. But while he hated addressing large groups, Barr seldom missed an opportunity to sermonize the MOMA trustees. When they called in 1930, Barr willingly gave a Thanksgiving eve lecture at the Samuel Lewisohn home. The list of the twenty lantern slides he borrowed from the Metropolitan for this occasion suggests that he avoided flagrant Modernism and instead dwelled on wide-ranging issues of connoisseurship. Among the slides he showed were ancient mosaics and textiles; a Courbet painting; a Pollaiuollo etching about which in 1926 he had written his first published article; and *The Dance*, a 1909 Matisse which enchanted him, even though he did not then know who owned it. As he used the museum's exhibitions and catalogs, so Barr used even this casual evening's talk to propagandize for works he eventually wanted for the museum. In this case, it took more than thirty years for Matisse's ode to primitive joy, *The Dance*, to enter the museum collection, a gift from Nelson Rockefeller in honor of Alfred H. Barr, Jr.

Despite his reluctance to speak in public, lecture invitations poured onto his desk in one of the two cramped cubicles which served as the whole staff's offices at the Heckscher Building. "Having until recently been an academic person, I have very little faith in lectures," he declined one such invitation. Refusing another, he wrote, "I have offended so many people . . . by my criticism of teaching both undergraduate and graduate and it seems to have done so little good that I really am quite happy to lie low for a time." Often he accompanied his rejection with a list of other speakers along with surgically frank opinions about each one. Among the five or six best lecturers on modern art, he replied to one invitation, was his old Princeton professor Frank Jewett Mather, but "for the nineteenth century only." Ralph M. Pearson "would perhaps be less expensive," while NYU professor Leo Katz was "inclined to oratory, but his fervor has made a deep impression . . . especially . . . among the older generation." Barr's contemporary, Meyer Schapiro, of Columbia University, was "a very brilliant dynamic character" who "might lecture interestingly though most of his work has been confined to the early middle ages."

Within the museum's family, Barr's presence was so ubiquitous and so intense that he sometimes overwhelmed and often distanced those he touched. "He was so concentrated," said Eliza Bliss Parkinson Cobb, an early member of the MOMA advisory committee and later museum president. "He expected such explicit answers from everyone, it made me shy. He didn't make light relationships." Edward M. M. Warburg, another early advisory committee member, called Barr "the guru." "Everyone had to follow his thinking," said Warburg. "He was shy, but awkward would be a better word. He was also puritan beyond belief, not prudish but weighed down with the prospect of so many Augean stables to be cleaned." Warburg remembered not only Barr's "absolutely unsmiling, pinched face" but also his gales of laughter over Warburg's Jewish jokes. Helen Franc, who had studied with Barr at Wellesley, considered him "a fantastic perfectionist. He demanded excellence in all things. He had impeccably high standards and insatiable curiosity," but he was also "a great showman, with a wonderful flair for publicity." Philip Johnson marveled that "his interior life was so rich that he didn't need many friends. He was not a socializer; he was silent, introspective, nerve-racked."

The two men had met in the late spring of 1929, when Barr was teaching at Wellesley, where Johnson's sister Theodate was a student and where his mother was president of the alumni association. Johnson had already bought his first modern painting, a Paul Klee costing seventy-five dollars, and spoke enthusiastically about starting a museum of modern art. "I'm starting one in the fall," Barr replied curtly. "Why not include architecture," Johnson suggested, and Barr shot back, "Why not?" This exchange, as condensed as a Mondrian painting, blossomed into a warm, lifelong friendship, an alliance no outsider and no happening could crack. During the middle thirties, when Johnson returned from a trip to Germany with glowing admiration for Hitler, the museum's liberal adherents were so angry they refused even to speak to him. But Barr continued right on with the friendship, even though he violently disagreed with Johnson's point of view. "I had disgraced myself by admiring the Nazis," Johnson soon realized, but he never forgot Barr's unshakable loyalty. Barr could always count on Philip Johnson to give the museum any art that the trustees found too shockingly strange. No matter how bizarre the items Barr wanted, said Eliza Bliss Parkinson Cobb, "Philip always bought them and Alfred always got them."

When he first met Barr, Johnson would relate at his friend's memorial service more than half a century later, "all I had was enthusiasm. All I had was a thirst for knowledge. Alfred had the knowledge and the ability to communicate that knowledge changed my life—a Saul/Paul conversion—to the cause of architecture." Johnson was four years younger than Barr, the son of a prominent Cleveland attorney. While studying classics at Harvard, he had read an article on modern architecture by Henry-Russell Hitchcock and soon became fascinated with the as-yet-unnamed stark and angular style embraced by the Bauhaus architects and a few other Europeans.

During the MOMA's early years, when they lived in the same building, Barr and Johnson spent many a night in impassioned argument over the aesthetics of the new style, tripping over its lack of a name. Hitchcock, who often joined them, had referred to the progressive architects as New Pioneers in his 1930 book, *Modern Architecture*. As he had criticized the book for its opaque writing style, so Barr resisted Hitchcock's uninspiring name for the new movement. As the three young aesthetes were debating the latest inventions of modern architecture one evening in 1931, Barr came up with the name that neatly described the new style, that resonated with history, and, above all, that would stick—International Style. He saw in the designs of Le Corbusier, Ludwig Mies van der Rohe, J. J. Oud, Walter Gropius, and others the first new Western mode of architecture since the thirteenth century, a style "as fundamentally original," he would write, "as the Greek or Byzantine or Gothic." The name was an echo of the fifteenth century's international style of painting, so called because artists in many European countries began to use oil paints, linear perspective, and secular subject matter as part of the High Renaissance. "He coined the phrase," Johnson later said, "Russell Hitchcock wrote the book, and I was the drummer and screamer-arounder."

To Johnson, a wealthy, young, and restless intellectual with no pressure to get a job or find a vocation, the Museum of Modern Art became a harbor and Alfred Barr was its beacon. Traveling through Europe, Johnson wrote long, chatty, opinionated, and affectionate letters to "Dear Alfo" and signed them "Pippo." The Bauhaus at Dessau, he confided, was the most beautiful building he had ever seen: "It has beauty of *plan* and great strength of design. It has majesty and simplicity which are unequalled." Barr was not so sure that the sterile, gaunt Bauhaus style would last; rather, he considered it a reaction to previous excesses of eclectic ornament. He expected architectural decoration to return one day, and when it did, he speculated, it would not derive from geometry or abstract painting but rather "from mechanical devices, such as steam radiators, electric bulbs, hydrants, mailing chutes, radio dials, electric fans, neon tubes."

Shortly after the Museum of Modern Art opened, Barr was already urging Hitchcock and Johnson to organize an exhibition of modern architecture, but the two were temporarily diverted in 1931, when the Architectural League of New York organized an offensively conservative exhibition billed as new design. In a mixture of protest and high jinks, Johnson and Hitchcock, with help from Barr and his staff, set up a counter-exhibition in a storefront on Seventh Avenue. It was titled "Rejected Architects," recalling the notorious Salon des Refusés in Paris at which the Impressionists, rejected by the academy, first showed their works. The American rebels hired sandwich men to shuffle back and forth in front of the League's exhibition, bearing signs that read: "See Really Modern Architecture, Rejected by the League, at 903 Seventh Avenue." To help spread the word, Barr asked the director of the College Art Association to let Johnson give a speech on rejected architects, rather than Oscar Stonorov, an architect whose work Barr judged "fairly good, but his English accent is fairly unintelligible." Johnson had already written Stonorov's speech for him and Barr saw to it that he gave it, as well.

Hitchcock and Johnson's "Modern Architecture: International Exhibition" finally opened at the MOMA on February 10, 1932. Various versions of it would travel around the United States for seven years, carrying the stripped and geometric gospel of Gropius, Mies van der Rohe, and Oud to such unlikely corners of the country as the Sears, Roebuck store in Chicago and Bullock's Wilshire department store in Los Angeles. Barr wrote the foreword to the exhibition's two-hundred-page catalog and also got publicist Edward Bernays to apply his persuasive talents to obtaining front-page publicity for the exhibition in the *New York Times*. (Bernays was no stranger to controversial ideas; he was the brother-in-law of Sigmund Freud.)

The progressive architecture so passionately advocated in this widely traveled exhibition alerted many American architects to the International Style and impressed them not only with its simple beauty but also, in those lean Depression years, with the cost-cutting potential of unornamented facades and modular interiors. For Barr, close cooperation with Johnson brought within reach the realization of one of his long-term aims for the museum: establishment in July 1932 of a department of architecture. For Alfo, Johnson not only funded this department, paying his own salary and that of a secretary, but also hired English film critic Iris Barry as the MOMA librarian. She would become curator of the museum's film library three years later, when Barr was finally able to convince the trustees of the need for such an unheard-of department in a museum.

With architecture officially within its domain, Barr exulted that the museum already was becoming "very different from what the noble gentry wanted." His persistent propaganda was dispersing willy-nilly the high-minded fog banks of "art appreciation" in which many trustees dwelled and firmly planting their feet in factual, historical scholarship. They had wanted an institution something like London's Tate Gallery or Paris's Luxembourg Museum, dignified public showcases where unproven contemporary works could rest until the severest critic of all—time—quietly rendered a final verdict about their worth. Today, the artists of the past receive frequent revaluations by art historians and also by the vagaries of public taste. When the Museum of Modern Art was established, by contrast, the trustees believed that the test of time was infallible; the museum's role was simply to present untested work until a "real" museum in the future rejected or accepted it.

By hiring Barr, however, the trustees were tangling with an evangelical whirlwind, a scholar with a flair for communicating complex ideas in simple language, a connoisseur who was quotable in newspaper headlines. Because of him, their museum was moving toward becoming a center for all that was new and provocative in the visual arts, a missionary chapel proclaiming the gospel of Modernism, loudly and persistently.

The trustees were not so much opposed to the newfangled departments for which Barr incessantly lobbied as they were cautious in the face of financial problems aggravated by the Depression. Moreover, almost all of them were collectors of painting and sculpture; they found it difficult to see aesthetic value in works like photographs or mass-produced objects, which appeared to have little monetary value and no prospects as investments. Contributions for the first year's budget of some $75,000 had trickled in slowly and almost entirely from a few trustees. Total membership also lagged; only 434 people had paid a minimum of $10 to join. But such modest resources only spurred Barr to a grandiose—and

totally unsuccessful—effort, in the spring of 1931, to raise an
endowment of $3.25 million.

In the closely argued, fact-laden pamphlet he wrote in support of
this effort, Barr seemed unaware that the American economy was
sinking into a dangerous morass, that banks were closing and
farmers were destitute, and perhaps he had not even noticed that
former business executives were selling apples on the sidewalk
right off Fifty-seventh Street. Instead, he boasted that 257,312
people had ventured into the museum during its first sixteen
months, making the three cramped rooms in the Heckscher Building the sixth most visited art museum in America. For its size,
however, it obviously ranked first. He proudly pointed to the infant
institution's profound impact on American culture, quoting from
glowing newspaper and magazine reports and from letters he had
solicited from museum officials and university professors. He also
subtly argued the investment possibilities of supporting modern
art. The artists whose works had been shown in the museum's
opening show had been scorned as "unintelligible and ridiculous"
during their lifetimes, he reiterated; now canvases by these same
men were bringing as much as $100,000. Seurat's *A Sunday After-
noon at the Grand Jatte* had sold for $200 shortly after the artist's
death; the Art Institute of Chicago had paid $25,000 for it in 1925;
but only five years later the Institute had refused an offer of
$400,000. In a crassly worded moral that only a speculator could
love, Barr underlined that "this represents an increase in 'bid'
value of about 200,000 per cent in forty years and about 1,500 per
cent in the last five years."

Barr was not sure if this tract had struck the right note, but he
knew an experienced fund-raiser who could point out its strengths
and weaknesses and who was considered a master of persuasion.
Apologizing for not having written for two weeks, he sent a final
draft of this brochure to his father, the professor of homiletics in
Chicago. Of the man who had raised an endowment for his Baltimore church in record time, Barr asked "for criticism on how our
points are made, what should be left out, what should be included."

Like an effective sermon, Barr's brochure pricked New Yorkers'
pride in a vein similar to that of the *Harvard Crimson* article five
years earlier, in which he had called Boston a modern art pauper.

First he flattered, calling New York "a double-ended funnel through which Europe and America exchange ideas as well as merchandise." Then he shamed, asserting that the city's public collections of modern art were far smaller and less advanced than those of fifty smaller cities in Europe and half a dozen in the United States. Finally he prescribed, declaring that existing museums, like the mighty Metropolitan, could not possibly encompass recent art because it "is as complex a subject as modern science and fluctuates more rapidly."

Because it owned virtually no art, the MOMA had to borrow almost everything it exhibited, an especially difficult task since the lending institutions could expect nothing in return. Most of the museum's trustees were collectors, and "the aggregate of their collections, if brought together," Barr yearningly pointed out, "would form probably the most important collection of modern art in the world." Though he knew that the times were not right for raising purchase funds or even for soliciting substantial donations of art, Barr had always carefully tracked the ownership of works he coveted. As he visited museums and viewed pictures in private homes, he would scribble down not only the titles of what he saw but also his private grades for them. After visiting the Adolph Lewisohn collection, he marked Cézanne's *Uncle Dominic* "C-plus" and *Madame Cézanne* "B." He gave Lillie Bliss's Cézanne, *Large Still Life*, an "A," but her *Madame Cézanne* rated only "A-minus." Duncan Phillips's Gauguin, *Tahiti*, merited just "C-plus," while Paul Rosenberg's *Yellow Christ* was a straight "A." Much later, when the museum's collection was bulging, Barr would tell collectors which of their treasures he would deign to accept, but in 1931, Barr would have welcomed even "C" works. Yet, the problem of building a collection which would be perpetually modern loomed on the horizon.

Abby Rockefeller sympathized with Barr's desires to form a permanent collection. She alone had contributed one-third of the museum's operating funds to date and had promised to give the museum all the modern works she owned. While she continued to seek Barr's advice on her personal art purchases, she also gave him $500 in 1931 to buy prints for the museum during his annual summer visit to Paris. Modern art prices were so low that Barr actually could buy a number of important graphics for such a modest sum. At least one Paris dealer also gave the museum a free Picasso print, "as testimonial for the pleasure . . . I had by making your acquaintance."

For Abby Rockefeller, the small sums she spent on her own purchases were mere pin money, not serious investment. For reasons of patriotism more than esthetics, she bought primarily Americans: Arthur B. Davies, Walt Kuhn, Stuart Davis, Yasuo Kuniyoshi. For reasons of thrift, she bought a vast number of graphics and in 1940 gave sixteen hundred etchings, lithographs, dry points, and woodcuts to the MOMA print room named after her.

Abby Rockefeller's relationship with the young man who had barely passed muster at Seal Harbor in 1929 became more cordial and social. The previous winter she had asked him to suggest the names of amusing, young French speakers whom she could invite to dinner with Henri Matisse, people who perhaps could blunt her husband's outspoken dislike of modern art. Though shy and distant, Junior had no scruples about calling the museum "Abby's Folly." Barr had suggested a few possible dinner guests, but he himself was unable to attend. Marga was having her tonsils out and in her absence, Barr was spending a week at Philip Johnson's country place. A few months later, Abby ventured timorously to address Barr by his first name. To an "old-fashioned New Englander, it comes a little hard," she wrote, "to get out of the habit of calling people by their titles rather than the informal and nicer way of calling them by their first name." Along with the new intimacy, however, Abby expressed gentle criticism of Barr's last-minute style in administration of the museum. Perhaps he and Goodyear should "work the museum on the Russian five-year or ten-year plan."

That a Rockefeller could admire an administrative device invented by the Russian Bolsheviks gives some idea of how radicalized even American plutocrats became as the Depression deepened. But Abby Rockefeller's suggestion also conveyed her worry that Barr was not making enough long-range plans for the museum, or was even a gentle rebuke at his inability to delegate authority or to create an efficient administration. To be sure, Barr toiled for inhumanly long hours, organizing one interesting exhibition after another, and seemed to be visible everywhere on the New York art scene. He spoke to every reporter who called; he often guided visitors personally through the museum; he thoughtfully examined the work of every artist who cared to bring a portfolio to his office; he answered every letter that arrived, no matter how incoherent or misguided. Saturdays he spent touring New York galleries and on Sundays he often caught up on paperwork.

Nevertheless, each exhibition was a new exercise in frantic last-minute improvisations, partly because Barr insisted on perfection in hanging and labeling pictures and in the accompanying catalogs. These were not the pallid listing of titles and works on display which museums then considered more than enough to guide the public. Rather, Barr insisted on producing an ample pamphlet, if not a book, for each exhibition. He considered the catalog far more important than the exhibition, a point of view that museums today share. But in the early thirties, no one had ever heard of comprehensive catalogs. Philip Johnson still recalls Barr's rage when he arranged an architecture exhibition without a catalog. "If I had to work for you," Johnson cried, "I wouldn't," although he would later concede that Barr was right. Exhibitions come and go, but catalogs are forever.

Along with his famous wall labels, Barr wrote most of the catalogs himself in a fluent style that painlessly enticed the reader to learn. He included piquant biographical details and concrete scholarly background about each artist, along with pungent aesthetic judgments. He insisted on illustrating as many items as possible and gave such mundane details as dimensions, name of the lender, and provenance (history of ownership). He buzzed restlessly over the text, first writing in longhand, then overscribbling draft after typed draft; given a clean retyping, he would scribble and scratch afresh. The limpid prose which readers lapped up and critics adored did not gush forth freely onto the page, but rather dripped painfully, sporadically, and, worst of all, slowly. Barr also insisted on meticulous layout, illustration and design; often he would order large blocks of type reset because the look of a page offended his sensitive eye.

More than reliable information, Barr's catalogs also contained a subtle subtext pleading for understanding and further study of puzzling art. But, like a master evangelist, he inserted the message so adroitly that the reader absorbed it along with the fascinating facts. In the introduction to a catalog for a Paul Klee exhibit in 1930, for example, Barr remarked that the artist's work "sometimes suggests the painting of primitive peoples. But there are in Klee's work qualities other than the naive, the artless, and the spontaneous. Frequently the caricaturist which he might have been emerges in drawings which smile slyly at human pretentiousness. . . . At times he charms by his gaiety or makes the flesh creep by creating a spectre fresh from a nightmare."

"Like everything you do," wrote founding trustee Frank Crowninshield of a 1941 revision of this essay, "it is a perfectly balanced combination of learning and interest." He wryly complained of "the many, many colds in the head which I have contracted by standing, with bared head, in your presence—my hat in my hand, my mind in a state of wonder!" Prose that could evoke this kind of awe from the sophisticated editor of *Vanity Fair* took time, and although Barr's catalogs were so valuable that many are still in print today, the trustees were frustrated indeed when the gorgeous catalogs sometimes arrived weeks after an exhibition had opened.

They were especially irritated because many of the works in the museum's early exhibitions were for sale; the catalog served as an essential guide to the quality of each work and also as a checklist for desirable items. The lack of any funds for buying art frequently prompted Barr to write to particularly generous trustees, like Abby Rockefeller, urging them to see this or that show. Beyond getting them involved with the museum, he was hoping that they would buy some of the works and later give or will them to the museum. Often Barr was able to persuade dealers to loan precious works to the museum because its exhibitions, in many instances, were more effective than their own gallery shows in promoting sales. Barr would borrow items he particularly coveted and was surprisingly successful in eventually acquiring his wish list. Of the 123 works in the 1931 exhibition "German Painting and Sculpture," for example, sixteen—more than 12 percent—ended up in the MOMA collection, most of them before 1939.

The space in the Heckscher Building was obviously too small to accommodate much of a permanent collection and only the most

modest temporary exhibitions. In October 1931, the trustees leased
a five-story limestone town house with a sixty-foot frontage at 11
West Fifty-third Street on condition that $80,000 for renovations
could be raised over a three-year period. The landlord was John D.
Rockefeller, Jr., whose home on Fifty-fourth Street backed up
against it. Such was the deflationary effect of the Depression—and
the persuasive power of John's wife, Abby—that the rent for the
entire building was $8,000, two-thirds of what part of a floor in the
Heckscher Building had cost two years earlier.

While the building was being remodeled, Jere Abbott was per-
suaded by the trustees' executive committee to accept the director-
ship of the small museum at Smith College, the very same job that
Margaret Scolari would have held if she had not married Alfred
Barr. It was a budget-cutting move. Abbott later claimed that
Barr had never told him he was on the way out; a chance remark by
the museum's front deskman, Pat Codyre, had conveyed the news.
However, Barr wrote to Paul Sachs about his chagrin at losing
Abbott: "I do not feel that the trustees realize his value and tend to
consider him merely as a lieutenant to me." Sachs consoled Barr
with a reminder that "the times are very unusual; that everyone
has very serious and unexpected problems." For Abbott, the new
job helped him to deal with his chagrin over Barr's marriage and
the breakup of their bachelor quarters at the Hotel Bristol. "Alfred
certainly enjoyed his power," Abbott recalled bitterly many years
later. Abbott saw himself as the only member of the museum's
staff who "kept the museum from being entirely Alfred's." To the
end of Barr's life, Abbott would write to him warmly and affec-
tionately, even though the replies he received were guarded and
distant.

The exterior of the museum's new building gave little hint of the
shocking works to be viewed inside. Its entrance was slightly
raised from the sidewalk and flanked by Ionic columns. Wrought-
iron balconies curled around the third-floor windows and a heavy
cornice masked a fourth floor housing servants' quarters and a
penthouse above that. Although cut up by awkward walls, the
interior was spacious enough for a permanent display of what few
works the museum owned, as well as several temporary exhibitions. Monk's cloth concealed most of the Edwardian ornament,

although the ceilings of what had been the drawing room, living room, and dining room still intruded elaborate plaster cartouches and dentils into spaces now filled with Modernism rampant.

It was not puzzling aesthetics that stirred controversy when the first exhibition held in the new building opened in May 1932. Planned as a show of American muralists, it proved so naively altruistic that it almost destroyed the museum. The organizers were members of the junior advisory committee, a group of lively young art aficionados organized at Abby Rockefeller's behest as a training ground for future trustees. The committee included Lincoln Kirstein, Philip Johnson, Monroe Wheeler, Eddie Warburg, James Johnson Sweeney, Lillie Bliss's niece Elizabeth, and Abby's son Nelson. Sons and daughters of affluence, they went along with fiery young Kirstein's argument that if their elders could only view the unappreciated works of American muralists, "all those rich people would want to have their houses painted."

Far from flattering wealthy patrons, however, most of the murals submitted were designed to enrage them. Even before the show opened as the centerpiece of the museum's installation at its new building, controversy rent the board of trustees. The discussion was especially heated over a depiction by Hugo Gellert of J. P. Morgan, John D. Rockefeller, Sr., President Herbert Hoover, Henry Ford, and Al Capone wielding a machine gun behind a pile of moneybags titled *"Us Fellas Got to Stick Together"—Al Capone.* Some trustees wanted to cancel this offensive exhibition entirely; Sam Lewisohn, who usually slept through all the meetings until something of interest came up, opened one eye, trustee Eliza Parkinson recalled, and murmured sarcastically, "I thought this museum needed money."

Most of the trustees agreed that it was too late to cancel the show; the artists, apprised of the trustees' displeasure, threatened to hold it elsewhere. Barr considered persuading Gellert to remove the offending work. In a letter to the artist he drafted but never sent, Barr claimed that the museum's executive committee had a policy forbidding "any representation of a living person which has any malicious intent." Barr wanted to assure Gellert that the museum did not object to depictions of "class struggle as such," but it did object "on the basis of the personalities that are lampooned,

who may be indirectly responsible for the future of the museum."
As a compromise, Goodyear suggested that scrapping the catalog
might mollify some trustees, but Barr disagreed because this
would be gravely unfair to the other artists in the exhibition and
defeat its original goal: "to provide illustrations of work by potential mural painters other than those of the [conservative] school of
Rome."

A flurry of fence-mending followed. Nelson Rockefeller called on
J. P. Morgan, on his grandfather, and on the Rockefeller family
attorney, Thomas M. Debevoise, and explained the museum's dilemma; the Rockefellers' public relations counsel, Ivy Lee, was
consulted; and shortly Barr was able to send Abby Rockefeller a
heartfelt cable: "Problem has been extremely difficult hope solu-
tion will be satisfactory." Given the hard times and the widespread
radical militancy of the day, the critics dealt rather gently with the
show. It was "a riot of propaganda," with few redeeming virtues,
wrote one, but its worst feature was the "rather terrifying picture
of what may happen to our public buildings if all the young experi-
mentalists were given free rein." In the face of the brouhaha, Abby
Rockefeller displayed her typical tolerance for views she abhorred
by buying Ben Shahn's crackling *Sacco and Vanzetti* from the
exhibition and, three years later, giving it to the museum.

The advisory committee's provocative exuberance reflected the
crusading euphoria of the staff Barr gradually gathered around
him. His tiny budget meant minimal salaries, but no one seemed to
mind in the heady atmosphere of campaigning for a sacred cause.
Barr's secretary, Alice Malette, gladly accepted thirty-five dollars
per week. As assistant director, Jere Abbott was paid only eighty-
one dollars per week, but he cheerfully minded the store while
Barr summered in Europe and Vermont, dusting picture frames
and buying several small fans when the summer heat reached the
boiling point. The chance to be part of the museum's modernist
mission attracted a variety of earnest, enthusiastic young people.
Monroe Wheeler moved from the advisory committee to the library
committee and then into a full-time job arranging exhibitions of
prints and book illustrations. He was grateful that Barr allowed
him to do "absolutely what I wanted," even taking books apart so
that all the illustrations could be displayed and then having them

rebound. A former student of Barr's at Wellesley, Ernestine Fantl, turned up to volunteer and soon was hired by Philip Johnson as secretary of the Department of Architecture.

Abbott doubted that there ever had been "a serious plan" for running the museum, pointing to "the extraordinary number of crises." Certainly, Barr's administration was so casual that people sometimes joined the staff while he was away or by invitation of whoever was around. Elodie Courter, for one, had her eye on a MOMA job all through Wellesley and had visited all the museum's exhibitions. After graduation, she wandered in one day in 1933 and was put right to work, typing captions on two thousand slides, although she had no typing skill. Soon she moved into supervising traveling exhibitions and stayed on for almost a decade. Ione Ulrich dropped by one afternoon in 1932 on the off chance that there was a job in the accounting department. Told that the sole bookkeeper had just left, Ulrich blithely announced, "I'll be in Monday." There was no money to pay her, she was informed, but she doggedly repeated, "I'll be in Monday." When Ulrich gave the lawyer for whom she worked her resignation, he offered to match whatever the MOMA was paying. But Ulrich cheerfully replied, "You can't pay me what I'll get there." The following Monday, she marched into the museum and stayed for twenty years. No museum staff was more dedicated than devotees like her, but some trustees reasonably wondered whether a permanent organization—and eventually a major cultural institution—could be built out of the melée, which resembled more an impromptu picnic than a dignified banquet.

Like the staff, the museum's collection grew in a sporadic, haphazard fashion. With no budget at all for purchases, Barr had to be grateful for donations, mostly castoffs from trustees. The first gift painting was Edward Hopper's brooding *House by the Railroad*, for which Barr effusively thanked trustee Stephen Clark. This picture's existential loneliness and surreal shadows were not much appreciated in 1930, nor was the artist's straightforward technique considered innovative or particularly modern. Hopper's works also were not especially valuable; in 1923, two years before *House by the Railroad* was painted, the Brooklyn Museum had bought a Hopper for $100, his first sale in ten years. In a 1929 article on Otto Dix, Barr had lumped Hopper vaguely with other Americans who were faintly reflecting German painters' new-found interest in subject matter under the rubric of Die Neue Sachlichkeit, the New Realism.

Nor could Barr have been very enthusiastic about the other early gifts to the MOMA collection. Among the seven paintings and seven sculptures which came to the museum before 1931, only the Hopper, Wilhelm Lehmbruck's *Standing Woman*, and Aristide Maillol's *Summer* and *Desire* were what today would be called "museum quality." Looking back on the museum's early acquisitions, Barr himself later worried about the collection's "opportunistic" early development. When he supplied background for Goodyear's history of the museum's first ten years, Barr wrote in 1941 that "it would satisfy my sense of order as director to have it recorded that the museum's development has been, at least partially according to plan."

The museum's motley collection reflected confusion over whether a modern museum should—or could—have a permanent collection at all. "The value of all contemporary art is debatable," Barr had written in 1929, "and much of it is certainly transitory, no matter how important it may seem to be to us at present." As Goodyear described the museum's role in 1929, "When a creative artist has not yet attained recognition from other museums . . . this institution [should] give him a full representation in its collections," but the MOMA's place should be that of "a feeder" to other museums; "where yesterday we might have wanted twenty Cézannes, tomorrow five would suffice." In 1932, in a broadcast about the MOMA's first permanent building, Barr agonized over the collection's scope. "That which is modern today will not be modern in 1952 or 1982," he said. "Our permanent collection will therefore be continually changing." He seemed to be agreeing that the MOMA would relate to the Metropolitan as Paris's Luxembourg related to the Louvre.

But in another segment of the broadcast, Barr conveyed his intense ambivalence about this concept. "To live," he said, "we need the bone and sinew of a permanent collection which has strength and vigor, which looks toward the future but which stands upon the finest work of the recent past." How to remain modern while still building a strong collection? It was a dilemma, perhaps insoluble, which would dog Alfred Barr to the end of his career. He often talked about winnowing out the older works when they were no longer modern, but few of the items that entered the collection ever left. As late as 1977, the museum still retained all but four of the first fourteen works it acquired.

Although acquisitiveness seems to be a basic trait of all museum people, Barr was motivated by additional considerations. As he contemplated the other art museums in New York, it seemed unlikely that any of them would create a collection that would show the public a comprehensive and balanced survey of Modernism. The Whitney, then located in four adjoining town houses on Greenwich Village's Eighth Street, showed and collected only Americans, and rather conservative ones at that. Beginning in 1932, it sponsored a biennial exhibition of representative contemporary works; its founder, Gertrude Vanderbilt Whitney, gave $20,000 for purchases. But critics complained that while the museum's interior was "decorated with the fastidiousness of a boudoir," the spaces were unsuited to showing pictures. Nor did the biennial give a true cross section of what American artists nationwide were doing; New Yorkers had contributed more than 100 of the 157 paintings on display.

At the Museum of Non-Objective Art (which became the Guggenheim) the eccentric director, Hilla von Rebay, watched the founding of the Museum of Modern Art with jealous rage. "It is sponsored by wealthy people and always crowded," she reported to her protégé, Rudolf Bauer, a mediocre painter whose works she lavishly bought. When Barr tried to borrow a few paintings from her museum's large collection of Kandinskys in 1931, von Rebay urged Solomon Guggenheim, her patron and lover: "Guggi . . . refuse, that is no company for you."

The Metropolitan also seemed to view the upstart in the Heckscher Building with lordly disdain. In the almanac of significant art events it published for 1930, it listed the anniversaries of such distant museums as the Walker Art Gallery in Liverpool (England) and the Toledo (Ohio) Museum of Art, but there was not a word about the opening of the MOMA, less than a two-mile walk from the imposing temple of art on Fifth Avenue and Eighty-third Street. In 1931, Goodyear and the Met president William Sloane

Coffin discussed the possibility of allowing a joint committee to buy American pictures with the Met's $15,000-per-year Hearn Fund. They would be shown at the Modern for ten years and then either return to the Met or be sold to other museums. But the idea never went beyond talk.

That Barr took no part in these discussions indicates how heavily the trustees weighed in shaping the museum's basic policy. Like a minister accommodating his deacons for the greater good of the church, Barr trimmed his clear vision of what was truly modern and designed quite a few exhibitions during the early years to mollify the conservatives on the board. In the spring of 1930, for example, he showed Jean Baptiste Camille Corot (died 1875) and Honoré Daumier (died 1879), much to the critics' approval. He also showed early watercolors (1916–1918) of Charles Burchfield, a painter of romantic landscapes who was a special favorite of Abby Rockefeller. When Julien Levy opened his avant-garde gallery in 1931, Barr resented and perhaps envied Levy's freedom to exhibit the latest provocations in paint. "A gallery like mine took the novelty out of his hands," Levy crowed, "by giving shows before he did."

In the fall of 1930, Goodyear insisted that Barr postpone an exhibition of German art scheduled for December because he thought Barr was giving too many shows for Europeans. But when he selected the works to include in the exhibition four months later, Barr took advice from no man. When Germany's leading modern art authority, Julius Meier-Gräfe, offered to select what should be shown, Barr not only politely ignored the offer, but also one of the four painters Meier-Gräfe deemed most crucial. Time has proven Barr's judgment more perceptive than Meier-Gräfe's. Almost all the artists he chose to show are still considered leading German Modernists more than a half century later. The *Times*'s Jewell bemoaned the exclusion of half a dozen artists well-known at the time, but only one of those he mentioned, László Moholy-Nagy, has stood the test of a half century.

A look at the works of the one painter Meier-Gräfe recommended that Barr ignored gives a revealing sidelight about Barr's taste. Lovis Corinth reveled in lavishly painted luscious nudes, erotically posed. This was not a kind of painting that ever appealed to Barr.

Perhaps because of his innate puritanism, perhaps because they were too reminiscent of Boucher's sly eroticism or the excesses of flesh in Rubens, Alfred Barr was put off by prettiness in painting. He once rejected a lushly beautiful painting for hanging in an exhibition because, he told Edward Warburg, "it would seduce the public." Often when a collector asked his advice on a purchase, Barr discouraged his interest in an attractive picture, saying, "You'll get tired of it." Barr frequently justified his austere taste in art with his favorite quotation: "Art teaches us not to love, through false pride and ignorance, exclusively that which resembles us. It teaches us rather to love, by a great effort of intelligence and sensibility, that which is different from us."

For the 1931 exhibition of German art, Barr used the catalog to deliver another stinging sermon about Americans' neglect of Modernism. In Germany, he marveled, more than fifty museums owned works by one or more of the artists in his show. He was awed that "even in small towns the museums have their figure by (George) Kolbe or (Ernst) Barlach, their painting by (Erich) Heckel, (Carl) Hofer or (Max) Beckmann, their watercolors by (Paul) Klee and (Ernst) Nolde." A city like Dresden boasted more than 700 modern works in public collections, Hamburg had 1,577, and Essen, 774; Munich and Berlin had entire museums devoted to modern art since Impressionism.

The *Herald-Tribune*'s Royal Cortissoz gave the exhibition a dose of his customary bile. "The last word in Teutonic 'expressionism,'" he called it, featuring "crude and dull pictures . . . the crudest, most raucous and least interesting of modernistic groupings we have seen in a long time." One visitor to the exhibition, aghast at what he saw, was moved to sarcastic doggerel, and the *New York Times* considered it relevant enough to print in its Sunday art pages:

Dot Sweetness it iss ausgespielt,
Each dog he hass his day;
De prize dog iss der Schweinehund—
Shoost now he hass hiss say.
To hell mit heart, to hell mit head—
All tings but buts and gall are dead.
Ve painds mit an indensity

Vat's simply an immensity.
For dis iss our brobensity,
And iff dey takes offensity
It shows deir stupid density.
De louse has over our liver crawled—
Der Katzenjammer it iss called.
Down mit der Traumerei und Schwaermerei
Hoch, hoch die Schweinerei.

The ignorance and transparent hostility in these lines must have enraged Barr. But as mockery strengthened the early Christians, so Barr could only defend what he believed in all the more fiercely. As he had written in his catalog, Germany was not only in the front rank of appreciation for modern art but also the home of the Bauhaus, the world's first community for the integrated pursuit of all the progressive visual arts. Berlin was vying with Paris as the Western world's cultural center and Munich was not far behind. But within less than two years, all that would fall to a horde of raving philistines that beggared the Biblical description. The arts in Germany would suffer a blow so grievous that they would not rebuild even in half a century. By a strange twist of circumstance, Alfred Barr would be an eyewitness to the opening scenes of the disaster.

5
BUILDING THE CONGREGATION

A friend submitted an anonymous sample of Barr's handwriting to a graphologist in the spring of 1933. While Lena Mayer-Benz's elaborate letterhead boasted that she was admitted to practice as an expert witness in the German courts, Barr's friend and psychiatrist, Dr. Otto Garthe, clearly considered her report on the handwriting of a "29-year-old American" as a wonderful joke. But her closely typed two-page assessment was surprisingly close to the mark.

He shows "distinct aesthetic refinement and a cultivated intellect," she wrote. "He draws others to him, forming a wide network of adherents. . . . He is uncommonly versatile . . . one is tempted to say, unlimited avenues of development are open. . . . Personally, he is a user-up of men, a devourer of men and his days overflow with varied encounters with people, experiences and interests. He demands excitement, variety and change." But his complex personality, she warned, "will produce . . . anxiety . . . that . . . will demand more physical and psychic strengths than he commands. . . . The new always beckons . . . he will always follow the same pattern: seduced by yearning toward an unreachable, always receding *fata morgana.* The only successful therapy involves a months- or even years-long narrowing of outside experience."

The graphologist had no idea who the subject was, nor that a year earlier Alfred Barr had come close to nervous collapse. Physically frail and emotionally intense, unable—and unwilling—to delegate any but the most menial task associated with *his* museum, he struggled in the spring of 1932 with increasingly severe bouts of insomnia, complicated by painfully stinging eyes. By early June, Abby Rockefeller was so concerned that she suggested he see a doctor. Referred to a specialist in nervous disorders, a Dr. Davis, Barr was told that he was suffering from nervous exhaustion. Dr. Davis prescribed sleeping pills but pointed out that "a long rest with complete freedom from responsibility was the most essential means of regaining normal sleep."

Reluctantly and in haste, the trustees arranged to give Barr a year off on half pay. They brought in two men as substitutes: Philip Johnson's friend Alan Blackburn to mind the store and Holger Cahill to fill in the blanks Barr had left in the exhibition schedule. Cahill was a big man, a Viking of Icelandic stock, bluff, self-taught, and in love with things American as only an immigrant's son can be. He had developed the Newark Museum's American collection and was Abby Rockefeller's adviser for American primitive art. He immediately unleashed "a flood of Americana," as Goodyear described it, within the Museum, exhibitions with such dubiously modern themes as "American Folk Art: The Art of the Common Man in America, 1750–1900" and an array of art objects from ancient Aztec, Mayan, and other early Latin American cultures titled "American Sources of Modern Art."

Alfred and Marga meanwhile prepared to spend a restful year in Europe. Marga sailed alone in June and spent a busy summer socializing in Paris and researching the ownership of the Picassos in an exhibition at Galeries Georges Petit. Later, she went to Italy to visit her mother. Barr stayed in New York, planning as much as possible for the museum's year in his absence. In mid-September, he joined Marga in Italy. After spending Christmas with Marga's family in Rome, they traveled to St. Anton and stayed for six weeks until, Barr wrote, "we could no longer stand the discipline of the *Skimeister.*" Still he remained sleepless, as Marga recalled, "always exhausted, always exhausted, always exhausted." A German woman they met in St. Anton recommended "just the man," Dr. Otto Garthe, a psychiatrist in Stuttgart.

The Barrs went directly there, expecting to enjoy some leisurely months, making and renewing contacts among modern artists, dealers, scholars, and museum folk, while Barr was under treatment. A New York doctor had previously suggested that Barr consult a psychoanalyst, and Dr. Garthe, whose wife, Margarethe, was a sculptor, proved congenial. The psychotherapy, Barr wrote to Abby Rockefeller, was "a natural step in curing insomnia." She, however, doubted that it would work. "I have gotten a very strong impression," she replied, "that often psychoanalysis adds a new complication rather than removes the old one." But the worst complication Barr faced was simply being in that place at that time. Germany in the winter of 1933 was hardly the place for a nervous man seeking restful sleep.

City streets seethed, while the rhetoric of Armageddon filled the air and the printed page as Hitler pressed Germany toward dictatorship. To a visitor, the Byzantine political machinations in Berlin may have been obscure, but there was no mistaking the menace of Hitler's brown-shirted bullies roaming the streets. They baited Jews, brawled with Communists, and beat anyone who refused to give the Nazi salute: "Heil Hitler!" Yet, in a series of turbulent elections, peaceful German burghers supported the National Socialists in record numbers and on January 30, 1933, as the Barrs were settling into their modest pension in Stuttgart, Adolf Hitler became chancellor of Germany. On February 27, the Reichstag fire climaxed another violent election campaign in which, on March 5, the Nazis won 44 percent of the vote, slightly less than in the previous summer's election. But other parties, frightened by the chaos, supported an enabling act on March 23, which gave Hitler dictatorial powers for the next four years.

"Stuttgart took its revolution very calmly," wrote Barr. "Many people knew of some acquaintance who had been granted the 'protection' of prison for racial or political reasons, but no one seemed to know how many had been thus treated . . . the flag and flagpole merchants did an enormous business; the swastika was everywhere. . . . The surviving newspapers resounded with the glory of the National Resurgence. Rathenau Street, named for a Social Democratic statesman murdered by the Nazis in 1922 was re-named Göring Street . . . there were parades by night and day." But after the turmoil of the previous nine months, the city seemed peaceful. He was surprised, wrote Barr, "at the thoroughness and rapidity with which the new order invaded every business and profession, every intellectual and cultural activity."

Within weeks, the Nazis wrecked the world's leading art establishment. With hardly a whimper of protest, they purged the finest scholars and museum directors in Berlin, Hamburg, Düsseldorf, Mannheim, Cologne, Chemnitz, and Karlsruhe, some because they were Jewish and others simply because the Nazis detested scholars or intellectuals. "These changes appeared one by one in tiny news items," Barr reported sadly. But no news items at all announced the disappearance of hundreds of paintings by modern artists or the closing of galleries of modern art. Some sixteen thousand works by modern artists of every nationality eventually were purged. Many of them ended up in the private collection of Hermann Göring, who offered them around at bargain prices to foreigners like William L. Shirer, if they paid in dollars.

Nor were events in Stuttgart conducive to Barr's quest for a good night's sleep. On March 12, 1933, barely a week after the Nazis took control of the Württemberg government, they closed a show of Oskar Schlemmer paintings at the Stuttgart Civic Gallery. A reviewer in the local Nazi newspaper called the pictures "unfinished . . . decadent," and saw no reason for exhibiting them except "to show the insolence of the 'artist' who has sent such half-baked rubbish on tour." The paintings were hidden away in the basement, an example, Barr wrote, of treating works of art like "persons who, politically or racially anathema to the regime, are put in jail, in *Schutzhaft* [protective detention]."

A few weeks later, the Barrs attended the first Nazi meeting on art in Stuttgart and were aghast at hearing the Württemberg minister of education rant that "art is not international . . . nor is there any such thing as international science. . . . If anyone should ask 'What is left of freedom?' he will be answered: there is no freedom for those who would weaken and destroy German art." This mass meeting had been called by the *Kampfbund Der*

Deutschen Kultur (League for Struggle for German Culture), which even before the Nazi takeover had denounced an urban plan by Gropius as "an enemy fortress in the midst of the Fatherland" and Le Corbusier as "the Lenin of architecture." In the seats of honor, the American couple saw the leading officials of the state of Württemberg and "behind them, row on row," wrote Barr, "sat painters, sculptors, musicians, architects, teachers, critics and many of the most active amateurs of the arts in Stuttgart."

After the orchestra had played Bach's Second Brandenburg Concerto, Dr. Otto zur Nedden, a Tübingen professor newly appointed to head the *Kampfbund*, proclaimed "a German academic freedom," without "insidious foreign influence." The Barrs listened in horrified fascination as eminent Tübingen scholar Max Wundt denounced contemporary philosophy as "besieged by un-German influences," while Prof. Adelbert Wahl called for a total cleansing of German culture. "The widely held contemporary belief that art is international is absolutely misleading," ranted another speaker. "What does not issue out of the depths of the spirit with conscious responsibility toward German culture, is not art in the German sense of the word." To Alfred Barr, the veteran of many a bitter skirmish with American philistines, these words may have sounded vaguely familiar. He was encouraged by his observation that the audience seemed restrained; hand clapping was "sporadic." He had scrutinized one row of ten listeners and found that "two clapped regularly after each statement, but five never clapped at all."

But he soon realized that he was in the midst of a uniquely sinister happening. This was not a genteel, civilized debate over the nature of art; these speakers were not at all like the conservative, perhaps misguided, critics of modern art with whom Barr had so vigorously debated in the past, and this audience harbored no will at all to resist the madness. Indeed, a shockingly large segment of educated Germans also cheered as modern paintings disappeared from public view and as modern artists and scholars were publicly humiliated. Hardly a murmur opposed even the absurd decree that steep, sloping roofs were to be added over "un-German" flat roofs.

Not a corner of German culture escaped the Nazi boot. In early

May, Barr attended a reception for the Württemberg minister of education for which the invitation said, "attendance obligatory." He noted that "lining the steps on either side of the portal were brownshirted troops of the National Socialist *Sturmabteilung* (S.A.) standing with rifles in their hands. Between their ranks, the artists filed."

Fed up, the Barrs moved to Ascona, an artists' colony in Switzerland, in June, and Alfred fought his horror and fury in his usual manner—with the pen. On the balcony of their room he lay "as naked as possible in the sun," Marga recalled, furiously writing four articles about what he had seen in Germany. He was confident that Americans wanted to know about the Nazis' persecution of modern art and artists. However, one rejection letter after another from America's leading magazines indicated forcefully that editors were not interested. Some thought Barr's observations too narrow and too localized, while others doubted that the Nazis intended literally to carry out the draconian program set forth by Hitler. Even a modernist crusader like Philip Johnson returned from Berlin with the belief that the Nazis would soon mellow.

Barr tried desperately to raise the alarm. "The journalist in Berlin or Munich has no idea of the extraordinary narrowness which dominates the Nazi movement in the provinces," Barr wrote to his friend Lincoln Kirstein, who was then editor of an avant-garde magazine, *Hound and Horn.* "I have had my eye on the innumerable articles on Nazi Germany in other magazines and have found nothing in any way like [these]." Nevertheless, Kirstein published only one of Barr's articles, "Nationalism in German Films." The remaining three essays finally appeared in 1945, in *The Magazine of Art* where Barr was on the editorial board.

"I wrote the articles in a rage," Barr explained to its managing editor, John D. Morse, "intending them to serve as warning propaganda, but such was the indifference in this country toward the cultural crisis—as distinguished from the political and racial issues—that the articles met with little interest. For propaganda purposes, I adopted a very objective and factual style, intending far more objectivity than I felt." But even though his articles had finally been published, he still grieved that it took so long. In 1948, when *Harper's* magazine published an article about art under the

Nazis by Prof. Hellmut Lehmann-Haupt and sent Barr a postcard announcing it, he tartly fired back: "It is now almost fifteen years since the editors of *Harper's* rejected an article I wrote on exactly the same subject. I understand they were not interested at the time."

Barr did insert a terse account of the Bauhaus's sad fate in the MOMA *Bulletin* for June 1933. Forced to leave Dessau in 1932, the Bauhaus reopened in Berlin as a private school under Mies van der Rohe. "In April 1933," Barr wrote, "the National Socialist storm troopers forcibly removed the students and faculty from the old factory where they had been holding classes. No explanation of this move has been issued by the government. Classes are at present being held in the houses of the various professors."

"The future is uncertain."

Predictably, considering his zest for involvement, Barr soon moved beyond the role of reporter into active intervention. While still in Europe, Barr was writing letters on behalf of German scholars who were forced to leave. In May 1933, he asked the director of London's Courtauld Institute to help Erwin Panofsky, an art historian fired by the University of Hamburg for being Jewish. He was writing not simply to help Panofsky, Barr said, but "because I think you now have the opportunity to secure the services of one of the most remarkable minds at work in the history of art." Panofsky's colleagues, attempting to stop his dismissal, had called him "the greatest living art historian."

Panofsky was no particular friend of modern art, but his warm lifelong relationship with Barr was based on loyalty to all art scholarship and to those who practiced it with skill. By 1934, when Panofsky had settled at Princeton, he was writing to Barr on behalf of young H. W. Janson, one of his most brilliant students at Hamburg. "I feel that persons of this caliber should be . . . given an opportunity to develop outside of present Germany. In a way, these loyal and intelligent Aryans who cannot bring themselves to agree with Nazi principles . . . are in a worse position (psychologically speaking) than even the Jews." Brought to America with Barr's help, Janson would write a brilliant art survey textbook which to date has gone through three editions and twenty-three printings.

Returning to his MOMA desk in the summer of 1933, Barr found the first trickle of what would become a torrent of desperate appeals for help from German artists and scholars. "It is impossible to receive another post in Germany in the present direction," wrote Dr. Justus Bier, director of Hannover's Kestner Gesellschaft, one of Germany's earliest and best museums of modern art. He had been dismissed because he was a Jew. "Therefore I am constraint [sic] to look out for a new existence in foreign country." Barr promised to place Bier's case "before an American committee organized to assist some of the intellectuals who are leaving Germany. You may rest assured that everything possible will be done for you."

Bauhaus painter Josef Albers's appeal for help in the summer of 1933 set off a flurry of activity at the MOMA. Barr found a job for him teaching at Black Mountain College, an avant-garde school recently founded in North Carolina by nine disaffected Florida professors. The school had no funds for faculty and the immigration authorities insisted that immigrants have means of support. "Unfortunately, Albers' not being a Jew," Eddie Warburg wrote Barr, "my usual contacts are fairly useless as my friends are only interested in helping Jewish scholars." But so excited was Warburg at the notion of having "the nucleus for an American Bauhaus" that he put up $2,500 and persuaded Abby Rockefeller to add $500 to furnish Albers's salary for two years. Pragmatist Philip Johnson was ecstatic about this coup; he considered Albers "very useful in all the industrial arts and typography."

Eager and rested (although insomnia would sorely trouble him for the rest of his life), Barr plunged back into the museum maelstrom. He was probably none too sorry to have missed some of Holger Cahill's lesser efforts, for example "Fruit and Flower Paintings" and "Objects of 1900 and Today." And he was probably glad to note that he had been missed. Summing up the MOMA's season in June 1933, *New York Times* critic Edward Alden Jewell called it a "very plump lean year."

But the following season would be plump indeed, at least in terms of publicity. Its centerpiece was the nationwide tour of a single painting, which Barr had set in motion early in his sabbatical. He had borrowed the sensational picture from the Louvre, the first instance, the publicity trumpeted endlessly, of the august

French museum lending a work to America. The triumphant progress of *Whistler's Mother* across America garnered paeans of patriotic piffle. Billed, on no grounds whatever, as "one of the six most popular pictures in the world," James A. McNeill Whistler's painting, formally titled *Arrangement in Grey and Black No. 1: The Artist's Mother*, painted in 1872, drew duly gaping throngs.

Newspaper headlines emphasized how the artist had been driven to work in Europe by America's provincialism and how this very picture had been spurned in America during the 1880s, only to be snatched up by the Louvre for $400. But none of the stories mentioned that, in life, Mother Whistler was hardly the paragon of motherhood enshrined in the icon her son painted. A stern Presbyterian, like Alfred Barr's mother, she confiscated her small son's toys for strict Sunday observance and would willingly have seized his paintbrushes too, if he had let her. Like, perhaps, Mother Barr, she would have much preferred that her son become a Protestant preacher rather than mingle with a loose artistic crowd.

For the nationwide tour, her likeness had "travelled like a returned transatlantic flyer, preceded by police escorts and surrounded by armed guards," wrote Barr anonymously in *Fortune*. He obviously gloried in the publicity spotlight focused on his museum by the exhibition, even if the press releases had inflated the insurance on the painting by 100 percent, from $500,000 to $1 million. In May of 1934, the picture returned to the Museum of Modern Art after its eighteen months' odyssey, for a final three-day display during the Mother's Day weekend—and a final orgy of publicity. Pres. Franklin D. Roosevelt's mother, a lady as strong willed as the mother in the painting, was on hand to pose with it, although she refused to speak on a nationwide broadcast on the NBC network.

While he later deplored all the hoopla and claimed no hand in "the excessive popular interest" surrounding *Whistler's Mother*, Barr unquestionably helped to amplify the picture's final fanfare in America. The old lady appeared on Mother's Day stamps that year, the picture "mutilated," as Barr indignantly wrote to postmaster James A. Farley, by the addition of a vase of flowers. The artist would be "enraged," Barr fumed in the letter, which he also sent to the *New York Times*, "by the adulteration of his design on the stamp." Though he knew it was far too late to change the plates, Barr nevertheless enclosed a sketch of an alternative stamp, faithful to the original and designed, the compliant *Times* reported, "by an impartial institution like the Museum of Modern Art."

Barr's backdoor efforts to maximize the MOMA's exposure in the *Times* had been extraordinarily successful. Three days after the newspaper reported copiously on his cavils about the Whistler stamp, it reprinted verbatim his MOMA *Bulletin* essay "The Meaning of Modern Art," complete with footnotes. "Modern art cannot be defined with any degree of finality, either in time or character," he had written, "and any attempt to do so implies a blind faith, insufficient knowledge, or an academic lack of realism."

While adroitly avoiding a definition, however, Barr was even then pondering the museum's fifth-anniversary exhibition, to be held that fall, which would illustrate his view of Modernism. He wanted it to "suggest what an ideal permanent collection of the Museum would be." Like a missionary preacher firming up the faith of the newly converted, Barr's selection again reached back to the familiar and much-loved Impressionists and to the big four he had featured in the MOMA's opening show, Gauguin, Seurat, van Gogh, and Cézanne. Bonnard's lusciously colored confections were balanced by Vuillard's dusky Impressionist interiors before the viewer was coaxed into more daring terrain: Modigliani, Derain, and Picasso.

Some two weeks before the fifth-anniversary show's opening, the museum sponsored a talk by Gertrude Stein. The Colony Club ballroom was crammed with the curious, their number limited by Stein to five hundred. Wearing a voluminous brown dress with a silver brooch at the throat, America's most avant-garde expatriate marched to the podium and without introduction began to read an essay titled "Pictures." She never discussed her friendship with Matisse and Picasso, but told how she saw only the gold frames at the Louvre and enjoyed sleeping on the red benches of Italian museums. Her audience "listened intently for nearly an hour to the frequently puzzling involutions and repetitions of her diction and went away afterward to argue," reported the *Times*. Few agreed on what Stein had said, but "most of those present had been entertained."

The anniversary exhibition which opened a fortnight later also entertained visitors while providing a few mild shocks to remind them that they were in the presence of The New. As one mounted the stairways to the upper floors, "the atmosphere chills," wrote critic Forbes Watson. The pictures shown were more contemporary; then came photographs of modern architecture and objects of industrial art. "When the visitor, having reached these altitudes, comes upon a kitchen sink in Monel metal, he is likely to be conscious of a ringing in the ears and is hereby advised to descend to lower planes before his nose begins to bleed."

In his catalog essay, Barr suggested an "unfinished conclusion" about the origins and directions of modern art: the nineteenth-century big four; the abstractionist rebels of 1905 to 1920, such as Picasso, Braque, and Derain; the return to subject matter following the First World War; and the interest during the 1930s in mural painting, the Freudian subconscious, and nationalist myth. What Barr was describing, however, was more the judgments of the taste-making avant-garde rather than the activities of all artists. Barr's overly simple schema ignored nineteenth-century painters of the subconscious like Odilon Redon as well as 1920s explorers of abstraction like Wassily Kandinsky and Piet Mondrian.

With his gift for persuasive prose, Barr often argued most convincingly when his opinions were still unformed. Only a year earlier, in an internal memo about loan exhibitions, he had struggled to define modern art. He tried to argue that all art was divided into only two categories: ancient and modern. The modern, therefore, "may be said to have begun historically toward the end of the thirteenth century, the end of the sixteenth century, or the end of the eighteenth century, depending on terminology." Popularly, however, modern could mean any "art which seems 'advanced' or 'difficult.'" By still another criterion, modern could mean "whatever resembles modern art in medieval or baroque, Egyptian or Cretan, Chinese or Mayan, Benin or Papuan." After spreading the widest possible net, Barr suggested that it was "one function of our museum to exhibit these discoveries and resurrections of the 'modern' art of the past."

By contrast, Abby Rockefeller's ambitions for the museum had been far more modest—and, compared with Junior's lavish giving, her financial contributions were also modest. During the museum's first five years, while her husband was spending $450,000 on the Museum of the City of New York, $1.5 million on the Metropolitan, and $5.6 million on the Cloisters, her own gifts to MOMA amounted to some $200,000. She had simply wanted the new museum "to seek out . . . important new works of art as they were being created—without the benefit of time to test their intrinsic worth." She was echoing an argument Barr frequently used to elicit funds for acquisitions and to justify mistakes in judgment that are inevitable when purchasing works before the paint is dry. "The value of all contemporary art is debatable," Barr had written in 1929, "and much of it is certainly transitory." The trick was in distinguishing the debatable and the transitory from important new works, an exercise which continues to bedevil collectors and museums.

Judging by her own collection, Abby Rockefeller did not commit large sums to modern art possibly because of her husband's anti-pathy to it, but also because her own tastes were conservative. When she later gave the museum a massive gift of works from her collection, she insisted, much to Barr's chagrin, on keeping her name only on the more conventional items. She gave the more adventuresome pieces anonymously, "partly for modesty," Barr later explained, and "partly because she did not like them." After her death, Barr told her biographer, Mary Ellen Chase, that Abby showed better taste "in her clothes and surroundings . . . than in her collections." She did not care for "the more radical forms of modern art, or those forms which discovered the expressive power of what is ordinarily called ugliness."

When consulted by Abby Rockefeller, Barr gave eloquent lectures to make sense of what he liked. Abby's daughter-in-law Blanchette, who would become the MOMA's president some four decades later, recalled a consultation in Abby Rockefeller's private gallery over possible purchases for her collection: "Alfred was a born teacher . . . we . . . listened to him speak about the selection he had assembled, fascinated by his slow, meditative analysis of each work. After considerable discussion, he was careful to see that Mrs. Rockefeller made her own independent choice." Barr was proud of his role as her Grey Eminence, always trying politely to nudge her toward his own refined taste. When she was remodeling

Sixteen-year-old editor Alfred Barr (second row, second from left) poses in 1918 with the staff of *The Inkwell,* newspaper of Baltimore's Boys' Latin School.

In early letters to friends, Barr affected a chop adapted from the signature often used by Albrecht Dürer.

Abby Aldrich Rockefeller, a MOMA founding mother, and her husband, John D. Rockefeller, Jr., leaving the White House after dinner with Pres. Franklin D. Roosevelt in 1935.

A dog lover and canny art collector, A. Conger Goodyear served as MOMA's president for its first ten years.

Edward M. M. Warburg became interested in modern art at Harvard in the late twenties. By 1938, he was a youthful member of MOMA's board of trustees.

The mother of Pres. Franklin D. Roosevelt was persuaded to pose with *Whistler's Mother* in 1935—but refused to be interviewed on the radio.

Nelson Rockefeller and Barr flank New York's Mayor Fiorello
LaGuardia and a sculpture of him by Jo Davidson at a Municipal
Art Exhibition in 1934.

MOMA trustees brought in Thomas D. Mabry, Jr., in 1935 to relieve Barr of administrative duties. A reproduction of Picasso's *Woman in White* is in the background.

Barr poses in front of a giant blowup of a Walker Evans photograph in 1938, two years before the museum started its Department of Photography.

A young museum visitor admires a towering Jacques Lipchitz
bronze, acquired for the museum by Barr in 1937.

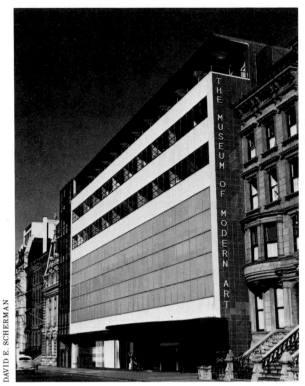

The museum's permanent building at 11 West Fifty-third Street opened on May 10, 1939. Barr thought a famous European modernist should be the architect, but the design by Philip Goodwin and Edward Durrell Stone won raves.

Olga Guggenheim enjoyed riding around Manhattan in her chauffeured limousine while Dorothy Miller told her museum gossip. Mrs. Guggenheim eventually gave more than $2 million worth of masterpieces to the MOMA.

a bathroom in 1933, Barr tried to get the job for Philip Johnson. Abby insisted on Donald Deskey, who had also designed her art gallery, but Barr boasted to Johnson that he had at least "saved her from having special custom-made bathroom furniture."

But while practicing subtle tact with the Rockefellers, Barr could be curtly arbitrary among his peers. In 1934 he was one of three jurors for the Carnegie International Exhibition Prize. Asked for their criteria, *New York Times* critic Elizabeth Luther Carey mentioned merit, and National Academy painter Gifford Beal cited workmanship and intelligence. Barr avowed, "I have no beliefs." Pressed for how he would judge the pictures, he snapped, "By looking at them."

Some of Barr's arrogance stemmed from frustration with the trustees' persistent confusion about what, if anything, the museum ought to collect, not to mention the lack of funds with which to purchase same. The MOMA founders had seriously considered the German concept of a *Kunsthalle*, a space for exhibiting works borrowed from individuals or other institutions. If the museum were to own works, its organizers had vague ideas about the content of such a collection. Goodyear had written in 1931 that the MOMA collection "will have somewhat the same permanence that a river has. . . . When a creative artist has not yet attained recognition from other museums . . . this institution . . . [should] . . . give him a full representation." But the MOMA should be "a feeder" to the Metropolitan and other museums in the same way as the Luxembourg functioned as a way point for works that might end up in the Louvre. In a 1932 MOMA booklet, Barr emphasized that "the composition of the collection will change; the principles on which it is built will remain permanent. . . . After an intermediate period in the permanent collection of the MOMA, many . . . works will find their way into . . . other museums." So adamant were the trustees about the principle of an ever-changing collection that they seriously considered a rule that the museum could not keep in its collection any work by an artist dead more than fifty years.

The question remained academic for some years, since the entire collection up to 1933 consisted of twelve paintings and ten sculptures. However, when Lillie Bliss died in 1931, she had willed the museum a magnificent array of thirty oils; thirty-six watercolors, drawings, and pastels; and fifty prints by such masters as Cézanne, Gauguin, Matisse, Modigliani, Picasso, Seurat, Degas, Derain, Pissarro, Redon, and Renoir. However, the MOMA could receive the bequest only when her executors deemed it "sufficiently endowed and . . . on a firm financial basis." Failing that, the pictures would go to the Metropolitan Museum of Art. At first, her brother and executor, Cornelius, considered a $1 million endowment sufficient, but in March 1934, on the last day permitted by the will, he accepted the $600,000 scraped from Depression-thinned pocketbooks by some 125 supporters.

"New York can now look London, Paris, Berlin, Munich, Moscow and Chicago in the face so far as public collections of modern art are concerned," Barr exulted. Without the Bliss collection, New Yorkers would still "have to hang our heads as a backward community." Beyond puffing local pride, however, acquiring the Bliss collection irrevocably altered the museum's dimensions. Where previously Barr's emphasis had been on borrowing and exhibiting the best examples of the widest variety of visual arts, he would henceforth also be a caretaker for valuable paintings and sculptures. While the Bliss will permitted the museum to sell works in the bequest, the proceeds had to be spent on other purchases. Before, Barr had been a carefree voyager steering the museum toward the most adventuresome shores; now he was the captain of a more imposing, yet less nimble, vessel laden with precious cargo. Not that Barr objected to his new role; to his father, no stranger himself to basking in parishioners' largesse, Barr rejoiced at the gift of "two score paintings valued at many hundreds of thousands of dollars. It would form a magnificent nucleus about which we may build."

As the Bliss treasure trove seemed assured, Barr sketched for the trustees a torpedo to schematically represent the ideal collection. Its nose would be "the ever-advancing present, its tail the ever-receding past." In painting, this would mean that the bulk of the collection "concentrated in the early years of the twentieth century, tapering off into the nineteenth." There was no indication, however, that as the torpedo sped forward it would lose any of its tail. Whimsically, Barr had added a propeller representing art even of the distant past which might have influenced some modern artists: Byzantine panels, Rembrandt, Coptic textiles, pre-Columbian figures, African masks, and Scythian metalwork.

This was the adventuresome Alfred Barr, who was always seeking out the new, the experimental, the original. But there was also a traditionalist Alfred Barr, whose first-rate education in art history and connoisseurship taught him to gather in beautiful objects, to sort them into their historical niches, and to display them for the public's edification. Despite precarious finances, Barr himself was building a personal collection which ranged across the centuries and included Russian icons; a seventeenth-century landscape in the manner of Arcimboldo; a Diego Rivera drawing; a 1919 Burchfield watercolor, *Freight Cars*; and Charlot's *Mama Spank*. This conservative Alfred Barr, in the same report, urged the trustees to exhibit at all times the treasures the museum had accumulated—the Daumier, the Picassos, Bliss's finest Cézanne, the Lehmbruck and Maillol bronzes. Such a permanent exhibition, he argued, will give "a weight, an anchorage, a ballast" to the museum's ensemble.

A fast-moving torpedo or the dead weight of ballast? This irreconcilable conflict would trouble Barr for the rest of his career. Had the trustees adopted a policy that no work more than fifty years old could remain in the collection, the museum would have to unload the van Goghs by 1940 and most of the rest of Bliss's treasures by the mid-1950s. This prospect was more hideous than any collector or curator could bear, the hoarding instinct being a basic personality trait of such individuals.

Furthermore, Barr was advising a host of collectors, especially those who could be expected to give works later to the museum. In December 1933, he arranged for John Hay Whitney to buy Edward Hopper's *Night Windows* for $1,500, a price Barr thought so niggardly that he apologized to the dealer who sold it. The bargain price, however, made it that much easier for Whitney to give the picture to the museum in 1940. Sidney Janis, who later became one of New York's most successful dealers in modern art, had begun his notable collection with three Klees bought from the MOMA's 1930 show. (It would be almost four decades before these pictures came permanently to the museum.) By the summer of 1935, Janis's collection was ample enough to be shown at MOMA, although "there was some hesitation lest the display of a private collection set an awkward precedent." But its quality, thanks to Barr's advice, was irresistible; among the sixteen works exhibited was Henri Rousseau's *The Dream*.

Barr's counsel was not reserved for big donors only. "Always, of course, offer about half or two-thirds of what is asked," Barr counseled an amateur collector by mail in 1932. "If you get several prints always make a lump sum offer considerably lower than the total. . . . This goes for America at present as well as for Europe always." In 1934, the MOMA *Bulletin* announced that each donor of $100 or more would be entitled to "professional advice of the director, by appointment, on modern art." And when department store magnate Samuel J. Bloomingdale asked Barr to suggest some suitable pictures for his living room, the museum director replied by return mail with a list of appropriate galleries to shop.

Those intimately involved with the museum, of course, received correspondingly detailed advice and often were alerted to bargains of particular interest to Barr. When Oskar Schlemmer's *Bauhaus Stairway* was expelled from the Stuttgart Museum, Barr was so enraged that he cabled Philip Johnson to buy the picture, "just to spite the sons of bitches." Johnson bought it for $500 and it came to the museum in 1942. (He kept a second Schlemmer bought at the same time.) Otto Dix's *Portrait of Dr. Meyer-Hermann*, which had enchanted Barr when it was part of the MOMA's 1931 exhibition of German art, also was bought by Johnson for under $1,000 and entered the museum's collection a year later. Again on Barr's advice, Abby Rockefeller had purchased Max Beckmann's *Family Picture* from the same show and gave it to the museum in 1935.

The museum's directors and trustees had a responsibility to see that "its fluent and receptive character may not be swallowed up in the pride and weight of possession," warned an *Art News* article in 1932. "But there seems little danger in that direction from a body of men and women as alive to the best interests of modern art as the executives of the Museum of Modern Art."

Logic and professionalism, however, dissolved before covetousness. When Barr had acquired pictures by herculean effort, it seemed unlikely that they would ever be disgorged from the museum's collection, no matter how old they became. Furthermore, the museum's benefactors were learning that a timely gift to the museum did wonders for the value of works by the same artist still in their private collections. Finally, the MOMA's acquisitions budget was so tiny that it seemed ludicrous to speculate that some day the museum would have a surfeit of treasures.

During the museum's first six years, Barr disposed of only $1,000 in purchase funds. Nevertheless, the museum's collection grew steadily as Barr honed his skill in bargaining with dealers and in finding donors for pictures he coveted. In June 1934, for example, he offered dealer Julien Levy $250 for Salvador Dali's *The Persistence of Memory*. Levy had been asking $400, but Barr countered that there were no buyers when the picture had recently been offered for $300. He would find a donor, Barr assured Levy, and to help spur interest in other avant-garde pictures Levy stocked, the gift would be announced just before the museum's fifth-anniversary show that fall, when maximum publicity would focus on modern art. Within two weeks, Barr had persuaded advertising queen Helen Resor to buy it for the MOMA. The picture is "one of the most famous paintings of the last few years," Barr crowed to Abby Rockefeller. "It seems now to have caught the imagination of everyone who has seen it."

Once a work of art had attracted Barr's lustful eye, he would pursue it for decades if necessary, until it was safely installed within the museum's walls. Barr's enthusiasm for Picasso, for example, went back to his eager perusal of *The Dial* during his student days, and he industriously gathered almost all of the Spanish artist's landmark works into the MOMA collection. As early as 1934, Barr was on the trail of *Three Musicians* (1921) a seminal work of synthetic Cubism. The picture could be had for less than $8,000, Barr informed Abby Rockefeller; perhaps she would put up half, with the rest paid by sewing machine and thread heir Stephen Clark. Abby might have been willing, but canny collector Clark declined, despite "as many blandishments" as Barr could muster. It took fifteen years before Barr's desire prevailed and *Three Musicians* came home to West Fifty-third Street, courtesy of Mrs. Simon Guggenheim.

Barr also stalked Henri Rousseau's *Sleeping Gypsy*, as it fell into the hands of creditors of a Swiss art dealer. The picture could be had for $15,000, and again he approached Clark without success. Clark worried that some experts doubted that the painting was by Rousseau, but Barr countered that "even if it were not, it would still be an extraordinary painting." Nervously, Barr waited for five years before he was able to persuade Mrs. Simon Guggenheim to buy it for the MOMA.

Sometimes it seemed as though no modern work was too minor or peripheral to escape Barr's acquisitive zeal. When two collections of French Surrealist books came on the market in 1935, Barr urged Walter P. Chrysler to buy them for $750, even though many of the items were already in the MOMA library. The duplicates could be sold to other museums or libraries, Barr suggested, "probably paying for half the cost." And when the owner of one of these collections, French Surrealist poet Paul Eluard, confessed that he was penniless, Barr also picked up his "excellent" Dada collection for fifty dollars more.

As the building at 11 West Fifty-third Street filled with goods, the original notion of the Museum of Modern Art as a feeder to the Metropolitan receded toward the far horizon. As early as 1931, Abby Rockefeller had wondered "how we are going to remain modern and at the same time satisfy donors that the pictures they give will not be disposed of in a manner that would be objectionable to them." Still, the rhetoric of cooperation between the two museums continued. At the dedication of the MOMA's first home in May 1932, Met president William Sloane Coffin affirmed that the election of two MOMA trustees, Cornelius N. Bliss and Nelson Rockefeller, to the Met board sealed the cooperative relationship among New York's major museums; both the Cloisters and MOMA would feed works to the Met, just as the Cluny and Luxembourg nourished the Louvre. But Barr disagreed. He approved of cooperation, he avowed, even of lending works to each other, but "we do not wish . . . to become merely the feeder to other museums."

A few days later, perhaps to mollify some trustees, Barr sounded slightly more conciliatory. Appearing with Coffin on radio station WJZ, he conceded that "no other institution includes so wide a public as the Metropolitan and to it should go, ultimately, the finest works of the foremost modern artists. . . ." *New York Times* critic Edward Alden Jewell thought this meant that "the much discussed

Luxembourg-Louvre sort of relationship . . . is about to become a less rhetorical reality."

For decades, the rhetoric would linger on—even as the reality receded. In 1934, Coffin tolerantly averred that the MOMA "believeth all things, hopeth all things, endureth all things." But, he demanded, "when the so-called 'wild' creations of today are regarded as the conservative standards of tomorrow, is it too much to hope that you will permit some of them to come to the Metropolitan Museum of Art, leaving space on your walls for the new creations of the new day?" The question would hang in the air for some years, but ultimately the MOMA answered it without involving the Met; it simply built bigger buildings.

An observer during the late 1980s might well wonder why the Luxembourg-Louvre model so mesmerized museum folk during the thirties. Even Alfred Barr seemed unable to openly question the French notion of the ideal art museum as the supreme showcase of aesthetic goods. The only explanation is that France in the thirties was still considered the epicenter of all artistic judgment. The French had pioneered the whole concept of a museum. American artists and architects still went to Paris to study. American collectors still went to Paris to shop although, as Barr wrote to a jobless friend in 1932, "I am afraid my wealthy supporters are at present so poor that they are not even considering going to Europe . . . When your fortune has been reduced from ten to five million, you decide to stay in America and economize."

Only decades later, when the best of modern art had long been snapped up by other museums and collectors, did the French realize that they needed a *real* museum of modern art, unconnected with the Luxembourg or the Louvre. Then, in building Beaubourg, they relied on the model developed by the American barbarians at the Museum of Modern Art and eagerly borrowed the works Barr had squirreled away on the MOMA's walls and in the capacious basement.

But in the early thirties, few people, even in the art world, had much of a notion of what a modern art museum should ultimately be. Even if he had wanted it, Barr could not expect sound advice on how to build his museum—it was simply unprecedented—but the advice came nevertheless. In the maddeningly woolly, prolix style

typical of thirties art writing, *Art News* thought "this comparatively new depot stands an excellent chance of developing into one of
the most powerful and progressive art centers that have yet been
evolved in either Europe or America ... the only truly international
art center in America designed to reflect the changing tastes and
traditions of a world that is being shot through transition after
transition with comet-like rapidity." In a similar vein, art critic
E. M. Benson in 1934 conceded in *The American Magazine of Art*
that MOMA's opening had been "like a breath of fresh air in a
Pullman car," and its first show "one of the most important art
events and the one that etched itself the deepest." However, "its
influence among that small nucleus of friends that originally welcomed it with open arms is beginning to wane."

Nothing could have been further from the truth. Not only had
attendance and membership in New York steadily grown, but tens
of thousands of Americans across the country were getting their
first glimpse of the new art through the museum's traveling shows.
By the mid-1930s the exhibitions which the MOMA had begun
shipping around the country in 1931 were drawing unheard-of
crowds.

The first of these, "A Brief Survey of Modern Painting in Color
Reproductions," started modestly with a tour to seven New York
City public schools. This exhibition was typical of many in which
Barr gently, steadily, resolutely coaxed the viewer from the familiar nineteenth century into the unfamiliar twentieth. It opened
with a couple of Daumiers calculated to appeal especially to the
thirties' preoccupation with social realism. It dwelled long and
lovingly in the nineteenth century, including a seductive Manet,
van Gogh's *Landscape with Cypresses*, Degas's *Race Horses*, and
Utrillo's *Banks of the Seine*. It also appealed to American patriotism by showing Albert Pinkham Ryder's *Toilers of the Sea* and
Winslow Homer's *Nor'easter*. Tiptoeing gently into the twentieth
century, a mild Picasso and Modigliani's *Portrait of a Girl* reassured the visitor that modern art was, after all, not so baffling.
While Mondrian's *Rectangles* of 1910 might have provoked some
viewers, the show also included Corot at his sweetest, neatly tying
abstract modernism to the nineteenth-century French painter
most represented (often by fakes) in American museums.

Like a missionary building his chapel on the site of a pagan shrine, Barr emphasized the strong bonds between modern art and traditionalism, rather than modern art's revolution against the past. The catalog Barr prepared not only told interesting stories about the artists and their pictures but also gave the history of the type of color reproductions on display, noting that the preliminaries for printing these plates sometimes cost more than $3,000.

Packaged in three stout crates weighing 638 pounds, complete with instructions for hanging, catalogs to be sold for twenty-five cents, and publicity releases and photos for local newspapers, this exhibition crisscrossed the country for three-week stands at such unlikely habitats of modern art as the Federated Women's Club of Richmond, Virginia; the Junior League of Houston, Texas; the Society of Fine Arts in Evansville, Indiana; the Art Club of Augusta, Georgia; the Kentuckiana Women's Institute in Louisville, Kentucky; and Kresge's Department Store in Newark, New Jersey. The rental for a three-week show cost less than forty dollars, plus freight to the next exhibition point. An interesting art show, ready to hang and available at a low price, seemed to be irresistible. By May of 1939, the show had been exhibited fifty-five times.

Similarly packaged, a collection of photographs of modern architecture had by July 1932 traveled as far as the De Young Museum in San Francisco, the Denver Art Museum, and the St. Paul School of Art. Concurrently, a selection of models of modern architecture had been exhibited at Sears, Roebuck in Chicago and Bullock's Wilshire in Los Angeles; as well as at major museums in Cleveland, Toledo, Milwaukee, Philadelphia, and Boston. In its first ten years, the museum would send ninety-one exhibitions on the road for three-to-six-week bookings at 1,363 places.

For Barr, the immediate result of such outreach was a deluge of demands on his time. The University of North Carolina's daily *Tar Heel* wanted a weekly feature on modern art to syndicate among college papers. United Press asked him to write a 1931 year-end wrap-up on modern art. Hallie Flanagan, a Vassar drama teacher who would later head the Federal Theater project, asked for help with organizing a Futurist show to accompany a series of student productions of Futurist plays. The architectural magazine *T-Square* wanted regular contributions from Barr on modern architecture.

Reluctantly, Barr declined these requests and many others.

Returning unread a graduate student's article about Daumier, he wailed that it was "almost impossible to do any kind of critical study outside of museum routine. I regret this situation extremely." He also shared writing assignments with others. Helen Franc, then a needy graduate student, helped him with the article "Painting and Sculpture" for the 1933 *Collier's Encyclopedia*. She received the entire payment—$31.25. The following year Katrina Van Hook helped out, glad to receive the same piddling pay. "The great secret in writing," Barr advised her, "is to jot down things as you think of them or come across them before you begin systematic review of periodicals."

Though he passed along as much work as he could to needy art scholars, Barr's restless curiosity and irresistible urge to sermonize trapped him in a squirrel cage of toil—a prison as loved as it was lamented. Every crank and student who addressed a letter to "Director, Museum of Modern Art" (or some such thing) received a considered answer, mostly by return mail. Responding to a casual inquiry from a prisoner in the penitentiary at Dannemora, Barr sent not only several copies of the Museum *Bulletin* and a book about American art but also a sympathetic letter, concluding with: "Will you please let me know how long your term is?"

Barr regularly read the papers of college seniors and, of course, the odd doctoral thesis on modern art. He courteously told a stamp collector that he had no expertise, rendered an opinion as to the value and provenance of an obscure sixteenth-century Spanish painting, and frequently agreed to see young women fresh out of Sarah Lawrence and inquiring about a museum career. Asked for an article about school architecture, Barr sensibly passed the assignment on to Philip Johnson. But he could not resist adding a few paragraphs: "What I write will be frankly controversial. . . . I feel quite strongly on the subject having had a good deal of experience in observing the extraordinary extravagance and waste, as well as the bad taste, of architects in schools and colleges."

Indeed, academic architecture was only one bête noire which Barr enjoyed flaying. Scarred by his early exposure to fake Gothicism both in his father's Baltimore church and at Princeton, he abhorred "so-called collegiate Gothic" for its lack of functionalism. This style, he wrote, "with its small windows, the expensive masonry, the leaded glass, carved moldings and copings and irregular planning, now seems to have been fastened both upon large universities and many smaller colleges not only by the sentiment of alumni and faculty but also by the propaganda of architects." This diatribe, fired off in March of 1932 when Barr was suffering the worst of his insomnia, must have puzzled the recipient, Prof. Yandell Henderson, who had mildly written to ask Barr to support higher salaries for Yale faculty.

On almost any subject, at the slightest provocation, Barr vigorously voiced his opinion. A printed brochure from the New York Philharmonic Chamber Orchestra elicited an enthusiastic letter from him: at last the orchestra had developed a program imaginative enough to challenge his preference to "sit at home and play my victrola." On Lincoln Kirstein's founding of the School of American Ballet in 1935, with George Balanchine as artistic director and maître de ballet, Barr was prophetic. It is "a valuable and much needed project," he wrote to Eddie Warburg, the school's general director. "While it is true that its methods and aesthetic ideals are imported, this can also be said of every other artistic medium . . . on this side of the Atlantic. To expect a full-fledged native ballet overnight is absurd. . . . It should be given general support so that it may have a chance to prove its value over a period of years."

Barr especially relished attending an informal art history study group organized by Meyer Schapiro. It met intermittently beginning in the spring of 1935 and included James Johnson Sweeney, Robert Goldwater, Jerome Klein, Louis Lozowick, Erwin Panofsky, and (occasionally) Lewis Mumford. Of the group's meetings, the man who in youth had sat through many an interminable sermon wrote: "Often the members are bored, either by too specialized papers or by too long papers—I might say that I myself was not bored for I have the questionable faculty of being interested in almost anything."

While intellectual discourse fascinated Barr, ordinary socializing often tormented him. He hated to be up late in the evening and when they were invited out, always asked Marga apprehensively when she thought they might be able to leave graciously. Marga worried about accepting so many invitations without reciprocating. In December of 1934, she determined to pay back their social obligations by having an eggnog party on Christmas Day, from 11:30 A.M. to 1:30 P.M. Marga, who always reveled in the company of the famous, stopped worrying whether the party would succeed when the poet Marianne Moore, a friend of the Barr family from Baltimore, appeared, wearing her trademark tricorne hat.

Alfred's shyness kept the Barrs from entertaining at home, even though Marga suggested that the museum's stingy expense account was the cause. Having people over made Barr "very anxious," Marga told an interviewer. Although shyness also distorted her personality, Marga said that she would have enjoyed entertaining at home far more than she did; "we never had an intelligent get-together," she said. When she did organize a cocktail party, he would arrive home late and then "begin to move pictures in a sort of anxious, housewifely way." Later, he would keep taking her aside to ask when the guests were leaving, shutting the door on the last few stragglers in relief. "He would never go out to dinner with the last remaining few," said Marga.

When it concerned his museum, however, Barr was far from shy and briskly tackled the minutest detail of its operation. He not only selected the works to be shown in the traveling exhibitions but also developed precise instructions for packing, shipping, and insurance. When the 1932 traveling show of modern architecture was being assembled, he suggested two versions: a larger one with photographs, blueprints, and models, and a smaller, cheaper one with just photos. He emphasized the need for publicity and investigated distributing the catalogs for these and other shows in cheap paperback editions through bookstores. He constantly searched for printers to turn out mass editions of inexpensive reproductions. On the eve of the museum's fifth-anniversary show, he complained to the staff about "atrocious lighting in several rooms, filthy wall coverings and awkward chimney breasts."

But none of these multitudinous sidings diverted the express train of Barr's ultimate plan for the museum. He was determined that his temple would include *all* facets of the visual arts, even some which the trustees may not even have realized they wanted. Thus, in 1932, he renewed a campaign to start a department of film.

Barr's passion for films probably began in 1924 while he was a graduate student at Harvard. A fine arts professor there, Chandler Post, often took students to the movies "as an extracurricular diversion," recalled Julien Levy, who was then an undergraduate. "He would lead us in whistling at Gloria Swanson when, her black curls stowed under a cap, she chose to volunteer for the foreign legion. It was most unusual for an art professor at that time to be interested in and guiding students to film." A decade later, it was still rare for an intellectual to admire that quintessential mass medium: the movies. During his 1928 sojourn in the Soviet Union, Barr had searched out Sergei Eisenstein, and he pronounced *Potemkin* "certainly one of the great twentieth century works of art." His 1934 article "Nationalism in German Films" demonstrated his extensive knowledge of the previous decade's significant films, as well as his dismay at how the Nazis had prostituted the great power of the moving picture.

Despite Barr's fervent pleas, the MOMA founding trustees had refused his request for the film department. But military history was one of Barr's many hobbies, and the strategy and tactics he mustered during his five-year campaign to bring movies into the museum were worthy of a Julius Caesar. Lobbying for a film department, he had dragged the gentle maiden lady Lillie Bliss to the Little Carnegie theater to see Carl Dreyer's grim and gruesome 1931 masterpiece, *The Passion of Joan of Arc*. He took to sending some of the trustees postcards recommending current films "that seemed to me works of art." In a 1932 report on how the museum should expand, Barr regretted that, unlike in London, Paris, and Berlin, "that part of the American public which could appreciate good films . . . has never been given a chance to crystallize." Attempting to overwhelm the trustees with a spate of then-obscure names, Barr suggested that even the works of "such masters as Gance, Stiller, Clair, Dupont, Pudovkin, Feyder, Chaplin, Eisenstein, and other great directors are, one can hazard, practically unknown to the museum's board of trustees." He called films "the only great art peculiar to the twentieth century," but the trustees remained unenthusiastic about an art form which one could not hang on the wall or place on a pedestal.

Nevertheless, a motion picture committee, chaired by Edward M. M. Warburg, somehow started in 1932. The museum *Bulletin*

somehow began printing thumbnail reviews of current movies in
June 1933. In the next year, Lincoln Kirstein, Nelson Rockefeller,
and Frank Crowninshield formed a film society for private showings arranged by Iris Barry, an English film critic who had
somehow become MOMA librarian, her salary paid by the ever-
obliging Philip Johnson.

Hired in 1932, Barry arrived on the job while the Barrs were in
Europe. Johnson thought her "brilliant . . . beautiful . . . the belle of
Bloomsbury," Marga Barr recalled years later. Despite a formal
education which ended at the Ursuline Convent at Verviers, Belgium, Barry wrote "with the enviable ease of the educated British." Alistair Cooke remembered her as "a small, trig brunette
with an Eton crop, a pair of skeptical violet eyes and a belly laugh
that responded like a Geiger counter to the presence of a stuffed
shirt . . . [she was] long on mockery and short on tact."

Her official job was MOMA librarian, but it was understood that
she would be in charge when a film department materialized. Barr
frequently "parked" talented people to run the MOMA library
while he patiently pushed a new museum department toward
reality. Barry's replacement at the library, for instance, was Beaumont Newhall, who would head the department of photography
when Barr had wangled it out of the trustees. Soon after she
arrived, Barry was stressing the need for starting a film library.
"By the fall of 1934," she wrote later, "it had already become
impossible to see any of the great Chaplin comedies, the bulk of
D. W. Griffith's epoch-making pictures or, indeed, any American
film made before 1932. Classics of the French, Italian, Swedish
and German cinema were equally invisible, as were the avant-
garde pictures of the 1920's or examples of the new school of
documentary films then being evolved in England. What little
remained extant from the past was in the form of sadly worn and
often incomplete prints, which were unlikely ever to be replaced."

Faced with this urgency, a small group met in Abby Rockefeller's home to explore adding a department of film to the museum's program. Abby "connived with me in launching the film
library," Barr later admitted, but at the same time, she worried
about including films that might be objectionable on what she
called "Freudian grounds." Still, by February 1935 a museum

committee was studying how to fund a film department and Barr revealed that of several hundred colleges polled on whether they would book MOMA-sponsored film series, 84 percent of those replying said yes. With the prospect of such support, rental fees could be expected to substantially fund the new department; there might even be a profit. In May 1935 the film department received a $100,000 Rockefeller Foundation grant plus $60,000 from trustee John Hay Whitney, a principal investor in *Gone with the Wind*, and Iris Barry became curator of the first film library ever associated with an art museum.

Though the trustees shied away from making a woman—and a foreigner at that—the head of a museum department and therefore named her husband, John E. Abbott, as director, Barry was the film library's spark plug. By July of 1935, the couple was ensconced in Hollywood's rakish Garden of Allah apartments, and Barry bubbled to Barr that she and her husband had acquired the first animated cartoon ever produced, *Gertie the Dinosaur*. Furthermore, Mary Pickford was donating seventy-five films and urging all Hollywood to be generous to the museum's film collection. "At the moment, the whole structure is seething like dough," Barry wrote to Barr, "but films we must have!" After a month, she wrote him that Hollywood was "not to be missed," although "they are not interested in films here, only in making them." Still, she exulted, "we are now getting the films, no fooling and nobody will ever know how hard it was."

In its first three years, the film library accumulated 288 titles, enough footage that a full viewing would take sixty-eight eight-hour days. Most of them were contributed by studios whose vaults Iris Barry industriously combed. She had also gathered the world's largest collection of books about film and was receiving seventy-five phone inquiries, thirty letters, and ten personal visits every day. As Barr was giving modern art its history, so Barry was unfolding the history of movies, assembling programs like "The Development of Narrative," in seven reels; "The German Influence," in thirteen reels; "The Rise of the American Film," in eleven reels; and "The Film and Contemporary Life," in fourteen reels. Shipped around the country, these programs attracted enormous audiences: 13,450 for a seventeen-session course at Dartmouth

College; 1,800 for five sessions sponsored by the Junior League of Wilmington, Delaware; 500 for one showing sponsored by the Tacoma (Washington) Newspaper Guild; 2,000 for five sessions at the San Diego Fine Arts Gallery. In its first two seasons, the MOMA film library's programs were viewed by 100,000 people.

Never had a museum-sponsored program attracted such throngs. A museum, after all, had always been a sedate, even somnolent, temple of art. Appreciation of art came with wealth and education. It was an exclusive pursuit and most professionals attracted to museum work had to have independent means; they were men who could affect tailor-made suits and opulently entertain trustees despite their pitifully small salaries. Their work left them with their white collars immaculate and their hands soft and manicured. Not quite like the director of the MOMA's department of film, who informed Barr, some weeks after the department began exhibiting films, that he was "completely worn out by having to operate the machine here for three showings this afternoon because the 'hired operator' didn't show up."

The crowds that came to look at movies and stayed to look at art sometimes were treated to other edifying spectacles. When Maurice Sterne had his first one-man show at the MOMA, newsreel cameramen and photographers were invited to shoot Sterne's wife dancing the hula in a grass skirt in front of his paintings of Bali and the South Seas. On that occasion, an unseemly argument broke out among the staff and, finally, no pictures were permitted. To avoid such embarrassing imbroglios while keeping the museum perpetually in the limelight, Barr in 1934 hired effervescent, redheaded—and shrewdly professional—Sally Newmeyer as a full-time publicity agent. No other museum anywhere would have dreamed of such a bold bid for the limelight. Museums spoke in hushed whispers, not in shouts to the press. However, most other museums had government support or ample endowments and, furthermore, abhorred the very notion of reaching out to the common man and woman. But then, to a missionary like Barr, this step had ancient precedents: had not Jesus charged Peter and Paul to travel about and spread the gospel? Had not Abby Rockefeller's father-in law hired publicist Ivy Lee to convince the public that

John D. Rockefeller was not a pinch-penny robber baron at all, but an enlightened philanthropist?

Newmeyer enthusiastically showered the press with irresistible morsels. When Albert Einstein arrived at the MOMA fifteen minutes before closing time on a bleak January afternoon in 1935, Newmeyer arranged to keep the lights on and the guards on duty as long as the famous scientist wanted to stay, but not before telephoning the *Times*. "He declined to be interviewed," the newspaper reported the next day. "After all," Einstein remarked, "one must have a little pleasure for oneself without giving it away." Heralding the arrival of Fernand Léger for the opening of his 1935 show at the museum, Newmeyer alerted city editors, ship news reporters, and photographers that the French Modernist "has decided and amusing views about [New York]. He should be an ideal subject for an interview. He speaks very little English, but . . . the French Line will furnish an interpreter."

In the spring and summer of 1935, Barr assembled an exhibition that would keep Newmeyer busy—and the MOMA on front pages—for the rest of the year. Furthermore, it would provide a handsome windfall for the museum's budget and bring prospective converts to modern art flocking to museums elsewhere in the United States in record numbers.

The Barrs were in Europe in early June when they learned that the world's greatest van Gogh collection—272 paintings and drawings—was about to be locked up in a warehouse, possibly for many months. The collection's owners, the Kröller-Müllers, had been buying modern art at minimal prices since 1907. Originally, they intended to build a museum for it on their estate at Hönderlo near The Hague. But in 1930 they lost all their money and moved the collection to their home in The Hague. The Dutch government had bought the Hönderlo estate at below market and had promised to pay for its upkeep once the museum was built, but now the Kröller-Müllers could no longer afford to keep even the Hague house and the precious van Goghs were headed for a vault. The Barrs rushed to Holland. "If this had not been a transitional moment," Barr excitedly reported to Goodyear, "we would have had almost no chance. As it is we can, I believe, borrow as much as we wish . . . on condition that we pay some form of rental." The exhibition could be highly lucrative, Barr thought; a Berlin museum had in 1927–1928 reaped a $20,000 profit from admissions to a similar show, enough, he noted, to buy a good van Gogh.

Goodyear and Thomas Mabry, Barr's assistant, hastily lined up four major museums across the country who would pay the MOMA $1,750 each for a chance to show the pictures. Later, four others joined. In Europe, meanwhile, Barr surpassed the "combined forces of Machiavelli . . . Castiglione . . . and Bismarck," Goodyear exulted, to borrow thirty-five paintings and an equal number of drawings for the largest single exhibition of van Goghs ever held. The Kröller-Müllers had asked for $10,000; Barr persuaded them to accept $7,500. Then he rushed home to write the catalog and talk to reporters. Publicity, he told Mabry, "will be of urgent importance . . . Miss Newmeyer should read Meier-Gräfe's biography [of van Gogh] and all the English translations of the letters."

Newmeyer, however, was far too busy churning out press releases on her mimeograph machine to indulge in scholarly research. While the Barrs were still in Europe, the press was informed that Goodyear was embarking to help Barr in borrowing additional paintings for the show from European museums. Later, there was news that New York department stores were preparing window displays to tie in with the show and that van Gogh blue and yellow was the most fashionable color scheme for fall. As the show's November 5 opening approached, Newmeyer almost daily doled out interesting tidbits to the press: a van Gogh sunflower painting for which the poor artist had hoped to receive $100 had recently sold for $50,000; the 127 works to be shown were insured for more than $1 million; when the pictures by "the great modern artist" arrived in New York, they would not be examined by customs at dockside, but would be taken, "heavily guarded, under customs cord and seal direct to the museum and held unopened until the customs inspector arrives to examine them, a courtesy usually extended when shipments are particularly valuable and fragile."

When the public responded to this publicity drumbeat by swamping Fifty-third Street, forming a queue averaging three thousand people, and waiting in the cold to enter the museum, further publicity went out. One release gave tips on how to pronounce the artist's name, explaining that an average of ninety people each day were phoning the museum for information, but "many seem reluctant to say the name of the Dutch painter and phrase their questions in such a way that the operator must say it." After frequent updates on the throngs in attendance, the museum announced that a record 123,339 had passed through the exhibition in six weeks. Among them was First Lady Eleanor Roosevelt, who had returned to the show five times. Most of the paintings then traveled around the country for almost a year, drawing record crowds—and massive press coverage—wherever they went: more than 100,000 at the Boston Museum of Fine Art; 227,540 in San Francisco; and similarly unprecedented throngs in Chicago, Philadelphia, Detroit, Toronto, Minneapolis, and Kansas City. When the exhibition returned to New York for a farewell viewing in early 1937, 19,002 visitors crammed the MOMA within two weeks. Altogether, 878,709 Americans had paid twenty-five cents each to see the works of an artist so maligned, so unappreciated that he had sold only one painting in his lifetime.

The overall message of the van Gogh show was that a great, innovative artist could easily be ignored, could perhaps even be driven to suicide, by an uncaring public. Its corollary was a warning that the public scorned difficult or puzzling art at its peril; that distorted or abstract work by contemporary artists, ignored or maligned today, might well be hailed tomorrow as masterpieces.

The van Gogh blockbuster was a personal triumph for Alfred Barr in many ways. Not everyone within the MOMA family had been enthusiastic about yet another show of a long-dead, figurative artist. The young turks of the advisory committee thought van Gogh passé and his influence on contemporary painting minimal. Others believed the show was too expensive, although it was hard to argue with a profit to the museum of some $50,000. Still others were embarrassed by the crude publicity which even the *New York Times* printed. When the van Goghs arrived in New York, for example, the *Times* ran a photo headlined "Self-portrait of Mad Dutch Artist." The caption explained that it was a three-quarter view showing "only one ear as he had cut off the other in a fit of madness."

Such publicity alienated quite a few museum directors. A letter from Louis LaBeaume of the St. Louis Art Museum complained to the Association of Museum Directors that "the public will flock as to a fire . . . or the scene of a crime" when publicity includes "sensational ballyhoo . . . often based on . . . tragic episodes in the life of the painter or . . . quotations of extravagant monetary value." Barr was so stung by this reproach that he demanded—and received—an apology. In a letter to all the museum directors who attended the meeting at which LaBeaume's charges were aired, Barr insisted that MOMA was "not responsible for the ballyhoo." While the museum's news releases did "draw attention to the ironic contrast between van Gogh's life and his posthumous success," he blamed American newspapers for exaggerations and distortions. He had deliberately avoided borrowing van Gogh's self-portrait showing his bandaged ear, Barr said, to discourage sensational publicity. To his chagrin, he claimed, the *Times* printed its offensive caption beneath a three-quarter self-portrait executed several months before the ear incident. Some fifteen years later, Barr was still defensive about the van Gogh publicity. "I did my damnedest," he wrote, "to keep both the commercial value and the morbidly sensational elements of van Gogh's life out of the exhibition."

Barr may have been truly remorseful about the van Gogh publicity excesses, but he was clearly of two minds about how far to go in getting the museum's message before the public. However tasteless the van Gogh publicity, it nevertheless had educated millions of Americans about a great artist and attracted nearly a million of them to look at his work. The trustees and MOMA donors who owned van Goghs had additional reasons to be pleased; henceforth, the values of their pictures marched steadily upward into the stratosphere. Where Barr had guessed in 1935 that $20,000 would buy a nice van Gogh, the artist's lesser work would sell a half century later for more than $30 million.

For Barr personally, the van Gogh show had settled a spiritual debt. Its success, he said, was "just what the artist himself would most passionately have desired. . . . His popularity depends on those very qualities which shocked and puzzled people not only during his lifetime but for thirty or forty years after his death. . . . For it is only recently that his gay, decorative, exaggerated color, his tortured drawing, his flat, unconventional perspective and the direct and passionate emotionalism have attracted rather than repelled the general public."

What Barr did not mention was the artist's intense religious fervor, which had driven him to preach, ever so clumsily and unsuccessfully, among the Belgian miners before he had begun painting in earnest. Moreover, the story of van Gogh's life—suffering, scorn, misunderstanding, persecution, a violent death, and finally, posthumous acceptance and adoration—was a parable for the lives of many religious martyrs, foremost among them Jesus Christ.

It is significant that van Gogh was among the few modern artists who sought inspiration in Christian themes. In a secular century, Alfred Barr continued to be religious; he devoted much time to encouraging modern religious art and to urging Christian churches to commission artists to create it. This theme took on increased urgency for Barr during the spring of 1935, when his father was struggling to recover from a severe stroke suffered in the early winter of 1934. The old clergyman must have relished his son's passion for van Gogh and his plans for sharing it with so many Americans. Perhaps he was at last content that his son, in his own way, was gathering in souls.

6

CONVERTING
THE HEATHEN

T his is not a traditional museum," Alfred Barr had warned
Beaumont Newhall at his hiring interview in 1935. "This is
a continual opening night; this is a three-ring circus. The
pressure is great. We are understaffed. Everybody must pull the
load." Arriving on the job as the new MOMA librarian a few weeks
later, Newhall found Barr perched on a camp stool, "surrounded by
a blaze of Van Gogh paintings." Barely glancing up, Barr ordered
him to take off his coat "and help me hang this show."

The two men had first met at Harvard, where Newhall had been
a graduate student in Paul Sachs's museum course while Barr was
teaching at Wellesley. By the time he joined the museum, Newhall
had worked in several important art libraries, where his insouciant
personality and unconventional interests raised some stodgy eye-
brows. The Metropolitan had fired him, but the chief librarian of
the Pennsylvania Museum of Art, Paul Vanderbilt, considered him
"a born bookman" and blamed his firing on "too much sense of
humor." Vanderbilt was particularly impressed with Newhall's
"extraordinary natural curiosity and intellectual flair" and be-

lieved the MOMA would benefit especially from his intense interest in typography, photography, and cinema.

Some trustees were dubious. Eddie Warburg called him "a plodder," who might command a great deal of information but appeared to have little gift for serving it up to the public in an appetizing form. Walter Chrysler, though impressed by his knowledge, feared he was not " 'presentable' enough for ladies who might donate books, or even for gentlemen." Hiring Newhall was "all right by me," Barr laconically agreed, but insisted he become thoroughly familiar with all modern art and fluent in French and German. This was a considerable challenge to Newhall, who admitted many years later that his knowledge of modern art at that time hardly went beyond Cézanne. Sachs's museum course had familiarized him with the School of Paris, including Matisse and Picasso, "but the names of Rodchenko and Lissitzky and Theo Van Doesburg and the activity of the group De Stijl, yes even of the Futurist group, were hardly known."

In fact, Barr had grand plans for Newhall. Just as Iris Barry, Newhall's predecessor in the library, had moved on to form the MOMA's thriving film library, so, unbeknownst to the skeptical trustees, Barr was already plotting Beaumont Newhall's ultimate mission. Even as his appointment as MOMA librarian was being debated, Newhall was writing to Barr from Europe, describing his contacts with specialists in photography, especially the few familiar with such French pioneers as Louis Daguerre, Nadar, and Eugene Atget.

Within a year, Barr would stop Newhall in a corridor one day and casually ask if he wanted to put on a photography show; the trustees had approved $5,000 for it. Asked what kind of show might be wanted, Barr replied, "That's entirely up to you." Barr fully approved of Newhall's selections in three categories: pictorial, recent pictures; historical, landmark older pictures; and scientific pictures, which were often abstract. Such a didactic style for an exhibition was congenial to Barr's own ideas about art exhibitions. He did not believe that museum visitors should be given only beautiful objects to look at, insisting that they learn about the artist's place in history and the place of a particular work in the artist's oeuvre. But he did not want to be dull or pedantic about it.

Barr therefore edited from Newhall's catalog the technical discussions that might alienate trustees and visitors. Newhall happily went along: "The fervor of the Museum's early days has been compared to the early Christian Church," Newhall recalled, "for it was truly a crusade, and Alfred was our leader."

No one subscribed to this view of Barr more ardently than Dorothy Miller, the first person to whom Barr was willing to delegate any judgment about painting and sculpture. Slender, vivacious, a thick braid of dark hair circling her head and striking pieces of handwrought modern jewelry usually circling her throat and wrist, Miller lived in bohemian casualness with her fiancé (and, later, her husband) Holger Cahill in Greenwich Village. She had graduated in art history from Smith College in 1925. As a woman, she had no hope of taking Paul Sachs's Harvard museum course and therefore had trained at the Newark, New Jersey, library and its associated museum. There she had met Cahill and began helping him create a valuable collection of American art, sponsored by a Bamberger department store heiress, Mrs. Felix Fuld. When her job was wiped out in budget cuts following the 1929 crash, Miller found work in Montclair, New Jersey, where a wealthy collector, Mrs. Henry Lang, had accumulated 2,500 items of American art, including 600 old Indian baskets. Miller deemed it the ultimate luxury when Mrs. Lang paid her to "sit and read for six months" to learn about Indian art and for two further years to catalog the entire collection.

During Barr's 1932–1933 sabbatical, Miller had helped Cahill with the shows of American art he had organized at the MOMA. And she had looked up in awe one morning, from her mundane task of pasting into an album the photos of Cahill's exhibitions, to note that her hero of Modernism, Alfred H. Barr, was back after his European interlude. "A few days later," she recalled, "I decided that MOMA was the only place I really wanted to work."

More than a year later, in June of 1934, Dorothy Miller sat in Barr's office as they discussed her heart's desire. She was wearing a "plain black dress and an outrageous summer silk hat in bright cerise," she recalled, as Barr lamented that his staff included "not a single trained museum person . . . only the beautiful daughters of trustees." If the trustees approved of hiring her, Barr warned in a follow-up letter, she would have to study German intensively to attain a reading knowledge. "It is not that we have much to do with German painting," he wrote, "but many of the best works on French and European painting in general are in German."

Miller would cheerfully have perfected Swahili and Urdu if it meant a job at the Museum of Modern Art. When the joyful telegram came—"Trustees approved. Start Sept. 1"—while Miller was visiting relatives in the South, she realized that no one had mentioned her salary. It turned out to be thirty-five dollars per week, less than what she had been paid for cataloging the Indian collection, but Miller didn't care: "I would gladly have worked for nothing. Besides, everything was very cheap. No one ever spent more than fifty cents for lunch."

Miller enthusiastically joined Barr in working "the eight-day week." Like Marga, she worried because Barr looked frail and *was* frail, "but he worked like an ox . . . there was hardly a weekend that the staff didn't work . . . for sheer love of the place." From September until June, Miller and Barr would spend Saturday afternoons together, dashing around to New York's avant-garde galleries: Valentine and Balzac, which featured French Modernists; Frank Rehn, Ferargil, Stieglitz, Downtown, and ACA, all of which had small stables of Americans; the New Art Circle, where Barr's old mentor J. B. Neumann showed Rouault, Klee, Chagall, Beckmann, Orozco, and Max Weber.

During the summer, Miller often stayed with the Barrs in Greensboro, Vermont. Sometimes, Marga and Alfred would first travel to Stockbridge, Massachusetts, and spend a few days in Miller's historic family house. Then Miller would drive them to Greensboro, a trip of about five hours. Alfred Barr never drove a car, while Marga gave up driving during the early thirties, after an accident. Miller recalls that Marga had driven into the elder Barr's garage in Greensboro and failed to stop. The car moved forward into the cabin's kitchen, where the Reverend Barr was frying a just-caught fish. At the impact, the fish leaped out of the pan onto the floor, as the Reverend Barr collapsed in wonderment and laughter. Marga was mortified, said Miller, and never drove a car again.

In Greensboro, Barr's museum labors continued on a more relaxed schedule. He left detailed instructions for the staff back in
New York but also suggested that "they must not follow my last
will and testament too closely, if better ideas present themselves."
Miller recalled that "we would usually work in the mornings. Then
we'd go for a swim, have lunch, and a brief nap." Afterward, the
Barrs and Miller would make car excursions to one of some twenty
destinations, all fancifully named after memorable bird sightings,
such as the Pileated Place or Seven Bob Climbing a Hill. Every
night there was a picnic lasting until the dark—and the mosqui-
tos—drove everyone indoors. Her intimate professional and personal relationship with Barr fueled recurring rumors that they
were having a love affair. Asked about it in 1986, Miller smiled
coyly and said, "It's not anybody's business. Lots of women were in
love with Alfred."

At the museum, Miller's first assignment developed and expanded to fill her entire career there, until she retired in 1968,
thirty-four years later. "Take these artists off my neck," Barr had
begged. Some telephoned ahead for appointments. Some carried
the recommendation of a trustee, an art teacher, or a dealer. Some
wrote letters and some had their wives write pathetic tales of an
artist's struggle for survival during a cruel depression. But most of
them simply appeared at the museum, hauling portfolios and
bulky canvases wrapped in brown paper. During her first year at
the museum, Miller saw eight hundred American artists. But, she
recalled, "there was almost never anything good. A lot of it was
pitiful." One such artist asked Miller if he should now give up his
part-time job running an elevator and simply paint. Horrified, she
replied, "Oh, no."

American art was the object of much pious chauvinism during
the thirties, but even its most optimistic boosters conceded that,
compared with the Europeans, it was second rate. Those who
collected the works of contemporary American artists, like Abby
Rockefeller, Duncan Phillips, and Gertrude Vanderbilt Whitney,
were seen as wealthy philanthropists cheering on a hopelessly
outclassed home team. Barr refused to make any special allowances for mediocrity, as he saw it. His calling was "setting and

maintaining standards . . . alert study and constant revision of judgement in many fields . . . protecting standards against internal and external pressures."

When it came to films, on which at that time there was no scholarly work at all, Barr could readily recognize the important contribution of the Americans and of Hollywood. He enthusiastically encouraged Iris Barry as she gave American films a history and an aesthetic. But when it came to American painting and sculpture, subjects which no one studied at the university level or wrote about in scholarly publications, Barr was polite but lukewarm. His entire education had been oriented to the great European tradition, of which he considered American art a derivative, colonial offshoot. Nor had much work by American Modernists been sanctioned in avant-garde little magazines like *The Dial*. As an art scholar, Barr looked for affinities among the works of contemporaries as a way of sorting out and relating diverse works. But the native twenties Modernism of Arthur Dove, Charles Sheeler, or Georgia O'Keeffe had not developed into a "school," like Cubism, or a "movement," like the Bauhaus. Like America itself, American avant-garde artists seemed to have no ideology except individualism and no coherent development that could be traced in other than European terms.

When Goodyear suggested in 1933 that the MOMA sponsor a show of artists from fifteen cities, Barr was sure it would be "mediocre . . . far more than our previous twentieth century American shows." The only justification for having such a show, he suggested, was that "good, bad, *and* mediocre works of art are all documents." Lacking aesthetic pizzazz, the show would be dull, Barr feared. Furthermore, New Yorkers would be unlikely to attend; they were "not much interested in the sticks." This from a man who had repeatedly told the trustees that an exhibition should not be judged first for its popular appeal, but for its intrinsic merits.

In 1934, Barr had provided some elaborate reasoning for excluding American artists from the museum's fifth-anniversary show. The Metropolitan and the Whitney had $30,000 a year to spend on American artists, he wrote Goodyear, while spending nothing on acquisition of European works later than Cézanne. Even the

Brooklyn Museum favored Americans over Europeans in its purchases. Thus, it was patently logical and fair that the MOMA
should buy only Europeans, he argued, while relegating the Americans strictly to loan shows. Moreover, buying works by Americans
posed prickly "problems of personal jealousy and prejudice on the
part of artists and their supporters."

In 1934, NBC organized a nationwide network radio series of
lectures on American art. Supported by the General Federation of
Women's Clubs, the American Federation of the Arts, the Metropolitan, and the Art Institute of Chicago, the series followed Barr's
notion of including architecture, objects of daily life, photography,
stage design, and films, and drew a surprisingly large and avid
audience; the book which grew out of the series *Art in America*,
went into at least three printings. But though Barr was listed as
coeditor with Holger Cahill, he simply suggested authors for some
of the chapters and edited what they wrote. Typically, he was
meticulous about the book's format, suggesting that there should
be more italic headings to "wake up" the columns of type. Cahill
had done a good job of the writing, he thought, except the section on
contemporary painting. However, Barr, who otherwise spent hours
and days revising material carrying his name, left Cahill's manuscript untouched; Americans did not seem to be worth his time.

Barr also was outraged by high prices for works by Americans.
"Hopper . . . is more expensive than Matisse or Picasso of the same
size. A Burchfield watercolor costs two to three times as much as a
Picasso watercolor," he complained to Robert W. Harshe, director
of the Art Institute of Chicago in 1936. Even without considering
that the quality of Americans was inferior, Barr implied, "the high
prices of Americans are enough to make one think twice before
purchasing them." Sculptor Elie Nadelman was asking $800 for a
single work, Barr wrote to Lincoln Kirstein, outraged that "we
were buying bronzes by Maillol, Despiau, Lipchitz and so forth of
the same size for very much less." Fortunately, Barr did not have to
think much about buying any Americans since Abby Rockefeller
donated large quantities of such works throughout the thirties.
Most of them were in the prevailing narrative style; if offered by a
less august donor, Barr would have instantly rejected them. The
181 objects by seventy-one artists she donated in May 1935, for

example, included a dozen watercolors by the Regionalist Pop Hart. Barr diplomatically told the *New York Times* that they were "generally acknowledged to be the finest group by this artist in any collection."

Only because of such gifts could Barr respond as indignantly as he did to accusations of slighting Americans. Sometimes he would wearily point out that during its first eight years, the MOMA had acquired 491 works by Americans, compared with 446 by artists from all other countries. Often, he would also remind critics of the museum's policy toward Americans—that forty-six of the first seventy-six MOMA shows had been devoted to American artists.

The numbers may have been there, but the spirit was lacking. Unlike Barr's other catalogs, those he wrote for exhibitions of Americans often looked skimpy, superficial, and hasty. A brief biographical sketch indicating whether the artists had or had not studied in Europe, a few photographs of representative works, and that was that. Where other shows were given a theme, like "Machine Art" or "European Commercial Printing," the local artists were exhibited as "Living Americans" (1930) or "Painting and Sculpture from Sixteen American Cities" (1933). At the first opportunity, Barr had fobbed off the troublesome Americans on his willing acolyte, Dorothy Miller. And so, during years when visitors to the Museum of Modern Art were learning about the great European pioneers of Modernism, they knew little of American innovators like Morgan Russell, Stanton Macdonald-Wright, Arthur Dove, Morton Schamberg, or Stuart Davis.

In this kind of reverse chauvinism, Barr was by no means alone. New York artist Edith Bry, whose career began during the thirties, recalled that getting a gallery show was virtually impossible. "One could trudge around to all of them," she recalled, "and hear nothing but 'Our stable is filled' or 'We only look on Tuesdays, but we're booked for the next month.'" For a woman, getting her work shown at all was virtually impossible. When the grand old man of the avant-garde in America, Alfred Stieglitz, offered his best Marsden Hartleys to Goodyear for an early MOMA show, he was told, "We only want the works of men owned by the trustees." Shortly after the founding of Abstract American Artists in 1935, a member lamented: "We don't have a single supporter—no critic, no dealer, no museum, no patron—and absolutely no public." Bereft of scholarly resources on American art, a victim of an education totally focused on European achievements, and married to a European to boot, Alfred Barr chose to remain sternly critical and aloof from the native avant-garde struggling for recognition. His fiercely discriminating eye stayed firmly fixed on the distant horizon across the Atlantic, the historic source, the beacon of modern art.

It was Dorothy Miller who in 1936 organized the MOMA's "New Horizons in American Art," a survey of hundreds of works created by artists of the Works Progress Administration (WPA). The many mediocre examples included for the sake of regional balance and stylistic inclusiveness seemed to bear out Barr's disdain for American art. A glance at the exhibition catalog's many illustrations of amateurish work demonstrates that government support for artists was no guarantee of artistic quality; quite the contrary, the WPA support encouraged many feeble talents to continue working. The whole purpose of WPA was to keep millions of Americans unemployed by the Depression at their trades, including artists, writers, and actors. While Barr was unenthusiastic about the overall quality of art produced with federal support, he agreed that "if the state assumes responsibility for the well-being of its citizens as a whole, the artist should certainly participate." When the WPA art projects were threatened with budget cuts in 1937, Barr wrote to the editor of the radical artists' publication *Art Front* to protest. It was not the artists, but the public which benefited most from WPA, he found. "I have listened to WPA music [and] seen twice as many WPA plays as commercial plays," he wrote, but he was noncommittal about the quality of the art the WPA brought forth, saying only that he had "studied with interest a large number of murals, easel paintings, and sculpture."

Dorothy Miller's husband, Holger Cahill, headed the WPA art programs and had written most of the catalog for "New Horizons in American Art." It reflected his belief that all artists, regardless of quality, contributed to culture. He liked to point out that the dozen or two early twentieth-century Parisian artists whom history would remember might not have produced their masterpieces if forty thousand lesser painters had not also been daubing away in

Paris at the same time. But whether the works of these lesser painters should be shown in the nation's leading museum of modern art was another question. In the two-paragraph foreword Barr deigned to write for the catalog, he called the exhibition "a visual report to the public" revealing "certain major trends in contemporary American art," but he was mute on what they might be.

While the exhibition included some works of Abstractionists such as Ilya Bolotowsky, Stuart Davis, Arshile Gorky, and Willem de Kooning, these were not illustrated in the catalog. In a review of James Thrall Soby's *After Picasso*, Barr hinted at his reasons for disdaining the work of these pioneers. Those who "still paint squares and circles with an air of virtue and discovery," he noted, ignored "the fact that excellent squares and circles were painted twenty years ago. But to the advance guard of today, such painting . . . is no longer interesting."

Compulsively involved in every trivial museum detail, Barr hardly had time to become interested in American artists, especially now that he had found a competent assistant to deal with them. Dorothy Miller was promoted to assistant curator of painting and sculpture in January 1936 and received a pay raise to forty dollars per week. Meanwhile, Barr was constantly distracted by crises. In February 1935, for example, the Tompkins-Kyle Marble Company threatened to attach the MOMA's Gaston Lachaise sculptures for collection of a bill. Barr had to beg Edward M. M. Warburg, the donor of one of these sculptures, to pay the $78.92 in order to avoid the "considerable embarrassment" of "a sale of Lachaise's work on the premises."

The threatened sale was averted, but accomplishing that diverted Barr from his curatorial and scholarly goals. In less than seven years, Barr had assembled and written forewords, if not the entire text, for nineteen of the museum's publications. Even more than the traveling exhibitions, these catalogs reached a wide audience; a total of 75,229 copies had been distributed in forty-six states, Hawaii, Washington, D.C., and sixteen foreign countries. Still, Barr felt himself falling behind in breaking new scholarly ground. "We keep running with our tongues hanging out, producing work which will count externally while our own sources of thought and information are gradually drying up," he wrote to his mentor, Paul Sachs. "I myself still have the feeling that I am coasting on the impetus of my few years' work in universities and colleges before coming to the museum . . . the very few scholars in our museum live completely hand to mouth so far as their intellectual work is concerned."

However, like many brilliant people, Barr often distracted himself. When the *Milwaukee News Sentinel* ran an article opposing public school use of reproductions of Gauguins, van Goghs, and Cézannes because they were "too modern or too extreme," Barr felt obligated to intervene. He was shocked, he wrote to the director of the Milwaukee Art Institute; "it would indeed be an extraordinary educational error . . . to deprive students . . . of the opportunity to enjoy the work of artists who are so important to the culture of our time." He tried to get a museum of modern art started in London and defended Maurice Utrillo against accusations from the U.S. Customs Service that he was not an artist because he painted scenes from postcards. He volunteered for several weeks of jury duty annually. He dug up illustrations and proffered advice to Helen Gardner, who was revising her authoritative textbook *Art Through the Ages*.

Though Barr himself had to take a pay cut to $9,000 per year during the mid-1930s, he tried to help others suffering because of the Depression. For Helen Franc, his former student at Wellesley who had gone on to postgraduate studies in medieval art and spoke three languages, he was begging the Carnegie Foundation for a secretarial job. His childhood friend Edward King was a more desperate case. The son of a well-to-do Baltimore banker, King had married a European princess and had a child. He had taught at Bryn Mawr, but colleges all over the country were cutting out teaching positions and it seemed unlikely that King could find more such work. "In a few months, they will be quite penniless," Barr wrote to the secretary of the Carnegie Foundation. Barr himself sent King a small monthly stipend and eventually found him a job as a curator at the Walters Gallery in Baltimore. At the same time, Barr was also sending money to his parents, while Marga went off to Italy to see her mother, taking along, Barr wrote to King, "a letter of credit."

And then, of course, there was Barr's more generalized evangeli-

cal do-goodism. This might involve writing to New York senator
Robert F. Wagner in support of the Federal Theater project in New
York. Or it might mean urging the Museum of Natural History to
purchase the carcass of a mammoth which the Russians had recently unearthed on Wrangel Island. "Outside of the Loch Ness
monster," wrote Barr, "I can't imagine a more marvelous (in the
literal sense of the word) specimen."

Barr also had to help out donors and trustees with seemingly
trivial matters. When Abby Rockefeller wanted to exchange a
Calder mobile for a better, more costly work, it was Alfred Barr
who conducted the niggling negotiation: Calder wanted an extra
ninety dollars; Barr offered seventy-five dollars. Because some
trustees had close connections to Yale University, Barr broke his
own rule against participating in picture juries and graciously
agreed, in the fall of 1936, to serve on the jury of an amateur art
show at the Yale Club.

To trustees who were studying a reorganization of the museum's
administration, Barr detailed his hectic, multifarious and often all
too mundane activities: directing staff, rewriting publicity, over-
seeing all the museum's programs, and meeting visitors. That
parade included trustees; members; artists; officials from other
museums; dealers and collectors "asking advice or, more often,
trying to push an artist or exhibition idea"; and foreign dealers,
artists, officials, and editors "many of whom have helped the
museum abroad and most of whom want something here." Each
year he met eight or nine times with the board of trustees or its
executive committee, four or five times with both the advisory and
architecture committees, and two or three times with the exhibitions and film library committees. Outside the museum, he was
attending two to twelve committee meetings annually, while turning down twenty or so more. Meanwhile, he was refusing forty
speaking invitations and ten art show juries each year. All the
while, he was also caring for the museum collection, handling
purchases, "interesting possible donors and placating would-be
donors."

After Jere Abbott's forced departure in 1933, the trustees had
searched diligently for an executive director who could relieve
Barr of committee work, business and finance matters, building

and staff responsibilities, membership and promotion, and publicity. Paul Sachs recommended another one of his ex-students, John Walker, but Goodyear doubted that he had enough experience for the job. Walker eventually joined the National Gallery in Washington, D.C., and went on to a distinguished career as its director. Instead, Goodyear favored Gordon Washburn, suggesting to Abby Rockefeller that "he would be a possible successor to Alfred if for any reason the post of director should become vacant." Instead, the trustees settled on Thomas Dabney Mabry, an intimate of Lincoln Kirstein, who had little museum experience and was remembered by museum associates as unable to "exercise the authority to which his position . . . entitled him." He moved into an office adjoining Barr's; a pass-through in the common wall allowed papers to be handed back and forth. Still, Barr complained that he and Mabry were "continuously overwhelmed with resulting confusion and exhaustion."

More than increased activities, Barr's insistence on rethinking every aspect of those activities accounted for the very pressures of which he complained. He was constantly searching for better ways to hang exhibitions. "I am just entering the second stage of hanging," he wrote to King, "where I can experiment with asymmetry. Heretofore I followed perfectly conventional methods, alternating light and dark, vertical and horizontal." Dorothy Miller believed that no one had Barr's gift for hanging pictures. When she had finished arranging a room of American watercolors, Barr found it too symmetrical, she said, lacking "an element of surprise." So he rehung the room. Arranging an exhibition of African art in 1935, Barr fiddled and fussed almost up to the moment the first visitors arrived, until 2:30 A.M. one day and until midnight the next. On opening day, he wrote to a friend, "I was in no condition to go out at all and went to bed immediately after dinner."

In 1936 Barr organized two exhibitions which were far more ambitious than any yet presented by any museum either in Europe or in the United States. They would seal his reputation as the world's leading historian of modern art. Moreover, they would serve as models for the kind of scholarly survey exhibitions called "blockbusters" today. They demonstrated a revolutionary new role for museums as educational institutions rather than dark, forbid-

ding, awesome, and largely puzzling places for the display of
aesthetic goods. Never had an art historian or critic attempted to
create a coherent framework encompassing all of modern art.
Never had a museum anywhere exhibited a series of works to
illustrate that framework. Barr's two blockbusters of 1936 also
proposed a way of looking at a work of art that minimized its
purely aesthetic, sensual qualities and instead emphasized its place
in the development of a particular artist's oeuvre and in the history
of art. Ultimately, this approach would squeeze most aesthetic
criteria out of the appreciation of modern art and leave only one
standard by which contemporary art could be judged. For better
or worse, that standard would be novelty.

The first of these landmark exhibitions, "Cubism and Abstract
Art," opened in March of 1936 amid controversy and criticism. The
brouhaha had begun weeks before the opening, when the U.S.
customs service impounded nineteen sculptures borrowed from
abroad because they "did not show natural objects in their true
proportions" and therefore were not admissible duty-free as art.
While works by such modern masters as Constantin Brancusi,
Alberto Giacometti, and Henry Moore remained fettered in red
tape, Goodyear fired off letters and telegrams to other museums
asking for their support in removing artistic judgment from philistine customs people and giving it to "those who are qualified." The
museum's publicity department fired off releases giving all the
horrid details. Although the *New York Times* reporter who visited
the offending works in a storeroom found them "decidedly . . .
esoteric . . . the odd forms . . . were not always recognizable from
the names," the sculptures were duly released on $100,000 bond.
The exhibition opened a week late.

The *Times*'s ponderous art critic, Edward Alden Jewell, knew
little about modern art and cared less about any works later than
Cézanne. He dealt with his bafflement over the exhibition by
churning out a three-column Sunday review, liberally quoting the
MOMA's literature and reproducing the cover of the exhibition's
catalog. About its merits or demerits, he was silent. In a news story
about the opening, another *Times* reporter noted that "scarlet fury
blazes once more over whether some paint on canvas is an immor-
tal work of art or a felonious outrage." The article drew an ironic

connection between the grim realities of the Depression and the artists' flight from subject matter: "There was no point in discovering that an engraved certificate purporting to represent $1,000 in negotiable securities represented nothing of the sort and then cavilling at a cubist for claiming that an arrangement of green rectangles was a faithful portrait of his mother-in-law."

More than bafflement, abstract art often evoked rage, even from respected art critics. Thomas Craven did not believe in going so far as to use embargoes or tariffs to keep French Modernism out of America, "but it is no longer necessary to pretend," he had written in a popular book in 1934, "that organized smudges, geometrical patterns and particles of unattached color contain spiritual values or psychic mysteries." Under the guise of criticism, Craven painted a crude portrait of the goings-on at MOMA. He claimed to have been present when Barr, "a pallid young man, born and raised in the Fogg Plant and top-heavy with lore" explained a Picasso to "the aesthetic old ladies who backed his museum and their bored husbands who, for some obscure reason, furnished the money." Craven called the Picasso being shown "not clever enough to be a good hoax: it was framed rubbish," and added he had never seen "a young man work so hard" as Barr did at this gathering. "He finished faintly and the old ladies cosseted him. No one understood or believed him and yet no one quite doubted him. . . . the men, hard-boiled old capitalists, were resentful and ashamed—the young rascal was giving their wives something they could not offer. While they were secretly convinced that the picture was not worth a dime, any one of them would have bought it on his wife's recommendation. And one like them did buy it for an enormous sum."

Not just crude Americans belabored Modernism, however. The respected English art historian Kenneth Clark seemed certain in 1935 that abstract art "has the fatal defect of purity. Without a pinch of earth the artist soon contracts spiritual beri-beri and dies of exhaustion. The whole cubist movement has revealed the poverty of human invention." Clark never did come to terms with the twentieth century; his magisterial television series and book, *Civilization*, abruptly concluded with Seurat and van Gogh in the late nineteenth century.

Abstract art in 1936 posed such an affront that the *New York*

Times was moved to editorial comment: "An overwhelming majority, when shown a cloudy half of a violin, or a dirty white canvas called *White on White*, or another canvas with a thermometer or a strip of newspaper pasted on it (this, they are told, is *collage*), doubtless feel quite justified in dismissing it merely as an example of childish charlatanry that requires more attention from the social psychologist than from the art critic."

Most people would have been crushed by this drumbeat of ridicule. But a man raised in a religious household knew that the noblest new ideas often attracted the greatest scorn. Such a man knew that righteousness would triumph: "The Philistines took him [Samson] and put out his eyes and brought him down to Gaza and bound him with fetters of brass; and he did grind in the prison house. . . . And it came to pass when their hearts were merry, that they said, Call for Samson that he may make us sport . . . and they set him between [two] pillars. . . . Now the house was full of men and women; and all the lords of the Philistines were there . . . and there were upon the roof three thousand men and women. . . . And Samson took hold of the two middle pillars upon which the house stood. . . . And he bowed himself with all his might and the house fell upon the lords and upon all the people."

Bible stories like these had been an intimate part of Barr's childhood, the fabric of the sermons over which his father labored each week. How to use them most effectively had been the elder Barr's specialty as a teacher of homiletics and also the subject of his two books. Although the father saw little of his son except during the summers in Greensboro, and may have deplored his lack of religious punctilio, he admired the craftsmanship of his missionary work. The old preacher may also have wondered about the strange kinds of images that his son found so compelling, but he was apparently convinced of the beneficial effects of great works of art. A former student wrote to Barr and described a communion in the old theologian's study during 1933. Barr's father pointed to a reproduction of a painting of Christ rising from the tomb and told the group about the illness which had forced young Alfred to give up his museum duties for a long rest. The painting masterpiece, the old preacher asserted, had exuded a "healing effect."

As Barr was assembling the Cubist show and meticulously laboring over the writing of its catalog in the summer of 1935, his father's health was failing. On September 2, the Reverend Alfred Barr died of a cerebral hemorrhage in Greensboro, Vermont, on the eve of his sixty-seventh birthday. He had never really recovered from a crippling stroke nine months earlier. The minister, the missionary, the preacher of Christian doctrine was dead. But there is no doubt that his son now mustered an extra measure of zeal and conviction in behalf of *his* chosen religion.

For the Cubist show, he assembled no less than 386 works, not only paintings and sculpture, but photographs and models of architecture, constructions, posters, furniture, stage designs, costumes, and films. A number of important works, especially by the avant-garde Suprematists and Constructivists who had so impressed Barr during his 1927–1928 sojourn in the Soviet Union, were represented only by photographs. The originals were hopelessly sequestered by Stalin's terror, while the avant-garde artists who had stayed in Soviet Russia were forced to disown their works and recant their theories. While assembling the abstract art exhibition, however, Barr had located a cache of hidden Suprematist works in Nazi Germany. He bought them and smuggled them out, tucking the drawings into magazines and rolling the canvases around his umbrella.

Six weeks before the show's scheduled opening, Alfred and Marga were still struggling to prepare the catalog for the printer, working Sundays and late into the night. When it appeared, barely in time for the opening, they had assembled every last shred of information about the works in the show and their underlying rationale. On the cover was a diagram which itself was an abstract composition of rectangles, arrows, and lines. Strongly resembling a Biblical genealogy, the chart attempted to depict all the relations and influences among the important artists and artistic movements which had swept across the European cultural landscape since 1890. In its cool rationalism, the chart's format displayed graphically the overwhelming influence of science on the arts during the twentieth century. Every aesthetic idea and movement appeared to have grown organically from earlier inventions or discoveries and hardly any seemed to have sprung purely from the imagination of individuals. After Cézanne, Seurat, Redon, Gau-

guin, and Rousseau, there were only groups, anonymous devotees of
a multitude of eccentrically named "isms."

Producing the catalog turned into a chaotic nightmare. *Time*
magazine may have exaggerated when it reported that Barr anxiously "gulped coffee and puffed cigarettes" and had only composed six pages of it three days before the exhibition opened. But
neither did Barr stick to the sedate schedule for producing the
catalog promulgated by the museum's director of publications,
Monroe Wheeler. Dorothy Miller described the book's production
as hasty, and Marga remembered the layout pages spread all over
the floor of the living room, when "a cat walked over it [all] messing
up the order and Alfred had to re-do it." While the catalog as first
published was a landmark of scholarship, it also included so many
mistakes that a second edition was published in June 1937.

Despite some errors which persisted into the second edition as
well, the catalog attracted considerable praise, most significantly
from artists who were participants in the movements Barr had
described. Wassily Kandinsky was delighted that "the plan of the
book and the method of tracing development are purely scientific,
which to my knowledge has been completely lacking in modern art
literature up to now." Himself the author of a philosophical treatise
on the spiritual in art, he especially appreciated the developmental
chart on the cover. The catalog clearly filled a crying need for
scientific, systematic, lucid literature about modern art. Once the
original editions sold out, Barr was constantly badgered to prepare
a new edition. In 1947, Barr's associate William Lieberman urged
him to allow reprinting of the 1937 work, but Barr refused unless
color plates were added. Then he refused unless the entire book
were revised, but he would not let anyone else touch it and was so
busy that he could not work on it either. For decades, broken and
tattered copies were bringing premiums in the used book market,
until 1974, when a paperback reprint was issued by the museum.

While Barr's preface proclaimed that the exhibition was "conceived in a retrospective—not in a controversial spirit," illustrations on the very next page confronted the reader with two posters,
one "overcrowded and banally realistic," the other "flat, almost
geometric . . . highly abstract." Both advertised the same event, a
1928 press exhibition in Cologne, and the reason for designing two

posters, Barr argued, was that "Americans would not appreciate the simplicity and abstraction" of the geometric poster, while the German public was quite accustomed to an abstract style.

On the pages that followed Barr enhanced the implication of his cover diagram that the history of cubism and abstract art could be traced step-by-step from the past with the same precision as the discovery of electricity or relativity. Reaching back into the Renaissance, he explained how the artists of that time "were moved by a passion for imitating nature" and how they had discovered the laws of perspective, foreshortening, anatomy, movement, and relief. Around the turn of the twentieth century, this "pictorial conquest of the external visual world had been completed and refined," Barr argued and therefore "the more adventurous and original artists had grown bored with painting facts."

Like a true evangelist, Barr anticipated the reader's struggle to comprehend the new vocabulary as well as the content of the new art. The word *abstract* was confusing, he admitted, but no more than the ethnological tag *Gothic* to describe French thirteenth-century art or the Portuguese word for an irregular pearl, *Baroque*, applied to European art of the seventeenth century. He insisted that "abstract art today needs no defense. . . . But it is not yet a kind of art which people like without some study and some sacrifice of prejudice." Like a first-rate sermon, it was calculated to persuade the reader with a gentle, reasonable, sympathetic, but unswerving, blend of fact and polemic.

In its 249 pages, the catalog included 223 illustrations. It gave brief chronologies of the many confusing "isms" and, unlike the flimsy listings of works which comprised the usual museum catalog of that time, it ended with a rich bibliography developed by Beaumont Newhall, 444 items, comprising virtually every word— in English, French, Italian, German, and Russian—ever published on the subject.

In the light of today's scholarship, Barr's catalog often appears simplistic and certainly incomplete. Even the casual reader will wonder why Barr drew no connection between the Renaissance artists' fascination with naturalistic details, scientific perspective, and anatomical accuracy, and the resurgent interest in science which was such a dominant feature of Renaissance culture. Rather than blaming boredom for the modern artist's turn toward abstraction, a reader today would readily consider the effect of photography and of films in displacing the artist's function of depicting reality and the increasing abstractness of modern science as a source of artistic inspiration.

Barr's friend, the art historian Meyer Schapiro faulted him for explaining the rise of abstract art "independent of historical conditions." With these code words, Schapiro identified himself with Marxism, a philosophy which then attracted many scholars because it seemed to offer a way out of the economic jungle into an egalitarian clearing. How could anyone be motivated by simple boredom, asked Schapiro, rather than by class antagonisms, historical imperatives, or changes in the mode of production? Historians tend to write history in terms of their own experience. During the thirties, that experience was filtered through the darkling glass of economic disaster. Nevertheless, Schapiro found Barr's catalog the best ever written in English, combining "a discussion of general questions about the nature of this art, its aesthetic theories, its causes, and even the relation to political movements, with a detailed, matter-of-fact account of the different styles." Even the *New York Times*, when it finally reviewed the catalog some five months after the exhibition closed, found it enlightening; it had brought clarity and detail to "a subject that has puzzled so many people and that is so frequently misunderstood."

The work featured in "Cubism and Abstract Art" was severe, cerebral, geometric, serious, pure, and, some thought, drab. It represented the Apollonian side of art and of human nature. The subject for Barr's second path-breaking exhibition of 1936, "Fantastic Art, Dada and Surrealism," was, by contrast, emotional, colorful, playful, erotic, and, many concluded, utterly zany. It expressed the Dionysian aspect of art and of mankind.

Newspaper readers could grasp the difference in an instant. The sober, doctrinaire Fernand Léger was wanly heralded in a 1935 MOMA news release as "the distinguished French artist . . . one of the four great Cubists." But when the flamboyant Surrealist Salvador Dali stormed into New York in the whirl of a great black cape and a blizzard of verbiage, readers knew they were in the presence of more than a quivering, curlicued moustache. How could anyone expect to understand his paintings, Dali ranted to a lecture audience in January of 1935, "when I myself, I regret to say, do not understand them either. . . . I am but the automaton which registers, without judgement . . . the dictates of my subconscious, my dreams, the hypnagogical images and visions, my paranoiac hallucinations . . . the only difference between myself and a madman is that I am not mad." At a fashionable New York dinner party, it was reported, Dali had eaten the buttons off his hostess's dress, exclaiming, "Permit me to do this as a token of my paranoiac esteem."

The Barrs had spent most of the summer of 1936 traipsing around Europe in search of representative works for the "Fantastic Art" exhibition. In pocket-size spiral memo pads, Marga supplemented Barr's hasty notes, filling in names and brief biographies of artists and titles of works. She kept track of appointments and made note of interesting restaurants and reasonably comfortable hotels. She added to his lists what museums and private collectors owned, what they were likely to loan, or prices of works for sale. She also did all of Barr's translating and interpreting, since, as she recalled much later, "he never managed very well in French" and "only slightly better in German." Like most Americans, "he was intensely bored by languages." These were chores that were essential to Barr's success, quietly done as matters of course, seldom publicly recognized; just a wife doing her duty.

For many weeks the Barrs stayed in Paris alternately avoiding the political squabbles of the Surrealist poets and taking their advice. On a tip from Paul Eluard, they trudged to a shabby one-room studio where, while potatoes boiled on a small stove, they were shown gruesomely graphic paintings by Richard Oelze. Barr borrowed his *Daily Torment* for the show, repelled by its "almost unbearable . . . morbidity," but fascinated by its "sense of absolute conviction" which "raised Oelze's work from the level of the clinic to the level of art, somewhat as the frightful diseases in [Matthias] Grünewald's *Temptation of St. Anthony* are justified symbolically as diseases of the spirit."

Barr's excitement in discovering a new artist dissipated quickly in the travails of gathering works for the rest of the exhibition. "The official 'run-around' has been worse than anything," he complained to Goodyear. "I had to write forty-seven letters and make eleven official calls in order to borrow four watercolors from the Louvre." This was especially galling since Abby Rockefeller was just then being feted in France alongside her husband, John D. Rockefeller, Jr., who had recently given $3 million to restore French national monuments. Yet she apparently deemed it unseemly to intervene directly with French museum people. Then Barr had "a rather harrowing fight," with the Surrealist poets who were trying to dictate what he should show. He was "very tired and fed up."

But there was no trace of world-weariness in the show which opened the following December. Indeed, its rambunctious blend of black humor and stark horror aptly reflected the realities of the year 1936. In March, Hitler's Nazi troops had goose-stepped into the Rhineland. In May, Mussolini's Fascist army marched in victory through the streets of Addis Ababa. In July an obscure Spanish general named Francisco Franco proclaimed a revolt against the Republican government; by November, his troops were besieging Madrid. And on December 10, three days after the opening of "Fantastic Art, Dada and Surrealism," Britain's King Edward VIII abdicated for the absurd, unheard-of reason that he wished "to marry the woman I love."

In such a nightmare world, it seemed perfectly reasonable that the New York department store Bonwit Teller would devote its Christmas windows to Surrealist themes and that Salvador Dali's window would feature a floor strewn with hundreds of teaspoons, a floating dinner jacket bedecked with dozens of cocktail glasses, and disembodied fingers dripping white fur nails reaching toward a manikin with red arms and a head consisting of red roses. Such a world was ready for Man Ray's metronome ticking past an unblinking paper eyeball, for Juan Miró's stuffed parrot perched above a wooden woman's leg, for drawings by children and by the insane, for Walt Disney's ramshackle machine called *Wolf Pacifier*, and even for Barr's most eccentric choice among the 694 works exhibited, Meret Oppenheim's *Object, 1936*.

Long after Barr's serious efforts to tie the scandalous works of Dadaists and Surrealists to fantastic visions by Dürer, Bosch, and Piranesi were blurred into a vague disquieting memory, the *Fur-lined Teacup*, as *Object, 1936* was soon renamed, would exude its seductive mystery. There it sat provocatively in a glass case, a plain cup, saucer, and spoon, covered with sensuous gray fur. A hoax? A bitter political commentary about the luxury of museum exhibitions in a period of mad dictators and frightful ideologies? A vaguely pornographic appliance? Though it could be had for only fifty dollars, even the museum's indulgent trustees refused to buy this mockery for the museum's collection. But Barr was so entranced with it that he bought it secretly, at first for "extended loan," then for the "study collection," and only in 1946 did he slip it into the permanent collection.

Unlike the reception they gave "Cubism and Abstract Art," few critics fumed over "Fantastic Art." Rather, they smiled and then matched the show's madness with their own flights of surrealistic prose. The *Times*'s Jewell suggested that "if you would go insane quite pleasantly and painlessly . . . beg of one of the attendants a lump of 1921 sugar out of Mr. [Marcel] Duchamp's sneeze-trap, drop it into Mr. [sic] Oppenheim's fur cup, stir well and then sit down to disintegrate at the hearth of Mr. Terry's *Fireplace with Waterfall*." He never did review the show, but indulged instead in verbal fripperies: "Dada rides in the saddle, messieurs, mesdames. The bars are down and the season of Exquisite Mal-de-lune has blossomed in all its splendor of hokuspochondria."

The *Newsweek* critic sniffed the exhibition's flamboyantly Freudian air and concluded that "no one could honestly brag that he came out as chipper as he entered. There was much too much symbolism hitting below the belt for even the most out-and-out extrovert not to feel some quiver of the unconscious." In the conservative Midwest, the Milwaukee Art Institute *Bulletin* announced that the show was coming, "trailing lurid, bold-face, spread-eagle headlines behind it. . . . The ordinary aesthetic criteria are not valid here. The preoccupations of flesh and blood life must be abandoned if we are to walk in the fuliginous twilight of an incredible dream world."

To convey the exhibition's theme on the most popular level, the MOMA news releases about the show pointed to the absurdly involved machinery drawn by cartoonist Rube Goldberg and "the animated fantasies of the world's best-loved Surrealist, Mickey Mouse." The show's months-long progress across the country had resulted in copious publicity: mentions in the *New York Times* at least once in every three days and generous spreads in all other leading newspapers, nine illustrated essays of three to five pages in *Life* magazine, and newsreels by both Paramount and Universal. Inside the museum family, however, the exhibition generated some dismay. Conger Goodyear conveyed to Abby Rockefeller his chagrin that a number of items were "ridiculous and could hardly be included in any definition of art."

Unlike the catalog for "Cubism and Abstract Art," the catalog for "Fantastic Art, Dada and Surrealism" did not contain a full essay explaining what the show was all about, because Barr did not trust himself to write it. In his preface, Barr simply referred to "the already very large body of writing about Dada and Surrealism" and followed it with a year-by-year chronology, mostly of European exhibitions, from 1910 through 1936. Irritated though he was with the squabbling Surrealist writers, he was also impressed enough to ask one of them, Georges Hugnet, to write essays about the movement's theoretical background and its leading practitioners.

Embarrassingly, a distinctly Dada devil dogged the catalog's first edition. Hugnet's essays arrived too late, and there was only a footnote promising that they would be published during the course of the show. The plates had mysterious gaps in the numbering. Some nineteen items were somehow listed as having been lent by the Metropolitan when in fact seventeen of them were represented only by photostats and two had been hastily borrowed from the Boston Museum of Fine Arts. Altogether, eight major errors were listed on a slip bound into the catalog's first edition. So many others were discovered later that Barr refused to allow a reprinting until he could get around to making corrections, which he never did. Nevertheless, the copious illustrations told the story, perhaps more forcefully than words, and the sensational nationwide publicity as the show traveled to six other museums for one-month stints did more to popularize modern art than many an earnest monograph could do. The exhibition's doors had barely opened, in fact, before its outlandish message crept into the culture at large: a Bonwit Teller advertisement on December 27, 1936, featured a Dali-esque limp watch and a disembodied eye, captioned, "She was a surrealist woman; she was like a figure in a dream." The hat she was selling had a heart dangling on a spring from a clock dial and was labeled, "Love springs at midnight."

Exhausting and challenging as the two blockbuster exhibitions of 1936 had been, they were perhaps less daunting than the surprise which arrived in Barr's personal life soon afterward—fatherhood. Few men took less interest in family life or children than Alfred Barr. While he realized that his missionary work would gain from an educational program for children at the museum, he rarely supervised the work done there and seldom communicated with the program's director, Victor d'Amico. Similarly, Barr did not take much interest in pregnancies or babies. Years later, when his friend James Thrall Soby told him that his wife had just lost a baby, Barr cheerfully replied, "That's good."

Alfred had never wanted children and Marga had agreed because "their life was too jumbled," said their close friend Helen Franc. But after six years of marriage, "Marga really insisted," said Dorothy Miller, although Franc believed neither parent cared to have a family. In October of 1937, their daughter was born. Helen Franc fed Barr beets for supper while Marga was in the hospital giving birth. The child was named Victoria, because, Barr sheepishly joked to close friends, she "represented the triumph of nature over reason." Perhaps because Marga had "insisted," perhaps because fatherhood then posed few responsibilities, Barr left the rearing of the child almost entirely to his wife.

Marga resisted the responsibilities of parenthood as well. During four long 1974 interviews with Paul Cummings for the Archives of American Art, the birth of their daughter was hardly more than a footnote to Marga's detailed account of her life with Alfred Barr. "Well, in 1937, I had a daughter," she told Cummings. Despite having a nurse, Marga chafed at being "more or less nailed into the house." When her baby was six months old, Marga accompanied Barr for a two-month stay in Europe and would never let the child interfere with what she considered "our campaigns": the never ending search for European art to be exhibited at the museum. In her year-by-year recollections of these "campaigns" in *The New Criterion* of summer 1987, Marga omitted any mention whatever of Victoria's birth.

As she grew older, Victoria disappointed Barr because she was dyslexic, right-eyed and left-handed, and therefore was not a bookworm. When she later decided to become an artist, both Barrs "did everything to dissuade her," said Dorothy Miller. "They knew too much about the hard times that artists have."

By 1937, when Victoria was born, the WPA art projects were mitigating the dire plight of artists trapped in the Depression. Aside from helping individuals who were starving, the WPA art projects did much to interest Americans in art, some of it modern. The hordes of artists working for their meager stipend, an average of $23.50 per week, built mountains of creative works. Visitors to thousands of post offices, schools, courthouses, and other public buildings could not escape the new art upon their walls. Artists aggressively exhibited their works, aided by government-sponsored marketing schemes. The statistics compiled when the projects ended in 1943 showed that government support had yielded more than 2,250 murals, 13,000 sculptures, 100,000 easel pictures, 239,727 prints pulled from 12,581 designs, half a million photos, and two million copies of 35,000 different posters. Furthermore, many artists had staffed the 103 WPA art centers from Gold Beach, Oregon (population 500), to Minneapolis, where a center developed into the Walker Art Center. Better educated than ever before and with more leisure time, due to Depression unemployment, some eight million Americans participated in these centers.

The WPA art tended to conservatism, and it included staggering quantities of marginal daubings and failed concepts. But among the 12,000 artists the programs aided were many who would become pioneers of the next wave of Modernism, including Jackson Pollock, Willem de Kooning, Mark Tobey, Morris Graves, Arshile Gorky, and Mark Rothko. These artists and many others were profoundly influenced by the European refugee artists and teachers who were beginning to arrive in America. Denounced by the Nazis as degenerate, Hans Hofmann, Joseph Albers, László Moholy-Nagy, and other refugees began to teach the European tradition of Modernism at American schools.

Much to Barr's frustration, the turmoil in Europe was also shaking loose extraordinary quantities of modern works of art while he had virtually no money for acquisitions. During the museum's first six years, he watched impotently as others repeatedly snapped up at bargain prices landmark works, among them Roger de la Fresnaye's *Conquest of the Air*, $6,000; Marc Chagall's *I and the Village*, $1,500; Giorgio de Chirico's *Seer*, $800; and van Gogh's *Starry Night*, $30,000. Picasso's *Three Musicians* was on the market for $10,000, and Barr quaked as it was being eyed by a Philadelphia collector, though "luckily he had spent most of his money on a Degas." Barr was disappointed too that the $20,000 profit from the van Gogh show had gone into the general budget, rather than into purchases.

Nevertheless, he was able to locate many bargains and if he had no money to buy, at least he would persuade the museum's patrons to acquire them. While borrowing works for the Cubist show in the summer of 1935, for example, he had asked Marga to visit an old friend of her father's, Giacomo Balla, to see about borrowing his Futurist *Dog on a Leash*. He was relieved when Marga cabled that the museum could borrow it and overjoyed that it was for sale for $600. In 1934 when he was more flush, Balla had asked $2,500, but Barr could not raise even the smaller sum; desperately, he persuaded Goodyear to buy this charming Futurist work. Barr hoped, in vain, as it turned out, that the museum president would eventually will it to the museum.

This was a time when sums that look ridiculous today could purchase extraordinary masterpieces. In 1935, Barr could have bought a Léger oil for $140, a Picasso gouache for $350, or a one-foot-high terra cotta by Henri Laurens for $35. During the summer of 1936, Abby Rockefeller gave Barr $2,000 to buy Surrealist art and he had snapped up eight Jean Arps for $282 and eleven Max Ernsts for less than $750. At the Surrealist exhibition itself, where almost everything was for sale, Barr had used another $2,000 from Abby Rockefeller to buy De Chirico's *Nostalgia of the Infinite*; two large Arp reliefs; a Giacometti construction, *The Palace at 4 A.M.*; and Miró's *The Hunter*. The six Juan Mirós he had bought between 1935 and 1938 had cost a total of $1,813. The museum's first Henry Moore, *Two Forms*, had been donated by Moore's patron and friend, Sir Michael Sadler, who had paid the sculptor less than $160.

Late in 1937, a shy, reclusive lady in pince-nez and a tightly finger-waved coiffure, whom no one had ever met before, appeared in Barr's office with a fairy godmother proposal. She had often visited the museum to peruse the collection, she told Barr. To his astonishment, she asked him to select a first-rate work of art for her to buy and present to the museum. The woman was the wife of a senator from Colorado, copper magnate Simon Guggenheim, and before her death in 1970 at the age of ninety-three, she would shower on the museum purchase funds of more than $2 million. The picture Barr selected for her first gift was Picasso's enigmatic *Girl Before a Mirror*. Mrs. Guggenheim, who lived on Fifth Avenue amidst the golden glow of her favorite Sienese primitives, did not like the picture at first. But she hoped to gain insight by "persistent contemplation" of the work and cheerfully wrote a check for $10,000.

That broke the ice. Abby Rockefeller had been hoping that other donors would appear to mute the gossip that the MOMA was a Rockefeller toy. In 1938, she gave the MOMA $20,000 for a purchase fund, while her son Nelson added $11,500. In the same year, Barr was able to engineer a complicated deal which brought in another landmark Picasso, his early Cubist masterpiece, *Les Demoiselles d'Avignon*. To buy this flamboyant experiment with the aesthetics of ugliness, he persuaded French dealer Jacques Seligman to substantially lower the price, then sold Degas's *The Race Course* from the Bliss collection to pay for the rest.

Just when the cultural tide seemed to be surging westward toward the New World, Alfred Barr was urged by his trustees to gather an exhibition which would show Parisians, and possibly Londoners as well, what America offered in the way of art. The man who had excluded American abstract artists from his "Cubism and Abstract Art" exhibition on grounds that these home-grown Modernists had already shown their work at the little Whitney Museum was now charged with showing the skeptical French that Americans were not all cowboys, Indians, gangsters, millionaires, and movie stars. Mindful of how patronizingly ignorant the French were, Barr's catalog reviewed for them the most basic facts about American history: that the frontier had ended in the 1890s, that waves of immigration had by 1900 swelled the American population to seventy-five million, that the United States

had become a world power with the completion of the Panama
Canal in 1914.

The idea of showing American art to the French had intrigued
Goodyear since the museum's early days. Even earlier, while the
Lost Generation was gathered in Paris, Washington collector and
connoisseur Duncan Phillips had attempted an American exhibition there, but French bureaucracy had defeated him. As for
Barr's plan, Abby Rockefeller was realistic about its potential
impact. She hoped that the Paris show would "have a tremendous
effect on the American people, even if it does not greatly impress
the more sophisticated and cynical French. I always suspect that
they do not admire anything produced outside of their own wonderful country."

Warming to his role as missionary to the French, Barr had
chosen the thousand-odd items that left New York aboard the
French line's SS *Lafayette* in late April 1938 to educate Parisians
about America's diversity and its people's restless, eclectic, inventive character. He had also picked works, especially the paintings,
to demonstrate the profound European influence on American art.
Barr was frustrated because the institutions which owned some of
the finest American paintings mean-spiritedly refused to let them
travel. Among the masterpieces left out were Thomas Eakins's
Rembrandtesque *The Gross Clinic*, Samuel F. B. Morse's stirring
portrait of Lafayette, Albert Pinkham Ryder's somber *Toilers of
the Sea* and *Jonah and the Whale*, Whistler's Impressionistic *White
Girl*, and Winslow Homer's *The Gulf Stream*.

Following his broad views on what comprised art, Barr intended
the paintings to give only a fractional glimpse of American art
while his selection of photographs, architecture, and films would
play to America's strengths. John McAndrew's catalog essay on
architecture featured only Thomas Jefferson; skyscraper pioneers
Henry Hobson Richardson and Louis Sullivan, who were trained in
Paris; and Frank Lloyd Wright, who had refused to attend the
Ecole des Beaux Arts. The typical American architect of the
previous fifty years had duly studied in Europe but, McAndrew
lamented, "has turned his back on most of the fundamental problems of architecture and gone into his library to find historically

accurate detail for the houses (and even the garages) of his clients."
Ignoring the dramatic skyline of urban America which invariably
impressed European visitors, McAndrew mourned that stylistically, "a city block in New York, Chicago or San Francisco will
encompass 2,000 years and 5,000 miles with bland unconcern."

Such abject modesty simply sharpened the fangs of Parisian
critics. The exhibition's opening in late May attracted an enormous,
enthusiastic crowd, but the reviewers' comments were inordinately
snide. As Abby Rockefeller had feared, the French were notoriously ethnocentric; moreover, a number of the bitterest critics
worked for Fascist papers and used the exhibition to beat their
chauvinist drums. The show was "very educational," wrote Raymond Galoyer in *l'Aube*. "We have become used to seeing their
Maecenases buy works of art to be transported homeward . . . [and]
. . . generously shower our land with gifts for the restoration of our
monuments . . . if Americans thus interested themselves . . . it was
because they had no art of their own." That the show included
works other than painting and sculpture, wrote Lucie Mazauric in
Vendredi, proved that Americans did not honor "the sort of hierar-
chies that confer upon painting and sculpture the highest value."
America would never "overtake the van. It has too poor a past."
Francois Fosca, critic for the rabidly Fascist, anti-Semitic *Je Suis
Partout*, asserted that he "would give all the contemporary paintings in the United States for a few meters of American films." Of
the paintings by the "so-called avant-garde," another Fascist, An-
dre Villeboeuf of *Gringoire*, wrote that they were "without origin,
without taste, marked alone by an originality that accentuates the
indecency of its arrogance, the puerility of its conceit out of fashion
with us in France."

While the French government donated $10,000, half the show's
cost, and while it had attracted large crowds, especially to daily
screenings of American films, it certainly had not budged the
French from their narcissistic smugness. In retrospect, Barr
would later write that he was "not surprised to find the French
enthusiastic about the films, impressed by the architecture, respectful toward the photography, but uncertain about the paintings." A plan to move the show to London during the summer of
1938 fell through because of ridiculously flimsy protocol: the Prin-

cess Royal was already engaged to open an exhibition of Canadian paintings and no other member of the royal family was available for another art show ribbon cutting. Furthermore, London was considered unable to support two concurrent art shows from the New World.

Snubbed by the Europeans, Barr was ironically being pounded at the same time by his most loyal MOMA trustees for insisting that a great European architect should design a new building for the museum. As early as 1934, it had been obvious that the compact four-story graystone housing the museum was outgrown. The staff offices, in what had been the servants' quarters, had been jammed from the day they had moved in. The Department of Circulating Exhibitions and the assistant curator of painting, plus their type-writers and secretaries, were all crammed into the second maid's hall bedroom; the publicity secretary and stenographer worked in the penthouse bathroom. In February 1936, the trustees spent $215,000 from the endowment and an additional $250,000 given by Abby Rockefeller to acquire seven parcels adjoining the existing building at 11 West Fifty-third Street. A new building on this large lot would face the end of Rockefeller Plaza, then planned to extend north from Fifty-first Street. By the spring of 1936, Barr joined Nelson Rockefeller and Goodyear on a building committee to plan an ambitious new structure on this prime site.

When a new building was first being discussed, Barr naturally dreamed about commissioning a great modern architect to design it. One possibility had been Le Corbusier, but the prospect of working with him evaporated abruptly when Barr was confronted by his abrasive behavior during an American lecture tour the previous year. As he traveled around the United States, accompanying a museum-sponsored exhibition of his work, Le Corbusier's irascible whims so exasperated the lecture tour's original organizer, Carl O. Schniewind, that he quit. Barr had then provided Le Corbusier with Robert Jacobs as "volunteer interpreter and general caretaker which, heaven knows, the great man needed." Sadly, Barr recalled many years later, "both the exhibition and the tour ended with acrimonious accusations. . . . [Le Corbusier's] chief complaint was that he was not allowed to keep all his lecture fees," while the museum paid all his expenses.

Just as the MOMA building committee began to meet, Barr became involved in the search for an outstanding European to fill a vacant chair in architecture at the Harvard Graduate School of Design. He corresponded almost daily with Dean Richard Hudnut, discussing various candidates, their special talents and availability. Barr agreed to approach Ludwig Mies van der Rohe with the job offer during the summer and, after he refused, to see Walter Gropius, who would accept the job as of February 1937. Thus, while Barr was in Europe skirmishing with the Surrealists during the summer of 1936, he was also trying to entice a prominent modern architect to teach at Harvard. This would be the man, he hoped, to design the new building.

But even as Barr was pursuing this delicate double mission in Europe, Rockefeller and Goodyear had already chosen their fellow trustee Philip Goodwin, a tame beaux arts designer, to do the work. "It seems to me that Mr. Goodwin would greatly profit professionally from collaborating with such a man as Mies [van der Rohe]," Barr wrote to Abby Rockefeller. "If, however, he refuses to collaborate and threatens to resign, he should be permitted to do so." Barr's strategy was to let Goodwin be the architect in name only while he persuaded Dutch innovator J. J. Oud, or Gropius, or even Mies van der Rohe to do the actual work. Nelson had seemed to favor Mies van der Rohe as well. But suddenly, just as the German Modernist seemed interested, Goodwin refused to work with a foreigner, and MOMA administrator Thomas Mabry urgently wrote Barr that "You had better issue an ultimatum immediately. . . . I'm afraid your technique of letting everyone fry until the last minute will not work." Goodwin was already "working away like a beaver." At Barr's request, Abby Rockefeller cabled to Nelson in a last-ditch effort to stop Goodwin, at least until Mies van der Rohe gave a definitive answer. But it was too late. Nelson, who was then chief executive of Rockefeller Center, replied that he favored Goodwin: "Plans now being developed are very satisfactory." The aide Goodwin chose for the project was the twenty-nine-year-old codesigner of Radio City Music Hall, Edward Durrell Stone.

Barr was crushed. "I cannot but feel that if we took second best, or, what is just as likely fifth best we would be betraying the standards of the museum," he lamented to Goodyear. But if anything was designed to make Goodwin dig in his heels, it was the insulting letter Barr fired off to get him to withdraw. While a generation of young American architects had tried to overcome "their anachronistic schooling," Barr wrote, "they have not had time . . . or experience enough to prove their mastery." The Europeans are "as obviously superior as Picasso is to [the American realist painter] Eugene Speicher." Some trustees might be "nationalistic," he granted, but "they do not hesitate to buy English clothes or French hats (if not French pictures)." To Nelson Rockefeller he exploded in a furious night letter, insisting that while he was "not personally resentful and hope Stone adequate," he feared the "museum losing position leadership." With that, Barr resigned from the building committee and, setting off consequences that would backfire drastically some years later, trustee Stephen Clark took his place.

Disgusted and humiliated over his defeat, Barr threw himself into major exhibitions and their catalogs, purchases, writing, and professional contacts, while taking little part in the new building's design or construction detail. But as Goodwin's plans emerged, Barr confided his disappointment to Philip Johnson, who fumed sympathetically: "I know you will snort," he wrote, "the building is Jewish. It looks like an upper Fifth Avenue front." Johnson wanted "a temple of art . . . the most beautiful and useless building in the world, small galleries, dark, cool and gorgeous . . . I mean a lot of wasted space. One should enter a museum up steps and one should be impressed and rather afraid to enter."

As it turned out, the genius of Barr and Johnson's idol, Mies van der Rohe, gave way before the tricky challenges of museum design. His only effort in that direction, the National Gallery, completed in Berlin in 1968, proved to be handsome but far from functional. An elegant glass box, its entire ground level lacked solid walls essential for hanging paintings; the picture galleries had to be crammed into the basement. Barr himself eventually moderated his views about the functionalism of the International Style. Some twenty-five years after the new MOMA building was opened, he advised another museum director who was planning a new wing: "If you are short on space you would do better not to have a glass wall."

Despite Barr's apprehensions, the new MOMA building was a sensational success. Completed almost a year behind schedule in the summer of 1939, at a cost of some $1 million, it was the first International Style building in America. *Architectural Forum* raved over its "efficient and flexible plan, superlative use of materials, color, and furnishings ... a thoroughly distinguished addition to the best modern architecture has produced." Contrary to Philip Johnson's notion, architectural historian G. E. Kidder-Smith marveled that "there was not a step between the sidewalk and the pictures." One walked in and immediately saw some art, with the sculpture garden beyond. Although the building was universally acclaimed, Barr, in his curmudgeonly way, never quite forgave Philip Goodwin for designing it. Even some years after the museum had moved into the new building, Barr grumbled about its architect: "I do not believe in his capacity as a designer in the modern spirit."

Looking down on the garden, a last-minute gift from John D. Rockefeller, Jr., Alfred H. Barr, Jr., might have paused to reflect on what he had wrought in ten years. Starting from a rented space in a nondescript office building, his museum now occupied a substantial chunk of the most valuable real estate in Manhattan. Instead of two harassed coworkers, the sleek offices down the hall, all democratically of equal size, bustled with people preparing books and catalogs for publication, assembling exhibitions both for the museum and for hundreds of other venues across the country, seeing artists, humoring trustees, attracting members. There was a registrar to keep track of the collection and of loans, and a bursar to handle a budget approaching $200,000. There was an executive director to deal with building maintenance, staff problems, schedules, and budgeting, and an assistant director to help Barr with a multitude of distracting details. And there was a publicity department to tell the world all about his wonderful museum.

"And David perceived that the Lord had established him king over Israel. . . . And let it be, when thou hearest a sound of a going in the tops of the mulberry trees, that then ... shall the Lord go out before thee, to smite the host of the Philistines."

7

PREACHING THE GOSPEL

Silver candelabra especially designed by Alexander Calder gleamed and flickered at a gala dinner party to celebrate completion of the MOMA's new building, two days before the official opening. Alfred Barr, who considered clothing worthy of aesthetic contemplation, noticed that Abby Rockefeller was wearing "a most glorious deep red dress by Lanvin; you know he cut everything on the bias. She looked magnificent." As the glittering guests sipped the last of three kinds of wine, Paul Sachs assured them that "in serving the elite," the museum "will reach better than in any other way, the great general public." Be bold, he urged; avoid "the danger of timidity." Goodyear lauded Barr as the museum's "pituitary gland, because this gland has such a profound influence on the growth of the body. The skeleton cannot prosper without it and when its activity is diminished, this leads to obesity and mental defects."

The new building opened with a grand public ceremony on May 10, 1939. Each speaker called by the master of ceremonies, Lowell Thomas, lauded the museum in terms of his or her own interests. Pres. Franklin Delano Roosevelt, who was anxiously watching totalitarianism run rampant in Europe, called it "a citadel of freedom." Motor magnate Edsel Ford, whose chrome-bedecked chariots Barr had often deplored, appreciated the museum's interest in industrial design. He did not wish "to boast . . . about the beauty of the automobile," Ford said, but could not resist noting that the car "is designed for contemporary use entirely . . . without the inappropriate patterns of ancient handicraft." Movie financier John Hay Whitney emphasized the museum's support of "the liveliest visual art of the twentieth century." The new MOMA president, art collector Nelson Rockefeller, rejoiced that it enabled "people to see and enjoy the things that present-day artists are doing."

Although the broadcast of the opening over New York station WJZ elated many of the museum's supporters, Barr was furious about the flippant tone Nelson Rockefeller had used in describing some of the museum's exhibits. Referring to the notorious *Fur-lined Teacup*, Lowell Thomas had quipped that he heard that moths had gotten into it, to which Nelson Rockefeller replied, "There was a report, but it's just an ugly rumor." Barr sternly protested, "That the president of an art museum should make fun publicly of a work of art by a serious artist . . . I consider a pretty cheap and unnecessary conniving with the public's desire to laugh at anything it can't understand at first glance . . . the same kind of 'fun' was made of the work of Van Gogh, Cézanne and Whistler some fifty years ago." Barr's prim sense of propriety also was offended by the broadcast's "back-slapping and first-naming"; he called it "pretty undignified" and in "thoroughly bad taste."

This outburst may have been appropriate ten years earlier, when Nelson Rockefeller, at Abby's behest, had joined the museum's junior advisory committee and worshiped at the feet of Alfred Barr. But since he joined the board of trustees in 1932, Nelson had taken an increasing role in managing the museum. In 1935, he became treasurer and took over so many important posts that Abby wrote worriedly to Goodyear that she thought it was "unwise, unfortunate and inappropriate" for Nelson to head "all the important phases of the museum," as chairman of the committees for finance, building, and the 1939 World's Fair. In an effort to minimize the museum's Rockefeller connection, Abby left the board of trustees when Nelson replaced Goodyear as president in May of 1939. For Nelson, the museum experience was invaluable. Later, after he had served as governor of New York and vice-president of the United States, he would recall, "I learned my politics at the MOMA."

While Barr clearly was embarrassed by Rockefeller's vulgarity and worried about the impression it left on the decorous directors of other museums, he also was playing his own political game to put the MOMA's new president in his place. In his own remarks for the opening, Barr was deliberately spare and ascetic. He modestly described the museum as simply "a laboratory; in its experiments, the public is invited to participate." But there was no doubt that the building marked the MOMA's metamorphosis from a small, struggling institution to a landmark on New York's cultural scene. Abby Rockefeller had sent him—and every other staff member—a personal note raving over "the arrangement of the galleries, the decorations and furnishings, the lighting and the perfection of workmanship throughout. An unbelievable job has been done." Enclosed with each note was a month's salary.

The opening exhibition, "Art in Our Time," gave a generous demonstration of Barr's accomplishments in ten years as MOMA director. For the fifth-anniversary exhibition, only ten New York galleries had loaned works and all loans from private collections also had come only from New Yorkers. For the tenth-anniversary exhibition, Barr had gathered loans from twenty-two galleries, many of them abroad, as well as from the world's most prestigious museums: London's Tate Gallery, the Royal Museums of Fine Art in Brussels and Antwerp, the Art Institute of Chicago, the Boston Museum of Fine Arts, the Philadelphia and Cleveland museums. Artists who lent works included Stuart Davis, Alexander Calder, Isamu Noguchi, Constantin Brancusi, and William Zorach. The collectors represented spanned the continent: Edward G. Robinson and Mr. and Mrs. Ira Gershwin of Beverly Hills, California; Frank and Robert Oppenheimer of Berkeley, California; Duncan Phillips of Washington, D.C.; and many lesser-known collectors in Cleveland; Baltimore; St. Louis; Wilmington, Delaware; and Germantown, Pennsylvania.

To avoid intimidating out-of-towners attracted to New York by the 1939 World's Fair, Barr deliberately refrained from presenting a comprehensive survey like the two landmark exhibitions of 1936, and included many seductive works from the margins of Modernism. Renoir's *Luncheon of the Boating Party*, which Barr flatly called the artist's greatest work, was already fifty-eight years old. An even older Renoir, *Dancing at Le Moulin de la Galette*, allowed Barr to retell the parable of great artists scorned by their contemporaries. "When children amuse themselves with paper and colors, they do better," Barr quoted an 1877 French critic of Renoir. The public of that day "thought the Impressionists were either crazy or incompetent," he explained, obliquely warning the viewer to withhold judgment on more provocative, more recent works.

In a decade, Alfred Barr's religion of modern art had grown from an obscure sect with a handful of mid-Manhattan devotees to a nationwide movement with strong middle-class roots. Membership committees for the Museum of Modern Art functioned in twenty-one cities, among them Detroit, Louisville, Houston, Minneapolis, Montreal, New Orleans, Palm Beach, Hartford, and Washington. Whereas in 1932 three traveling exhibitions had been shown in fifteen places, thirty-eight shows were on the road in 1938 and 1939, exhibited in 143 places. At the mother church itself, some 112 exhibitions had attracted about 1.5 million visitors.

Along with giving modern art a history with his path-breaking exhibitions, Barr had also provided it with a literature. His fifty or so exhibition catalogs had revolutionized this genre. More than mere lists of works, wrote one critic, they "satisfied the cognoscenti and interested the laity by combining an elegance of format, a scholarly precision and a richness of data ... with a clear, readable style." Agnes Mongan, his old mentor at Wellesley, wrote that "a library on contemporary art is unthinkable without them. I would lay a wager that no shelves in any museum library are more steadily or more eagerly visited than those which contain the Museum of Modern Art catalogs." Barr saw the catalogs not only as educational tracts but also as "one of our most important membership selling points."

The idea of selling memberships at all had been a MOMA innovation, born of Depression necessity, and by 1939 close to seventy-five hundred people were paying a minimum of ten dollars each per

year to join. Though nonmembers had to pay for admission beginning in 1939, attendance nevertheless rose by 380 percent, largely
because the twenty-five-cent ticket included free admission to
films shown in the new auditorium. What with lectures and perfor-
mances keyed to exhibitions, a museum store and restaurant, and a
sculpture garden, the Museum of Modern Art was blossoming into
a lively cultural center, a place to meet friends, the only museum in
midtown Manhattan. Alfred Barr's little classroom had become a
multi-sided cultural institution, a model for museums all over the
world.

Memberships and other money-making enterprises furnished
only about one-third of the museum's funds. The rest came from
donations, principally from the trustees, and among them Rockefeller contributions were overwhelming. In 1940, for example,
Abby Rockefeller gave $55,000 to the general budget, $55,000 to
the building fund, and $5,000 to the film library, in addition to
seventeen paintings, 1,423 prints, one photograph, and fifty-nine
posters. During the year ending in 1941, some $323,000 of the
museum's $605,000 budget came from the trustees, more than one-
third of the total from Abby Rockefeller. In 1943, Abby Rockefeller
again gave $50,000 for the general budget, $127,000 to the building
fund, and $5,000 for the garden.

With deficits every year and such dependence on Abby Rockefeller's generosity, Barr had to struggle and scheme to fill the
gaping holes he perceived in the museum's primary raison d'être,
the collection. True, in its first decade, the museum had acquired
271 paintings, ninety-seven sculptures, and constructions, 308
watercolors, six pastels, an uncounted number of drawings, and
149 prints. In 1940, the collection was insured for $707,664, but its
quality was uneven, skewed by what the trustees had deigned to
donate. Americans, for example, comprised some 40 percent of the
items, but only 14.7 percent of the value. The costliest items were
also the oldest: if the trustees carried through with their original
notion to pass nineteenth-century works on to the Metropolitan,
almost 45 percent of the collection's value would vanish. The weight
of twentieth-century works by the School of Paris also was overwhelming: 34 percent of the total value, compared with only 3.6
percent for modern Germans and a scattering of Russians, Mexi-

cans, and English. There appeared to be no reasonable balance in the collection and much of it was frankly mediocre. Describing the museum's holdings in 1941, Barr emphasized the need for "more works of real quality and historic importance." Only half the paintings were "really useful" for exhibition and only one-eighth "could be considered worthy of an ideal collection."

His ideal painting collection, as he sketched it out in 1941, would resemble a cathedral, with twenty-nine bays, each twenty-four feet square. Three would be devoted to late nineteenth-century Europe, three to Expressionists, two to Cubism and abstract art, and two to fantasy and Surrealism. Two bays would show only Picasso, while two more would cover Matisse, Léger, Miró, and other French pioneers of Modernism. The later French masters also would occupy two bays, with one each given to the European classical and realist reaction to Modernism, and to the Neo-romantics. Of the six bays he gave Americans, two were for "masters," two for young artists, and one each for American scene and watercolors. Mexican painters would occupy two bays, South Americans one, and the remaining two were for "popular painting" (now called "naif").

Although the nineteenth-century share of the collection seemed dangerously bulky, Barr could not resist compiling a list of more such works that he wanted. For the first three bays alone, he still coveted a Monet or Pissarro; a late Degas pastel; a great Cézanne landscape and a great figure composition; an important Seurat and two drawings; an important Gauguin; a good Toulouse-Lautrec and two lithographs or drawings; a van Gogh landscape, figure, still life, flower piece, or interior; a Rousseau portrait and an "important jungle picture"; two Redon lithographs; an Ensor; three Munch prints; and early examples of Vuillard, Bonnard, and Rouault.

Like his earlier catalogs, the 384-page book accompanying "Art in Our Time" included many borrowed twentieth-century works which Barr yearned to own. But this time the list was more than an empty dream. A number of masterpieces loaned by Europeans were trapped in America when the Second World War broke out in September 1939 and their owners, faced with an uncertain future, decided to sell. Others belonged to refugees from the Nazis with pressing financial problems. Frightened by the prospect of war,

many dealers sent works on loan to the MOMA for safekeeping. The
longer they were displayed, as it turned out, the more opportunity
there was for Barr to cajole a donor into a generous purchase. For
the most important such works, there was now Mrs. Guggenheim's
ample checkbook, an example and a spur to others.

But the most controversial source for great works of modern art
in the summer of 1939 was an auction in Lucerne, Switzerland, on
June 30. It confronted Barr (and many others) with an agonizing
moral dilemma. On the block at the Fischer Gallery were some 125
of the finest examples of Modernism in all the world—Gauguins,
Braques, Chagalls, Matisses, Klees, Mondrians, Modiglianis, and
works by the greatest German Expressionists, Ernst Nolde, Oskar
Kokoschka, Max Pechstein, Ernst Ludwig Kirchner, Franz Marc,
Otto Dix.

They were part of a monstrous Nazi seizure of all modern works
from German museums and private owners during the previous
year. Branded as decadent, they were first dumped into a Berlin
warehouse: 1,290 paintings; 160 sculptures; 7,350 watercolors,
drawings, and prints; and 230 portfolios. After the Nazis' self-
styled art connoisseur Hermann Göring hauled off what he wanted
to his opulent hunting lodge, Karinhall, the Nazis tossed most of
the remainder, at least four thousand works, onto a huge pyre in the
courtyard of Berlin's main fire station and on March 20, 1939,
incinerated everything. To a few dealers they gave about seven
hundred items to sell for foreign currency. The works to be auctioned in Lucerne were considered the choicest among all this loot.

Aghast at the obscene spectacle, many dealers boycotted the
auction. Others formed a ring to keep the prices down. By this
generally illegal maneuver, they agreed not to compete against
each other but to let just one person bid, to keep the price low, and
settle the matter of ownership later in a private auction of the
works among themselves. Less than two months after this sale, the
MOMA announced it had bought from the Buchholz Gallery five
important items sold in Lucerne and they were being added to the
"Art in Our Time" exhibition. They were Derain's *Valley of the Lot
at Vers*, stolen from the Cologne Museum; Ernst Ludwig
Kirchner's *Street Scene* and Wilhelm Lehmbruck's *Kneeling
Woman*, both taken from the Berlin National Gallery; Paul Klee's

Around the Fish, pilfered from the Dresden Gallery; and Matisse's *Blue Window*, seized from the Essen Museum. Barr blandly told the *New York Times* that the "more cultivated elements in the Nazi Party" were "very much embarrassed" by Hitler's art theories and sorry to lose the pictures as well as "Germany's reputation as a cultivated nation."

Actually, the Barrs were in Paris while the auction took place and had given exiled German art dealer Curt Valentin, who owned the Buchholz Gallery, money donated by Mrs. Resor and others to bid. "I am just as glad not to have the museum's name or my own associated with the auction," he wrote to MOMA manager Thomas Mabry on July 1. Many French dealers, artists, and newspapers were outraged that anyone had bid on art stolen by the Nazis. "I think it very important," Barr added "that our releases . . . should state that [the works] have been purchased from the Buchholz Gallery, New York." Barr handsomely repaid Valentin for his services by sending trustees to shop in his gallery and by stopping there himself about once a week. When the dealer applied for American citizenship in 1943, Barr vouched for his good character.

Barr's uneasiness over the morality of buying art stolen from German collectors and museums lingered on for decades. In 1944, after the MOMA had bought a number of other works stolen from German museums, Barr noted that although *Time* magazine reported the items in the Lucerne auction had been worth $250,000, the sale brought in only $135,000. To an Associated Press reporter a decade later, Barr implied that the MOMA had actually boycotted the auction and thereby had lost the best Munch ever on the market. After thinking "a long time," eighteen years in fact, Barr decided that he had acted correctly in accepting—and keeping—the stolen works. By then, the Nazis had been long defeated and, to Kenneth Donahue, then curator at the Ringling Museum of Art in Sarasota, Florida, who was wrestling with the same issue, Barr rationalized that similar works were now available to German museums. "I frankly thought it was a good thing for the Germans as a whole to have some reminder of their collective guilt and folly. Perhaps I am being not only Calvinistic but Jesuitical since I want to keep the pictures here. But in any case, you're safe on the first count (legal); your conscience must guide you on the second (moral)."

The museum world's deepest secrets deal with purchases, the sources, and especially the prices paid. Nevertheless, it is known that, in addition to educating or delighting the public, the MOMA exhibitions have long provided a sophisticated selling device for dealers and an elegantly discreet shopping expedition for buyers. This system began as early as 1936, when a price list accompanied "Fantastic Art, Dada and Surrealism" on its nationwide tour. An André Breton collage went for $5 then, a Kandinsky watercolor for $75, Henry Moore's *Reclining Figure* for $210, Rene Magritte's *Mental Calculus* for $275, and Paul Klee's *Mask of Fear* for $1,000.

Among the 255 modern works listed in the "Art in Our Time" catalog, sixty were lent by galleries or artists and therefore can be considered almost certainly for sale. Another forty of the most valuable items belonged to trustees and many of these would end up in the museum as gifts or bequests. In fact, during the next few years Alfred Barr would gather in an extraordinary number of masterpieces. In addition to the haul from Lucerne, Barr acquired a number of important twentieth-century works which genuinely broadened the MOMA collection: Alfaro Siqueiros's *Echo of a Scream*, given by Edward M. M. Warburg, for example; many German Expressionists; and sculptures by William Zorach, George Kolbe, Jacques Lipchitz, Renee Sintenis, and Raymond Duchamp-Villon. Yet, the pull of the nineteenth century proved irresistible.

In the annual report for 1940–1941, the trustees reiterated their goal of making the collection "permanent as a stream is permanent"; the period the collection was to cover would be "approximately the fifty years previous to the ever-advancing present." Yet the cover of this report itself belied this plan. It featured "the most important single gift of the year," van Gogh's irresistible *Starry Night*. Barr had traded some works from the Bliss collection for this unquestionable masterpiece, but the acquisition raised an insoluble dilemma. The picture had been painted in June 1890, and thus was already more than fifty years old. If the Met collected important works from the last fifty years, Barr rationalized, the

MOMA would never have acquired *Starry Night*. But how could a modern museum keep on acquiring historic works while also pursuing the contemporary cutting edge? The conflict highlights the ambivalence which continues to rage in the breast of every imaginative museum director. Attracted to the study of art history by the beauty of existing works, trained as a historian as well as a connoisseur, Barr was perpetually torn between the quest for the new and the lust for the old. "Watch and pray that ye enter not into temptation: the spirit indeed is willing, but the flesh is weak."

Perhaps Barr had taken the irrevocable step toward the beauty of the past in 1939 when he persuaded Mrs. Guggenheim to give the MOMA Henri Rousseau's mysterious *Sleeping Gypsy*. The last acquisition of the legendary American collector John Quinn, the *Sleeping Gypsy* had capped a collection of some 500 paintings and 300 sculptures, the world's most extensive privately owned gathering of modern art. Quinn had been buying avant-garde art with increasing obsessiveness ever since the Armory Show of 1913 showed Americans the latest creations of the wild young Europeans. When he died in 1924, Quinn's collection included more than fifty Picassos, twenty-seven Brancusi sculptures, nineteen Matisses, Redons, Picabias, and eleven Seurats, virtually a corner on this artist's oil paintings. Ignorant and uneasy about modern art, Quinn's heirs hurriedly disposed of his treasures.

When the *Sleeping Gypsy* was auctioned with the rest of the collection in Paris in 1926, Jean Cocteau had described the picture in the auction catalog as "a phenomenon, a unique piece, the hub of the wheel, the dead center, the heart of the hurricane, the sleep of sleeps, the silence of silences . . . painted poetry," while a Paris newspaper headline asked: "Which idiot will pay the Big Price for *The Sleeping Gypsy*?" A dealer, Henri Bing, paid $15,600 for it and eventually resold it in Switzerland for an unknown price. Perhaps its owner, like so many others in that troubled time, thought the picture would be safer in America. More likely, the picture was already for sale when Barr persuaded its owner, Madame E. Ruckstuhl-Siegwart, to send it on its first transatlantic voyage. At the time, no dealer would touch the painting, Barr later revealed, because its authenticity was questionable.

When Barr announced, early in 1940, that the *Gypsy* would

henceforth sleep at the MOMA, he avoided Cocteau's lyricism, calling it simply "one of the great masterpieces of modern times . . . unique in the concentrated power of its composition and the dreamlike fascination of its subject." Restorer Carolyn Keck was enraptured by the chance to clean the painting. "It was her greatest treat," Dorothy Miller remembers. "She begged Alfred to let her do it." Then one evening Keck excitedly phoned Miller. "You have to come over immediately," Keck insisted. "Come for dinner! You've got to come and see the sky!" Miller and Barr rushed over to her Brooklyn studio (Marga was in Europe) and "it was just delirium tremens," Miller recalled. The cleaning had uncovered a sky full of stars. When the cleaned-up *Gypsy* returned and hung in the MOMA place of honor, some weeks later, the entire staff held a celebration. "It's as if we'd had a copy," observed Monroe Wheeler, "and now we have the original."

Before the Second World War ended, masterpieces would come thick and fast into the MOMA collection. From among the works shown in "Art in Our Time," Braque's *The Table* was bought by sale or exchange of a Bliss collection work in 1941; Bonnard's *The Breakfast Room* was given by Stephen Clark in 1942; Mrs. Guggenheim financed purchase in 1942 of Léger's huge *Luncheon* and in 1945 of Chagall's *I and the Village*; Max Beckmann's *The Departure* was given anonymously (probably by his dealer Curt Valentin) in 1942. More than seven feet tall and ten feet wide, this shocking triptych documents Beckmann's own horror and despair as brutality trampled over civilization in Germany. He had begun *The Departure* in 1932 on the eve of Hitler's takeover. As he completed it in 1935, he wrote to a friend, "I am trying to use intensive work to get myself through the talentless insanity of the times. After a while this political gangsterism becomes ridiculously unimportant, and one feels best in the islands of one's soul." To his dealer, Valentin, Beckmann described *The Departure* as "a kind of rosary . . . which . . . tells me truths which I cannot express with words and did not even know before. . . ."

Beckmann fled to Holland in 1937, after 590 of his works were confiscated by the Nazis, and a number of them exposed for public ridicule as "Degenerate Art." Through Barr's influence, he was offered a summer job at the Art Institute of Chicago in 1940, but the American consul in The Hague refused to grant him a two-year teaching visa because he feared Beckmann would become a public charge. Then on May 10, the Nazis invaded Holland and throughout the war years and beyond, the artist diverted his pain and isolation into feverish work. In 1947, he would write to his dealer Valentin: "I am in urgent need of a terrible lot of canvas. . . . Also I don't have any Cremser white or Prussian blue. I'll take anything, I'm in the most fruitful working period!!! . . . The last bed-sheets have been painted."

The horror Beckmann had conveyed in *The Departure* would haunt Alfred Barr on a daily basis, as desperate refugees begging for help commandeered ever larger chunks of his time. The Barrs, of course, had witnessed the coming of the Nazis during their stay in Germany in 1933. To his despair, no American magazine had printed his shattering account of the tragedy. Then, Barr had been an acolyte, sitting at the feet of the German prophets of Modernism. Now the tables were turned and suddenly it seemed as though the entire German modern art establishment—artists and architects, art historians, critics, and museum directors—was looking to Barr and to his fledgling museum in New York for aid.

Among the first of the Bauhaus teachers to arrive in the United States was Josef Albers. Offered a job at Black Mountain College, a new progressive school in the hills of North Carolina, he arrived in 1933 on a nonquota visa guaranteed by Philip Johnson and Edward M. M. Warburg. Within four years, Barr was glowing about the Bauhaus's impact in America: "The forces of reaction have turned Germany into a first-rate military power and a fifth-rate power artistically. But the misfortune of the German people has been the good fortune of others . . . our culture has recently been enriched by the presence of such voluntary exiles as Gropius and Albers. Through them, may the resolutely modern spirit of the Bauhaus be given an American rebirth!"

"I lost all my money and all my pictures," Berlin dealer Alfred Flechtheim wrote to Barr from London in 1935. "The only things I didn't lose are my name, my experience, my knowledge of nearly every French modern picture, my connections in Europe." He wanted Barr to find the money for "nearly the only thing I saved," a Lehmbruck. Abby Rockefeller bought the *Standing Youth* for the

MOMA in 1936. Soon, however, Barr was sorrowfully turning away a host of tempting art bargains. Paul Westheim, an eminent German art critic who had fled to Mexico with his superb collection of German Expressionists, for example, offered the MOMA thirty paintings, hundreds of drawings and prints, and ten sculptures, all for $10,000. There were no funds to buy anything, he was told.

Like many others who were preoccupied with rescuing victims of the Nazis at that time, Barr tried to help those he deemed most forgotten. Despite Hitler's strident rhetoric, no one in the West then dreamed that the annihilation of European Jews was at hand. Though he abhorred anti-Semitism, Barr perceived that "the Jews after all have their fellow Jews representing immense wealth to look toward," whereas "the Gentiles . . . have been comparatively neglected." When Alexander Dorner, director of the Hannover Museum and professor at the technical high school there, was fired, Barr recommended him for a job at the Harvard Graduate School of Design. "He is a Gentile," he wrote to Dean Hudnut, but had been persecuted by the Nazis because he was "too much involved with modern art and architecture." Asked to help yet another European art specialist in 1937, Barr sounded weary: "Both our professional and commercial art circles are filled with recent refugees from Germany (many of them Jews but also, in the last two years, many Gentiles)."

By no means were all the refugees abject supplicants. Ludwig Mies van der Rohe had tried to maintain the Bauhaus in Berlin and had even attempted several commissions for the Nazis. When he stepped off the SS *Berengaria* in New York in the fall of 1937, he was greeted by MOMA trustee Helen Resor and whisked away to Jackson Hole, Wyoming, to design a vacation house for her there. He chatted with Frank Lloyd Wright at Taliesin, Wisconsin, before settling in Chicago to head the architecture department at Armour Institute. There, he immediately brought in two Bauhaus colleagues, Ludwig Hilbersheimer and Walter Petrhaus, while warning that America could not simply import a superior foreign culture; American culture would flourish only "through the harmonious unfolding of its own powers and possibilities."

However, by then the centuries-long effort to import European culture into America was no longer a matter of isolated missionary efforts like Alfred Barr's. As Hitler and the Nazis marched on jackboots toward war, European culture embarked in wholesale waves for the United States. During the late thirties and early forties, the American art world was assimilating the cream of Germany's scholarship; as New York University art historian Richard Offner put it: "Hitler shook the tree and I picked up the apples." But the influx did not simply reproduce what had existed in Europe; rather it mingled with native ingenuity and curiosity and a democratic impulse harnessed to Americans' perpetual quest for self-improvement. The mixture would ultimately bring America world leadership, not only in scholarly studies and in museum management but also in the creation of new styles of art.

During the late thirties, though, no one had time to assess theoretical consequences; the urgent task was to save people from all too physical threats. As Barr's office at the MOMA became a clearing house for information and aid, he ceased haggling over whether refugees were Jewish or not and worked heroically to provide whatever might be needed. In that process, he also gleaned many precious apples from the tree of European scholarship.

Meyer Schapiro, for example, sent Barr a former film critic for the *Frankfurter Zeitung*, Siegfried Kracauer, who had some weird notions about how totalitarianism was prefigured in German films of the twenties. Barr steered him to Iris Barry, who helped him to get Rockefeller Foundation support and two Guggenheim fellowships. He then wrote *From Caligari to Hitler*, one of the earliest scholarly studies of the movies. When young John Rewald arrived from France, he brought several hundred pages of unpublished letters from Camille Pissarro to his son. First Barr tried through Paul Sachs to get Harvard University Press to publish them. Unsuccessful, he then tried to get Rewald a Guggenheim fellowship, to amplify the study of Cézanne which had been his doctoral thesis at the Sorbonne. Refused again, Barr got the New York manager of Durand-Ruel Gallery to give the MOMA a tax-deductible contribution which he then gave to Rewald. "This book should be written," he said. The work became Rewald's path-breaking *History of Impressionism*, published in 1946 and currently in its fourth revised edition.

The American Abstractionist painter Lyonel Feininger had lived in Europe since 1913 and had married a German. Barr had met him in 1927–1928 during his visit to the Bauhaus and had included three of his works in "Cubism and Abstract Art." When the Feiningers appeared at the Museum of Modern Art after being expelled from Germany, Barr sent them to Dorothy Miller, who rented them her summer house in Stockbridge, Massachusetts, for the next six years at $100 per month. (One evening, a man dropped in to ask for donations to the local hospital. He saw the pictures on the walls and was awed. Feininger, who had spent his youth as a commercial illustrator, was equally awed when the man introduced himself as Norman Rockwell. They became good friends.)

For each famous name, however, there were dozens of promising young artists known mostly to other refugees, or scholars familiar only to specialists. By the spring of 1939, Barr's office was sending out to any agency that might be able to help a "sketchy and unclassified list of some German, Austrian and Czech refugees and would-be refugees who have come to our attention." Art historian Erwin Panofsky, whom Barr had earlier steered to Princeton, was concerned about painter Edward Bargheer, still in Germany. Paul Sachs at Harvard was looking after art historians George M. A. Hanfmann, Hans Huth, Jakob Rosenberg, Georg and Hanns Swarzenski, and Emmanuel Winternitz. Journalist Annie Fried had been settled in Newark, New Jersey; sculptors Waldemar Raemisch and Walter Cohn, Viennese painter MOPP (Max Oppenheimer), and teacher Wilhelm Dessault were all in New York. Dr. Heinrich Schwartz, the former curator of Vienna's Belvedere Museum, had been "in serious trouble in July 1938 [and] hasn't been heard from since."

After the Second World War broke out in September 1939, the plight of those left in Europe dangerously worsened, as American efforts to save them foundered not only for lack of funds but also in a morass of government red tape. Many of the Germans who had fled to France, among them the artists Hans Schiefer, Max Ernst, and Hans Bellmer, were inexplicably arrested and locked up in squalid camps as "enemy aliens." Others, like Kurt Schwitters, who was safe in London, were starving. The German master of collage and inventor of environmental art begged Barr to buy a picture, to be delivered after the war, and Barr had to reply "we already have three and I am afraid I could not persuade our committee to purchase another sight unseen."

English painter and satirist Wyndham Lewis was stranded by the war in Canada and begged Barr to sell some of his paintings. "My stay upon this continent has been unbelievably unprofitable and unpleasant," wrote Lewis. "I want money very badly to keep alive." Barr answered that he would try to help, recalling with amusement Lewis's satirical description of him in a 1940 essay: "There he is, thinking up some new outrage. . . . I have seen him surrounded by millionaires examining some leering monstrosity upon the walls of his so-called museum. He looks like a defrocked Jesuit."

After the fall of France in June 1940, Barr made Marga responsible for working closely with Varian Fry of the Emergency Rescue Committee. Threading her way through confused bureaucracy, Marga wrote the needed letters for Barr's signature. Fry had been at Harvard with Barr, studying Greek and Latin, and later, after the Depression had wiped out his fortune, had been considered for a job as MOMA librarian. Even after the United States entered the war in December 1941, he traveled repeatedly to unoccupied France, scooping up refugees like a modern Scarlet Pimpernel. Barr provided him with an affidavit to bring out German art critic Andreas Becker, and Marga raised guarantees of support to enable Fry to obtain visas for a number of threatened artists, including Marc Chagall, Jacques Lipchitz, André Masson, Jean Arp, and Wassily Kandinsky. Later Barr would recall wryly how he persuaded the MOMA trustees to buy a bronze bust of the Spanish Communist firebrand called *La Pasionaria*. Barr considered the work of its sculptor, Jo Davidson, pretentious and overpriced, and deplored his radical leftist politics. It was "a negotiation not without comedy," Barr recalled, but he went along with the arrangement because Davidson promised to give all the proceeds to the Emergency Rescue Committee.

Adroitly, Barr picked his way through the ideological causes of the day, choosing to support moderates and liberals, while resolutely avoiding the taint of Communist fellow-traveling. In 1942, he refused to support a campaign to free Earl Browder, the chairman of the American Communist Party, who was imprisoned on a

trumped-up charge of passport fraud. However, when the Joint
Anti-Fascist Committee asked to use his name as a sponsor of a
fund-raising dinner, Barr enthusiastically agreed. Though the
committee included some well-known Communists, it was also
cooperating with other anti-Fascists in rescuing refugees from
Europe.

In the midst of the turmoil, the State Department and other
bureaucrats were still attempting to apply their own critique to the
work of the artists fleeing for their lives. Marcel Duchamp's friend
and patron Walter Arensberg asked Barr to help rescue the enigmatic Dadaist after exhausting his own government contacts.
Arensberg described his efforts to enlist help from attorney-gen-
eral Francis Biddle through his brother, artist George Biddle.
Barr doubted that this attempt would succeed, "for George has
come out against artists of Marcel's type with almost hysterical
fury."

When the exits from Europe finally slammed shut, late in 1942,
Barr and others had brought to America a surprisingly large
creative group. Between 1933 and 1944, some 717 artists and 380
architects arrived—and many of them, for good and ill, settled in
close proximity to the Museum of Modern Art. Barr now could
personally consult Fernand Léger about his inspiration and work
process and about the real meaning of his *Le Grand Déjeuner*,
which Barr had rechristened *Three Women* because "I think it
suggests an interesting relation to [Picasso's] *Three Musicians*."
Barr had coveted the picture for more than ten years, he wrote to
Léger, asking for advice on framing and hanging it and whether it
needed cleaning. Barr also could stroll over to Mondrian's pristine
studio and pay him thirty dollars to restore his 1925 *Composition*,
which Philip Johnson had just given to the museum.

Right on his doorstep, Barr was once again in the midst of the
contentious Surrealists, his puritan soul torn between admiration
for their bold leaps into the unconscious and revulsion for their
eternal, left-wing political wrangling. His meetings and correspondence with their self-styled Magus, André Breton, "were not entirely friendly," he would write later, "since on occasion I had to
ignore his rather tyrannical efforts to control relations between the
Surrealist artists and our museum. I'm afraid he was also exasper-

ated by the fact that our museum did not ask him to lecture." But these quirks, Barr hastened to add, did not "diminish at all his greatness as a poet and champion of Surrealism."

The Surrealist sideshow amused or outraged many members of the New York art establishment, but the wartime refugee who would leave the most lasting imprint was a diminutive, outrageous riptide of a woman, the rebellious daughter of an American copper dynasty, Peggy Guggenheim. Simultaneously weak and willful, impulsive and canny, she had lived in Europe ever since the twenties in a restless search for fresh sensation. She arrived by air from Lisbon, with an entourage typical of her scrambled life. The eleven who straggled off the Pan American Clipper on July 15, 1941, included Guggenheim; her lover, Max Ernst; her two children, Pegeen and Sindbad; their father, Peggy's former husband, Laurence Vail; his current wife, Kay Sage; and their five children, Jacqueline, Bobby, Apple, Kathe, and Clover.

Also arriving was Guggenheim's extraordinary collection of modern art. She had accumulated most of it during the previous three years, seized by the kind of casual whim that wealthy people sometimes indulge when boredom yawns. In 1938, she had opened the Guggenheim-Jeune Gallery in London and had bought one work out of every show, "so as not to disappoint the artists." Relying on advice from art critic Herbert Read and artist Marcel Duchamp, she had held exhibitions for Jean Cocteau, Yves Tanguy, Antoine Pevsner, Henry Moore, Calder, Jean Arp, Schwitters, Picasso, Braque, Brancusi, and Miró. She had given Kandinsky his first London show and, at Read's urging, was planning to open a museum of modern art there.

When war broke out, Guggenheim fled to Paris with a list of artists from Herbert Read and the funds for the London museum in her pocket. "I decided to buy all the works of art that we had meant to borrow," she wrote later. "I put myself on a regimen to buy one work of art a day. Nothing could have been easier. The Parisians were expecting a German invasion and were delighted to sell everything and flee . . . everyone pursued me mercilessly. My phone rang all day and people even brought me paintings in the morning to bed, before I rose. I went to all the artists' studios and all the galleries and made many new friends."

As the Germans approached Paris, Fernand Léger told her that the Louvre would store her collection in the country, and so she crammed everything into a one-cubic-meter crate. Then the French museum officials told her the works were not worth saving, so she managed to haul the precious crate along roads clogged with refugees to a remote barn in unoccupied France. After many further vicissitudes, she had the paintings and sculptures repacked along with some old blankets and casseroles and shipped to New York as "household effects." For a collection which now included the works she had bought in London, plus several Klees and Picabias, a Cubist Braque, and works by Gris, Léger, Gleizes, Marcoussis, Delaunay, Severini, Balla, Van Doesburg, Mondrian, Dali, de Chirico, Brauner, Magritte, Lipchitz, and Giacometti, she had paid less than $40,000.

Guggenheim was disappointed that Barr would not leave Greensboro, Vermont, to greet her and her kin upon their arrival. "His books on modern art had been my Bible for years," she wrote, "so I was naturally longing to meet him." Barr, however, was more interested in meeting Max Ernst, whose works, Guggenheim wrote, he was "crazy about." When they did meet, in the fall of 1941, she was surprised that he looked like Abraham Lincoln and thought him "shy but very charming." But she soon "hated his cagey quality" and the way he would "fuss and fuss and bargain, and drove me crazy with his indecision." Eventually, Barr gave Guggenheim one of the thirteen Maleviches she claimed he had in the museum cellar, in exchange for an Ernst. And Guggenheim gave Ernst "the money that was not involved in this exchange."

Once installed in a luxurious remodeled brownstone mansion at Fifty-first Street and the East River, with Ernst and her collection, Guggenheim invited the Barrs to dinner "in a state of great excitement to know what he would think of them." She was relieved that they "thought I had some very fine things" and embarrassed that Marga asked some tactless questions about Ernst's recent affair with the artist Leonora Carrington. But Barr also deplored Guggenheim's extravagance. When she asked him for a contribution to bring Theodore Van Doesburg's widow, Nellie, over from Europe, Barr at first declined because "$881 seems awfully high—most of our refugees came over for from $350 to $400." Then, in a handwritten postscript, he pledged ten dollars. To pay for the rest, Guggenheim sold a Henri Laurens sculpture and a Klee watercolor, a sale she later called one of her "seven tragedies" as a collector.

For Barr, the entry of the United States into the Second World War threatened tragedy of a different kind. Soon after Pearl Harbor, the museum took steps to protect its collection in case of air raids. The most important works in the basement, many of them European loans stranded because of the war, were sent to a skyscraper warehouse. Some twenty-two of the most valuable items displayed on the museum's third floor had to be moved every night to a sandbagged strong room. A number of these, like Rousseau's *The Dream* and Picasso's *Three Musicians*, belonged to collectors; Barr shrewdly hoped that by being kind to their precious properties he would eventually acquire the works for the museum.

The war also meant that there were no more trips to Europe for the Barrs and no chances to borrow or buy the works of European artists. American museums showing more traditional works suddenly discovered that their colleagues elsewhere in the country had plenty of worthwhile works to loan out, but Barr had, since the MOMA's founding, looked to Europe as the sacred spring of Modernism. In 1940, he still cavalierly dismissed native artists: "America is not yet, I am afraid, quite the equal of France." In honor of American Art Week, however, he urged Dorothy Miller to stress the number of exhibitions she had arranged of American art works and to emphasize that no other museum had done as much as the MOMA "to further the interests of American photography, American films, American architecture, and American industrial design."

His acquisitive drive thwarted, Barr gladly accepted $26,000 from Nelson Rockefeller for purchases in Latin America. In the summer of 1942, while Lincoln Kirstein combed South America, Barr set forth on a six-week buying spree in Mexico and Cuba. A youthful assistant in the MOMA design department, Edgar Kaufmann, Jr., accompanied Barr, "to clean his shoes and speak Spanish."

"He's very delicate," Marga warned Kaufmann as she issued detailed instructions on how to care for Barr, to see that he got enough sleep and ate properly. But like two mischievous boys away from home, they got into trouble almost at once. In Laredo, Texas, Barr insisted on sampling an exotic drink called Dr. Pepper and, Kaufmann recalls, immediately got "deathly sick." Kaufmann idolized Barr and thought it "glorious, just glorious" to "play nursemaid." After Barr recovered, they headed for Mexico City, where gallery owner Iris Amor offered expansive Latin hospitality. She was "tiny, not too beautiful, very intelligent and high-toned, quietly dressed, the daughter of a wealthy family," said Kaufmann. "And she was married to a bullfighter." The two Americans were lionized by the Mexican art establishment, visiting galleries, meeting artists, and buying many works at what Kaufmann thought were "laughable prices." A good Orozco painting could be had for $700, although it took some shrewd bargaining, Barr reported to the trustees, to bring down prices "raised in the belief that the museum was fantastically rich and would therefore buy extravagantly." Best of all, from Kaufmann's caretaker standpoint, Barr's health thrived: "All that hot Mexican food and strong liquor didn't faze him."

After a brief stopover in the Yucatan to visit Mayan archaeological sites, Kaufmann and Barr flew to Havana, Cuba. They were surprised to be greeted at the airport by the wife of an artist, Maria Luisa Carreno, Kaufmann said, "splendid looking in white shorts and elaborate makeup." Though they had never met her before, she insisted that the two Americans stay with her and her husband, painter Mario Carreno. For a dinner party on their first evening, Maria Luisa appeared in a long, clinging dress, her face and head covered with laurel leaves. It was "surrealism alive," Kaufmann recalled more than four decades later. He also remembered his anxiety over Barr's health: if Marga had known about the bohemian life they were leading, Kaufmann thought, "she would have had a fit." Though he had only $500 to spend on Cuban art, Barr himself found the experience "one of the most unforgettable in my life," he raved to the Carrenos, soon after his return to New York. It was "so compact . . . of work and play, of new pictures, new scenes and new people, of the instant and cordial friendship of you two . . . and of your friends, of the rumor of distant malice, of incidents dramatic and funny, gay and instructive."

Kaufmann, the son of a wealthy Pittsburgh department store owner, was enchanted by his travels with Alfred Barr. Some months after returning from this jaunt, young Edgar offered to give the museum $750 every three months for purchases to augment the collections of the industrial design and architecture departments. "I would like you personally to decide how the money is spent," he wrote to Barr. Kaufmann also persuaded his mother to donate $300 and added $800 of his own to help Barr buy Mexican art works "as you see fit."

Back at the museum, however, Barr had sober second thoughts about the two hundred bargain canvasses and sculptures he and Kirstein had scooped up in Latin America. They obviously were not up to the quality Barr expected in works from Europe, and many did not measure up to the more tolerant criteria Barr applied to works by Americans. To museum president Stephen Clark, Barr wondered "whether we should make allowance for the general mediocrity or backwardness of any national school or whether we should set a standard similar, say, to that which we maintain for American painting." The answer remained vague, mostly out of respect for Nelson Rockefeller, who had financed Barr and Kirstein's collecting trips to Latin America and whose family had vast financial interests there.

When it came to exhibiting art of the most exquisite quality, Barr sometimes could not resist abandoning Modernism altogether. In 1940, he was beguiled by the chance to exhibit twenty-eight Italian Renaissance and Baroque masterpieces, which had been shown at the 1939 San Francisco World's Fair and also in Chicago. The Metropolitan, the natural New York venue for such a show, had declined because the $35,000 rental fee would have required an admission charge, which the Met's charter forbade. As a city-supported institution, the Met also was under pressure to reject the show on grounds that exhibiting any Italian paintings helped to legitimate Mussolini's Fascist regime. New York mayor Fiorello LaGuardia refused to attend a dinner celebrating the exhibition's opening at which the Fascist Italian ambassador to the United States was a guest of honor.

But Barr insisted that art was unpolitical, and showing these masterpieces was another great publicity and attendance coup, not to mention, as he justified it to the trustees, a money-maker for the museum. Between January 26, when 7,206 viewers set a one-day attendance record, to April 7, when the last of 290,888 visitors departed, the museum netted $64,400—and a bonanza of publicity. The works in their copper cases weighed ten tons and, newspapers were told, were worth $26 million. A troop of mounted policemen met them at the pier. Photographers could shoot the nighttime arrival of the masterpieces at the museum under special flood-lights. The museum would be open until 10:00 P.M. each evening. The pictures would never travel outside Italy again. Visitors could vote for their favorite painting, and when they picked Titian's *Pope Paul III* instead of Botticelli's *Birth of Venus* or Raphael's *Madonna of the Chair*, as expected, Barr congratulated "the New York public . . . upon its good taste."

A few months later, when the president of IBM, Thomas J. Watson, asked Barr to help him form the world's first corporate art collection, Barr wrote in the company's magazine about the public's fundamental interest in "the best, the finest, the strongest, the most beautiful." He admitted that the public was slow about making up its mind, "so that the great revolutionary individual whether in religion, science and invention, or art often has a hard time of it." The public had foolishly and carelessly "martyrized many of the great innovators, burned them at the stake, crucified them, laughed at them, as in the case of Whistler, or simply let them starve or go mad, as in the case of Van Gogh." He ended on a sunny note: "Given time, society ultimately repents if it has been wrong, honors great achievement and even takes [innovators] to its heart." Barr's relationship with IBM was the first of many strong links that the MOMA would forge with large business corporations.

Whenever anyone suggested that he was an arbiter of taste, Barr furiously denied it. But there was no denying that when the war cut Americans off from the Europeans whose judgments they revered, Barr increasingly stepped into the void. A German refugee in

January 1942 sent samples of a friend's paintings to Barr, calling him "the High Court" in judging art. Robert Schuppner's Surrealist works, Barr decisively replied, are "not particularly original or good in quality." When he first saw the work of Grandma Moses, on the other hand, Barr deemed her "really talented" and suggested that her work be considered for exhibition at the Museum of Modern Art.

Barr's interest in the aesthetics of commercial design also brought in a raft of requests for advice. The National Park Service asked him to consult on redesign of its concessions and gift shops. The Castleton China Company wanted him to help choose ten artists to create decorations for its dinnerware. When Montgomery Ward asked for his advice about postwar redesign of its appliances, Barr had no qualms about denouncing the industrial designers who had restyled many consumer products during the thirties. "Their designs are aimed at sales appeal of the most superficial kind," he wrote. "They are, to my mind, a very important element in the vicious circle which during the past ten or fifteen years has contributed so much and so cynically to the disadvantage both of the consumer and of the honest retailer." He cited pencil sharpeners senselessly streamlined, refrigerators with curved tops so that no plates or bottles could stand on the top, and the new stoves with ovens below the burners, "giving salesmen a talking point" that they were table top height, while giving "the housewife a backache."

Whenever he suspected a doubter of modern art, Barr was prepared to accost him or her with his gospel. For those visitors who might pass by the books and catalogs for sale at the museum, Barr drafted a handbill designed to convert skeptics. "*If you dislike modern art,*" he wrote, "the Museum welcomes you, believing that its collections and special exhibitions, its explanatory labels and sympathetic gallery guides (or gallery tours) will interest you and convince you that the art of our time—*your* time—is worth your attention even if some of it puzzles you at first. (But watch out! With some unprejudiced study you may even come to enjoy it!)"

For the more sophisticated, Barr tailored an equally compelling message. He bluntly accused art historians of willfully ignoring the art of their own time. In the November 1941 *College Art Journal*, the very first issue of the first American scholarly art periodical, Barr pleaded for college courses and research into Modernism. Shaming academics for their narrowness, he noted "how absurd this exhortation would be if addressed to our university physicists or economists, astronomers or psychologists, political historians or biochemists." Barr asserted that his belief in "the cogent importance of twentieth century art lies not so much in the greatness of its achievement as in this one simple, obvious and overwhelming fact—the twentieth century happens to be the period in which we are living . . . It is our century: we have made it and we've got to study it, understand it, get some joy out of it, master it!"

Barr's teacher at Princeton, Frank Jewett Mather, Jr., heartily, elegantly, disagreed. In the next issue of *College Art Journal* he argued that studying contemporary art, literature, or history was "obviously . . . the negation of a liberal education. . . . In any balanced curriculum . . . the present must always have a standing rather marginal than central." As for Barr's suggestion that graduate students could get firsthand research data from living artists, Mather professed to "shudder at the results" elicited from "pumping" living artists like John Marin, Thomas Hart Benton, or Salvador Dali; students had better stick to elucidating the work of long-dead artists like Masaccio's teacher, Masolino, or Van Eyck.

Having had his say in the first issue of *College Art Journal* and having been refuted in the second, Barr stubbornly insisted on having the last word. He brought up his reserve artillery: James Thrall Soby, his closest friend and colleague at the MOMA, wrote a three-page defense of modern art for the magazine's third issue. In addition, Lawrence Schmeckebier, a Syracuse University art historian, asserted that though it was much easier to study the dead— "They will not change their minds or talk back"—art professionals "cannot escape the modern artist." In the lead article of the periodical's fourth issue, Beaumont Newhall, director of the newly established MOMA Department of Photography, urged the study of photography as a branch of art history and Robert J. Goldwater wrote on modern art in the college curriculum. What with two reviews of a Henri Rousseau exhibition at the Museum of Modern

Art and a review of a book about Rousseau, some fourteen of the journal's thirty pages dealt with modern art. Within a year after this cannonade, Barr was named to the editorial board of the College Art Association, the journal's publisher, and the field was his. There would continue to be peripheral skirmishes, but whether modern art was a legitimate area of academic study never was seriously questioned again.

Like any successful general, Barr not only harassed the enemy but constantly braced his own troops. At the MOMA, no detail seemed too minute for him to notice. "There is a pretty bad ashtray on one of the library tables," he wrote in a staff memo. "If we have no other to put in its place, I think we should buy a new one. Thanks." He was embarrassed when the *New Yorker* noticed a John Ferren relief hanging upside down and urged that when it went on tour, the top and bottom be clearly marked. He was annoyed about bad typography in an index published by the film library and distressed that a pamphlet about the index which he also thought ugly would for months affront the public's eye on the museum's front counter. To Monroe Wheeler, he complained that signs in the lobby were poorly thought out and even that the type font Wheeler had chosen for a Pavel Tchelitchew catalog contained ugly capital G's and K's.

He demanded no less of himself. He patiently answered the most trivial letters; a thank you, for example, from the teacher of a group from the Bronx High School of Science who had visited the museum. He fretted that the exhibition catalogs perhaps contained too much advocacy, "without enough critical skepticism." When the trustees wondered whether special exhibitions or the permanent collection were attracting more attendance, Barr personally counted the number of visitors on a Sunday. Comparing results for the same week in 1942 and 1943, he reported that the permanent collection almost invariably outdrew temporary exhibitions, an argument he considered helpful in persuading the trustees to establish a permanent collection.

Settled in its new building, the museum's activities expanded geometrically. In a typical week in late January 1943, it was offering fourteen public lectures, fourteen film showings, a do-cents' meeting, an exhibition opening and another closing, five continuing exhibitions, a two-day conference on art in American education and society, three traveling exhibitions departing and two in preparation, and a class for high school students. Barr insisted on ultimate responsibility for all these activities, while also supervising each department's acquisitions, loans, labels, exhibitions, and press releases. When the new building opened, he had been named to the board of trustees and early in 1940 became vice-president. Though he was a member of the accessions committee, he refused a vote "because I much prefer to be overruled than outvoted. Such an arrangement gives me a chance to give my professional opinion, putting full responsibility for going against that opinion on the shoulders of the committee. If I was simply outvoted, it would be rather easier for the committee to have its way in the case of a difference of opinion." This elegant strategy worked so well, Barr boasted, that "no work is ever purchased without the full approval of the Director."

Still, even a master strategist like Alfred Barr could not manipulate every museum activity and every trustee. Time and again since the earliest days, the trustees had worried about the museum administration's hectic ad hoc atmosphere. But in adding staff and attempting to rationalize the chain of command, they had not reckoned with Barr's voracious missionary appetite for new fields and new responsibilities. The business people who formed the majority on the board of trustees did not appreciate that a museum is not a business. Part school, part philanthropy, an entertainment as well as a storehouse for precious objects, the kind of museum Barr was trying to build was unique. But while realizing his large vision, Barr was overwhelmed with pedestrian details.

As early as 1933, when Barr returned from his sabbatical, Conger Goodyear had tried to ease him out of the museum directorship. The newly hired administrator, Alan Blackburn, needed a suitable title, Goodyear wrote to Barr, casually adding that Abby Rockefeller had suggested that "it might even prove best for you to take the title of curator and for the time being make Alan acting director." The museum president attempted to lure Barr out of the administrative side with flattery: "You would be entirely free to devote your time to the aesthetic activities for which you are so obviously qualified." But though Barr had returned to the museum bearing a letter from a Swiss physician attesting that his health was still frail, he declined to step aside. To trustee Frank Crowninshield, Barr mocked certain museum directors, "Men who are primarily executives and 'contact men,' good at getting money or giving lectures, or addressing Saturday Rotary luncheons."

Later that year, Goodyear was again irritated at Barr's refusal to bring in guest curators, even though he was too busy to do all exhibitions himself. Barr suggested that trustee Stephen Clark arrange a show he particularly favored and Goodyear exploded. Barr should not fob off on a trustee "what are properly part of his duties," Goodyear wrote to Abby Rockefeller. "He should understand that we are to specify what his duties are and that if he does not fulfill them we must get someone in his place."

Two years later, Abby Rockefeller again complained about administrative messes at the museum. A new secretary had been hired while the incumbent was still in office. A curator had been appointed without the approval of the department chairman. A plan to use endowment funds for land and the new building had been approved before anyone had explored whether the land or funding for the building could be obtained as a donation. She was most disquieted that an expert had been brought in to study the museum's operations, but his recommendations had been ignored.

Near the end of 1936, even-tempered, loving Abby Rockefeller became enraged at Barr's sloppy management. The immediate trigger for her wrath was that several donors who had promised the museum generous gifts reneged because no one had gotten them to sign pledges. While she still had the highest respect for Barr's catalogs, she wrote to Goodyear, "he is neither physically nor temperamentally fitted to cope with the intricate problems of the management of the museum or the management of the trustees, if I may use the expression." She urged that they find "a museum director who directs, one who has the confidence and sympathy of the trustees and who is able to help raise money as well as interest people in giving their collections." Goodyear replied that it had been evident to him "for a long time . . . that Alfred is not temperamentally fitted to handle many of the problems that should devolve upon a director." Still, Barr was responsible for the museum's "unquestioned success" and the ticklish problem was to "adjust Alfred to a new and subordinate position."

The matter remained unresolved, but again in 1938, a reorganization committee diagnosed "chronic administrative difficulties" and recommended making Barr art director under an administrator. Barr resisted. In a letter to the trustees, he blamed the problems on "inadequate time, space, money and physical facilities" and on the "disparity between the rapidly growing complexity and bulk of the museum's program and the inadequate size and training of the museum staff."

In a postscript which he never sent, Barr was pessimistic about his future at the museum. "I do not have the strength to continue," he wrote. "My heart and energy have been consumed in the museum for nine years and I am still unable to find the time and energy not only for administrative duties but also for the work of a curatorial, scholarly, or educational nature for which I am, I believe, best suited." Perhaps at the urging of Marga, who was "nailed into the house" with an eighteen-month-old daughter to raise, he added, "Also I am unable to enjoy a normal social and domestic life." Then he unlimbered the ultimate threat: "I believe that the power in an art museum should be centered in a person of sufficient knowledge, vision, passion, skill, strength, courage and integrity to guard the institution against hurry, compromise and mediocrity. I believe that the last nine years have proved that I am not that person; and I am willing *now* to withdraw to a curatorship of, say, painting and sculpture, providing this were a real and not a nominal withdrawal."

Most of the trustees in 1938 (to some of whom Barr probably conveyed these black feelings orally) could only blanch at such a drastic prospect. To them and to most of its public, Alfred Barr *was* the museum. Furthermore, the new building was under construction; the collection was growing rapidly and a major exhibition was to open that summer in Paris. Granted, Barr and president Goodyear had their disagreements, but there was always Abby Rockefeller to smooth things over and Paul Sachs to support Barr with her. Nelson Rockefeller, who succeeded Goodyear as MOMA president in 1939, also revered Barr's scholarship and taste, as did John Hay Whitney, who was vice-president.

Nevertheless, they were determined to bring a stronger administrator into the museum, and during the summer of 1939, while the Barrs were in Europe gathering loans for a definitive Picasso exhibition scheduled for the following November, the trustees dismissed executive director Thomas Mabry. Without Barr's knowledge or consent, they replaced him with John E. Abbott from the film collection and at the same time made Monroe Wheeler director of publications. Abbott at one time had been a stockbroker and the trustees had confidence in him as a "money man." Barr's friends on the staff cabled the news to him in Paris and he cabled back: "Sit tight until I return." When he got back, Barr told Beaumont Newhall, "Well, it just had to happen and I couldn't do it." Newhall concluded, along with other staffers that "he didn't have any power any more."

As the museum's staff had grown, rivalries and tensions escalated. Edgar Kaufmann recalled that working there was "incredibly exciting," but there was also "a great deal of inside maneuvering." The staff was not "one happy family, but one *un*happy family." Abbott exacerbated the stresses with needless intrigue and just plain stupidity. Barr responded by withdrawing into intellectual and curatorial work. He resisted making important decisions and sometimes appeared unconcerned with the practical problems of budgets and trustee relations that his staff brought to him. Early in 1940, Nelson Rockefeller decided that, like in a corporation, the museum's top management should sit on the board of directors. In what they described as an effort to promote better cooperation among the museum's administrators, but was really a move by the board to get tighter control, the trustees appointed Abbott, Barr, and Monroe Wheeler to the board.

Only six months later, however, Nelson Rockefeller bowed out of active management of the museum when he went to Washington as Coordinator of Inter-American Affairs. A few weeks later, Abby Rockefeller and Stephen Clark, the new chairman of the board, began pressuring Barr to write a book on modern art. To free him from museum responsibilities, the trustees made Monroe Wheeler director of exhibitions as well as of publications.

These nagging skirmishes dragged on for several years until the wartime winter of 1943, when the climate for Barr at the museum turned frigid. Nelson Rockefeller and Jock Whitney were in Washington. Philip Johnson and Eddie Warburg were in the army. Founding trustees Paul Sachs, Frank Crowninshield, and Duncan

Phillips were now voteless honorary trustees. The board fell into the grip of conservative, elderly trustees led by president Stephen Clark, the severe, humorless, black-clad heir to the Singer sewing machine and Clark thread fortunes. During the twenties, he had accumulated some of the choicest modern works of the previous decades, but he was frankly dubious about the more recent art which intrigued Barr. In 1933, he had questioned the need for acquiring the Bliss collection, particularly since getting it required heroic fund-raising. He had also resisted the museum's involvement with films, photography, and industrial design and served still as a trustee of the Metropolitan Museum of Art, where the MOMA's lively publicity and innovative exhibitions were viewed as unseemly pandering to the mob.

Some of Clark's notions about proper displays of art must have struck Barr as distinctly tacky. In the late 1920s Clark had remodeled a gym on the top floor of his gray Gothic mansion on Seventieth Street between Madison and Park avenues as a Matisse room, with blue curtains, red-checked tablecloths, polka-dot pillows, and crockery imitating the paintings on the walls. When Clark proudly displayed this room to the artist in 1930, Matisse had been appalled. After Clark became MOMA president, Barr's relations with him remained cool; he always addressed him as Mr. Clark. Barr also treated him tactlessly and patronizingly. Asked to review the text for a speech Clark was about to give, Barr abruptly asked him to change the opening and closing paragraphs in tones appropriate for a student paper: "I think what you have already written is good," he wrote, "and it will be better still when you have given it a little more time."

A Christmastime exhibition in 1942 of an elaborate shoe-shine stand by a Sicilian immigrant had enraged Clark and his conservative coterie. Struggling young sculptor Louise Nevelson had noticed a man carrying an ornate shoe-shine box on the street. When she learned that its owner, Joe Milone, had a whole stand at home, all elaborately decorated, Nevelson notified Barr. The work was "as festive as a Christmas tree, a baroque shrine or a super–juke box," Barr told the *New York Times* as the stand was unveiled in the museum lobby on December 21. Years later, Barr was still impressed with the work. It was "really beautiful and touching," he wrote in 1953, "done with love and enthusiasm by a Sicilian boot-black—perhaps wishing to create out of New York jetsam the equivalent of a Sicilian painted cart."

To Clark, by contrast, museum art consisted of a costly object in a gilt frame or on a polished pedestal, not a riotously painted shoe-shine stand. When he learned of an exhibition of the naive works of retired Brooklyn slipper manufacturer Morris Hirschfield, planned for the summer of 1943, Clark was livid. Collector (and later, dealer) Sidney Janis had been pushing the show for many months and Barr, hoping to encourage Janis's enthusiasm for the museum, had reluctantly agreed to it for the summer, when atten-dance was light. The public reacted with sneers and laughter. All the models had only left feet, someone pointed out, because Hirschfield's slipper samples were always made for the left foot only. Even more irritating was Janis's pedantic analysis of the pictures. He mounted photographs and texts beside the paintings and spun an elaborate web of threads to connect the points in the text with the relevant parts of the picture. *New York Times* critic Howard Devree said it looked "as if Hegel were pausing to demon-strate a lollipop."

Clark had had enough. Despite his annual gift of $50,000, the museum had run a deficit for the previous two years. And now it was a laughingstock as well. When the trustees straggled back from their summer homes, he mustered a majority of the executive committee and on October 15, 1943, he summarily demanded Barr's resignation.

8

IN THE WILDERNESS

B ewilderment and outrage swept through the museum's staff at the news of Barr's dismissal. No one seemed to know what had happened; who, if anyone, was in charge; and, even worse, what would happen next. The confusion gave rise to an irresistible myth. Barr himself never hinted that Goodyear and even Abby Rockefeller had not been totally satisfied with his administration of the museum and had been searching for almost ten years for some way of bringing in a competent administrator while retaining Barr as the museum's aesthetic soul. Nor did he tell anyone that he had considered resigning five years earlier. And so, varnished by countless retellings, the legend for decades obscured the truth.

The myth begins with a dour and difficult villain clothed in funereal black, Stephen C. Clark, who senselessly and ruthlessly ambushes our frail and innocent hero, Alfred Barr, in the fullness of life. Clark hated Barr, it was said, because "he was infernally jealous of Alfred's knowledge of modern art." Grievously wounded, the hero retreats to his bedroom for thirty days, his wife faithfully bringing food he hardly touches. He wanders at last in Central

Park, indulging his passion for bird-watching, where his grief begins to heal. Stoically, he returns to the institution which has just rejected him and now refuses to leave. In a cramped corner of the library, he monkishly pursues his research and writing, gliding in and out like a ghost, while former colleagues beseech him for advice.

This is the fable that Dorothy Miller's memory knitted over the many years since the events took place. Philip Johnson painted a similar scenario almost forty years later. "He may have won many battles, but it seemed to us he had lost the war," Johnson emotionally recalled in his memorial tribute to Barr in 1981. A lesser man would have been broken, he said, "but we underestimated our bulldog. . . . Finally he was allowed to work in a tiny cubbyhole. . . . He refused to leave the building. He had a fierce and fearless loyalty. . . . It never crossed his mind, against the advice of many of his friends, to desert the museum."

Marga Barr's published recollections highlighted the precise details of Barr's firing, as they illuminated his extreme reticence. October 16 was a gray Saturday and Marga suggested they take in an afternoon movie. Only on the way home did Barr tell his wife about a letter from Clark received in that morning's mail. In three single-spaced pages, Clark complained that Barr had still not produced the book on modern art that Abby Rockefeller and Clark had asked him to write. "The amount of time you are able to devote to unimportant matters and to philosophical discussions in the course of a presumably busy day has been a constant source of wonderment to me," Clark wrote. The "relatively unimportant work" Barr was doing did not justify a $12,000 salary, he added. Henceforth, he would be advisory director, at $6,000 per year. Once he had revealed the letter to Marga, their apartment "took on a sense of nightmare," she wrote. "A[lfred] won't go out. He won't dress. He won't eat. He sits at his desk formulating answers to Stephen Clark." For months, Barr languished in pajamas and robe on the living room couch, Marga told an interviewer in 1974. He did not respond even when she kneeled beside him proffering his favorite, an old-fashioned cocktail, in hopes that he would then eat.

Barr's own correspondence and MOMA records tell a less melodramatic, far more interesting story, with lights and shadows softening the sharp edges of the myth. If Barr retired to his bedroom or to his couch at all after ostensibly being fired from the museum, he emerged less than two weeks later and calmly told the MOMA coordinating committee on October 27, 1943, that his work of recent years had been hampered by "heavy pressure in an atmosphere of emergency." It was impossible for one man to do all that he had attempted, Barr said. "Now, in order to find time and peace of mind for writing, it has seemed best that I take the position of Advisory Director." He sounded rather pleased that he would no longer have to deal with administration and petty curatorial matters and optimistic about having more time to write and to spread the Modernist gospel outside the museum.

Nor had the firing been a bolt from the blue. Barr was present in February of 1943, when the MOMA trustees had discussed at great length the possibility of relieving him as director and creating a research chair for him instead. However, the incumbent's duties, as they emerged, sounded to him suspiciously like those of the director, without the title: study and writing; consulting with and advising staff; editorial advice on museum publications; and exhibition and display of painting and sculpture. After Barr pointed out that these were already his central assignments as director, the trustees kept him on but urged him to concentrate on study and writing. This was a hopeless assignment so long as his title implied full responsibility for the museum and all its works.

In April of 1943, James Thrall Soby was appointed assistant director of the museum, Clark wrote to Barr, specifically "so that you would have plenty of time to devote to your literary labors." A few days later, Barr sent Clark a tantalizing speculation on the work he intended to write: a comprehensive, yet popular, history of modern art. "Should it be primarily a record, an explanation, a justification, or an appreciation?" he wondered. How much historical background should be included? If American art were covered within the Western tradition, Barr feared it would seem "secondary and retarded." Barr also wondered whether he should start with Impressionism or in the twentieth century, whether the book should be a series of studies of particular problems and movements, or a conventional survey. "Should the emphasis be upon ideas and pictures or upon personalities?"

As he so often did, Barr clarified his thinking on paper. He agonized over his inability during the previous dozen years to keep up with serious studies of modern culture. "Whatever knowledge I have accumulated has been the result of hurried visits to artists' studios and dealers to borrow or buy pictures, and forced marches while preparing catalogs." He felt out of touch with the world of scholarship after more than a decade of reading "only for specific purposes" and had only "the most casual knowledge of the work of Whitehead, Maritain, Wyndham Lewis, Sorokin, Spengler and others who have written on the general critical state of modern culture." Therefore, he feared that his book would be too superficial. Barr may have been intimidated by a two-week visit to Cambridge, where he discussed his project with Paul Sachs and other Harvard professors.

Yet, Barr also relished the prospect of writing an important book and set out some details of what he planned: "a succinct history for the general reader, but, I hope, with enough clarity, detail, and balance so that it can be used by the student and teacher." It would begin with Impressionism, although the late nineteenth century would be merely "a springboard" for the twentieth. The book would not be a work of propaganda because "the time for that is passed. Where defense is called for, I shall try explanation. . . . I shall not permit myself the luxury of dogma." Research would be difficult, Barr explained, because of "a curious anomaly that exact facts about the work of many modern artists are harder to come by than if they had lived in the fifteenth century." More than facts, however, Barr planned an ambitious—perhaps impossibly ambitious— "*visual* demonstration, a revelation of modern life . . . the life of the mind and the heart—of poetry, wit, science and religion, the passion for change or for stability, for freedom or perfection."

Such a grandiose plan tremendously impressed Clark and Abby Rockefeller, who received a carbon copy of it. No one, not even a multifaceted genius like Alfred Barr could have written a book to fit his blueprint. Naively, however, the trustees believed that a brilliant man told to study and write would be able to do it, persevering steadily, undistracted by intriguing byways or time out for cogitation. "He was always extraordinarily absorbed," Marga told an interviewer. "You never knew what would be coming up next or what he would want to do next." The trustees were unaware that the pure and limpid prose did not flow as freely as it read; indeed, writing, for Barr, was a painstaking exercise, an ordeal. Then he would attack his penciled drafts with nervous, black, emphatic revisions. What with constant improvements and polishing, Marga said, "the pieces of foolscap that were used were unimaginable because it was rewritten and rewritten and then typed with spaces and corrected. It was an extremely slow and laborious process." Thus, he often suffered infuriating pangs of procrastination. Important letters, even telegrams, rarely emerged from his office without a few final swipes of the pencil.

As well as clarifying his intellectual or aesthetic views on paper, Barr often dealt with conflicts and rage by slashing assaults upon a page of text. In a crossed-out segment of a much-edited letter to Abbott written soon after his dismissal, Barr chewed over recent events. Although the trustees had assigned him the primary duty of research and writing the previous February, he had found it impossible to ignore "the supervisory work I felt obliged to do so long as I was generally responsible for the intellectual and artistic work of the museum." He thought he might have been able to delegate other duties gradually but for the defects of "a curatorial staff continually broken up by the war."

As some of his critics had noticed, there was a Machiavellian side to Alfred Barr. He could be tactless and stubborn, but he could also be maddeningly evasive. When his point of view was challenged, he seemed to lack the vocabulary of compromise or conciliation. A colleague who for years dealt with Barr found one trait particularly enraging. Presented with a particular proposal, Barr would agreeably nod and sympathetically smile, while the supplicant exulted over how easy it had been to win over Alfred Barr. Just as the visitor was leaving, Barr would inexplicably dig in exactly where he had been before, unconvinced, unyielding, inscrutable. After such a session, taciturn Stephen Clark would rush fuming out of Barr's office and down the corridor, screaming, "What does he want? What does he want?"

In 1938, when the trustees criticized his administrative style, Barr had written out his resignation and then held it back. A shrewd bargainer, he was not above threatening to resign, especially when there was little likelihood that his resignation would be accepted. With a new building under construction and an ambitious tenth-anniversary exhibition being planned, the trustees desperately needed Barr's curatorial skills and he was counting on that need. Submitting his resignation then would have forced the trustees to decline. Still, Barr did not tempt them. In 1943, after Clark had fired him, however, Barr used his martyrdom to maximum effect. Was not Jesus Christ wronged, persecuted, scorned, and mocked? Crowned with thorns, Barr would emerge from his modest corner of the library more powerful than if he had stayed in the director's office.

In the cool of a decade's distance, Barr would sketch his portrait of an ideal museum director, stressing some of the qualities he felt lacking in himself: "administrative, promotional, financial and diplomatic ability and . . . understanding of and sympathy for professional integrity—all this in addition to some professional achievement in his own field." He compared this paragon to a college president, although a successful minister comes immediately to mind. "I had some abilities as a writer, curator, showman . . . and perhaps a modicum of professional integrity," he wrote, "but . . . I was inadequate as a fund-raiser, general administrator and diplomat." Still touchy in 1953, he wrote to Dwight Macdonald, who was working on a *New Yorker* profile of him, that "the really able and successful museum director . . . can wisely gain his point or take his stand without sacrificing his personal or professional integrity, but . . . without unnecessary conflict. Obviously I was unable to do this." Barr suggested that "inconvenient" museum people might become more effective if they studied the writings of Renaissance diplomat Castiglione, a contemporary and disciple of Machiavelli who described the essential talents of a courtier.

In 1944, however, a controversial article in *Harper's* suggested that Barr himself was not only a Machiavelli but a Talleyrand and Svengali as well. "Whisper-voiced, he rarely smiles and when he does the effect—in the apt phrase of one of his friends—suggests soil erosion. His appearance gives the impression of no great strength of body or of will," wrote Emily Genauer. Yet he had ruthlessly imposed his quirky taste upon intimidated trustees, creating a collection of "Sure Things and Shockers." In its first fifteen years, Genauer charged, the museum had become "the most highly publicized museum in the world." Yet, "its course has been overprecious and erratic . . . again and again, it has sponsored the fashionably odd rather than the fine, the decadent rather than the original, the spectacular rather than the sincere." She also pointed to gaps in the collection: no Ossip Zadkine, but thirteen Arp collages; no Oskar Blümner and only one George Grosz, but eighteen Max Ernsts. As the art critic for the *New York World Telegram*, Genauer had covered the museum since its opening, and even forty years later she recalled her thrill at getting the *Harper's* assignment: "It was exciting how many trustees resented the museum's policies."

The article raised a great flurry of memos within the museum and some of the trustees may have regretted firing the MOMA's most eloquent and knowledgeable spokesman. Barr was so pained by Genauer's charges that almost ten years later he was still framing defensive replies. Until the article appeared, he wrote to a colleague, he never had a reputation for "politicking and silent maneuvering." He was still astonished to be compared with "both a Svengali and a Machiavelli." Genauer disapproved of the museum because "her tastes were different from ours," Barr wrote. "Consequently she assumed that I must have put over what to her were deplorable policies and actions thanks to my diplomatic ability. Actually, I believe I had the reputation and still have for tactless, stubborn insistence rather than for expert maneuvering."

Though Barr lacked the talent for hiding his contempt for people he didn't like, he tried mightily to get along with Stephen Clark. He located pictures that the willful collector might be interested in, including an 1850 view of New Haven, where Clark had attended Yale University. When Clark mailed Barr two frosty paragraphs asking him to serve on the committee on the museum collections in 1944, Barr graciously agreed. Later, he told Clark that "your interest in the collection is greater than that of any trustee. . . . I value your judgement in painting more than that of anyone else on the board." When the committee was considering purchase of a Vuillard, he invited Clark to stop by in his office to study the picture more closely. If Barr ultimately failed in achieving tact and diplomacy, it was clearly not for want of trying. Clark was worth cultivating, not only for his influence among conservative trustees and for the $50,000 he contributed annually to the museum but finally, perhaps, for the superb Matisses he hoarded in the tastelessly converted gym at his mansion.

Whether Barr's banishment to the library was a political ploy gone awry or a deliberate retreat from unwanted responsibilities, the move opened the way for the next phase of Alfred Barr's ambitions for the museum. By 1943, all the departments he had originally envisioned were established in a building designed to suit. The canvas had been sketched; the underpainting was done, and much of the rest was niggling detail: smoothing disputes among contentious staff, romancing trustees, fiddling with exhibitions, raising funds. The one great mission as yet undone was to develop a collection which would coherently—and exquisitely— illustrate the gospel of modern art according to Barr. Barr's greatest challenge now would be to convince the trustees of his views on the most important modern artists and which of their works should be in the MOMA collection. That would take research and writing, the very tasks to which he had just been exiled. Thus, the picture that would so often be embroidered, of an upright, simple scholar toiling in the solitary cell he was granted after refusing to leave the museum, simply does not stand up to the facts. "Of course Alfred would not leave," Marga said many years later. "It was his museum. The museum was his mistress." More pertinent, perhaps, is the teaching of Peter: "Be clothed with humility: for God resisteth the proud, and giveth grace to the humble."

The MOMA staff wore a pathway to the library cubicle where Barr worked, Dorothy Miller recalled, to ask about museum business. Humbly, Barr explained that he had no "power or responsibility" although, of course, he was still a member of the board of trustees. When Nelson Rockefeller's brother Laurance inquired whether he could buy his wife a small Maillol or Despiau from the museum's collection for Christmas, Barr rather gleefully told James Thrall Soby, "This is a question that under present circumstances you and Dorothy [Miller] will have to decide."

Soby, one of the closest friends Barr ever would have, was an art journalist and collector who had been brought in to relieve Barr

Barr chose Picasso's *Girl Before a Mirror* as Olga Guggenheim's first gift to his museum. It cost all of $10,000 in 1939.

Another Guggenheim, the flamboyant Peggy, arrived in New York from Europe in 1941, complete with a motley entourage and crates of modern masterpieces.

Barr's fascination with well-designed, everyday objects led to the museum's Department of Design. Curator Greta Daniel displayed an array of her treasures in 1952.

René d'Harnoncourt specialized in primitive art when Nelson Rockefeller brought him to the MOMA in 1944. After he became MOMA director in 1949, d'Harnoncourt considered his principal task to be the care and feeding of Alfred Barr.

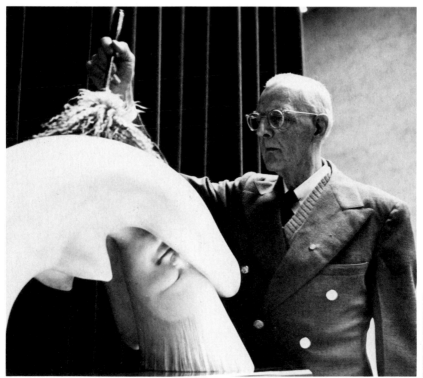

Dusting Jean Arp's *Human Connection* is guard Thomas Feast, onetime butler for the Du Pont family.

Edgar Kaufmann, Jr., accompanied Barr as translator on a wartime collecting trip to Mexico and Cuba. Later he was director of the MOMA's Department of Industrial Design.

The lively displays arranged by Barr attracted all kinds of visitors to his museum. These two women stroll past Wilhelm Lehmbruck's *Standing Youth*, a 1936 gift from Abby Rockefeller.

Barr's lifelong friend Philip Johnson became an architect after founding the museum's Department of Architecture in 1934.

The Abby Aldrich Rockefeller Sculpture Garden, designed by Philip Johnson, remains an oasis of calm in strident mid-Manhattan.

Dorothy Miller and Barr surrounded by
masterpieces in the museum collection.

Top row from left: Picasso's *Ma Jolie*, Braque's *The Table*, Gorky's *Agony*, de Chirico's *Nostalgia of the Infinite*. Second row from left: Matisse's *Bather*, Marin's *Camden Mountain Across the Bay*, Hopper's *House by the Railroad* (the museum's first acquisition), van Gogh's *Starry Night*. Center (sculptures): on left, Arp's *Human Condition*; on right, Lachaise's *Egyptian Head*.

Barr's acquisitions, like this Jackson Pollock, often baffled or even angered museum visitors, but they kept coming back for more.

Alfred Barr, Jr. at a MOMA board meeting. Clockwise around table, from extreme left: René d'Harnoncourt, director; George Stillman (partially obscured), secretary; Philip Goodwin; Mrs. G. Maccoloch Miller, president of the Whitney Museum; A. Conger Goodyear; Alfred H. Barr, Jr.; William S. Paley; Mrs. John D. Rockefeller III; Monroe Wheeler (partially obscured); Wallace K. Harrison; Edward M. M. Warburg; James W. Halsted; Steven C. Clark; Charles Keppel; Mrs. David M. Levy; John Hay Whitney, chairman of the board of trustees.

during the January 1943 reorganization. Genial, loyal, amusing, and long-winded, he was Barr's eyes and ears—and vote—on the "coordinating committee" of trustees which, along with administrator John Abbott, was conducting the museum's day-to-day business. Born to wealth, Soby had been involved with the junior advisory committee and in 1942 was elected to the board of trustees. Though he would write definitive monographs on the Italian Futurists and on Giorgio de Chirico and also serve several years as art critic of the *New Republic*, he worshiped Barr and would be a crucial go-between when the time came to bring him out of the wilderness.

In the immediate aftermath of the firing, the trustees were inordinately successful in obscuring what had taken place. It was not an era when journalists covering cultural institutions risked their reputations as gentlemen by delving beneath bland public announcements. Whatever feuds were simmering, they never bubbled into public print. When the *Times*'s Edward Alden Jewell spent two days at 11 West Fifty-third Street near the end of January 1944 to ascertain who was in charge, he came away with a long list of names, many prominent, but was told that "no one man . . . could fill a post demanding specialized knowledge in so many directions."

Stephen Clark himself soon realized that Barr was indispensable. A month after Clark had fired Barr as director, he appointed him to the acquisitions, exhibitions, and architecture committees. When Barr sent him a copy of a speech and an article in the *College Art Journal* a few months later, Clark replied that he "could readily understand why [the speech] was considered the best . . . delivered at that meeting." And the article, he wrote "bears out my contention that you should give more and more of your time to a field in which you particularly excel." Two proud, opinionated men sequestered by stubbornness and shyness from fluent intercourse with others, Clark and Barr tried as best they could to reach clumsily out to each other. In 1945, Clark sent Barr the closest he could get to an apology. "I want to tell you how greatly I appreciate the splendid work you are doing at the present time and hope you realize how much more important and effective you are in your present position than you were as director of the museum, much of whose time was taken up with a lot of trivialities. You occupy a unique and very distinguished place in the world of art and if you go on as you are now going you will leave behind you a reputation as the foremost art critic of our time. That amounts to a great deal more than anything you could do in the capacity of director." As a scholar who interviewed Barr at length about the museum's collecting policy noted, Clark "would no more have thought of asking him to sever all ties with the Museum than Barr would have thought of taking a job anywhere else."

However, the salary cut to $6,000 was a serious blow. His 1929 beginning salary of $10,000 had been cut to $9,000 for several years during the mid-1930s. In 1939, he received a raise to $12,000. Out of his salary, he had meticulously paid all of Marga's expenses abroad, even though her command of languages and willingness to manage pedestrian details made her an essential participant in his European journeys. In the fall of 1939, the Barrs had moved to a larger apartment at 49 East Ninety-sixth Street, and by 1944, the Barrs also had the education of their seven-year-old daughter to consider.

A year earlier, Marga had reluctantly taken a job teaching art history at Spence's, an exclusive East Side finishing school for girls. She felt "humiliated . . . to go and teach in a school because I had taught at Vassar." She said that she consented only after a friend warned her that she would never work professionally again unless she took the job. However, the extra income certainly was a factor in her decision, and also the school's convenient location, only five blocks from the Barrs' new apartment. Spence's must have been delighted to have such a qualified teacher on the faculty; she stayed on for thirty-seven years, inspiring a number of future scholars, including Joan R. Mertens, curator of Greek and Roman art at the Metropolitan. However, shy Daisy Scolari Barr, who often hid her diffidence behind harsh remarks, remained insecure. She did not regard it as a mark of her value to the school that she was permitted to hire a substitute in the late spring each year, when she had to accompany Barr to Europe. Rather, she saw the arrangement only as a desperate measure to keep her job, explaining, that was why "I was able to cling to it."

In February of 1944, a few months after Marga began teaching at Spence's and probably at her urging, Barr wrote Clark a long letter reviewing his financial needs in the light of what he had accomplished for the museum: "It is not too much to say that the purchases and exchanges which were made on my recommendation have increased in value more rapidly than those made by any other American museum during the same period." Since top curators at the Metropolitan were then getting $12,000 per year, Barr suggested that $15,000 "would be a fair salary."

Clark replied the very next day in one curt paragraph, saying that he was astonished at Barr's request. Some ten days later, Barr retracted his salary demands. "I now understand that the financial problems which you have to face are more difficult than ever," he conciliated. "Believe me, there is nothing I want more than to work in harmony with you for the good of the museum." This episode illustrates Barr's curious ambivalence about money. When it came to buying pictures for the museum, he was known as "a tight-fisted bargainer . . . cagy . . . the shrewdest museum director I ever dealt with," said dealer Sidney Janis. But when it came to financial dickering for a proper salary, Barr was anxiously reticent. Like the pastor of a wealthy church, Barr insisted on expounding correct dogma while remaining somewhat awed by his parishioners' financial resources. The rich are not to be underestimated, he had written to an assistant a few months earlier. "They are often interesting and intelligent and more enlightened than the humble." In his personal life, too, Barr played the role of the faithful pastor. He was abstemious, if not stingy, wearing well-worn clothes and searching out bargain restaurants for lunch. Architectural historian G. E. Kidder-Smith, who first met Barr in 1940, described him as "the uptight Presbyterian Minister of Art."

In that role, Barr arranged an impressive funeral for Piet Mondrian, on February 3, 1944. The Dutch consul general in New York had never heard of the artist and had to be "prodded" to attend. Barr gave a moving eulogy. "He seemed able to live without the consolations of love or religion," Barr said of the artist whose stark, rectilinear paintings he had admired for two decades or more. "Although Mondrian's work may lack variety, fantasy, sensuality, richness of human association," he added, "it does possess an extraordinary power—a power so subtle and intense that during the past twenty-five years it has influenced the arts of practical design throughout the world." He then raved about Mondrian's last painting "based on his enthusiasm for our popular music—as if some great musician had taken material from folk dances for his final masterpiece of counterpoint."

The picture was *Broadway Boogie-Woogie*, a mosaic of primary colors which Barr had persuaded a donor to buy for the museum's collection some nine months earlier, for $800. Largely because of Barr's enthusiasm, prices for Mondrians escalated steeply; five years after the artist's modest funeral, Barr was surprised to see one of his drawings offered by Knoedler's for $7,000. Soon after the MOMA's Mondrian retrospective in 1945, Sidney Janis bought up every Mondrian he could find in Europe, doling them out at great profit to collectors shopping in the gallery he opened in 1947. A 1910 figurative Mondrian sold at auction in 1962 for $27,687 and by 1969, an abstract composition went for $44,550.

Clearly, Barr's imprimatur was beginning to have a powerful effect not only on the public's aesthetic judgments, but also on art prices. This power added to the appeal of his new post as director of museum collections. If Barr harbored any real desire to leave the museum, he could have taken his pick among a multitude of tempting offers. The Denver Art Museum wanted him as director. A dozen publishers begged to bring out his history of modern art and, by March 1944, Barr was assuring Paul Sachs that if he wrote such a work, Harvard University Press would have first call on it. Simultaneously, Northwestern University asked him to be chairman of its art department, but Barr replied that he had every reason to believe that his situation at the MOMA "will develop in a satisfactory way."

Barr also won generous support from art professionals and the art public. Marion R. Becker of the Cincinnati Modern Art Society called his resignation "a great blow" and said she could hardly imagine the MOMA "*being* at all without you." Isabel S. Roberts, director of the Brooklyn Museum, wrote that Barr's "contribution to the appreciation and understanding of modern art can certainly never be equalled." When Barr offered his resignation from the executive council of the American Association of Museums, its president, Lawrence Vail Coleman, begged him to reconsider: "We

need you and we need what you now stand for very much." Poet
Marianne Moore, who was an old neighbor from Baltimore,
mourned that for her and her friends, "interest in the museum dies,
in proportion as you leave it to itself."

But Barr had no intention of leaving the museum to itself.
Indeed, as he was being fired as director, he was also launching the
most potent tract for modern art ever written. It was potent
because it was written for a huge new audience, a mass no one
previously had considered as possible converts to modern art. It
was a tract because its format and tone were models of sectarian
persuasion. As a youngster, Barr had of course been steeped in the
story of the early Christian church, of the early converts who came
from wealthy and aristocratic families and of the church's evident
success in appealing to the masses. Just as the early church spread
its influence among humbler Romans, even slaves, so Alfred Barr
now sought to convert the wide public with his message. "And he
said unto them, 'Go ye into all the world, and preach the gospel to
every creature.' "

Barr's vehicle was a small booklet, with new chapters beginning
every page or two, and replete with pictures. Ostensibly designed
for high school students, *What Is Modern Painting?* appealed to the
skeptic but also to a surprising multitude of sophisticated art
connoisseurs. Barr said he "wrote for people who have had little
experience in looking at paintings, particularly those modern
paintings which are sometimes considered puzzling, difficult, incompetent or crazy." His booklet "intended to undermine prejudice, disturb indifference and awaken interest so that some greater
understanding and love of the more adventurous painting of our
day may follow."

In his first two sentences, Barr jumped right into the most
frequent popular critique of modern painting, attacked it as prejudice, promised understanding and love, and suggested that learning more is a pleasurable adventure. No professor of homiletics
could have asked for a more persuasive model of proselytizing
prose. The whole booklet was mercifully brief, forty-eight spacious
pages including bibliography, generously illustrated, informa-
tively captioned, attractively printed on good stock, and bargain-
priced at twenty-five cents. Before the final, final, final revision

went to press, Barr had tested its prose on children, housewives, and even farmers around his summer place at Greensboro, Vermont. He would mark any questionable wording and rewrite it. The final tract even included discreet guides to pronouncing unfamiliar names: Go-ga(n), Sayzann, Ma-tees. "For if the trumpet give an uncertain sound, who shall prepare himself to the battle? So likewise ye, except ye utter . . . words easy to be understood, how shall it be known what is spoken?"

Moving subtly from familiar pictorial paintings to more abstract work, Barr spoke directly to his reader, guiding him or her into seeing new meanings in the paintings and also suggesting the strong emotions that artists often express. Again and again, he addressed the readers directly: "What is your first impression? . . . Which way of painting means more to you? . . . Have you open eyes and a free mind? . . . Can you feel what [this artist] felt?" He began with illustrations of familiar American scenes and gradually led the reader into more complex European works. And finally, he shared his own view that quality in a work of art "cannot be measured or proved or even analyzed with any logical satisfaction . . . in the end what makes a great work of art great is always something of a mystery."

Barr himself called the little booklet "an instrument of propaganda in the original and best sense of the word." Some ten years after its first publication, Barr told MOMA publications director Monroe Wheeler that he would gladly accept reduced royalties if the museum would bring out a new edition at a lower price. Barr noted that he had written *WIMP* (the absurdly misleading acronym by which the booklet had become known internally) to explain painting because this was the museum's principal medium, "the medium subject to the most serious misunderstanding on the part of the public and this misunderstanding involves the most sinister implications. In other words, *WIMP* is a political tract as well as an exposition of an art."

More than any single publication on modern art before or since, *What Is Modern Painting?* broke down the barrier between modern art and the masses. From the unlikeliest sources, such as the editor of the plebeian *New York Daily News*, came praise for its simplicity, lucidity, and common sense. High school and college teachers welcomed its plain-spoken accuracy, while the director of the Philadelphia Museum of Art raved: "Marvelous. I am giving it to trustees, secretaries, doubters, evangelists." Scholars tend to scorn works written for the masses, but *WIMP* seemed to beguile them as well. Perhaps the highest compliment, wrote Horst Janson in the *College Art Journal*, was that in discussing truth, freedom, and perfection, Barr "was able to give force and meaning to . . . vague, overworked concepts." As a teacher at Washington University, Janson was particularly delighted that the MOMA had developed a traveling exhibition and sets of lantern slides to accompany the booklet. He was one of the young German scholars Barr had rescued during the thirties and would become no mean popularizer himself as the author in 1962 of *History of Art*, an all-time best-seller among art history college textbooks.

The smooth and satiny fabric of Barr's prose stretched seamlessly over the elegant pages he designed, with no hint of the perfectionist quibbles, the obsessive polishing, and the eleventh-hour panic beneath. But to a group of museum directors discussing the future of art museums as educational institutions in 1946, he admitted that the MOMA's scholarship was "sometimes a hand-to-mouth last minute effort to meet an exhibition or catalog deadline." Results did emerge from "this frenzy," he said, "even though the research involved may be hasty and superficial." Still, he thought the work worthwhile, although some would call it "a kind of superior journalism produced too often in the atmosphere of a newspaper office." Without referring to his own enforced concentration on scholarship, Barr told the group that the public should be convinced that museum research "is not some recondite game, but an essential and fundamental activity, even a means of confirming our faith in our own usefulness to a democratic republic."

So soon after his firing, research and writing may well have been a test Barr devised to assess his own usefulness. But everything he ever wrote was a supreme test for all those associated with it: the secretaries who stolidly watched as Barr's pencil nervously slashed through the latest clean retyping of the manuscript; his wife, Marga, who often worked with him through the night as the last scribbled-over proofs were locked up; his "publisher," Monroe Wheeler, the MOMA director of publications who wheedled and cajoled late manuscripts out of him for almost forty years (and who, decades later, was still enraged with Barr for his persistent, apparently limitless need to procrastinate).

And yet, out of the pipeline stuffed with memos admonishing haste, setting schedules, quibbling over details of paper and type, seeking just the right illustration, and making cogent excuses, always cogent excuses, for missing deadlines, publications did eventually emerge. In 1946, the museum brought out Barr's landmark study, *Picasso: Fifty Years of His Art*. The very title is a monument to Barr's shameless penchant for delay. It was originally supposed to be a light reworking of his hasty catalog for the museum's 1939 exhibition, "Picasso: Forty Years of His Art." But the revision had languished as Barr was distracted by his duties as museum director and the always useful but time-consuming byways which engaged his quicksilver mind. It was Barr's seeming inability to find time for his writing that so exasperated Stephen Clark and was the ultimate reason for Barr's dismissal as MOMA director. But when the book finally appeared, an idealized catalog for a mythical, ideal exhibition, it was a model of all that Clark expected from such a work—coherent, concise, complete, original, and a beautiful example of modern typographic design. It is dedicated to "Margaret Scolari-Fitzmaurice, advisor and invaluable assistant in the Picasso campaigns of 1931, 1932, 1936, and 1939."

Though cut off from his subject by the war, Barr had moved swiftly after Paris was liberated from the Nazis to obtain information about Picasso's latest works and activities. He described the artist's role in the resistance and the triumphant exhibition of his wartime works which followed soon after the liberation of Paris. The text confronted Picasso's joining the Communist party at that time, while also mentioning that his studio was open once a week "to crowds of bewildered G.I.'s and other allied troops on sightseeing tours." To illuminate the murky beginnings of Picasso's career, Barr unearthed many early drawings and paintings. They showed the influence of Toulouse-Lautrec, Vuillard, and Gauguin on young Picasso as well as the acute observation and brilliant draftsmanship that proved that the artist had not chosen distortion and abstraction, as some critics still muttered, because he could not draw.

During their few face-to-face meetings before the war, Picasso had been typically uncommunicative. Childish and self-centered, he basked in the limelight, while running critics and scholars a merry chase for facts. To fill out the meager information from the artist himself, Barr had fired off innumerable questions to those said to be close to Picasso: his secretary, Jaime Sabartes; critic Georges Hugnet; dealer M. Paul Rosenberg; and a young American art scholar who had visited Picasso while serving in the U.S. Navy, Lt. Cmdr. James S. Plaut. They helped to fill the book's factual gaps, Barr wrote, because "Picasso himself has left many questions unanswered."

Producing the book so shortly after the end of the Second World War was a tour de force—and a revelation. European collections were still largely inaccessible and virtually all the illustrations came from works in the United States, many of them belonging to Picasso himself and left at the Museum of Modern Art for safe-keeping when the war broke out in 1939. But the five-page list of works in American museums revealed that in less than two decades since the MOMA's founding, Picasso's works had been acquired by twenty-seven American institutions. In New York alone, art lovers could view thirty-eight works, including the MOMA's twenty-four (plus *Guernica*, on permanent loan). The Art Institute of Chicago had twenty-three Picassos and the eccentric Dr. Barnes of Merion, Pennsylvania, boasted twenty-nine, but the work of the twentieth century's leading painter also could be seen in Baltimore, Buffalo, Cincinnati, Cleveland, Columbus, Detroit, Hartford, Honolulu, Los Angeles, Oberlin (Ohio), Rochester, St. Louis, San Francisco, Toledo, Washington, D.C., and Worcester, Massachusetts. The list foreshadowed the preeminence of the United States in collecting, exhibiting, studying, and, finally, in creating modern art as it emerged during the postwar years.

The MOMA's Picassos reflected Barr's opinion of Picasso's massive output. Most of the twenty-four paintings in the museum's collection dated from the artist's earliest periods; only six were painted in the twenties, only two in the thirties (including the magnificent *Girl Before a Mirror*), and one was dated 1941. A few months after the Picasso book was published, Barr excitedly reported to Clark that Mrs. Guggenheim had inquired about purchasing *Guernica* with her fund. Then the museum's committee on the museum collections studied the matter, but nothing came of it; some four decades later, the museum had to reluctantly send the masterpiece to Spain, pursuant to the artist's will.

As Barr described Picasso's recent activities, he engaged perhaps his own longings as a creative individual in a nearby field: "Neither the Nazis nor the Communists officially approve Picasso's painting. Quite the contrary. Yet under the Nazis and after his profession of Communism he kept on painting the way he had before, without regard to political theories about art. Responsible only to himself, he works out of his own inner compulsion. Take it or leave it, he says in effect, I can and will paint in no other way. In a world in which social pressures—democratic, collectivist, bourgeois—tend to restrict the freedom of the exceptional individual, Picasso's art assumes a significance far beyond its artistic importance."

While the author of these words may also have briefly yearned to kick up his heels and thumb his nose at social pressures, especially when his ego had been bruised, his Calvinist background did not permit him to succumb directly to such fantasies. Rather, he preferred to pour such bohemian daydreams into writing about the artists who lived them. Perhaps Barr really hated losing the director's job; yet, in addition to writing, he quickly plunged into a multitude of other activities with a gusto that indicated relief more than grief.

With his old mentors at Harvard, he explored the possibility of completing the Ph.D. he had been working on in 1929 when the museum called. In 1940, Barr had proposed to Paul Sachs submitting his catalog for "Cubism and Abstract Art" as his dissertation, the only requirement he still had to fulfill for the degree. Too busy even to mail a book and spend an afternoon defending it before a committee of professors, Barr had done nothing further until 1946. This time he offered the Picasso book, grateful that the Harvard rules were so flexible that he could "submit a work for the doctor's degree twenty years after I took my general examination." In his abstract, Barr wrote that the book "neither argues an interpretation nor offers any final conclusions. But it does attempt a balanced, condensed, accurate survey of Picasso's art." In its thoughtful mélange of plates and commentary, "the text is servant to the pictures." A few weeks after submitting the book, Barr was officially awarded his doctorate and invited to participate in the Harvard commencement on May 1, 1947.

Though he was supposed to be relieved of museum duties to concentrate on writing, the trustees could not resist asking him for advice, and Barr could not resist giving it. Less than three months after he was fired, Barr was editing a wide-ranging report to the trustees on the museum's collections. The new building was not yet five years old, but he was already bemoaning the lack of space. Only seventy-five paintings, thirty-five sculptures, and a dozen drawings could be shown in the third-floor galleries reserved for the permanent collection, while "three or four times as much space is needed." If only the museum could provide twenty galleries instead of the present seven, there would be space for "the most comprehensive and interesting collection of modern paintings in the world . . . with further acquisitions and extended loans from trustees, the collection could also be the finest in quality." Such a collection would show the public authoritatively "what the museum stands for in each of its departments . . . a permanent visible demonstration of . . . its scope, its canons of judgement, taste, and value, its statements of principle, its declarations of faith."

The words sounded bold and precise, but underneath them raged a conflict that split the trustees and warred within Barr himself. What is modern? Is it innovative, contemporary work, always stretching backward from the present into only the very recent past? Or is modern a style, like Gothic or Baroque? If so, would the modern style which began in the late nineteenth-century reaction against Romanticism inevitably give way, like those older styles, to a new kind of art with a new name? It was a conflict which had plagued the trustees from the beginning and which continues to be discussed at the museum today, even though the issue has been resolved in favor of historical style for some time. In 1944, however, there was still a chance that the museum would somehow dwell forever in the ever-advancing present. The collection's scope, Barr suggested, should be "the visual arts of all countries during the past fifty or sixty years with the greater emphasis on the recent part of this period." A mysterious, undefined "metabolic process," he expected, would eliminate older works as new ones were added.

Barr himself had been uncertain as to how modern should be defined. In 1936 he wrote that it was "a relatively elastic term" for painting, sculpture, moving pictures, architecture, and other visual arts, "original and progressive in character, produced especially within the last three decades, but including also 'pioneer ancestors' of the nineteenth century." Among these, he reached back as far as Delacroix and Daumier, the Barbizon School of the 1840s, and Realists like Courbet. He even suggested that all art should be included which had "to contend with indifference, ignorance and often bitter ridicule from the academic artist, the critic, and, for a time, the general public." In 1943, he wrote that the museum had no business collecting or showing "the art of the past . . . art previous to fifty or sixty years ago," except for certain works desirable for "specific educational purposes."

When the museum was founded, the idea of showing the art of the previous fifty or sixty years seemed to encompass the contemporary and its immediate ancestors in a neat package. But fifteen years later, concentrating on the same time span would mean that some of the greatest and most valuable masterpieces in the collection would soon have to be discarded. So alarmed by this prospect were some trustees that they were still discussing it six months after the matter had first been broached. Barr himself wavered perpetually between his thirst for novelty and his yearning to accumulate wonderful and important pictures from the past. He also worried that those trustees who owned valuable older works would not dream of giving them to the MOMA unless the museum could guarantee that they would remain in the collection. Barr tried to reassure one such collector, MOMA trustee Samuel Lewisohn, that "for the time being, we should include a number of first-rate works by such artists as van Gogh, Renoir, Cézanne, Toulouse-Lautrec, Gauguin, Degas and others, particularly in those aspects which look forward to or actually develop in the twentieth century." Even the museum's *Uncle Dominic*, painted by Cézanne in the 1860s, should be retained, Barr argued, as "a remarkable example of Expressionism forty years before its time."

In yet another revision of his views on the collections, a memo written in 1944, Barr completely abandoned any "metabolic process" or any notion of the MOMA collection as a stream, flowing ever forward into the present while shedding the past. He suggested three surprisingly concrete starting points for the MOMA's collection: living painters of the generation born in the 1860s, such as Bonnard, Signac, and Matisse; the earlier Impressionist generation of Renoir, Degas, and Cézanne; or even the late eighteenth-century pioneers of the romantic and classical movements, such as Goya and David. "So long as the Metropolitan continues to spend $90,000 on another Sargent," Barr wrote, "while remaining satisfied with one inferior Daumier and one minor Delacroix, not to mention inadequate examples of David, Cézanne, Renoir, Degas, and the entire omission of Chasseriau, Redon, Pissarro, Sisley, Seurat, the modern museum would have good reason to form a really fine nineteenth century collection."

Underlying all the agonizing about the collection was an extremely controversial auction sale the trustees had contrived for the spring of 1944. Defying Barr's strenuous opposition, they decided to raise money by selling forty-five works from the MOMA collection, along with sixty-three items owned by various trustees. An anonymous statement from the museum assured the public that the works by such artists as Bellows, Cézanne, Delacroix, Derain, Dufy, Eilshemius, Hartley, Lachaise, Maillol, Matisse, Picasso, and Redon duplicated works it was retaining and that no works by living artists from North or South America were included. Also, the names of the original donors would be attached to new works bought with the proceeds. While official announcements downplayed the event, the catalog produced by the recently organized Parke-Bernet Gallery for the auction scheduled for May 11, 1944, obviously traded on the museum's fame. Its name was bold and large, while much smaller type announced "additions from members of the museum's board of trustees and advisory committee."

Edward Alden Jewell tantalized readers of the *Times* on the morning of the sale, as he wrote, with more discretion than reportorial zeal, that the auction was "much discussed," that it included "many items of real consequence," and that "the result will be watched with peculiar interest." The next day he described a capacity crowd but tactfully omitted what *Art News* called a "mass stampede of sightseers, collectors, dealers and museum personnel."

By later auction standards, the proceeds seemed pitifully modest: $20,000 (the highest price) for Corot's *La Grande Metairie*; $16,000 for Cézanne's portrait of his wife; $4,600 for Matisse's *Nue de Dos*, and $5,600 for Picasso's *La Statuaire*. A number of items sold for less than their insurance values: Redon's *Seated Nude*, for example, was insured for $1,700, but brought only $250; Derain's *Guitar Player*, insured for $3,500, sold for $2,600; Pop Hart's *The Mella Brook*, for which Abby Rockefeller had paid $450, sold for $90. Altogether, the museum netted $55,189, while the other sellers split $36,489.

As Barr had feared, the benefits to the museum were paltry, while the damage reverberated for many years. Twenty-five years later, James Thrall Soby still cringed at the "slaughter . . . I don't think we've yet lived down the blunder." In the view of many, the auction diminished the prestige of the trustees as they were seen riding the coattails of the museum's good name for their own benefit. Even worse, it made donors leery that treasured works they gave would soon be unceremoniously sold or, as the mealy-mouthed verb for it would later have it, de-accessioned. Barr's grandiose vision for the MOMA collection notwithstanding, Samuel Lewisohn, for one, gave his superb collection of nineteenth- and early-twentieth-century masters to the Met some seven years later.

The year 1944 marks the beginning of the MOMA's transition from a hell-raising enfant terrible in the art world to a sedate, authoritative institution, parallelling Alfred Barr's personal progression from brilliant wunderkind to forty-two-year-old wise man. His catalog for the fifteenth-anniversary exhibition that year for the first time extolled the museum's permanent collection. "Strictly speaking," (where it had never before spoken strictly) the MOMA's role was as "a repository of possessions of certain value and presumably permanent interest," said the foreword, taking pride in a collection "magnificently increasing from year to year." Explaining why the exhibition, ironically titled "Art in Progress," still dwelled so lovingly on the early years of Modernism, James Thrall Soby wrote that "art is traditionally long and there is no indication that the great painting and sculpture created between roughly 1880 and 1929 have lost their capacity to inspire and instruct contemporary artists."

Indeed, many acute observers of the cultural scene during and just after the wartime years believed that Modernism—perhaps even Western culture itself—was played out. Wyndham Lewis, who had been an early devotee of modern art, in 1940 knelled the death of abstraction with some glee: "At last the Cube, the Cone, the Cylinder are still forever . . . the Equilateral Triangle has breathed its last. Braque's abstract bric-a-brac is fast becoming junk. . . . Brancusi's Egg has gone to join the Dodo's." In *College Art Journal*, an art historian rejoiced that "modern art has outlived its function. . . . Its creators . . . will become one with the . . . dinosaur." Art critic Clement Greenberg told readers of *The Nation* in 1944 that "both the golden and silver ages of modern art are over seemingly—at least in Paris"; he feared that the philistines were again on the march. Looking back on the previous half century and its culminating horror, the Second World War, T. S. Eliot was even more pessimistic about culture as a whole. "I see no reason why the decay of culture should not proceed much further and why we may not anticipate a period of some duration of which it will be possible to say that it will have *no* culture."

This was the kind of pessimism that usually inflamed the missionary in Barr. Now that the museum had unchained him from petty duties, he was free to ride the circuit, preaching the gospel of Modernism, where in the past he had turned down almost all speaking engagements, ostensibly because he lacked time, but actually because he felt insecure at the podium. "I am not an expert lecturer and tend to stutter a bit," he wrote in answer to one request, and to another, "I dislike lecturing beyond words." In fact, he had always been a persuasive, humorous, and engaging speaker and may have felt deficient only in relation to his childhood image of his father sermonizing his congregation from the pulpit. In 1942, Barr had declined an invitation to give the prestigious Mary Flexner lectures at Bryn Mawr. When the invitation came again three years later, Barr cautiously felt out the trustees, then happily accepted.

The overall theme for the six lectures he gave in February and March of 1946 sounded a bit devotional: "Dogma and Practice in Modern Art." The titles of the individual lectures seemed downright theological, moving from description and commentary to moral imperatives: "Art Should Be Modern," the rise and decline of the machine; "Art Should Be Pure," with a glance at utilitarian consequences; "Art Should Be Marvelous," the visual poetry of enigma and fantasy; "Art Should Be Intense," depicting anxiety, violence, ecstasy; "Art Should Be National," varieties of racial and regional self-esteem; and "Art Should Be Social," the state of the world, propaganda, and prophecy.

Despite his modesty about his lecture talents, Barr knew exactly how to charm the young women at Bryn Mawr. One of them remembered thirty-five years later how he had juxtaposed a slide showing a Mondrian painting with another showing a commercial linoleum pattern to illustrate how life imitates art. Most impressive to her was how he told students gathered around him after one lecture of "his pleasure at seeing a student who stood and stood before some work he had hung up as part of an exhibition there—and looked and looked. And in that instant I learned how to stand and look at a picture. Such a little hint, but his whole being was caught up in the smallest remarks and I was forever magnetized."

In the school newspaper, his appearance was immortalized with a piece of doggerel titled: "T'ain't what 'cha do, it's the way that 'cha do it!"

There was a sly mentor named Barr
Who gained fame through a course at Bryn Mawr.
Those bespectacled tarts
Took a look at the arts
But found HIM more intriguing by far.

This cagy old sage made his start
By shattering heart after heart—
Said one, "Get the preacher
I'm mad for that teacher
Though I don't know beans about art!"

He fed them Picasso
Like sips of curaçao.

He stressed that Daumier
Was here, but *to stay*.

He delivered a sermon
On romantics like Berman

And flashed on Renoirs
like five-cent cigars.

He gave them a shock
With their first Cubist Braque

Then hoped that O'Keeffe
Would bring some relief.

From Courbet to Kane
The moral grew plain:

For Barr's tidy survey
Did most of all purvey
That the best way to interest a female in art
Is to lower the voice and aim straight for the heart!

Enamored as the students were of Alfred Barr, they had slim
resources indeed if they desired to read about Modernism on
campus. A list of the entire holdings on modern art in the Bryn
Mawr library, sent to Barr when he was first invited to lecture,
might explain his sermonizing mood. Less than two pages long, the
list included a survey, *Modern Artists*, dated 1908; a 1917 gem,
The Ideals and Tendencies of Modern Art; a scattering of books on
Impressionists and Post-Impressionists, with only eleven works
about more recent art; a few old MOMA catalogs; and runs of five
current periodicals that occasionally featured modern art, and two
which had ceased publishing in the early 1930s.

No wonder that, despite the MOMA's evident success, and despite
the burgeoning audience for modern art all over the United States,
Barr still worried about his new religion's ultimate triumph, the
more so in view of the rash of public predictions that avant-garde
art was moribund, if not dead. The new museum public was an
unknown, possibly dangerous, mass, Barr told museum colleagues
in 1944, "a chaos of mind and feeling, inattentive, undisciplined,
and irresponsible," and, worst of all, "almost unexplored." When
the war ended and eight or nine million people returned to civilian

life with "fresh and critical eyes," they would pose "an overwhelmingly important challenge to our capacity for popular education."

In fact, a survey among the millions of servicemen who passed through New York during the Second World War indicated that the Museum of Modern Art was the fourth most popular tourist attraction, ranked right after the Statue of Liberty, the Empire State Building, and Rockefeller Center. (The Met was sixth.) Barr was still wary of the masses even when it was clear several years later that veterans were eagerly swamping museums and all other educational institutions, soaking up the learning they had missed during the war—or foregone during the Depression. In 1947 Barr was still worried that American freedom itself could threaten artistic experiment, that "democratic pressures of ignorance and indifference," notably the popular press's irreverent attitude toward experimental art, were sometimes as deadly to the creative spirit as totalitarian censorship. Barr had recently tried to convert the president of the United States, with far from brilliant results. Harry Truman wrote to Barr:

> I appreciate very much your note . . . enclosing me a book on modern painting. . . . It is exceedingly interesting. I still get in almost the same frame of mind as after I have had a nightmare when I look at these paintings.
>
> Some of them are all right—at least you can tell what the painter had in mind. Some of them are really the "ham and egg" style.
>
> I do appreciate highly your interest in trying to convert me to the modern viewpoint in art, but I just can't appreciate it, much to my regret.

Many of the museum's trustees were not much more sophisticated about modern art. Invited to a warehouse in 1945, where the museum's entire collection would be on view, economist Beardsley Ruml begged off, writing: "You know I don't know a damn thing about modern art or any other kind of art and my judgment on the collection isn't worth anything. But sometime if you want to give me a lecture on what the collection means and what you are trying to do with it, I will come up and be glad to exploit you." Those who attended the viewing delivered themselves of comments like these, recorded by a secretary: van Gogh's *Starry Night*—Miss Aldrich "said the sky was like a hooked rug"; Degas's *Dancers*—"Sam Lewisohn thought it bad"; Picasso's *Demoiselles d'Avignon*—"Mrs. Guggenheim said Barr had suggested she squint at it in order to get the pattern without the subject. She said she had been squinting ever since [but] does not like [it]"; Tchelitchew's *Hide and Seek*—"Mrs. Warren would like to put her foot through and collect insurance. Mr. Soby got mad."

During the war years, the American art world had concentrated on muddling through until the nourishing ties with Europe could be reestablished. There was no precedent for believing that the transatlantic cultural relationship would ever shift from what it always had been: the mature European tradition as the wise parent, America and other far-flung outlands as the grateful, imitative children. But the war's last bullet had hardly been fired before flimsy letters to "Modern Museum" or some such approximation and with the vaguest sort of address began appearing in the mailbags at 11 West Fifty-third Street. Barr was supposed to be sequestered with his research and writing, but no one else at the museum knew what to do with these pathetic requests. Some begged for just a few postcards or slides showing modern art. A Berlin artist wanted the museum to help him salvage several sculptures buried in a 1943 bombing raid. Another artist offered to exchange a painting for a set of oil colors and brushes, materials unavailable in postwar Germany. He enclosed a grandly engraved first prize certificate from 1937, a pathetic relic from another age.

The museum filled so many requests from professors and museums for all the catalogs it had published since 1939 that the supply was immediately exhausted. Barr's secretary, Mimi Catlin, carefully answered every request in fluent German. In an ironic turnabout, Barr used funds originally contributed to aid refugee artists and scholars to send library packets abroad. In the summer of 1946, librarian Bernard Karpel shipped sixteen complete sets of MOMA publications to major European art libraries as well as to institutions in Peking, Canton, Nanjing, Manila, and Tel Aviv. There was more than a missionary impulse behind such large-scale shipments of sacred texts. When Paris gallery owner Louis Carré requested catalogs in the summer of 1945, the MOMA staff went to great lengths to send twenty-four, even though almost all were already out of print; Carré might be expected to give the museum special deals on works by important artists he represented, among them Jacques Villon, Léger, and Picasso. When Katherine Dreier wanted materials sent to German scholars, Barr rushed them off in hopes of cementing relations with this cantankerous lady whose collection he coveted for the museum.

Barr enthusiastically corresponded with German art historians who had survived the Hitler years. "I am delighted to know that you are well and still an active warrior for the cause of freedom in modern art," he wrote to Dr. Hans Hildebrandt, whom he had first met in 1933. Along with the letter, he sent seventeen precious MOMA catalogs. When Barr learned that Germany's largest art library, at the University of Munich, had been wiped out by a single bomb—"all, absolutely all," a distraught professor wrote— Barr arranged a complicated deal to help: the MOMA bought a George Grosz drawing from a German dealer who then donated the $176 in proceeds to purchase 123 slides and twenty-two books to be sent to Munich.

When the refugee funds ran out, Barr sought donations from Edgar Kaufmann, Edward M. M. Warburg, and Nelson Rockefeller. Barr himself contributed $300 to the program. This kind of largesse from a man who usually gave five or ten dollars to worthy causes indicates that Barr may have been suffering some guilt for his role in the Museum of Modern Art's purchases from the "Degenerate Art" auction of 1938, although he never suggested returning any of these items to the museums from which they had been stolen by the Nazis. Certainly it was ironic that the MOMA donated a Paul Klee catalog to a Lübeck museum whose entire Klee collection had disappeared. One stolen watercolor, *Tänze zu Ungeheuer zu Meinem Sanften Lied*, Barr's secretary carefully reported, was now in the Guggenheim Museum.

But more than artists, works of art, and scholars had migrated to the United States because of Nazi persecution. There may have been a hint of what really was happening in letters from respected German art historians such as Dr. William Grohmann, who called the Museum of Modern Art's catalogs "the best publications about modern art which we now have." A few months after Paris was

liberated, Barr had asked René Huyghé, chief curator of the
Louvre, to write a series of "letters from Paris" for the *Magazine of
Art,* where Barr was a director. So eager were the French for
contact with America that Huyghé's letters went to New York in
the diplomatic pouch. But when the first one arrived, Barr was
dismayed. "I am afraid that Huyghé has yielded to the overwhelming French habit of generalized rhetoric when writing about art,"
he confided to the magazine's editor, John D. Morse. On Huyghé's
promise that his next letter would contain "more specific news,"
Barr urged that it be printed. In 1938, the French art establishment had lambasted the exhibition of American art Barr had sent
to Paris. Now it was Barr's turn to carp and cavil.

He was annoyed early in 1947 by a letter from Germany which
had appeared in the *Magazine of Art* because of its "highly subjective, over-rhapsodical writing" about art works which one could
appreciate only by seeing them. Otherwise, he snapped, "one reads
it with boredom or irritation." Again, he complained that the
article padded a few sparse facts in a cotton wool of rhetoric. These
were straws in the wind; no serious observer would yet have dared
to suggest that the continuous cultural flow from Europe to America of four centuries would reverse its direction and that during the
postwar years American culture would begin to dominate Europe.

While Europe was cut off during the war, Barr had thrown
himself into promoting the study of American art, old and new, in
American universities. He may have questioned the aesthetic quality of American art, but as a scholar he felt obligated and even
intrigued by it. His personal collection held an eclectic blend of
Americans: a Thomas Cole landscape, three trompe l'oeil paintings
by John F. Peto, and a portrait of Marga by Maurice Grosser. The
agenda Barr drew up for a meeting of the College Art Association's
Committee on American Art History, of which he was chairman
early in 1945, indicates the low esteem academics held for the study
of American art then. Barr himself had written that "American
art is in the end more valuable to us for what it tells us about
America than for its contribution to any international tradition."
Still, he wanted scholars to consider carefully whether the field was
important enough for university-level research and publication,
whether graduate study should go beyond the M.A., whether grad-

uate students should be allowed to concentrate on American art later than 1900, and whether film or industrial and commercial design should be included.

Such suggestions were unenthusiastically received at that time. When Barr urged the head of New York University's Fine Arts Institute, Philip McMahon, early in 1945 to pioneer serious studies in American art, especially since the postwar world "is likely to be characterized by strong nationalism," McMahon declined. His department was dominated by Central Europeans, he explained, most of whom "seemed to think that there was no American art and one frankly said so."

While the efforts to create a viable academic field for American art were serious enough, they smacked of the kind of home-team boosterism which Americans have always found irresistible. For Barr, they seemed to be a way to keep busy so long as there was no chance for leisurely summer trips to Paris, Rome, and Amsterdam. Instead of exciting visits to galleries and to artists' studios, there were the modest consolations of conferences in Chicago and correspondence with American academics. However, Barr also had been on the jury which selected paintings for the first spring salon in 1943 at Peggy Guggenheim's gallery. Along with James Johnson Sweeney, Soby, Mondrian, and Marcel Duchamp, he had selected about forty paintings, among them exciting abstract works by Jackson Pollock, Robert Motherwell, and William Baziotes. Here was a new kind of painting to engage Alfred Barr's proselytizing talents.

With such activities, and without even beginning serious work on his history of modern art, Barr was busier than ever. In June 1945 he reported to the trustees that in addition to the Picasso book and the Flexner lectures, he was preparing an entire special issue of the *College Art Bulletin* devoted to American art and was on a multitude of committees: inside the museum, he continued on the committee on the collections and a subcommittee on acquisitions; outside, he was serving on a committee choosing American paintings for exhibition in London and on a committee for New York State art legislation. He worked hard inside the College Art Association, as a director on the executive committee and chairman of the committee on research in American art. He carried on an immense correspondence with the Cubans he had met during his visit to the island in 1942, and in 1944 wrote a long article for *Gaceta del Caribe*, pleading for support for Cuba's modern artists. On the advisory council of the *Gazette des Beaux Arts*, a wartime publication of the Wildenstein Galleries which featured articles by such luminaries as Sir Kenneth Clark, Henri Focillon, Bernard Berenson, and a flock of exiled European museum directors, Barr was the only individual even remotely connected with modern art.

He also began to pour fire and brimstone upon organized religion for ignoring modern art, especially the Protestants, whom he considered particularly backward. Churches should use "really great art of the past in reproduction in place of the tawdry and vulgar sentimentalized pictures one ordinarily sees in church and Sunday schools," he urged one Protestant leader, and they should also commission works from the best living artists. Yet his mission toward organized religion was resolutely ecumenical. He encouraged Eloise Spaeth to assemble an exhibition of modern religious art at the Dayton, Ohio, museum where she was a trustee and became active in a foundation for contemporary religious art organized by Spaeth and her husband, Otto, both prominent Catholic laymen.

Barr also tried desperately to find the time for active participation in a conference on science, philosophy, and religion organized in 1946 by Louis Finkelstein, president of New York's Jewish Theological Seminary. To the first meeting of a subsection on art and religion Barr fired off a barrage of searching questions: "Why are contemporary religions not interested in art, past or present? Are the clergy knowledgeable? Why are contemporary religious artists outside the churches? Are churches afraid of real art and real images? Does iconoclasm still live? Are artists more estranged from religion than the general public?" He would "write more on this interesting subject at another time," Barr promised, but, beyond attending innumerable meetings—and begging off because of conflicting obligations from innumerable others—he never did.

He was busier than ever before. Indeed, it was clear that the less the museum demanded from Barr, the more involved he became in public issues involving all kinds of art, not just modern. He joined the cries of outrage among art historians, for example, when the

American military governor of Germany, Gen. Lucius D. Clay, shipped two hundred masterpieces of German painting to the National Gallery in Washington. The excuse for what Barr considered simple plunder was that German museums had no heat or lights and the works could deteriorate. Barr may have felt some residual pangs about his own decision to bring works the Nazis had stolen into the MOMA collection and now spoke out vociferously against removing masterpieces from German museums for a tour across the United States and perhaps even keeping them permanently as reparations. Barr also was furious when he learned that the occupation powers planned to destroy all German war memorials erected since 1914 and to burn all Nazi books. It was "not a question of the destruction of good or bad art," Barr fumed, "but the principle involved, that is, the art of any nation, enemy or otherwise."

When the war had erupted in 1939 no one had imagined that a modern art movement of more than perfunctory interest abroad could arise in the United States. True, by the spring of 1942, a great spectrum of New York galleries was showing American Modernists. In addition to an American Abstract Artists group exhibition, John Ferren showed at the Willard Gallery, Max Schnitzler at the Pinacotheca, Edwin Dickinson at Passedoit, James Guy at Ferargil, and John Marin and Arthur Dove at An American Place. At the MOMA, by contrast, shows of Americans continued to emphasize realism, regionalism, and geographic surveys. In 1940, protesters gave out handbills to some thousand artists invited to the museum to preview an exhibition of newspaper cartoons. Headlined in Gay Nineties circus type, the handbill demanded to know what was modern about John Singer Sargent, William Harnett, and Winslow Homer, who were then being shown. The tenth-anniversary exhibition had contained too many nineteenth-century artists, its signers complained, while a more recent exhibition, "Modern Masters," had included only Americans who were dead for at least twenty years. Of the fifty signers, Barr responded, eighteen had already been shown at the museum since it opened. But the charges that the museum was unfair to modern American artists lingered. In 1944, art historian Meyer Schapiro reported to trustees that "serious artists have criticized the Museum for its failure to show more important and stirring work."

When the museum sponsored yet another show featuring American romanticism and magic realism, the Federation of Modern Painters and Sculptors wrote the MOMA an open letter deploring its "increasingly reactionary policies . . . toward the works of American artists" even as it concentrated on "such ephemeral fads as the output of certain refugee surrealists and . . . American scene illustration." The reply of Barr's friend James Thrall Soby, who was then in charge of painting and sculpture, was haughty indeed. He asked all seventy-nine artist-members of the Federation to verify that each had approved of the letter. Clement Greenberg wrote that this tactic reminded him of the "Stalinist telephone-pressure campaigns of the late Thirties." The conservatives at the MOMA wanted only "the romantic, the realistic, the descriptive, the immediately erotic, the chic," he feared, and suggested that the museum might become "an educational annex to the Stork Club." The Museum of Modern Art did not "exist for the direct benefit and patronage of artists," Soby fired back; its mission was not "to lead artists, but to follow them—at a close yet respectful distance." The museum was doing more for American artists, he insisted, by exhibiting and touring their works than by buying them. Public acceptance would be "a far more important contribution to the support of living painters and sculptors." Barr agreed and wrote to Lincoln Kirstein, "It is strange how with all the whoop-to-do about our buying American art, that nobody gives any money for that purpose." In a postscript he suggested vaguely that Kirstein "would be surprised if you knew how much money we have spent on American painting during the past five years."

All their adult lives, art professionals like Soby and Barr had watched American art lurch from feeble imitations of European discoveries to militant nativism to occasional geysers of originality unsustained by either steady patrons or a critical mass of younger artists elaborating on the new direction. So it was particularly shocking when a rank amateur, a giddy outsider, both to the art world and especially to American art, began to recognize, foster and, in short order, impose a bold new aesthetic upon this tired cycle. With characteristic impetuosity, Peggy Guggenheim had leaped into the turgid pool of the American avant-garde and boldly plucked forth one pearl after another.

Between spectacular fights with Max Ernst and parties at which the guests disrobed "to show how detached one could be," Guggenheim rented a top floor at 30 West Fifty-seventh Street and proceeded to plan a gallery there. She paid a brilliantly idiosyncratic Austrian emigré architect, Frederick Kiesler, some $7,000 to decorate it and bragged that the place "would not be known to posterity for [Guggenheim's] collection of paintings, but for the way [Kiesler] presented them to the world." Those hundreds who contributed a dollar each to the Red Cross to attend the opening on October 20, 1942, were bemused by its *doyenne* bustling about in a new white dress with one Tanguy earring and one by Calder, "to show my impartiality between Surrealist and abstract art." They were startled that by Guggenheim's order all the paintings were unframed. They were stunned by Kiesler's design: in the Surrealist area, paintings mounted on baseball bats protruded from the wall and the lights flashed on and off every three seconds; in the Abstract and Cubist Gallery, some paintings dangled on strings from the ceiling in the center of the room. The Klees were on revolving wheels which automatically moved when a viewer stepped through an electric eye, and reproductions of the Duchamps (he had not done original works for many years) were visible only through a peephole in the wall.

Guggenheim's exhibitionistic flair may have been a bit much for ascetic Alfred Barr, but there was no denying the quality of her collection. A man accustomed to badgering donors for piddling purchase funds, Barr winked at Guggenheim's flamboyant bohemianism, while he marveled at what she owned. Her gallery "immediately became the center of the New York vanguard," he would write. When he participated in the jury for her spring salon early in 1943, he began to lose his skepticism about the Americans. Yet, he was cautious about buying their works for the museum. From the one-man show Guggenheim gave for Pollock in the fall of 1943, he and Soby selected only one work, *She-Wolf*, which took them six months to sell to the trustees. The next Pollock arrived at the MOMA in 1952, a gift from Guggenheim. From Motherwell's first one-man show in 1944, Barr also bought just one work, a mixed-media collage on cardboard called *Pancho Villa, Dead and Alive*. Guggenheim gave William Baziotes his first one-man show in the same year, but the MOMA did not acquire any works by this artist until 1947. Nor was the MOMA interested in any paintings by Mark Rothko when Guggenheim held his first one-man show in 1945; not until 1952 did Barr persuade Philip Johnson to buy Rothko's *Number 10* for the museum.

Today, the years when Peggy Guggenheim streaked across the New York art scene are seen as the glory days of Abstract Expressionism, a term coined by *New Yorker* art critic Robert Coates for the group which also included Clyfford Still, David Hare, Adolph Gottlieb, Hedda Sterne, Ad Reinhardt, and Jackson Pollock's wife, Lee Krasner. In 1983 a French observer even concluded that New York then stole the idea of modern art. Bowled over by Guggenheim's rescue of European avant-garde works, mesmerized by her "search for the extreme," and succumbing to her "flair for business," grumbled Serge Guilbaut, the New York art public began to support its own artists and snubbed Paris.

It is difficult to imagine Peggy Guggenheim guilty of premeditating such villainy. If anything, her chaotic private life, which she insisted on spreading across the public print in her 1946 memoirs, paints her as a sadly muddled buffoon. Written in the summer of 1945, "as she lay upon the sands of Fire Island and wept," according to *Newsweek*, it revealed how she became interested in art "during a lull in her love affairs." *Time* thought the memoirs of the "tense, ink-haired heiress" were stylistically, "as flat and witless as a harmonica rendition of the *Liebestod*," yet "all too frank." Reviewer Harry Hansen called her book "a testimony of reckless bohemianism," while art critic Katharine Kuh wrote that this "vulgar" book "has done the cause of modern art no kindness by mixing it irrevocably with a compulsive recital of her own decadent life." Guggenheim's scandalized family dispatched agents, it was said, to bookstores all over the country to buy up and destroy all extant copies.

With this gamy fanfare, and given the MOMA's lukewarm response, New York did not so much steal modern art as have modern art thrust upon it. When the war ended, many of the European exiles like Hans Hoffmann, Marcel Duchamp, Hans Richter, and Max Ernst decided to stay on, enriching the postwar American art scene. Those who returned to Europe, among them André Breton, Fernand Léger, André Masson, Jean Hélion, and Marc Chagall, arrived on a continent exhausted by war and divided by politics, and in a culture drained of imaginative vitality.

At the Museum of Modern Art the end of the war meant the end of Stephen Clark's confused caretaker regime. Although no clear administrative leader had emerged, the museum family had flourished under Clark's reign; membership had doubled and attendance had reached half a million per year. Nelson Rockefeller was reelected president in 1946 and John Hay Whitney replaced Clark as chairman of the board of trustees. Soon, they were exploring ways to bring Alfred Barr in from the wilderness and back into the museum's central councils—but without restoring him as the museum's director. In July of 1946, the trustees' executive committee drew up one of the organizational charts of which it was so fond, and it showed Barr as director of research in painting and sculpture, among five equal staff directors. But he would be removed from the board of trustees and would lose control of curatorial departments and programs. Through Soby, who served as a go-between in these negotiations, Barr refused. By September, he was insisting on continuing with his writing, both for the museum and outside, and offered to abandon "all my vestiges of curatorial functions if I am to take on the time- and thought-consuming trouble of working with Clark and Nelson forwarding the interests of the collection in the five-ring arena which the trustees are setting up." He also expected to delegate the exhausting task of hanging exhibitions since "under the plan there is no more reason why I should install painting than pots and pans or photographs." He was pessimistic that Soby could negotiate a satisfactory arrangement and signed himself, "yours, hardboiled and as ever, looking out for himself and trying the patience of his best friend."

A few days later, Soby suggested to Barr that he confront the trustees with "infidelity," perhaps by seriously considering a job elsewhere: "You not only wouldn't be at the museum but you *would* be somewhere else; hence the museum would lose status as center of authority." The only time Clark was "really shaken," Soby reported, was on learning that Barr might leave the MOMA, possibly for the Fogg Museum at Harvard. Using Soby as an intermediary, Barr then wrote out exactly what he would require to stay at the MOMA: control of $5,000 per year for purchases and the right to buy works costing $500 or less without committee approval; selection of all objects to be "eliminated"; technical care of the collection; approval of all loans, installations, and labeling; and approval of all publications, films, telecasts, and publicity. All staff working on the collections would be responsible to him. After taking up all these duties, Barr believed that "writing may have to take a secondary place."

In January 1947, his new role began to emerge as the trustees gave in to all his demands and more. He could spend four months each year on writing and editing museum publications devoted to subjects unrelated to the collections. In March, he was officially named director of the collections and moved back into the office he had occupied as museum director. He did not "attach any 'symbolic importance' to this room," Barr assured Nelson Rockefeller, "but it is quiet, comparatively isolated and was designed for hanging and studying important pictures which are under consideration for purchase." The job was not new, Barr explained to a colleague, "but simply the responsibility for the Museum Collections which has been my principal interest since the beginning in 1929."

Obdurately, single-mindedly, Barr had wagered his professional life and won. Typically, Barr had fought for control and not for money. He was still making $10,000 a year, the salary which the trustees had thought so outrageously high when they hired him almost sixteen years earlier. In 1946, the Bryn Mawr lectures brought in another $1,000 and other lectures and writing totaled perhaps $850. He got no royalties on any of his museum publications, not even the best-selling *What Is Modern Painting?* To Soby he confided that he needed an income of at least $15,000 or else they would have to "lower our standard of living more even than we've had to do the past three years."

He complained, but it was obvious that money was never important and never would be important in the life of Alfred Barr. Stephen Clark, at about the time he had fired Barr, had lectured a museum staff member on rich people's feelings about money:

"Money is not just money; it's a symbol. You waste a penny or a thousand dollars and it's the same thing." To Barr, his years in the wilderness bore out a different text, remembered from his youth: "Ye that know righteousness . . . fear ye not the reproach of men, neither be ye afraid of their revilings. For the moth shall eat them up like a garment, and the worm shall eat them like wool: but my righteousness shall be for ever. . . ."

9

DEFENDING THE FAITH

Sheltered by the ambiguity of his new title, Alfred Barr charged back into the mainstream of the museum's activities. During the next few years, his influence in the councils of the museum and in the art world would become so pervasive that his title was insignificant. Director of the museum collections became an authoritative mantle for Barr just because it was so vague. Inclusive without the unmistakable heft—and burden—of being simply museum director, the title as Barr defined it became an official license to pursue the multitude of interests clamoring for his attention. Although he was still supposed to spend several months of the year locked up with his writing, and although the new title implied that he would devote the rest of his time to curatorial pursuits, he operated more like a one-man flying squad in the battle to defend and define modern art. Whether he learned of a critic faulting the museum or sniffed the smoke of a distant skirmish over Modernism, Alfred Barr charged righteously forth into the fray. "Behold, I give unto you power to tread on serpents and scorpions, and over all the power of the enemy: and nothing shall by any means hurt you."

The war against the Nazis and the Japanese had been won in 1945 by the forces of freedom, but as young American artists themselves turned increasingly to Modernism, the nation's conservative majority of artists, critics, museum people, and even politicians were gathering for yet another drive to turn back the progressives in the art world. In March 1947, a respected furniture designer, T. H. Robsjohn-Gibbings, published *Mona Lisa's Moustache*, an irritatingly intemperate attack on modern art. He claimed that painters did abstract pictures to "gain power . . . over beings they consider insignificant" and called art authorities who supported them "victims of necromantic systems." In hysterical, italic-ridden prose, Robsjohn-Gibbings worked up to his final, absurd accusation: "In 1914 Kandinsky arrived in Russia and three years later came the Revolution." This tirade received a glowing *New York Times* review from the director of education at the Boston Museum of Fine Arts.

Robsjohn-Gibbings had provided "damaging evidence" that modern art was a fraud, William G. Dooley had written, "all to the good because for twenty years no literate or plausible attacker has appeared." To extirpate this heresy Barr first called a council of war at the museum and then did not rest until he had forced the poor man to recant; he even wrote to Dooley's boss to complain. In a subsequent column, Dooley explained that he was being ironic, that the book was the second-best work of its kind in a field of two. Barr also gloated that he had persuaded his friend Jacques Barzun to do "a masterly dilapidation" of the book in *Harper's*.

"The conservatives of course are always hoping that art will return to something they like—and sometimes it does," Barr wrote to Nelson Rockefeller. But it was up to the art critics to provide "open-minded elucidation, as well as evaluation." To improve the critical climate, Barr had tried in 1946 to persuade Holger Cahill and James Thrall Soby to apply to the *Herald-Tribune* for the job of art critic when arch-reactionary Royal Cortissoz finally retired. Both men declined and Barr was left to mend his relationship with the outspoken critic of the MOMA who got the job, Emily Genauer. As for magazine editors, columnists, caption writers, and popular essayists, Barr concluded that they were "less concerned with enlightening their readers about modern art than with the easy and profitable confirmation of popular prejudice." While "most artists can read," he noted, "few writers can see—and thus the blind continue to mislead the blind."

Barr also protested repeatedly against the efforts of psychoanalysts to interpret modern paintings. When the *College Art Journal* published an article purportedly analyzing Picasso's psyche on the basis of his paintings, Barr protested such an invasion of privacy to the journal's editor. An artist "is peculiarly defenseless against intrusion not only into his private affairs," Barr wrote, "but also into the hypothetical secrets of his mind and soul." Barr inquired widely as to the credentials of the author of the offending article and pounced on the fact that he was only a student of psychoanalysis. In 1950, when a full-fledged psychoanalyst attempted a Freudian interpretation of art, Barr again exploded. "That these supposed scientists should publish so much half-baked guesswork about artists and works of art does no credit to their usually scrupulous profession," he wrote to the editor of *The Saturday Review of Literature*. To a museum member who asked him about psychoanalysis and art, Barr contrasted the intensive, lengthy therapy sessions required for a full analysis, against Freudians' cavalier interpretations of works of art "with very little knowledge of the artist and no first-hand opportunity to . . . study his personality through free association, dream narratives, etc." Perhaps with his own brief, unsuccessful psychoanalytic sessions with Dr. Garthe in Stuttgart in mind, Barr denounced the whole profession. "They have banded together into a block for mutual defense . . . so that they do not feel free to criticize each other publicly," he wrote. "I consider this a deplorable . . . form of censorship."

Sometimes a criticism as unthreatening as the pop of a cap pistol would send Barr rushing to the barricades. A museum visitor strolling through the galleries while waiting for *Casablanca* to begin in the movie theater wrote to Barr that he did not appreciate certain paintings. He considered Malevich's *White on White* "a geometrical doodle which I could reproduce in an hour," while another picture with "a hideous green face" (perhaps Peter Blume's *The Eternal City*) gave him "the creeps." Though he was not a writer, he concluded, "if your pictures are art, then this [letter] is a literary masterpiece." Barr replied in two single-spaced pages. He appreciated the man's frank opinions; for understanding of *White on White* he suggested a study of Malevich available in German; and he enclosed a news release about four drawings Abby Rockefeller had just given to the museum, with pertinent passages marked.

From the popular press, one could only expect "brass-bound Philistinism," as Barr in 1947 had described the policy of *The New York Times Magazine*. But when Boston's Institute of Modern Art broke ranks, Barr was truly outraged. In March 1948, the Boston museum suddenly decided to change its name to Institute of Contemporary Art and issued a blistering "statement of principles." It defended the artistic experiments of the early twentieth century but called more recent innovations "a general cult of bewilderment," rife with "double-talk, opportunism, and chicanery at the public's expense." Although "world chaos and social unrest" may have prompted the "excesses of modern art," the statement urged artists to "come forward with a strong, clear affirmation of truth for humanity." To Barr, such words were sharper than a serpent's tooth, for the Institute was a direct offspring of the Museum of Modern Art. It had grown out of the Boston Program Committee, a chapter of the MOMA founded in 1935. Four years later, it became a separate institution, directed by James S. Plaut, but many MOMA exhibitions continued to travel to its Boston gallery and relations between the two museums had previously been cordial.

It was, of course, not the first time that Alfred Barr had confronted the traditionalist art lovers of Boston. Back in 1927, however, when he had called the city a modern art pauper, he had been a solitary evangelist, preaching to a handful of adoring acolytes at Wellesley. Now he mustered the resources of a major cultural institution to beat off the Boston heathen one more time. The word *modern* is deliberately provocative, Barr argued in a response he prepared for MOMA trustees; it had been used "probably since the beginning of civilization to denote what innovators created and what . . . reactionaries disliked." He cited how the Roman emperor Nero's art critics deplored what was then called modern painting because it was influenced by "Egyptian charlatanism." He blamed the flap in Boston on a centuries-long trend in which "the public began to assume the right to criticize painting without ever taking the time or trouble to understand it as art."

Barr was even more alarmed when the Boston statement found vigorous support from Francis Henry Taylor, director of the Metropolitan Museum of Art. No friend of Modernism, Taylor had been heard to refer to the MOMA as "that whorehouse on 53rd Street." In December of 1948 he published an article in the *Atlantic* calling on artists to start painting works "the public can understand." Contemporary art was "divorced from ... common human experience," he charged, and had become "a form of private communication—when it communicates at all—whereby abstract associations of form and color convey intimacies scarcely less cryptic than those revealed on the psychiatrist's couch."

Taylor's attack was particularly embarrassing because only two months before the Boston brouhaha, the MOMA and the Met had at last announced an agreement whereby the older works in the Museum of Modern Art collection would gradually be sold to the Metropolitan. Representatives of the two museums had first met in 1934 to explore possible cooperation. In Abby Rockefeller's parlor, two trustees and the directors from each institution agreed heartily to "cooperate"—but not to the extent of exchanging pictures. The Met, the MOMA, and the Whitney had sporadically been bargaining over spheres of influence since 1943. The Whitney, in fact, had given up its autonomy in exchange for a home at the Met and nominal control of the Met's $15,000 Hearn Fund for purchases of American art. But the tripartite museum talks, as they were diplomatically dubbed, moved at the pace of international arms negotiations; one dinner at the Brook Club ended in "a violent free-for-all." In the summer of 1947, Barr wrote to Stephen Clark, who also was on the Met board of trustees, that he expected the talks to drag on and was "not very sanguine about a favorable conclusion." Mrs. Guggenheim, for one, worried that the museum's great Bliss Cézannes and van Goghs and her own costly gifts to the MOMA, including Rousseau's *Sleeping Gypsy*, would end up in what many considered the mausoleum on Fifth Avenue.

But early in 1948, a new tri-museum pact was announced. The MOMA would sell some forty works to the Metropolitan for a total of $191,000. Only the oldest, such as Daumier's *The Laundress*, and fourteen works of American folk art would immediately go to the Met. The rest would stay at the Museum of Modern Art for the moment, but as they aged and presumably lost their modern appeal, they would gradually migrate to the Met, with the last ones to move uptown on October 1, 1957. To a reporter, Barr explained once again that the MOMA wanted to concentrate on modern work, "done in our time (say within the last fifty years) and at the same time . . . modern in character—that is it must have new formal relations, new ideas or psychological approach." He anticipated that even the works of Picasso would be split between the museums for many years, with the early works, including those from the Blue Period, at the Met and the later ones still at the MOMA. But to one skeptical reporter, the ultimate fate of a masterpiece like van Gogh's *Starry Night* remained "the $191,000 question."

The immediate fate of lesser works, however, was already engaging passions on both sides. To seal the deal, the Met had agreed to let the MOMA have an indefinite loan of one of the few modern masterpieces it possessed, Picasso's 1906 *Portrait of Gertrude Stein*. The avant-garde writer and collector had willed the picture to the Met, but once it was installed at the MOMA, Barr persistently tried to persuade her heir, Alice B. Toklas, to let the MOMA keep the Stein portrait indefinitely. He sent her a photo showing the painting displayed "in the place of maximum honor" opposite the entrance to the museum. He asked Thornton Wilder, who corresponded with Toklas, to put in a good word: "I sincerely believe that the portrait is happier and in more appropriate company here," he wrote. But after only ten months, the Met's Taylor curtly demanded it back: "We have had many requests to have the picture shown here."

By then, the Whitney had already abandoned the coalition, even though the Met had promised to build a wing to house its collection and had given its director, Juliana Force, $40,000 from the Hearn Fund to buy contemporary American art. The Met did not want to show "advanced art," Force complained. Indeed, one of the Met's most active board members asserted that each time he had to pass through the single gallery where modern paintings were displayed, "he looked only at the floor." The Whitney then moved next door to the MOMA garden on Fifty-fourth Street, "a grand plan," Barr wrote to Nelson Rockefeller. Such proximity would be "evidence of a friendly alliance between two independent institutions working in an overlapping field; it might serve as a block against present resentful hostility of some of our conservative friends."

One way the "conservative friends" on upper Fifth Avenue were expressing their "resentful hostility" was by opening a van Gogh exhibition in collaboration with the Art Institute of Chicago. Treading on turf the MOMA thought it owned, the Met mustered ninety-five paintings and sixty-five drawings, only seventeen of which had been seen in the great 1935 MOMA show. Once more the mobs tramped through an exhibition of glorious pictures by an artist reviled in his own time—some three hundred thousand people in thirteen weeks. But this time, the crowd milled through the Met and, at the salescounter near the exit, scooped up thirty-two thousand catalogs and countless tawdry van Gogh trinkets worth, the Met coyly said, "tens of thousands of dollars."

At the same time, the Met hired Robert Beverly Hale as its first curator of contemporary American art. The Met intended to buy and show works by living Americans "on a broad scale," Taylor proclaimed. The first step would be a competition with $8,500 in prizes, the *New York Times* announced on page one. But the reader had to turn to page forty-five to learn that the purchases of Americans would come from the Hearn Fund, whose $15,000 a year had been untouched so long that it now amounted to some $100,000. Although the MOMA–Met agreement lingered on officially until the Met paid the last of its $191,000 in 1951, true cooperation between the museums ended right then.

Even though it ran counter to the deepest acquisitive drives of all museum people, the intermuseum agreement might have worked in an earlier time, when art values were relatively stable and when new kinds of art did not appear every other Monday. But it was bound to fail in the superheated boiler of the New York art scene that began to unfold in the late forties and fifties. The American abstract artists discovered by Peggy Guggenheim before she fled New York in 1946 had grown from a handful to a swarm. Alfred Barr could have told the director of the Met that in treading into the field of contemporary American art, he would sink into a morass. The Met had no sooner announced its competition than twenty-eight of the most prominent abstract painters and sculptors proclaimed that they would boycott it. The jury, which included the lukewarm Modernists of the previous generation—Charles Burchfield, Yasuo Kuniyoshi, Maurice Sterne, and Eugene Speicher—was "notoriously hostile" to advanced art, they charged, and so was the new curator of contemporary art. Six weeks later, some seventy-five other artists who claimed to be just as advanced defended the Met's plans. The second group did include a few artists, like Milton Avery and Philip Evergood, whose works would stand up, but by and large they would be forgotten in the rush toward the new. The boycotters, by contrast, included a roll call of what would soon be called the New York School of Abstract Expressionists—Adolph Gottlieb, Robert Motherwell, William Baziotes, Hans Hofmann, Barnett Newman, Clyfford Still, Richard Pousette-Dart, Theodore Stamos, Ad Reinhardt, Jackson Pollock, Mark Rothko, Bradley Walker Tomlin, and Willem de Kooning.

Barr himself was feeling the heat from this explosive new movement. In a 1948 paper on the state of American art, he wrote that while the abstract-realist polarity was "crude and ambiguous," he was glad that the public had a choice. The artist should be free to create in any idiom, but "when one kind of art or another is dogmatically asserted to be the only funicular up Parnassus . . . those who love art or spiritual freedom cannot remain neutral." Yet he was cautious. During the 1948–1949 season, he had asked the trustees on the museum collections committee to help select the works to be shown in an exhibition called "American Paintings from the Museum Collections." He had tried to include artists with a full range of styles: pioneers like Maurice Prendergast and Max Weber; post-Armory Show moderns like John Marin, Frank Stella, Charles Demuth, and Arthur Dove; individualists like Georgia O'Keeffe, Peter Blume, Edward Hopper, Maurice Gropper, Ben Shahn, and Marsden Hartley; the experimenters of the forties, such as I. Rice Pereira and Loren MacIver; and finally a small selection of the current Abstract Expressionists. Again and again, Barr visited the show, trying to absorb the historic sweep and perhaps fathom the future direction of American art. But when he walked through it again with critic Clement Greenberg, he was told that it was "vastly disappointing." Greenberg raged at how "scandalously few" of the Abstract Expressionists were represented. "One sees how remiss the museum has been lately in its duty to encourage modern American art . . . how little, how woefully little the Museum has to show for the expenditure of so much money, space, time, energy and—at least on the part of some—devotion."

Until now, few articulate or knowledgeable critics had been writing about American art. In explaining Modernism as a whole, Barr had been virtually alone. Now he was suddenly being ground up between a noisy band of new art writers who eloquently beat the drums for this volcanic new art and a skeptical older generation of critics, collectors, and, most important, MOMA trustees. Barr was understandably cautious in buying newer works for the museum collections when Stephen Clark, for one, snapped that "they don't have much to say." In selecting works for exhibitions of current American art, Barr and Dorothy Miller were careful to include representatives of a variety of styles. Yet, he was hurt when *New Yorker* critic Robert Coates called a 1952 "Fifteen Americans" exhibition "a grab-bag." The museum had sponsored perfunctory surveys of this kind since its founding without getting rapped in print. "Golly," Barr wrote to Coates, "when I think of the sweat and soul-searching that went into "Fifteen Americans" it does make me pretty mad to have you damn it." To Nelson Rockefeller Barr insisted that the show was "the most compelling and dramatic demonstration of the vigor of our art that I have ever seen—at least our contemporary art."

But the vitality of new American art had caught even Alfred Barr by surprise. Until now, the artists Barr had championed had all been of an older generation and mostly Europeans. Suddenly a covey of brash young Americans were flinging paint pots at the canvas, challenging the Metropolitan Museum of Art on the front page of the *New York Times*, defiantly posing on the pages of popular picture magazines, and calling the Museum of Modern Art stodgy and middle-aged. Moreover, these artists were taking over more galleries every month and the prices for their works were rising steeply. In a 1949 "closeout" by dealer Samuel Kootz, prices for the likes of Baziotes, Gottlieb, or Motherwell were $500 to $900, and for each purchase by a museum, Kootz threw in a free painting

of the same size. But only two years later, the MOMA had to pay
$1,800 for a Rothko, and in 1953 de Kooning's *Woman I* cost the
museum $3,500.

The price inflation for Americans reflected an even steeper rise
in the prices of European Modernists. Just before the Second World
War, a Monet might fetch $3,000. Another Monet, stolen from
Hitler's air raid shelter in Munich just as the war was ending in
April 1945 had been traded to a farmer for a pound of butter. But
only a year later, Monet's *Seine at Bougival* brought a record
$11,000, and ten years later, a Monet would sell for more than
$70,000. When Sidney Janis opened his New York gallery in 1948
with an exhibition of Fernand Léger, he sold only two pictures,
both of them after the show officially closed. One went to what
would become the Guggenheim Museum for $2,800 and the other to
a friend for $600. That year Barr bought a Léger colored litho-
graph for the MOMA for $30. In 1949, he was offered "a very fine
old Léger" for $950. But only four years later, an early (1919) Léger
sold in Paris for over $6,000.

In 1949 Barr boasted that he had been able to buy three first-
rate Chagalls, a Kirchner landscape, a Karl Hofer, and a small
Derain "for very little more than $10,000." He was surprised that
Matisse's *Goldfish* had sold for as much as $15,000 and suggested
that most French pictures were "overpriced by about 50%." But the
prices of older French works were going through the roof. In 1953,
Barr was shocked that David Rockefeller was considering purchase of a Gauguin still life for "hold your breath"—$85,000. How-
ever, the museum itself was contributing to the price rises. During
the thirties, a Paul Klee oil sold for about $500. But after two large
Klee exhibitions at the Museum of Modern Art, in 1940 and 1950,
the same works were soon selling for ten times as much.

Ever since Lillie Bliss had made her collection during the
twenties and thirties, Impressionist and Post-Impressionist paintings had sold at fairly steady prices, depending on size, quality, and
decorative appeal. Up to the end of the Second World War, the
pictures she had given to the Museum of Modern Art in 1934 had
appreciated moderately, at about the same rate as any other gilt-
edged investment. But around 1950, several factors combined to

turn the genteel, refined art market into an overheated bazaar. For one thing, a great many wealthy people fell in love with the sensuous, gorgeously colored paintings from the last half of the nineteenth century and became avid collectors. While the carefree leisure pursuits that the Impressionists so often painted were remote from the reality of late nineteenth-century France, war-weary twentieth-century collectors adored their nostalgic love letters to "the good old days." At the same time, numerous museums, especially in America, decided to modernize their collections and entered into the same marketplace. Finally, brazen and well-financed auctioneers, such as Christie's, Sotheby's, and Parke-Bernet, invaded the arena previously dominated by cultivated dealers. The first hint of what this combination of forces wrought came in 1952, at the Gabriel Cognacq sale in Paris, when a Cézanne still life brought $94,286; a Renoir portrait, $64,285; and a Degas pastel, in a "wild flurry of excitement," $30,000.

It was this precipitous rise in the prices of pictures—and the end was nowhere in sight—that ultimately derailed the Museum of Modern Art from the contemporary track. Even if Alfred Barr had wanted to clean out the basement, to sell or trade older works in order to bring in the new, no board of trustees in the world would have agreed to sell works whose values were rising so swiftly. For, if Cézannes, Renoirs, Degas, and Gauguins were appreciating so madly today, one could expect the same for Picassos, Matisses, and Braques tomorrow—and even for Pollocks, Motherwells, and de Koonings the day after. The pact with the Metropolitan really fell apart over this underlying fact. The unprecedented rise in art prices led the MOMA board, in February 1953, to reverse all that the museum had represented since 1929, and it dominates the museum's policy to the present day.

Since the MOMA's earliest days, Barr had been trying to reconcile his enthusiasm for the newest, most revolutionary works of art with his affection for the earliest Modernists, the pioneers who had shaken and overturned the academic establishment and whose works, in tiny monochrome reproductions, he had perused so avidly in *The Dial* while he was a student at Princeton. With virtually no purchase funds, he had to rely on gifts and on the often capricious taste of donors. He had learned through bitter experience that, to attract gifts, the museum would have to guarantee that the works would remain in the museum's collection.

Furthermore, American tax laws offered extraordinary incentives for wealthy collectors to donate art to museums. A donor could promise a work of art to a museum, take a tax deduction based actuarially on what his gift would be worth when he died, and then keep the work for the rest of his life. How could the museum profit from this loophole unless it intended to create a stable collection? Collectors who during the thirties and early forties had put pin money into speculative art were able to promise works to the museum during the fifties and immediately deduct the substantial appreciated value from their taxes. Helen Resor, for example, had bought Paul Klee's *Vocal Texture of the Singer Rosa Silbers* in 1940 for $600. Fifteen years later, when Klees were bringing $14,000, Barr had no trouble in persuading her to donate the picture to the museum.

Literally thousands of art works would eventually come to the Museum of Modern Art—but only if there were a stable collection to take them in. Understandably, on February 15, 1953, MOMA board chairman John Hay Whitney announced "an important change of policy." The museum's original notion of passing on older works to other museums, he said, "did not work out to the benefit of its public. It now believes it essential for the understanding and enjoyment of its entire collection to have permanently on public view masterpieces of the modern movement, beginning with the latter half of the nineteenth century." By then, the MOMA's collection was considered the best of its kind in the world and certainly the largest: 829 paintings, 210 sculptures, 310 drawings, 4,000 prints, 2,500 photos, and 670 pieces of furniture, utensils, and other examples of modern design. For insurance, it was valued at $2.5 million. Most of these works were still expected to pass through and only "key pieces" would be kept, the museum announced, but clearly the lusty enfant terrible was on the way to becoming a stylish dowager.

Barr himself had contributed mightily to the transformation. After the early years of begging and bargaining, and then the years in the wilderness when purchases and all other museum activities marked time, he began to dispose of considerable acquisition funds soon after becoming director of collections. In 1949 and 1950, he spent some $90,000 on thirty-six paintings, eight sculptures, twenty-two drawings, 210 prints and portfolios, forty-eight posters, and twenty-one films. (About $14,000 of the total went for works by Americans.) In addition, through Mrs. Guggenheim's largesse, he brought in two extraordinary paintings which he had been tracking for decades: Matisse's *Red Studio* and Picasso's *Three Musicians*. The *Musicians* had barely slipped through Barr's fingers in 1936, when he attempted to wangle this massive monument of Picasso's synthetic cubist period through a complicated trade with Walter P. Chrysler. When the picture finally arrived at the MOMA, it completed Barr's plan to own a landmark work from each of Picasso's major periods: the *Demoiselles d'Avignon* of 1907, the *Three Musicians* of 1921, and the *Girl Before a Mirror* of 1932. As of 1949, Barr declared, the MOMA owned the most important Picasso collection in the world.

Only a year earlier, Barr had complained of overcrowding in the museum's galleries: just 15 percent of its paintings were regularly shown; only half of its sculpture and just 5 percent of drawings and 1 percent of all its prints could be exhibited at one time. But the fear of rising prices blew a powerful draft on the fires of acquisitive lust. However, a knowledgeable buyer could still winkle out some bargains, especially if he knew his art history—and even more so if he had written a good deal of that history.

In 1949, Barr bought wholesale from a MOMA exhibition of Italian Futurists. For only $5,500, supplied by Nelson Rockefeller, Barr purchased ten paintings, four sculptures, seven drawings, fifteen prints, and five portfolios of prints. At one blow, the museum went from owning a scattering of Futurist works to boasting the best collection by these artists anywhere outside Italy. When an Italian dealer then offered to sell him an Umberto Boccioni painting for $17,000, Barr called the price "preposterous" and reminded him that "there is almost no market for Futurist paintings in this country or . . . in Europe, outside Italy." Marga Barr noted in Barr's papers that "Alfred was so happy that he was able to get a splendid selection of Futurist work before the Italians tried to buy things up for their museums." Within three years, he was even happier when he added the centerpiece to that collection, Boccioni's *The City Rises*, for $5,800. When this painting was almost irretrievably burned in a fire at the museum ten years later, the insurance payment was $52,500.

Barr and Soby (who owned several first-rate examples of Giorgio De Chirico's brooding dreamscapes) had traveled to Italy in the summer of 1948 to gather works for this Italian Futurist exhibition. The Italian government offered to put a car at their disposal, ·while the American State Department, then eager to woo the left-leaning Italians, bought round-trip tickets for the Barrs and Soby. A Milan art dealers' association agreed to pay for shipping the works to the museum and back. Fifty-six of the items finally shown at the museum in the summer of 1949 were for sale, among them, of course, the choicest works already reserved by Barr for the museum. The trustees snapped up twenty-two of them, with Nelson Rockefeller buying "a whole bunch" before the exhibition opened. On each sale, the museum collected a 10 percent commission.

Once it became clear that gifts or bequests from collectors would become a major source of the museum's acquisitions, Barr began to guide them carefully into buying works that the museum wanted. When Barr failed in an attempt to buy a particular Braque for $6,500 for Nelson Rockefeller in 1949, he suggested that the museum president purchase another Braque priced at $14,000, though Barr had "reason to think I could get it for a lot less." The work would be a worthwhile purchase, Barr wrote to Rockefeller because speaking "with my usual institutional self interest!—it is quite unlike any Braque in the museum collection." As he traveled about visiting dealers and exhibitions, it became routine for Barr to pick out works that Rockefeller might like to buy, along with those he chose for the museum. His unique title may have been director of the museum collections, but in effect he was also director of the Goodwin Collection, the Burden Collection, the Rockefeller Collection, and many others.

Sometimes it was difficult to draw any line between what the museum exhibited or bought, and what the collectors on the board of trustees acquired. When the MOMA purchased a Marino Marini bronze *Portrait of Vitali* for $500 in October 1949, trustee Samuel Lewisohn got a cast of the same work for $550. When trustee Philip

Goodwin spotted a Braque he wanted in a 1949 MOMA exhibition, he asked Barr to write to its owner and ask whether the picture was for sale and at what price. When Philip Johnson bought a Baziotes for $333.22 in 1950, Barr did all the negotiating and promised the seller that "if the museum doesn't take it, one of our younger collectors will."

From the museum's first major exhibition of Abstract Expressionists in 1952, trustees bought sixteen works before the opening. Nelson Rockefeller bought at least one example of each artist's work, acquiring a Baziotes, a Gorky, a Motherwell, a Tomlin, three de Koonings, and, immediately after the opening, his first Jackson Pollock. Dorothy Miller, who had organized the exhibition "Fifteen Americans," naively wrote to Barr that she thought it "very important and also maybe a unique situation in the museum world to have trustees working so closely and with such enthusiasm with the institution and to support the most advanced contemporary art." But clearly the fifties were not the thirties. Experienced investors all, the trustees knew that when the Museum of Modern Art endorsed certain kinds of art, astronomical profits on those kinds of art were not far behind.

Barr's relationship with William A. M. Burden, who replaced Nelson Rockefeller as museum president in 1953, is typical of how intimately the museum's business could become intertwined with a trustee's affairs. Burden had been a MOMA trustee since 1943 and later became chairman of the committee on collections. A principal in a venture capital firm investing the considerable fortune he had inherited, Burden had served as assistant secretary of commerce for air and special assistant for research and development to the secretary of the air force. He was also an avid collector of modern art and relied heavily not only on Barr's advice as to the quality of art works but also on his encyclopedic knowledge of the art market and his shrewd bargaining ability. When Burden traveled to Paris in 1952, Barr gave him a full rundown of art galleries there, which artists they represented, how firm their prices were, and what sort of commission they charged. He also evaluated the newer artists in terms of how their works might fare in the future. "Younger men, especially [Pierre] Soulages and [Hans] Hartung," Barr advised Burden, are "both excellent and sound investments." He also encouraged Burden to acquire works by older men. "I heartily recommend" Picasso's *Still Life with Guitar*, Barr wrote to Burden, adding that the price seemed "reasonable, though not a bargain. This is a picture that I would like to see come to the museum eventually (if I may be so bold!)."

This correspondence took place well over a year before the museum announced it would form a permanent collection; clearly, discussions about the new policy were well advanced. And dealers and collectors well knew that Barr often served as a broker for works of art they wanted to sell. He wrote to British collector and art critic Roland Penrose, for example, that he had put Burden onto "the big, important early Tanguy you might part with. If he doesn't like it, please send me a photo and I'll try Nelson Rockefeller." As Burden's collection grew, he asked Barr's assistant, Olive Bragazzi, whether she would catalog it "when you have some spare time? I would be glad to pay a fair fee." When Burden built a new house in Mt. Kisco, his architects, Harrison and Abramovitz, wanted Barr to advise on how to hang the collection in it.

The aggressive, corporate scale of collecting among the museum's trustees offered a distinct contrast to the spirit of adventuresome amateurism which had motivated the museum's founders, as exemplified by Abby Rockefeller. When she died of a heart attack, on April 5, 1948, a newspaper editorial called her "the most unconventional and effectual patron of art which America had seen." Although she had sought Barr's advice as eagerly as the collector-trustees of the fifties, Abby was not interested in investment, but rather in "aiding struggling and even hungry artists." Her grandchildren recalled "a handsome woman, smelling of lilac and wearing extravagant hats, who became thick at the ankles . . . in her last years." Stephen Clark recalled a steadying force, smoothing over the museum staff's "bickering, jealousy, and dissension" throughout his stormy presidency during the early forties. "Everybody liked and admired her," he wrote, "and so great was her tact and understanding that, even when she had a disagreeable duty to perform, she left no scars behind."

Behind her dignity lurked a twinkling mischievousness. "Your father gave me a lecture previous to my going to the [museum] dinner," she wrote to one son, "about my talking to Mr. Clark all the evening about the museum, so I went very much chastened, but nevertheless with a small list concealed in my purse of things I really wanted to talk to him about." Two years after she died, Junior asked to be dropped from the museum's mailing list, explaining that he "just did not have time for art that baffle[d him]." Abby's influence on the next generation of Rockefellers remained profound. In addition to Nelson, her son David later served as MOMA president, as did Blanchette Hooker Rockefeller, the wife of another son, John III.

Soon after he became director of the museum collections, Barr embarked on a years-long campaign to woo the affections of another veteran of the amateur era of modern art. She was a cantankerous, elderly maiden lady, an unlikely art connoisseur who happened to own one of the world's most eclectic collections of early modern art. As Barr's father might have wooed the big donors to the church in Baltimore, so the son courted and humored and romanced Katherine S. Dreier.

One of five children of a stern, black-bearded German immigrant, who had made good in the iron import-export business, Dreier had been designated by her parents for a musical career. She instead chose to become a painter, while dedicating most of her energy to the Little Italy Settlement House, one of the first settlement houses in Brooklyn, and to a vacation house for working women founded by her mother. A large and rather clumsy woman, she cut an unlikely figure in the artists' and writers' salons she enjoyed frequenting. She expressed her opinions with Germanic authority and once casually remarked, "I am the reincarnation of Frederick Barbarossa."

Dreier claimed to have founded the first Museum of Modern Art, in 1920, when, with the aid of Marcel Duchamp and Man Ray, she established the *Société Anonyme*, subtitled Museum of Modern Art. She was the first American to own a van Gogh and had also bought early works by Joseph Stella, Francis Picabia, Man Ray, and Duchamp, with whom she was so enchanted that she once followed him to Buenos Aires. On annual buying trips to Europe during the twenties, she had scooped up for virtually no money examples of avant-garde work by just about every artist who claimed to be a Modernist. She exhibited her collection in various

American museums, accompanied by earnest tracts about the spiritual value of abstract art. But by the late thirties, many of the works Dreier owned had only historic value and her own fortune had been consumed by the Depression. Nevertheless, among the hundreds of works carelessly crammed into her house in Wilton, Connecticut, were valuable creations by Kandinsky, Klee, Schwitters, Malevich, Miró, Léger, and Jacques Villon.

Barr had been aware of Dreier's collection since 1927, when he had borrowed some works from it for an exhibition in Boston. He must have known that the *Société Anonyme* also was called the Museum of Modern Art, because that was printed at the bottom of her letterhead. And he may have had some guilt about appropriating this name when the MOMA was founded in 1929; at least he kept these three early letters from her in his private desk file, apart from later correspondence with Dreier. Some years after Dreier's death, Barr was still rationalizing his museum's appropriation of her collection's name. In a memo for his files, he claimed that during the summer of 1929, when the MOMA was getting organized, no one recalled the *Société Anonyme*'s other name, nor was it listed as such in the *Art Index*. When the MOMA organizers learned that "Miss Dreier felt badly about our using the name," Goodyear or Barr himself had written her to apologize or explain. Goodyear insisted that Dreier's use of Museum of Modern Art "was not known to our founders . . . When it was called to our attention, it was too late to make a change."

Barr may have forgotten about the name Dreier had given her collection but not about what it contained. He carefully avoided antagonizing her in any way. In 1930, he refused to review her book, *Western Art and the New Era*, for the *Saturday Review of Literature*. It is "a very muddled book," he wrote, but "as Dreier is a friend of mine and an important collector in modern painting, I do not feel that I could give an opinion about it."

Bitter about the MOMA's success—and especially about its appropriation of the subtitle of her museum—Dreier gave the bulk of her collection to the Yale University Art Museum in 1941. But she retained enough works, most notably Duchamp's *Large Glass*, to arouse Barr's acquisitive ardor. In 1948, after becoming a director of the largely defunct *Société Anonyme*, Barr persuaded Nelson

Rockefeller and several other trustees to give Dreier $500 to help her produce a catalog of her collection. When the work on it languished, Barr wrote several sections himself and frequently invited her to lunch, always tactfully inviting Duchamp as well. At the ceremony when Yale officially accepted her collection, Barr read a letter from Rockefeller apologizing to Dreier for "quite unwittingly assuming the second half of the *Société Anonyme* name. Since then," he flattered, "we have followed your lead not only in name but in several more important ways as our exhibitions and collections clearly show."

By then an original painting by Dreier herself had become part of the MOMA collection; Barr had bought her *Abstract Portrait of Marcel Duchamp* for $500. So abstract was this work that when it was exhibited among a group of new MOMA acquisitions late in 1949, the ultimate mockery of anti-Modernists came true: it was hung upside down. Though it was Dreier's mistake—she had hastily signed the picture in the wrong corner—the MOMA quietly printed a correct version in its next *Bulletin*, removed Dreier's scrawl, and got Duchamp to sign the work with her name in the correct spot.

Sometimes Barr resented all he was doing to court this cranky collector. "She was extraordinarily stingy in her acknowledgement of the days of work I put in on her catalog," he confided to Monroe Wheeler. "I raised nearly $1,000 for it from Yale graduates and by buying one of her pictures, but never a word." Instead, he would get carping letters: "I must confess, Alfred, that I do not like the present mode of presentation," she wrote, in her stiff and earnest Germanic style. "I like to go into a large rectangular room where the different men or periods are hung in groups and sit down and let them speak to me. . . . But this present mode of going from room to room, like a snake . . . is not conducive to study . . . I am at the mercy of the man who makes the program."

Despite Barr's forbearance in the face of such missives, despite his sending of light fixtures and even museum carpenters to Wilton, Connecticut, to devise the proper illumination for the *Large Glass*, despite the many lunches and the long, chatty letters written when Dreier was ill, the big prize Barr was after eluded him. "Although I started out to 'cultivate' . . . [Dreier] . . . I grew fond of

her. Also, I got to like that portrait of Duchamp," Barr confessed to
Soby soon after Dreier died in the spring of 1952. Having failed to
capture his objective while the lady was alive, Barr now hoped that
Soby would be able to persuade Duchamp, who was her executor,
to give the MOMA a good share of all her remaining works.
Duchamp was irritated that neither he nor his brothers, Raymond
Duchamp-Villon and Jacques Villon, had ever been recognized
with an exhibition at the Museum of Modern Art, but he also
appreciated its power to make reputations and lift prices. In 1953,
he gave the museum seven Klees, four Duchamps, two Kandinskys,
a Brancusi, a Léger, and a Mondrian. But the *Large Glass*,
Duchamp's erotic, enigmatic masterpiece, whose full name is *The
Bride Stripped Bare by Her Bachelors, Even*, went to Philadelphia, where most of Duchamp's other works were displayed as part
of the Arensberg Collection.

At about the same time, Barr began a delicate negotiation to
bring another long-sought masterpiece into the museum's collection. In 1933, with no funds at his disposal, he had watched impotently as Sidney Janis spent $33,000 for Henri Rousseau's lush
junglescape *The Dream*. In May 1953, Janis tantalized Barr with
the information that he was ready to accept $125,000 for the
picture from an unnamed New Yorker, a person who was not a
museum trustee and who had vowed never to give the picture to the
MOMA or even to put it back on the market. Barr thought the price
steep, but within a fortnight he was lunching with public relations
mogul Benjamin Sonnenberg, in the hope that he "might secure the
Rousseau for us by waving a want [sic]." Neither Sonnenberg nor
any of his wealthy clients were moved by Barr's wit, but Nelson
Rockefeller came through, paying Janis $31,250 in January 1954
and the rest a year later. When *The Dream* went on display at the
MOMA in September 1954, the *New York Times* reported a rumor
that it had cost more than any other work in the museum's
collection.

Single-minded as he seemed to be in building the MOMA collections, Barr nevertheless found the time to leap into an endless
sideshow of diversions. When Dr. Alfred Kinsey was beginning the
research on his monumental study of American sex habits, Barr
agreed to provide him with the names of artistic types who might

submit to a battery of questions about their intimate lives. When *Life* magazine pictured a black-haired mammoth on its cover, Barr wrote the editors about the stuffed mammoth he had seen in Leningrad in 1928, with "long, cinnamon-colored bristles," and wondered why neither the Smithsonian nor the New York Museum of Natural History displayed such a fabulous beast. In 1953, he found time to embark on a long correspondence with the president of New York's Fifth Avenue Coach company. In gruesome detail, he set forth the perennial litany of New York bus passengers' tribulations: rude drivers, empty buses inexplicably zooming past bus stops, long waits followed by a bunch of buses going in the same direction. After six months of tormenting the company president, Barr took his complaints to the readers of the *New York Times*: "I have had enough," he concluded his catalog of frustrations at the bus stop, and signed it "Irate."

In 1953, Frank Lloyd Wright published a tirade against current architects, especially the devotees of the International Style. As he did so often, a furious Alfred Barr took pencil in hand to denounce Wright's "jealous rancor and patent meanness of spirit. You are a great architect but you serve your greatness shamefully . . . In your magnificent old age . . . you might have shown a little generosity . . . instead you publish Hearstian . . . diatribes which reek with a vanity which can embarrass your friends and comfort your enemies." Barr polished several versions of this letter and then, his rage vented, never sent it.

While diverting himself with petty crusades, and expending great energy and talent to building the museum's collections, Barr also kept one foot in the world of scholarship. Princeton had cited him as "champion of contemporary things before they become respectable" and awarded him an honorary degree as doctor of humane letters in June of 1949. But Barr was still attempting to persuade academic departments of art history to permit graduate students to write dissertations about contemporary art movements. In 1950, Barr begged the conservative art historians at Princeton to accept William Seitz's proposal for a doctoral thesis about Abstract Expressionism. Barr argued that graduate students in other fields, such as natural or social science, had no difficulty when they proposed theses about "the present or recent past"; there was no reason to avoid studying contemporary art. The Princeton art department reluctantly agreed, largely because Seitz, himself an Abstract Expressionist painter, had firsthand information about the movement. Since no member of the Princeton faculty felt qualified to direct Seitz's dissertation, Barr happily agreed to become his adviser.

The academic atmosphere had always exerted a strong magnetism on Barr. Along with his father's tenure as a professor, Barr could recall an uncle who had taught at Princeton Theological Seminary for many years. The ruminative, speculative discussions among Paul Sachs's students at Harvard, the adulation of students at Vassar and Wellesley, the opportunities for leisurely study and writing during summer vacations and sabbaticals—all of these looked particularly attractive to a man beset by managing a staff, humoring cranky collectors, and rushing words into print. Barr's honorary degree from Princeton meant a great deal to him, Seitz's wife, Irma, recalled, although "he tossed it off," his ambivalence about the academic world unresolved. When Seitz took his oral examinations, Barr was pleased to stay overnight in Princeton with the Seitzes, a closeness between mentor and student of which the university disapproved. Barr was up at dawn the morning of the exam, binoculars in hand, to scout the neighborhood for birds. After Seitz received his Ph.D. in 1955, he was hired as a professor of art history, Princeton's first specialist in modern art. In 1960, Barr brought Seitz as a curator to the Museum of Modern Art, where he organized a major exhibition of Monet. There, an observant visitor once spotted him, the consummate connoisseur, gazing thoughtfully at a single painting for an entire day.

Ironically, Barr's most convincing argument to the stodgy Princeton professors had been that Abstract Expressionism was the first new American style to impress Europeans with its "originality, energy, and vitality." The irony of this argument lay in the evident European weakness in scholarship of modern art. John Rewald recalled that in the years just before the Second World War his mentors at the Sorbonne frowned upon his proposed dissertation on Cézanne and urged him to pick a subject no later than Delacroix. Nor had French postwar scholars caught up with more recent trends in modernism. Perusing an outline of *Celebrated*

Painters, a scholarly work planned by Bernard Dorival of the newly established Paris Museum of Modern Art, Barr found much of it "omissive and helter-skelter in the extreme" and exhibiting "extraordinary confusion of ordinarily accepted terminology, as well as ignorance of simple chronology."

When Barr and Soby made their first trip to Paris after the Second World War, they found the French resentful that so many first-rate French modern paintings were now in America, while local museums held only lesser examples of the most important artists of the previous sixty years. French scholarship suffered accordingly. In 1952, Barr dismembered a book about Mondrian by Michael Seuphor, for "too many loose ends, occasional disorder, gaps and outright errors . . . too frequently Seuphor has not looked hard enough at the pictures." But then, he added mockingly, "we do not expect American standards from European scholars working in the 20th century field."

By 1948, packets of catalogs shipped by the Museum of Modern Art were delighting art experts at renowned European museums like Vienna's Albertina and Hamburg's Kunsthalle and were much-sought additions to art libraries from Amsterdam to Belgrade. So eager were the Europeans for what they considered to be models of scholarship in Modernism that in 1949 the Museum of Modern Art arranged to sell any of its books wholesale in Europe at a 40 percent discount and gave any European museum a $100 credit for its first order. To stimulate sales, the museum openly asked for reviews of these works in foreign publications. Barr also saw to it that MOMA-sponsored shows of American art toured overseas, and by 1953, exhibitions like "The American Woodcut Today" and "Twenty-five American Prints" were traveling triumphantly around the European museum circuit.

On his annual trips to Europe, which resumed in 1948, Barr could see for himself that the war had devastated much of the continent's cultural vitality. Among European galleries, abstract art hardly counted; Mondrian, Kandinsky, and Malevich were virtually unknown. Klee's first exhibition at Paris's barren Museum of Modern Art in 1947 drew only 1,500 visitors and a large Léger retrospective attracted just 1,200 souls. As late as 1950, one could buy a Léger in Paris for $120. Where before the war Barr had remained silent about French shortcomings, he was now quite outspoken. To an assistant who gushed that Paris was "perfectly marvelous," Barr tartly disagreed: "Had you known Paris and the French spirit in the Twenties and Thirties as well as I, you would understand why I feel the way I do."

Nevertheless, in 1952 he laid plans for a comprehensive exhibition of American painting there. The Paris Museum of Modern Art's director, Jean Cassou, was "frank about [the] indifference, *chauvinism, méfiance* [suspicion] of [the] French," Barr noted, "but insists that they be shown foreign art anyway." Anxious to show the French how far the barbaric Americans had progressed since the disastrous 1938 show, he drew up a list of works that heavily emphasized abstract American art: John Marin, Arshile Gorky, and Stuart Davis of the older generation, and Pollock, Calder, David Smith, and Theodore Roszak to represent revolutionary new movements. Unlike the critical ambush for the 1938 exhibition, this time only the Communists denounced the show and Cassou begged the MOMA to organize a follow-up exhibition soon.

When the Museum of Modern Art agreed to send three of its most valuable works to Paris for an exhibition at the Orangerie in the spring of 1955, Barr insisted on extraordinary precautions because of "the notorious carelessness of French museums." Cézanne's *Still Life with Apples*, van Gogh's *Starry Night*, and Rousseau's *Sleeping Gypsy* should travel on U.S. Navy ships because the French merchant marine "has a bad record for fires and carelessness concerning cargo," Barr informed museum president Burden. He stipulated that the pictures were to be accompanied at all stages of their journey by "experienced American personnel," and a "commissioner" should be in Paris to guard the pictures and "above all, in case of accident, to control any effort on the part of French restorers to repair the pictures." Furthermore, he wanted an American conservator to inspect them daily and to be on hand when they were packed and unpacked. The French meekly agreed.

By then, Barr was unquestionably the world's leading authority on modern art. His catalogs of the thirties were collector's items and museum people in Paris "greatly admired and envied" his 1946 Picasso book, Janet Flanner (who wrote the *New Yorker*'s "Letter from Paris" under the pseudonym Genêt) informed him.

They "of course can never afford such completion and color, poor devils," she wrote. "That's Europe and America for you; they have the art, we have the money; even when they had the money they did not buy the art, not the moderns . . . anyhow." What sealed Barr's reputation, however, was a work he had been thinking about ever since the MOMA's sketchy 1931 Matisse exhibition but had tackled seriously only after being exiled in the library. This turned into *Matisse: His Art and His Public*, a book published in connection with the most complete retrospective of the artist's work ever held, which opened at the Museum of Modern Art in November 1951.

The book had suffered an inordinately painful gestation, even for Barr. Originally, he had planned only a revision of the catalog he had prepared for the 1931 exhibition. As usual, the revision stayed on his back burner, despite Monroe Wheeler's hortatory memos to get on with it. As soon as the war ended, Barr began giving John Rewald long questionnaires to present to Matisse on Rewald's annual visits to France. Elderly and ailing, the artist would get so tired of answering that he begged Rewald to "put it away." Matisse's daughter, who had been working for years on a *catalogue raisonné* of her father's work, refused to answer Barr's letters. Matisse's son Pierre had a complicated relationship with his father and seemed uninterested in the book. The eccentric Dr. Albert Barnes, who owned many of the world's greatest Matisse paintings, refused to admit Barr to his private museum in Merion, Pennsylvania, and forbade him to reproduce the works in his collection. But the work went forward "inch by inch," Barr reported, even though he lost much time "in clearing the way of misinformation which both Matisse and his French enthusiasts have been accumulating for fifty years."

In the summer of 1950, Barr passed up a trip to Europe and holed up in Greensboro, Vermont, with a dictating machine, in hopes that writing would come more easily that way. Two assistants at the museum typed transcripts and shipped them back to Greensboro for more of Barr's endless tinkering with text. Even though the final product, as always, read smoothly and lucidly, Rewald thought the book's organizational choppiness showed Barr's lack of "facility in writing." Yet by cutting back and forth among various subjects, Rewald said, Barr highlighted new relationships, turning the choppiness into a virtue. Stylistic quibbles aside, however, so packed was the book with new information about the artist and his works that, though Barr in his dedication called it a "work in progress," it remains a definitive study almost four decades after publication.

Reviewers could hardly find enough superlatives to describe *Matisse*'s virtues. "All manner of curious and heretofore unknown data has been unearthed with patience and discretion," wrote Katharine Kuh in the *College Art Journal*. "The total effect of dedicated honesty puts to shame the many haphazard and indiscriminate art books of today." Barr's meticulous chronology both of Matisse's travels and of his works impressed Benedict Nicolson, who reviewed the book in the *Art Bulletin*. He called the book a perfect example of American puritanism in art writing, so fully documented that it reproached European art writing, "where the wildest statements, based on no historical evidence, are allowed to go unchallenged because, in Europe, modern art is not normally treated as an academic study." Munich art history professor Dr. Franz Roh, president of the German Critics' Guild and editor of Germany's best art magazine, *Kunst*, called the book "a masterpiece. . . . This is how monographs about our leading artists should be written."

The outcome was glorious, but the creation of *Matisse* had been so agonizing that Barr diverted himself with fantasies of a Fulbright fellowship in Paris. Late in 1950, with the pressure to complete the Matisse book at its most hectic, Barr drafted a grandiose proposal for a year's study which would "cover the history of abstract art as an international movement," including its influence upon architecture and commercial art, its fate under both totalitarian and democratic regimes, and its ethical and philosophical as well as aesthetic meaning. The anticipation of such a magisterial project must have looked like heaven itself to a man who had spent several years niggling over whether Matisse sketched this flower vase in February or March of 1908, gathering hundreds of illustrations from scores of sources, and shepherding delicate color separations through the press.

For six months, while Monroe Wheeler badgered him for the last bits of copy and Barr decided whether to use pictures of the Barnes

Matisses without the mad doctor's permission, the Fulbright administrators and Barr dickered over the fellowship. Meanwhile, one of the first Fulbright scholars in Paris, Robert Goldwater, and his wife were writing Barr long letters about the miserable working conditions there. Not only had Goldwater and another Fulbright fellow, Millard Meiss, been unable to find an apartment, they were disheartened by antiquated research facilities and uncooperative archivists. "The fact is that art history here is still carried on in the tradition of the bourgeois scholar inheriting and building his own library and working 'privately,'" Goldwater despondently wrote. Meiss had found library research almost impossible and had quit in total frustration before his fellowship was half over. Just as Barr's travails with the Matisse book ended, so did his interest in the Fulbright. He suddenly discovered that the fellowship required that he lecture in French, a language he had never mastered. Moreover, the financial support was such a pittance compared with his museum salary that the whole project was out of the question.

The longing looks at the Fulbright may have been Barr's mid-life search for alternatives to his museum career. With Nelson Rockefeller pushing the appointment of René d'Harnoncourt to the long-vacant post of MOMA director, it was obvious that Barr would never recapture this position; it isn't clear that he even wanted it. Still, the Fulbright fellowships were intended for young scholars, not for a forty-nine-year-old acknowledged expert in modern art and not for a man who had recently refused to lecture at the prestigious Society for Contemporary American Art in Chicago, who had declined to write the definitive article on twentieth-century painting for *Collier's Encyclopedia*, who had refused to serve as visiting scholar in art at the University of Delaware or to lecture on modern artists at Brown University, who had rejected an invitation to give a paper at the American Society for Esthetics, and who had turned down a contract to write a two-volume history of art since 1790 for the authoritative Pelican series.

Instead of seeing the reality of an established, respected leader in a dynamic new field which was beginning to attract not only the cream of younger art scholars but also an unprecedented public, Barr often saw himself in the mirror of a reality more than twenty years old, as struggling, embattled, barely hanging on in the face of lethal onslaughts. In the late twenties, it was true, he had witnessed the German avant-garde ambushed by the Nazis and hounded into exile. And he had visited the Soviet avant-garde in its final autumnal flowering, before the killing Stalinist frost. But in the late forties, Barr was still reacting desperately over each conservative "boo!" He devoted immense energy and time to passing tempests, while complaining that he was "desperately busy" and that "some days here I go crazy sitting on the phone and rushing to meetings—an absurd life!"

Along with Dorothy Miller, Barr was still working almost every Saturday and many Sundays, but he felt he could "never catch up." With colleagues at the museum, he was gentle and constructive with advice. Frequently, he would drift off into "a dreamlike mood," said MOMA curator Alicia Legg, "and then one couldn't break through." Sometimes he would pass John Rewald in the hallway without even saying hello. Then, perhaps two days later, Rewald would feel an arm on his shoulder and turn to Barr's "How's it going?" One afternoon Barr quietly approached architectural historian G. E. Kidder-Smith standing on a balcony overlooking the sculpture garden. "Which one do you think is the best sculpture out there?" asked Barr. Kidder-Smith named Lachaise's *The Source*; Barr listened attentively without revealing his own favorite, if he had one.

He frankly admitted that his taste tended "toward a certain severity, rather than toward a sensual or hedonistic kind of painting." Over the years, Barr had also emphasized the historical importance or influence of a work of art from the determination of its quality, "a far more debatable and intangible factor." In his own surroundings, he was austere. The Barrs' apartment struck Rewald as monkish, with hardly any pictures on the walls, and his taste as "unsensuous . . . purely intellectual." Another colleague noted Barr's aversion to eroticism in art. Much as Barr admired the work of Brancusi, he rejected the sculptor's *Adam and Eve* for the museum because some of the trustees thought it obscene. Barr's austere taste also carried over into his characteristic exhibition style—uncrowded white walls broken at key places by a charcoal gray panel at right angles.

Occasionally, however, another Alfred Barr would emerge from behind the prim and pinched schoolmaster and scholar. Sidney Janis treasured several days he spent with Barr in Paris during the 1950s. Sightseeing and gallery hopping, Janis "discovered a different Alfred Barr," he said. "It was a revelation; he was amusing and interesting." To an English friend who had sent him a deerstalker cap, Barr confessed that he was "an irregular Baker Street irregular" and that he had worn the cap in Central Park "with good effect." A colleague at a museum opening once complimented Barr on his elegant tuxedo and was flabbergasted when "he unbuttoned the jacket to reveal . . . red suspenders."

Despite such rare frivolity, Barr was a classic workaholic, whose family could either join him in his work-related activities or adjust to his perpetual absence. Marga no longer pitched in with his desperate last-minute drives to complete an exhibition or catalog and sadly recalled that "when Alfred finally would come home he was too tired" for family or social life, "and he came home later and later." But she accompanied him on European foraging trips almost every summer, translating, taking notes, and keeping track of his busy schedule. Though she found Greensboro dull by comparison with Europe, Marga spent many weeks there during the summers, keeping their household and social life going while Barr did his writing.

While her parents were in Europe, Victoria was sent to summer camp, and during the winters, her father was seldom at home. It was a special occasion when he found the time to take her for an outing and even then, it was often related to his work; for example, an excursion to an exhibition at the Met when she was eleven years old. A disappointment to her father because her dyslexia hampered her school work, Victoria may well have decided to become an artist in order to gain her father's esteem.

Though she was intelligent and well-read, Marga was impulsively outspoken and could be vapid, snobbish, and cruelly tactless. At an art people's party she once turned to Joella Bayer, who was then married to gallery owner Julien Levy, and observed: "You and I got the last two real men in the world—and they're not very much men either." In a milieu which tolerated many variations of sexuality, Alfred Barr was remarkable for his abstemiousness and prudery. It is doubtful that his many close relationships with men, some of whom were homosexuals, ever went beyond intellectual intimacy. Nor is there any evidence that his marriage was particularly ardent. The Barrs generally slept in separate beds and the birth of Victoria seemed to surprise even her parents.

However, when Barr went off to Greensboro alone in the summer of 1954, because Marga needed a sinus operation, she wrote to him with exuberant affection:

> I watched and watched you from the platform before the train hauled out but you are not susceptible to magnetism. . . . I hope all is delightfully fresh and springlike there—as I remember Greensboro in its best moments. Do go see the columbine for me and if the one you planted thrives, do try to transplant some others.
>
> Walk and wander alone in the evening for the lovely and beloved hermit thrush. It evokes all that is best in calm hope and yearning.
>
> Never worry about me—the trouble with me is that I am an only child and I thrive on being alone.

Two weeks later, while recovering from her operation, she again wrote a long letter, full of social chitchat and news of mutual acquaintances. "My dearest love to you," she added, "and do go see some people, especially the [John] Gunthers. Ever amused at sheer existence." But Barr had little talent for casual socializing. A fellow guest at one lunch at the Gunthers' recalled such desultory conversation that "Gunther left the table for the companionship of a local plumber who was doing repairs in the kitchen." Though he worked a good deal during his sojourns in Vermont, Greensboro represented a vital safety valve in Barr's hectic life. Many years later, a young neighbor recalled being taught by Barr how to catch butterflies and mount them and Barr walking for hours along Campbell's Creek with young people, "supervising tadpole catching" and lecturing on how they changed into frogs. "We always prayed we'd be asked to go with him on whatever scientific quest he had in mind and often we were." At the lake, the boy watched Marga swim out to a raft, with a basket of mending on her head and Alfred joining her "with field glasses and an intent look." Sometimes when Barr was working on a book, the youngster visited Marga, who might be cooking green noodles and singing "Oh, my Bulgie, my little Bulgerino!" And sometimes the boy would encounter the Barrs on a late afternoon walk and listen raptly to their talk "about the beautiful light and the porcupines in trees and the special soup eaten on a hillside."

Although they may have struck a young neighbor lad as idyllic, Barr's summers in Greensboro were far from idle. When he and Marga spent time in the little Vermont vacation town, his secretaries at the museum industriously dealt with the content of heavy packets from Barr that arrived in almost every day's mail. They were stuffed with letters he had scribbled out, drafts of writings, and plans for exhibitions. Marga made the best of her isolation in Vermont, the price for being the wife of an important figure in the art—and social—world. The packets from Vermont often contained her housewifely instructions about checking accounts, mail at the New York apartment, or a pressure cooker to be sent up. Devotedly, the women in Barr's office—Mimi Catlin, Marie Alexander, Olive Bragazzi, Helen Franc, Betty Chamberlain, Betsy Jones— would see to it that he answered this or that important letter, met Monroe Wheeler's "final deadline" for some writing project, read a crucial report, or decided on an acquisition. Along with the latest museum gossip, they gave him sprightly reports about New York's beastly summer heat or blessed showers and sometimes wondered what to do about cryptic notes he had left on his desk.

In the fall, Barr would return to the barricades full-time. For years, he felt driven to answer mindless extremist attacks on modern art by an obscure congressman, George A. Dondero. No matter how ridiculous Dondero's charges that modern art was a Communist plot, Barr felt constrained to answer and to muster allies. After Eleanor Roosevelt spoke at the MOMA in 1949 about the problem of Russian censorship of the arts, Barr wrote to her that he was "deeply disturbed that the same problem has arisen in our country." To the Princeton graduate school alumni letter in 1950, he decried "the wave of reactionary hostility toward modern art. . . . The ignorant Congressman is apparently inspired by a group of academic artists, just as the Nazi and Soviet politicians were inspired and abetted by academic artists in Germany and Russia."

Barr leaped into action in 1951 when New York's conservative Francis Cardinal Spellman attempted to ban an Italian movie, *The Miracle*, because of the sacrilege he saw in its story of an insane girl who bears a child by a shepherd she thinks is St. Joseph. Barr fired off letters and cables to protest. When he persuaded a prominent Catholic layman and president of the American Federation of the Arts to deplore this censorship, Barr was so elated that he called an assistant at home: "We landed Otto Spaeth!" When the New York Supreme Court decided the issue, the dedicated women on Barr's staff thought it important enough to cable him in Europe: "Unanimous Supreme Court ruled out ban for sacrilege hooray."

Like a general still fighting the last war, Barr pressed all of his tremendous prestige and energy against a pillar which was already crumbling. Sometimes his impassioned defense breathed new life into the dying debate over modern art. In a December 1952 article in *The New York Times Magazine*, for example, Barr denounced the "fantastic falsehood" that modern art is "communistic." Predictably, that fervent sermon brought in one conservative response deploring that modern art "is destined only for the pseudo-elite," and another from radical leftist Rockwell Kent, who argued that abstraction was "the inevitable and perfect expression of a moribund culture . . . the cultural counterpart of the atomic bomb."

Although one could always find quotable jabs at Modernism along the extremist fringes of public opinion, the great moderate mass among educated Americans had by this time fully embraced the notion of abstract—or virtually any other kind of—art. Late in 1953, when Dwight Macdonald was preparing his amusing profile of Barr for the *New Yorker*, he was hard-pressed to find anything revolutionary or threatening about what had become a quintessential New York landmark, the Museum of Modern Art, or its "soul," Alfred H. Barr, Jr. "Shy, frail, low of voice and scholarly of mien," Macdonald wrote, "the austerity of his beak-nosed bespectacled face [is] reprieved only by the kind of secret smile one sees on archaic Greek statues or on the carefully locked features of a psychoanalyst." He was "the only person who can answer 'Have you got a minute?' with 'No.'" He was "intensely absent-minded" and "lacked any capacity for small talk." Though Macdonald found his personality "as low-keyed and ascetic as that of his creation is vivid and worldly," he was also impressed with Barr's passion, "having the scholar's greed for data, the intellectual's joy in refining the crude stuff of reality, the pedagogue's pleasure in instructing and explaining and the crusader's righteous zeal."

Interestingly, Barr did not reveal to Macdonald (or anyone else) his favorite pictures in the museum collection. Rather, he provided him with a list of the MOMA's "most important" acquisitions of the previous six years, including Picasso's *Night Fishing at Antibes*, Brancusi's *Fish*, Chagall's *Calvary*, and Maillol's *Mediterranean*. He also listed the museum's most valuable paintings: van Gogh's *Starry Night*, Rousseau's *Sleeping Gypsy*, Picasso's *Demoiselles d'Avignon*, Léger's *Three Women*, and Cézanne's *Bathers*. Perhaps there is a clue to Barr's personal favorites in the two pictures which appeared on both lists: Picasso's *Three Musicians* and Matisse's *Red Studio*.

Barr insisted on reviewing the drafts of Macdonald's articles, pounding them with penciled scrawls as pitilessly as he pummeled his own prose. He was troubled by "a slight sense of David and Goliath in the piece," Barr complained and thought that Stephen Clark and Nelson Rockefeller had been slighted, as well as d'Harnoncourt, Soby, and Miller. Furthermore, the MOMA did not disavow, as Macdonald's draft had claimed, his definition of an automobile as "hollow, rolling sculpture." Rather, as Barr edited it, "a notice was posted at a later show of cars: 'Automobiles are not expected to achieve the spiritual insight of art.'" As the profile crept contentiously toward publication, Barr was pleased that he had persuaded Macdonald to throw "the renaissance-condottiere atmospheric description of the museum's internal life into the past." To museum president Burden, Barr reported that "by dint of a great deal of time and argument," he had countered the "*New Yorker* compulsion to disparage." Having worked for days to incorporate Barr's revisions into his manuscript, Macdonald grumbled, "The hell of it is that your objections were so damned *reasonable*.

I've not hitherto felt forced to do anything like so big a job of revision on a manuscript."

Asking Burden to "say a few disarming words" to the trustees about the profile, Barr asserted, "I wish I had never got involved in this, but did so I suppose through the corruption of modesty and lapse of wisdom which affects people in middle age." The MOMA publicity department and the coordinating committee had urged him to cooperate with Macdonald, Barr explained, because they thought it would be good for the museum. Torn between modesty and pride, worried about offending trustees or donors, Barr fled to Milan as the two articles were appearing; he left a memo for d'Harnoncourt that he had done his "damnedest" to make the museum director look good.

Despite Barr's agile modesty, the *New Yorker* profile gave modern art the smart set's seal of approval: "It would appear that the highbrows have finally convinced the middlebrows that modern art is fashionable and even enjoyable," Macdonald wrote. The "lowbrows" who were still dubious, he wrote, included Harry Truman, Communists, and Pres. Dwight D. Eisenhower, who had responded to a Léger mural at the United Nations with, "To be modern, you don't have to be nuts." For the rest, the "nine-ring circus" at 11 West Fifty-third Street was not only a showplace for the best modern painting and sculpture but also "a community center, a movie theater, a library, a publishing house, a school, a provider of shows for other institutions, an arbiter of taste for everything from frying pans to country houses."

As the museum celebrated its twenty-fifth anniversary, articles in many leading American publications lauded its achievements and Barr as its guiding genius. But some magazines also were beginning to note the extraordinary profits to be made by following the museum's taste. *Vogue*, for one, devoted four pages to picturing "33 blue chips" as examples of the museum's "record of rewarding speculation." Among them was Brancusi's "whoosh of metal," *Bird in Space*, which in 1926 "might have cost $3,500, but now the price would be nearer $12,000." A dozen years later, cosmetics tycoon Helena Rubinstein would buy the twentieth of thirty fresh castings of this sculpture for $140,000. A Miró for which the museum might have paid $250 in 1936 would cost about $5,000 in 1954, the article said. By 1966, a comparable painting cost $85,000. Among Americans, the magazine mentioned Jackson Pollock, whose work sold for about $600 when the MOMA acquired *She-Wolf* in 1944 and was selling a decade later for $4,000. Within eight years, a Pollock would reach $36,300 and then escalate wildly into millions.

To coincide with the anniversary exhibition he created, Barr put together a sumptuous picture volume, *Masters of Modern Art*, and saw to it that some five hundred free copies of it were sent to scholars and institutions all over the world, even to two Soviet magazines he considered important. A *New York Times* editorial benignly commended the MOMA's "unique spirit and atmosphere. . . . Young couples hand in hand, [Helen] Hokinson ladies, students, artists, businessmen, children, rich collectors may be enthralled or annoyed, pleased or angered, excited or outraged, but they all enjoy themselves."

Enthusiastic reviews greeted both the exhibition and the book, although Barr confessed to Peggy Guggenheim that he had barely survived "the ordeal" of creating them. "I am too old now for these desperate institutional forced marches." Praise for Barr rolled in. *The Nation* thought the entire show was "a tribute to [his] wisdom and discrimination." Philip Johnson wrote that "the museum to me means Alfred Barr, no matter what changes in title might be involved." Thanks to his discrimination and knowledge, wrote a conservative English critic, the museum now owned "unquestionably the greatest collection of the advanced painting of our time in the world."

But a price had been paid for the accumulation of so much valuable aesthetic property. The book which attracted such admiration was not a scholarly study of a particular movement or group or country, as many of Barr's earlier catalogs had been. Rather, it displayed the masterpieces he had himself anointed—the gospel according to Barr, as it were. It contained little background information as to why this or that work or artist had been chosen. The book, like the exhibition it described, was more authoritarian than authoritative. For the first time, Barr insisted on printing the names of every donor to the museum. The list would prove "valuable and interesting," Barr explained without further details to Philip Johnson. However, such a crass list indicated that the museum's interest had perhaps tipped from exhibiting and collecting the most progressive art of its time to amassing goods. Accordingly, the most valuable of these goods—paintings—were allotted by far the greatest amount of space. Barr may have felt uneasy about this because he rationalized it at length in a memo to Richard Griffith, director of the museum's film library. He blamed "the general attitude of the board of trustees," the potential market for the book, and difficulty with illustrations for emphasizing painting so heavily and assured Griffith that the space allotment did not reflect a lesser status for films as art. Perhaps not in Barr's eyes, but in the eyes of trustees who were also collectors, painting clearly was fundamental.

Mingled with the praise for the exhibition, too, were disturbing flickerings of doubt. The museum seemed to have settled into placid middle age, wrote veteran critic Henry McBride, who had covered the MOMA's opening exhibition in 1929. "The array is quite wonderful," he wrote, "giving a resumé of the world's recent aesthetic activities with a thoroughness truly amazing." But he regretted that there appeared to be "no more rumpuses." In a review titled "Aging Modern," *Time* thanked the MOMA for giving the public "data on Dada, the dirt on Dali, Picasso's punchlines, Matisse's more colorful moments, and de Kooning's brash blooming," but worried that the recent decision to form a permanent collection "may be the Modern's first mark of increasing age." Even from within the museum family, there were rumblings of discontent. Edgar Kaufmann, who had developed the MOMA industrial design department into a lively and influential arbiter of everyday taste, left in 1954. "It was going off the track," he recalled many years later. "Instead of finding out what the world was doing, the museum was telling the world what to do." When the museum threw a giant birthday party for itself, President Burden pointed out that the artist is "the leader whose genius we follow. The vigor and excellence of his work is the lifeblood of all our endeavors." Yet among the hundreds of guests who swarmed elegantly through the

MOMA's brilliantly installed galleries on opening night, Marcel Duchamp and Edward Hopper were the only invited artists.

After twenty-five years on the barricades, Barr had successfully defended the faith against all its enemies. But after so many forced marches in the long campaign, had he stepped beyond faith into dogma?

10

EXPANDING THE CANON

F or the time being I have no leisure time at all," Barr lamented in the fall of 1956. "The museum year is worse than ever and I am twice as old as I was two years ago." His life had always been hectic, crammed with self-imposed duties and time-consuming diversions, but by the mid-1950s, the whirlwind of activities inside the museum was reinforcing a cyclone of excitement in the New York art world. A profusion of modern art galleries had sprouted in New York; no leisurely Saturday rambles among a few outposts of the avant-garde could suffice to give a clear picture of all the city's new artists and their works. By 1957, Barr was "ashamed to say" that he had not visited any artists' studios for three years. Striving to keep up, Barr had joined The Club, a lively, informal gathering of artists and art hangers-on who assembled at various Greenwich Village venues for heated discussions-cum-parties at 9:30 P.M. every Friday night. Most of the New York School artists drifted in and out, along with sophisticated critics like Thomas B. Hess, managing editor of the *Art News*, and Frank O'Hara, a poet and later a MOMA curator. Barr was an official member of The Club from 1955 on, but he seldom had time to attend and always had to be reminded to pay his twelve dollars in annual dues.

While Barr magisterially purchased expensive art for the museum and its trustees, he took scant interest in his own finances. After Stephen Clark fired him as MOMA director in 1943, he was paid only $6,000 per year; this amount gradually inched back up toward $10,000 per year, his starting salary in 1929. Clark was relentless in insisting that every penny Barr received from outside work should be turned over to the museum. When Barr became director of the collections in 1947, he bargained desperately over his duties and powers, but not over money. He did get minimal royalties for *Picasso: Fifty Years of His Art*, and later for the Matisse book, but he had to beg Nelson Rockefeller for even those. "The cost of living has caught up with my financial margin and passed it," he wrote to Rockefeller in 1947. "We have lowered our standard of living without being able to break even except through some very uncertain windfalls."

In 1954, when his daughter, Victoria, was at Radcliffe, he had to sell a Matisse to make ends meet. "I spent many hours pouring [sic] over the checkbook and as usual we are quite broke," Marga wrote to him in Greensboro in 1954. "Please don't cash any check without letting me know." While convalescing from an expensive sinus operation, she was calculating how much it cost per day to live in New York as compared with Greensboro. A few months later, Barr had to postpone a fifty-dollar donation to a memorial fund for dealer Curt Valentin because he was still paying Marga's medical bills. And even when he retired in 1968, a colleague told the MOMA's official historian that he doubted that Barr ever made much more than the original $10,000 per year. The Barrs' apartment was never redecorated after the days when Barr languished on his living room couch in pajamas and robe after being dismissed as MOMA director in 1943.

Far more than money, health problems afflicted Barr all his life. The sleeplessness which had forced him to take a year-long sabbatical in the early thirties continued to trouble Barr and sometimes flared up disastrously. In 1953, he was under doctor's orders to lie down for an hour before dinner "to help cure end-of-the-season insomnia." Flu, colds, and exhaustion frequently kept him from his museum office. Though he would try to carry on at home, he frequently felt the lash of duties undone, letters unanswered, writing postponed. In the summer of 1955, he fell ill with flu in Barcelona and was laid low with three relapses within a few months. Because of his sleep disorders, Barr was a connoisseur of all-night radio; a new program, "Music Through the Night," he wrote to David Sarnoff, president of NBC, in 1954, was "a vast improvement over Musak through the night." When he overheard a group of MOMA women employees one day chatting about an intriguing new product, stockings attached to panties, he stuck his head through the door, saying he'd heard of that novelty on all-night radio: "They're called panty-legs."

The growing complexity of the museum and of his role there did not seem to concentrate Barr's interests, but rather left him exposed to—and seduced by—a multitude of interesting, time-consuming byways. He carried on a long correspondence with Gleb Botkin, son of the last court physician to Nicholas II of Russia, who had founded a Chapel of Aphrodite somewhere in New Jersey and who called himself its chief Aphrodisiast. Barr never visited the chapel but believed Botkin was "a serious if eccentric individual." Barr was also intrigued by a Chicago designer who had developed a way of cutting women's clothes to fit without darts or pleats. "It seemed to me not only skillful and beautiful," Barr wrote of the sample Charles James had sent him, "but somehow to go way beyond the ordinary limits of the fashionable. It was, I felt, a work of art." More than simply complimenting his work, Barr actually offered to help James start a foundation to train disciples, to counter "the disintegrating effects of mass production and the numbing corruption of advertising." Sometimes it seemed as though Barr sought distractions from his distractions. During a fast-moving European trip, with memos and letters flying across the Atlantic, Barr suddenly discovered that he needed "badly to read about elephants" and asked his secretary to ship him the bestselling novel on the subject, *The Roots of Heaven*.

Like many brilliantly multisided individuals, Barr had developed a remarkably counterproductive working style to deal with stress and anxiety: the busier he was and the more ramified the decisions he faced, the more he was attracted by trivial, periph-

eral, and ultimately meaningless side issues. Having received a
postcard advertising a triangular watch, for example, Barr could
not resist writing a letter expressing his revulsion at both "the
vulgarity of the card's color and design, and . . . the design of the
watch itself." Commenting on an article by the director of the
Smithsonian, S. Dillon Ripley, Barr agreed, "I too am a strong
believer in the Abominable Snowman." He sent two postcard reproductions of religious paintings in the MOMA collection to a high
school sophomore writing a term paper on the world's major religions and referred her to the *International Journal of Religious
Education* for more data. To an inquiry from an eighth-grade class
in Elkhart, Indiana, about a "secret painting" Matisse was working on when he died, Barr sent a detailed reply revealing that it
actually was the design for a circular stained-glass window commissioned by Nelson Rockefeller as a memorial to his mother.

While wrestling with budgets worth millions and exhibitions
that would leave a lasting imprint on the history of art, Barr
exchanged literally dozens of letters with an elderly, poverty-
stricken, and completely unknown artist named John Cournos.
Back in 1937, the artist had apparently given some prints to Barr,
who had then passed them along to a gallery to be sold. The gallery
had closed long ago and almost thirty years later, the artist was
asking for either the prints or the proceeds of the sale. After two
years of correspondence Barr was unable to trace the prints and
finally sent Cournos a fifty-dollar bill, writing, "Just so you will not
feel under any obligation to me, let me explain that I found this in
the back seat of a taxi not long ago."

All of this smacked more of the pastoral work expected of a
conscientious minister than that of the director of a great public art
collection. William Seitz's wife, Irma, was flabbergasted when,
after a casual conversation about strange, unexplained phenomena,
Barr sent her a book that described all manifestations of sub-
humans since the Ice Age. He found it "tantalizing," he wrote.

To the editors of letters columns in New York newspapers, Barr
was a dream correspondent. He reacted to local events speedily,
sharply, concisely, and frequently. He was incensed that while New
York mayor Robert Wagner in 1957 refused to greet King Saud of
Arabia on grounds that he was anti-Jewish and Marshal Tito of

Yugoslavia because he was a Communist, the mayor nevertheless welcomed Fascist Francisco Franco of Spain. "If the mayor wants to snub tyrants, he should snub them all!" Barr wrote to the editor of the *Herald-Tribune*, signing himself "A Protestant (and a voter too!)." As in many of his letters to the editor, he asked to remain anonymous "since I do not want to involve the institution where I work."

Concurrently, Barr engaged in a protracted epistolary campaign against New York's imperious parks commissioner Robert Moses over plans to develop Central Park's bucolic Ramble. He deplored that Moses had "once more given way to his obsession for turning greensward into concrete. . . . This spring, those who used to find refuge from city sights and sounds by walking up the east side of the Ramble will find the sweet song of birds accompanied by the idyllic slamming of car doors, the grinding of gears, and the stench of gasoline. Yes, you guessed it! Another parking lot." This salvo was signed "Irate Rambler," and Barr accompanied it with personal letters to the *New York Times*'s managing editor and editorial page editor, urging it be published despite the newspaper's "reputation for avoiding any criticism of Robert Moses." Apparently the *Times* refused to print another anonymous missive on the subject because a second letter drafted by Barr, which appeared two weeks later—"What tact! What taste! What a triumph for the bulldozer and the concrete mixer!"—was signed by his secretary, Marie Alexander.

Ever since the thirties, Barr had waged a running skirmish against magazine and book editors over a popular layout device to bleed reproductions of paintings into the margin of a page. After trimming, small portions of the original would disappear, much to Barr's indignation. "One loses the sense of definition which the rectangular format of the canvas creates," Barr complained to the editor of art publishing house Harry N. Abrams. Barr fumed to Douglas Cooper, who had transgressed in a 1959 catalog of a Picasso exhibition, that "bleeding pictures is barbarous mayhem, comparable to cutting off the first and last lines of a sonnet." By the same token, verbal sloppiness often drew Barr's fire. After receiving a news release from an art film society which called *The Childhood of Maxim Gorki* "a classic of humanist cinema," Barr tartly demanded to know how this movie differed "from a 'humanist' point of view" from other recent biographical films.

For several decades, too, Barr persistently volunteered for jury duty in the New York courts, serving for weeks or months, even as he fretted about how distracting it was. "I am booked for a European lecture series in less than a month and have not been able to find the time even to outline what I shall say," he wrote to a friend in November 1958. "The situation is little short of desperate."

Certainly Barr would have been unable to indulge in these quixotic forays had not the helm of the museum been in the steady, competent hands of René d'Harnoncourt. A Viennese with vague Hapsburg noble connections, he had spent many years in Mexico, collecting folk art and dealing in antiques. In 1930, he married an American and emigrated to the United States. He directed a radio program, organized occasional exhibitions of primitive art, lectured in art history at Sarah Lawrence College, managed the Indian Arts and Crafts Board for the United States government, and worked with Nelson Rockefeller on Latin American art exhibitions. In 1944, with Nelson Rockefeller's enthusiastic support, d'Harnoncourt became a MOMA vice president for foreign activities and director of the Department of Manual Industries. Three years later, he was named chairman of the museum's coordinating committee and director of curatorial departments and in 1949 became the museum's director. It was typical of his smooth, reassuring manner to tell an interviewer that he planned no "startling innovations; things are going just perfectly."

From the beginning, d'Harnoncourt treated Barr as an indispensable resource. He accepted the post as MOMA director specifically on condition that Barr stay, and his aides frequently gnashed their teeth over what they saw as capitulation to Barr's prickly demands and sometimes quirky, inefficient ideas. At the same time, d'Harnoncourt tried to smooth the flinty edges of Barr's stubbornness. When Barr wanted to borrow some of Stephen Clark's pictures, d'Harnoncourt suggested he revise his letter to the dour ex-president to assure him that his precious objects would be shown only "within the museum walls" as Clark was "now so obsessed by the risk of travelling exhibitions."

Barr and d'Harnoncourt were almost the same age, but otherwise they were a study in contrasts. Physically, Barr was slender, slight, bespectacled, frail-looking, and pale, while d'Harnoncourt was a huge and hearty man, 6'6" tall, size 14½ shoes, a 37½-inch sleeve, "more than the average orangutan could say," he jovially told a *New Yorker* interviewer. Barr's education had been traditionally academic and his entire career had been devoted to the museum; d'Harnoncourt's schooling was eclectic and his career was a checkerboard of challenges. Barr's style was cool, puritanical, critical, ascetic, evangelical; d'Harnoncourt's was flexible, tolerant, easy-going, gemütlich. Barr's family had deep roots in the heartland of American Protestantism; d'Harnoncourt was "very Catholic," with a Central European aristocratic urbanity. Where Barr enjoyed confrontation and rigorous debate, d'Harnoncourt slid over disagreements on a carpet of Viennese whipped cream. Barr used his rapier intellect to drive a committee to his point of view; d'Harnoncourt patiently drew elaborately baroque embellishments on the agenda before him (later published as *d'Hoodles*) and then when the tedious committee wrangle subsided, calmly offered a decision.

The wonder of it is that these two dissonant personalities not only worked together harmoniously for more than two decades but also developed such genuine mutual respect and admiration. D'Harnoncourt frequently asserted that his primary task at the museum was the care and feeding of Alfred Barr. While Barr sometimes resented d'Harnoncourt and fiercely protected his domain, said Philip Johnson, "the two of them worked together because they had to, to keep the 'dowagers' happy." Furthermore, Barr could not help but admire the qualities in his nominal boss that he felt lacking in himself: "René was an excellent diplomat, subtle, sometimes with Viennese indirection but effective and iron-willed," Barr would say, "a publicist who did not have to write, an optimistic financier, an administrator through persuasion and kindness . . . very rarely did his subordinates feel a dominating hand."

Perhaps the two men worked together so smoothly because they shared the museum person's most pervasive secret vice: cupidity. While the art collector may struggle to pull the skimpy mantle of appreciation over his naked need to possess, the museum professional commands an ample cloak of scholarship, connoisseurship, and authority to muffle his comparable acquisitive lust. As a dealer in art and antiques, d'Harnoncourt had considerable practical exposure to the vagaries and vices of collectors. For Barr, the hungry years when little or no acquisition funds were at hand were an education in the most sophisticated stratagems for stocking the museum's collections. Together, Barr and d'Harnoncourt comprised a formidable team of patient, persuasive, resourceful shepherds, gently but persistently gathering great works of modern art into the museum's fold.

Aided by tax laws which allowed donors to take immediate, generous write-offs while retaining possession until they died, the two men developed refined techniques for attracting handsome gifts to the museum. The museum's frequent exhibitions of works from private collections during the late fifties did more than flatter the owners; the MOMA seal of approval also enhanced the value of these works and the museum's chances for eventually adding them to its collection. But many collectors also played coy games. Albert E. Gallatin, who was also a painter, for example, dangled his excellent array of early Modernists before a number of museum directors, attempting to get his own mediocre canvases into their collections. Gallatin invited Barr to lunch and pointedly told him that he had lunched with Henry Francis Taylor of the Met on the previous day. Gallatin insisted that he be named curator of his own collection and that the entire array be displayed during his lifetime. That was too much even for Barr's acquisitive lust. "I made no gesture toward it," he wrote, and the Gallatin collection ended up at the Philadelphia Museum of Art.

The collector finds the game of cat and mouse with museum folk so delicious, John Walker, director of the National Gallery observed, that he becomes "a master escape artist . . . refus[ing] to be pinned down because once that happens, the game is over." With this game in mind, Barr and d'Harnoncourt in 1958 began a series of exhibitions whose only unifying theme was that all the works shown had been given or promised to the Museum of Modern Art. Once a work was promised, the museum's attorney drew up a letter of agreement which would then become a part of the donor's estate. This would persuade the executors and heirs, said Richard Koch, the lawyer who wrote scores of these letters, "to take the wishes of the donor seriously." The periodic exhibitions of works given or promised were designed "to make sure that the donors stuck to their agreement," said Koch. "They would have been embarrassed to back out, once the work had been shown at the museum."

Even more than exhibitions of what they owned and what they were giving, however, donors craved intimate contact with the professionals at the museum. For years, Olga Guggenheim, the donor of many masterpieces, would telephone Dorothy Miller every two weeks or so and shyly ask if she had time for a visit that afternoon. Of course Miller had time. Over the years, she spent hundreds of hours in the back seat of Mrs. Guggenheim's black limousine, retailing museum gossip while the chauffeur drove aimlessly around midtown Manhattan. Curator William Seitz once declined an invitation to spend the weekend at the Pocantico estate of Blanchette and John D. Rockefeller III. D'Harnoncourt soon appeared in Seitz's office, asking, "What's this about you can't go for the weekend to Pocantico?" So, of course, Seitz canceled a previous engagement and went. In pursuit of donors, said art critic Hilton Kramer, "they all went and went and went." And when they got there, recalled Irma Seitz, it was enjoyable, although "when you visit people like that, well, you know you have to sing for your supper." On Sunday morning, Blanchette Rockefeller invited William Seitz into her gallery to show him a Rouault and a Picasso and to ask: "Which one should I buy?"

For a while, the museum even loaned parts of its collection to decorate the offices and homes of generous donors, but this practice stopped abruptly when a trustee who had given a valuable work spotted it hanging in the offices of a large construction company. Barr considered the donor's anger excessive but conceded that "the collection was formed for public use rather than for loans to private institutions." He cited this embarrassing case to David Rockefeller, who had requested similar loans to decorate Rockefeller Institute. Barr, Miller, and William Lieberman then selected works for the Institute to purchase. Soon afterward, David Rockefeller decided to form a collection for the Chase Bank, purchasing works of art from all the places where the bank had branches. Barr agreed to serve on the selection committee, provided that Dorothy Miller could be his deputy. Miller was gratified that the Rockefellers "believed in art" and found it "great fun" to visit galleries and artists' studios in behalf of the bank's collection.

Indeed, the line between official duties and private favors to benefactors became increasingly blurred. When Clare Booth Luce returned to New York in 1956 from Italy, where she had been ambassador, her secretary phoned the MOMA to ask d'Harnoncourt to supervise the hanging of her pictures. Mr. Barr would be acceptable for the task, she implied, and if both men were unavailable, "perhaps Mr. [Nelson] Rockefeller would do it, since he had been at the apartment several times."

"The successful curator," wrote John Walker, "is one who can sense and act upon the subtle nuances that influence collectors, nuances that often have very little to do with the intrinsic beauty or value of works of art." And so Barr willingly advised Texas department store magnate Stanley Marcus that $1,000 "would not be excessive" for a German Expressionist painting by Alexei von Jawlensky, "but $800 might be fairer." He provided museum employees to help a New York psychiatrist and his wife, a *New Yorker* staffer, in rehanging their collection; Dorothy Miller passed this task on to Lieberman, writing that "Alfred wishes to be good to them because they own several very important paintings by Klee, including *Mask of Fear*." Because some of the organizers were also collectors, Barr sat through a Hotel Pierre luncheon celebrating Israel's tenth anniversary and dutifully confronted supreme of fresh fruit fantaisie, stuffed chicken with French peas and candied sweet potatoes, salad, and fruit tarts. He persuaded Jock Whitney and David Rockefeller to lend their Utrillos to a Hadassah benefit exhibition because the sponsors, Mr. and Mrs. Siegfried Kramarsky, owned a van Gogh: "I have set my cap, or rather the Museum's cap, for the *Dr. Gachet*." The picture then was already sixty-six years old, hardly suitable for a museum of modern—meaning recent—art.

Such is the fickleness of donors, however, that *Dr. Gachet* and another van Gogh belonging to the Kramarskys were simply passed on to their children when the couple died during the 1960s. After loaning the second picture, a painting of part of a railroad bridge over the Rhone River, to the Metropolitan's popular blockbuster *Van Gogh in Arles* in 1986, the daughter coolly consigned the picture to Christie's, where it was auctioned on June 29, 1987, for $20.2 million. Her father had bought the picture in 1932 for about $8,800.

In 1956, such an immense windfall would have been unthinkable, but the profits to be made on works by what Barr called the nineteenth-century ancestors of Modernism were already substantial. The museum was confronting a painful paradox: there was precious little truly contemporary art to be acquired for free, since the people who collected recent works were not yet ready to give them away simply for a tax deduction or the social esteem of being a museum benefactor. Instead, the museum was harvesting gifts and bequests from the generation which was ready to think about its estates, people who still considered nineteenth-century artists like Vuillard, Toulouse-Lautrec, and even Renoir to be Modernists. The Museum of Modern Art was prepared to agree, even at the cost of keeping up with contemporary art.

For years, Barr supplied background information to the wife of MOMA president William A. M. Burden about collectors who should be invited to dinner parties for current or prospective donors. Among them were a Swiss banker who had just given the MOMA an "exciting" Kees van Dongen, *Modjesko, Soprano Singer*, painted in 1908; the donors of a fractional interest in Vuillard's *The Park*, painted in 1894; and the lender who might be persuaded to give Renoir's *Judgment of Paris*, a Rubensesque fandango of fatty female flesh, painted in 1914.

The museum also responded eagerly to help Burden with his private collection. Barr went to the museum president's apartment to advise on whether the chipped stone base of his Brancusi could be repaired. He then sent the sculpture to the museum's restorer to be repaired while the Burdens vacationed in Florida. Barr's assistant, Olive Bragazzi, who was cataloging the Burden collection, saw to it that Barr and the museum's registrar consulted on raising the valuations on some items. This would later give Burden a greater tax deduction when he gave works to the museum. In 1959, Burden shipped most of his collection to Belgium, where he served as United States ambassador. When he returned home for the Christmas holidays, the museum president asked Barr to supply some paintings from the museum's collection to hang in his New York apartment, so that it would look "relatively decent . . . especially for our New Year's Party on January 1." Barr obliged with Picasso's *Two Acrobats with a Dog* and Mondrian's *Trafalgar Square*, both of which had been on extended loan to the MOMA.

Barr had no qualms about providing trustees with such services. He saw the museum collection as "a collaborative effort in which our trustees take an active part, buying paintings for their own immediate use but with the intention . . . of giving them to us eventually." Thus, when the trustees began to invest in New York School pictures, "Dorothy [Miller] and I picked out the artists and almost all the paintings (or at least OK'd them) . . . bought by Nelson [Rockefeller], Blanchette [Rockefeller], Burden and . . . Philip Goodwin. . . . Now we are buying for David [Rockefeller]."

"There is no doubt that one of the principal joys of a museum director," John Walker wrote, "is finding works of art to buy with Other People's Money." Barr, however, was helping rich people to buy works for themselves and keeping his fingers crossed that they would eventually benefit the museum. (Quite often, however, it turned out that the donors also had their fingers crossed when they promised to do so.) In 1957, Barr sent Mary Lasker a list of galleries to visit, along with names of Abstract Expressionists he considered well established "though not necessarily the best." He also urged her to see the Whitney Annual from which she might buy a Theodore Stamos for $900 and a Philip Guston for $1,500. When MOMA trustee John Hay Whitney became American ambassador to Britain, Barr suggested he take along Loren MacIver's *Fisher's Island*, $1,800 at the Pierre Matisse Gallery. For museum president Burden, Barr located more costly items—a $40,000 Matisse, a "little van Gogh," a $20,000 Picasso watercolor. For a trip to Brazil, Barr provided Burden with a list of the best painters there. When Burden bought a Gris, a Picasso, and a Klee, Barr was "excited by the news." And when the museum president decided to take his profits on a Max Weber and a Rufino Tamayo, Barr suggested dealers who might be interested, adding that "Parke-Bernet is certainly the simplest solution, though many collectors, the museum included, are reluctant to offer any work by a living

American at auction. This reluctance is sound sentimentally, but certainly not economically."

For a sophisticated collector like Peggy Guggenheim, Barr found other favors to perform. When she established herself in Venice, he presented her with a sinuously carved wooden *forcole*, a gondolier's oar rest, which she in her eccentrically cryptic way called "most Venetian and at the same time un-Venetian." She exhibited it in her garden, where "those who don't know what it is admire [it] as a wonderful piece of modern sculpture, which is just what Alfred intended." More practically, he saw to it that Peggy Guggenheim was featured prominently—and relatively sanely—in Aline B. Saarinen's scintillating book about American collectors, *The Proud Possessors*. Still, Guggenheim remained fickle, and when she threatened to leave her collection to the city of Venice, Barr worried that "a long series of real or imagined lapses on the part of the museum" might be to blame and hastened to mention her more conspicuously in a catalog accompanying a European Jackson Pollock exhibition.

Barr maintained the world's most extensive files about works of modern art, including thousands of photos and nuggets of data on who owned what, exhibition catalogs, and research notes for exhibitions. Tucked among the banal entries he scribbled into a stack of notebooks during thirty-two years of foreign travel are tantalizing and revealing tidbits. In 1948, Barr hungrily described several Gris paintings for sale at Kahnweiler's for $250 each, a Rouault for $1,800, a Vuillard for $1,200, a Rodin for $1,450, a Vlaminck landscape for $1,350, and a van Gogh for $18,000. But Barr was largely window-shopping then; he still disposed of limited purchase funds. By 1956, direct purchase funds had grown considerably. In 1953 the museum had spent only $21,470 for paintings and sculpture, while in 1955 it spent $142,390. Moreover, purchase possibilities with John Walker's favorite currency, other people's money, had grown dramatically. "Can buy one, two, or three superb late Monet ponds, about six feet square," Barr wired Burden from Paris, "around $14,000 each or smaller cheaper, please cable."

In anticipation of future gifts, Barr prodigally cast bread upon the waters. He was punctilious about remembering the birthdays of artists' widows and sending condolences when artists died. He tirelessly visited collectors and commented admiringly on what they owned. Privately, however, he confessed that he yearned to see newer art. "You can't imagine how boring it is," he wrote to a friend, "to enter one house after another adorned exclusively with Utrillos, Modiglianis and Dufys." But to Dorothy Miller, for one, "he was a genius at wangling things out of people . . . his child was the museum; he would do *anything* for the Museum of Modern Art."

Yet when an outsider mildly criticized his spirited pursuit of pelf, Barr became exceedingly defensive. In a brief *Art News* editorial in 1957, critic Thomas B. Hess chided the museum for concentrating on collecting older Europeans to the neglect of the American Abstract Expressionists. The Pollock one-man show the previous winter and the recent purchase of a painting by Hans Hofmann, he remarked, "does not mean that [the MOMA's] collective bureaucratic stereotypes have become flexible." In a letter that took up more than a full page in the next issue, Barr testily reviewed the museum's attitudes toward American Modernists since its opening, pointed out that four trustees owned Abstract Expressionist works, and concluded sarcastically that "the museum welcomes and ponders thoughtful, informed criticism."

With suave René d'Harnoncourt as a model, Barr became increasingly adept at courting collectors, reinforcing their fantasies of being persons of exquisite taste and discrimination. Perhaps a missionary could be forgiven an occasional lapse of frankness or even a stray attack of greed when the cause was so obviously virtuous: to obtain the best works of art for the public's delight and education. While the discourse dwelled in realms of the beauty or, as the museum expression has it, the "importance" of a particular work, he managed discreetly to convey the coarsely commercial side of accumulating works of art. Only occasionally the rough edges of a collector's crassness obtruded too obviously and then Barr was outraged. He wrote in righteous anger to d'Harnoncourt in 1960, for example, when one art lover offered to buy a particular work for the museum on condition that he be given an appraisal of twice the purchase price before the end of the tax year.

If Alfred Barr had written an autobiography, however, he might well have agreed with John Walker that urbane handling of donors required a "protective vocabulary of meaningless adjectives and phrases . . . 'weasel words' " such as " 'interesting,' 'fascinating,' 'what an enviable possession,' 'I prefer picture X to picture Y.' " And he might have shared Walker's dismay that "the egotism of some collectors passes description. I have listened to some dilate upon the perfection of their works of art until I felt as though I were drowning in cold grease."

Verbally, collectors may dwell ad nauseam on the beauty they possess, but the love of art for art's sake seems to be a relatively slight motivation for those who buy works of art. In a 1953 survey by the French magazine *L'Amateur d'Art*, 43 percent of collectors said they were interested in investment and speculation; 17 percent wanted to decorate their homes, and another 17 percent cited love of art (no other reasons were given by more than 10 percent of the one thousand respondents). At a Brooklyn Museum seminar on the museum and the private collector in 1958, participants ranked their reasons for collecting. In order of declining importance, they were: furniture and decoration; investment or tax benefits; showing their taste, wealth, or social distinction; historical completeness; power now and glory posthumously; patronage; and, finally, love of art. The official chronicler of the Metropolitan Museum of Art, Calvin Tomkins, wrote that "many art dealers are convinced that the pure and selfless love of works of art for their own sake is so rare as to be considered almost nonexistent."

Collectors relish the excitement of the chase and the prestige of ownership, wrote Walker, as well as the pleasure intrinsic to viewing beautiful objects while making a secure investment, especially in inflationary times. But among Americans, he noted, "only a cynic would ignore [the] desire to add to the cultural heritage of the country through the enrichment of its private museums." In the United States, collections normally stay in a family for only one generation; thus, "it is axiomatic that the undertaker and the museum director arrive almost simultaneously." However, a worldly European dealer, Maurice Rheims, believed that even giving a work to a museum is less an altruistic deed than a way of making sure that no one else can possess that particular object. Collectors are notoriously fickle, he found, rewriting their wills frequently because they could not bear to see the ensemble they had made "dispersed by the disorderly and clumsy hand of . . . heirs."

Many subtle and overt drives have whetted collectors' appetites since ancient times, but during the last half of the 1950s, several new ingredients entered into the mix. In the past, people had sought objects of great beauty or intrinsic value—gold, jewels, objects of exquisite workmanship. But for those who collect modern works of art, another value comes into play: importance. A painting might be extremely ugly, like Picasso's *Demoiselles d'Avignon*, but is nevertheless enormously precious because it flagged a radical stylistic change in the artist's work and, in addition, enormously influenced other artists. Beyond mere connoisseurship, the contemporary collector also needs an expert to tell him which works are "important" and why. This is the crucial reason why Alfred Barr became such a pivotal figure among collectors of modern works of art. With his wide-ranging exhibitions and superb catalogs of the thirties and forties, and with his monographs on Picasso and Matisse, Barr had created a history of modern art. He had separated a welter of baffling and seemingly unrelated artists into coherent schools and convincingly related them to artists who had flourished centuries ago in other places, tying Expressionism, for example, to El Greco, or fantasy painting to Hieronymus Bosch. With the prestige of the Museum of Modern Art behind him, a prestige to which he was, of course, the chief contributor, his opinions carried tremendous weight. Within his schema, the ranking he assigned to modern artists continues to affect the prices paid for their works. Furthermore, Barr had created a vocabulary for knowledgeable discussion of modern works and had laid the foundation for the study of modern art as a respectable field for research at the university level.

Wherever modern art was discussed, Barr inevitably was the authority, and honors rained upon him. In 1955, he was named an honorary associate of the New York chapter of the American Institute of Architects, presumably for giving a name—and the prestige of numerous museum exhibitions—to the triumphant International Style. At the end of that year, when *Fortune* became interested in the "Great International Art Market," it was Alfred Barr who read, critiqued, and corrected the two lengthy articles prepared by Eric Hodgins and Parker Lesley. In 1957, he was a juror at the prestigious Sao Paolo Biennale art exhibition and he and Marga used the opportunity for rushed hops to Lima, Cuzco, Ouro Preto, and Rio de Janeiro. The University of Bonn awarded him an honorary doctorate in 1958, but he was so busy that more than a year passed before he could accept it. In the spring of 1959, the American Federation of the Arts, the erstwhile enemies of Modernism, presented Barr one of four fiftieth-anniversary citations as "our first and still our foremost scholar of modern art . . . a critic who clarifies instead of obscuring and who never stands between the reader and the work of art." D'Harnoncourt chaired the award committee, which also cited Duncan Phillips, Robert Woods Bliss (the brother of Lillie), and Paul Sachs. In the fall, Barr received the Commander's Cross of the Order of Merit from the West German government for introducing modern German art to the American public. Not to be outdone, the French government two months later made Barr a Chevalier of the Legion of Honor.

All at once, the Western art world was anxious to honor the man who had preached the gospel of Modernism so fervently for so long. However, behind all the honors lurked more than acceptance of a particular aesthetic; for the prices being paid for works by the earliest Modernists, the Impressionists, were astounding even the most jaded observers. The art market is "boiling with an activity never known before," the 1955 *Fortune* article noted, while the second installment, in January 1956, pointed to museums, "those stationary deposits recognized and held in veneration by every modern society," as the decisive force in conferring value on works of art. Moreover, the international market in art, which *Fortune* hailed as "perhaps the closest thing to a truly self-regulating enterprise . . . in the capitalist world since Adam Smith wrote *The Wealth of Nations*," was itself in a feverish revolution.

The Cognacq sale of 1952 had not only brought record prices for Impressionists but also signaled a radical change in the way pictures were sold: just as the aristocratic collector was being joined by the brash *arriviste*, so the dignified hush of the dealer's gallery was being crowded by the hectic chant of the auctioneer. The poorly organized Paris auction facilities were being replaced by sophisticated operations in London and even New York, where the chic went to see and be seen. At the Weinberg sale at Sotheby's in London, in July 1957, the bidding frenzy was such that seven early van Gogh watercolors and drawings, which, one authority stated, offered "about as much promise of genius as the drawings of Adolf Hitler," brought $80,000. In November the delirium moved to New York, where Sotheby's, recently merged with Parke-Bernet, was auctioning the collection of Georges Lurcy. As the main salesroom filled to capacity with an elegantly bejeweled throng including Chester Dale, Henry Ford II, nightclub impresario Billy Rose, Eleanor Roosevelt, and Metropolitan Museum director James Rorimer, the overflow followed the proceedings on closed-circuit television in two auxiliary rooms. The crowd cheered as bidders propelled prices toward new records and enthusiastically applauded the final rap of the auctioneer's gavel. "It was obvious that history was being made," wrote one observer who soon published a popular book titled *Art as an Investment.*

The international jet set now added to its global calendar the annual spring and fall "season" of art auctions. Perhaps the twelve hundred in evening clothes who gathered at Sotheby's in London for the Goldschmidt sale at 9:30 P.M. on October 15, 1958, were disappointed that there were only seven pictures on the block and that the bidding was over in just twenty-two minutes. But the expanded art world was stunned that two Cézannes, three Manets, a van Gogh, and a Renoir, all admittedly first-rate, fetched $2,186,800. Widely described as the definitive sale of the century, it heralded a spectacular price rise not only for Impressionists but also rippled forward to more recent works. At the Kirkeby sale in New York, five weeks after the Goldschmidt spectacular, a Bonnard brought $95,592, almost as much as a Renoir, and two Modiglianis reached $66,000, as much as a Degas. Two auction sales in May and July of 1959 confirmed that collectors were now willing to pay similar prices even for early, representational Picasso or Braque; in November, a mere drawing with touches of gouache by Picasso sold for $33,600, making it one of the most costly drawings ever sold from any period.

Among dealers, Impressionist paintings were known as "framed money," observed Elaine Cannell in a handbook tastefully titled *Good Taste: How to Have It; How to Buy It.* As the values of the older works outstripped the pocketbooks of all but the wealthiest collectors, savvy investors combed through the offerings by more recent artists. Many an art lover who had picked up a decent Braque in 1954 for $3,500 would have been elated to learn that a similar work auctioned five years later had brought $140,000. He or she might then have hastened to Alfred Barr with an offer to donate it to the Museum of Modern Art, provided the museum's appraisal was lofty enough to yield a fancy tax deduction, while the painting could lend its prestige to the benefactor's mantlepiece until he died.

As the European Modernists spiraled upward, the exciting post-war American Abstract Expressionists began to look more attractive to the growing public who speculated in art. The *Fortune* article had mentioned the names of de Kooning, Rothko, Pollock, Baziotes, Motherwell, Still, Franz Kline, and Ad Reinhardt as artists to consider if one wanted to dedicate $500 to $3,500 to an art speculation. At about that time, Sidney Janis had offered Barr Pollock's *Autumn Rhythm* for $8,000. Barr was unable to raise that sum, but after Pollock died in August of 1956, he suddenly decided that he wanted the work after all. By then, Pollock's widow, Lee Krasner, demanded $30,000, and Barr, said Janis, was "too shocked to answer my letter." Janis had no trouble selling the picture to the Metropolitan, which also was competing for modern American works, along with the Guggenheim and the Whitney museums. "Death is the greatest thing that can happen to an artist," English critic Herbert Read once cynically remarked. However, Pollock's death also lifted the prices of his living contemporaries; the funeral elegies for the flamboyant drip painter were hardly over before Janis got $10,000 for a de Kooning which a month earlier had not attracted $5,000.

Suddenly, the surveys of American art which Dorothy Miller had been organizing at the MOMA for twenty years excited rapt attention. Among the collectors who snapped up almost everything exhibited in "Twelve Americans" in 1956 was Blanchette Rockefeller, who took home Grace Hartigan's *Essex Market* for $1,200 and Franz Kline's *Accent Grave* for $1,350. Miller herself bought a Kline for $1,500 and was flabbergasted at the "mad inflation" this painting underwent; for a 1985 exhibition at Smith College, it was insured for $800,000. When Peggy Guggenheim paid a visit to New York in 1959 she was "thunderstruck" to find that art had become "an enormous business venture. . . . Prices are unheard-of. People only buy what is the most expensive. Some buy merely for invest-ment, placing pictures in storage without even seeing them, phon-ing their gallery every day for the latest quotation." Guggenheim did not regret having given the Abstract Expressionists their start, she said, but "I do not like art today. I think it has gone to hell."

Picking his way through this tide of greed, Barr worked hard to maintain his standards, while insuring that the museum eventu-ally—when all the promised pictures came home—would have a collection representing the best of contemporary work. He replied once again to the charge that the MOMA was neglecting and ignoring American Modernists by pointing out that the MOMA had shown an Arshile Gorky in 1930, bought a Pollock and a Mother-well in 1944, and a de Kooning in 1948. His delay until 1952 in buying a Hans Hofmann "may have been an error of judgement," he admitted, "but was not the result of indifference." The frantic market in modern works of art of the late fifties inevitably was affecting the work of artists themselves, especially the generation which followed the Abstract Expressionists. With the stakes so high, collectors were rushing around to artists' studios, attempting to snatch a bargain off the easel before the paint—if it even *was* paint—was dry. Dealers like Sidney Janis, Leo Castelli, and the two refugees from Vienna, Frank Lloyd and Harry Fischer, who founded Marlborough Fine Art, raced to supply the giddy market with the most recent scandal in paint.

When a youthful, white-haired commercial artist named Andy Warhol brought his portfolio to the Castelli Gallery, manager Ivan Karp admiringly studied his lively technique but hated the subject matter. "I don't know what to paint," conceded Warhol. So Karp disappeared into the back room and rummaged in the cupboard next to an old hot plate. "Paint this," he said, and plunked down a can of Campbell's tomato soup.

Faced with a fresh stylistic upheaval soon to be called Pop Art, Barr became cautious. He bargained hard in 1958 to spend more than $35,000 for yet another Léger to add to the eleven Légers the museum already owned; yet the following year, when dealer Leo Castelli offered to find a donor for Robert Rauschenberg's *Magician*, priced at $2,250, Barr claimed that the ephemeral debris in this "combine painting" would pose a conservation problem. He dithered until the donor retreated.

Caught between trustees who had barely assimilated what the Abstract Expressionists were about and the aggressive dealers representing the next wave of innovation, Barr relied on the prestige the Museum of Modern Art conferred to acquire a few examples of the new work at bargain prices or as gifts. From Castelli's first one-man exhibition for Jasper Johns, he selected several items, including one of the artist's mocking paintings of an American flag, priced at $900. The MOMA's acquisitions committee balked, Barr told the dealer, and so Johns eventually donated the picture to the museum. Similarly, Castelli sold the MOMA a $1,200 Frank Stella for $700, so that Barr could use his discretionary budget without bringing it before the committee. Being in the MOMA collection conferred a seal of approval on an artist's work while displaying it to a desirable array of potential collectors. No one was saying that artists were forced to donate works to the museum, but frequently a dealer would offer a particular artist's work on "indefinite loan" or would locate an unnamed "donor," usually the artist or the dealer, who was willing to give the work to the museum.

Ironically, the more contemporary art was accepted and valuable, the more cautious Alfred Barr became. Moreover, as others increasingly sought his opinion about contemporary art, he tended to become curt and even arbitrary. Aline Saarinen described Barr's role as a tastemaker in modern art as being comparable to Bernard Berenson's in Italian Renaissance art. Indirectly, she wrote in 1958, the MOMA's influence is "strategic. Even the most independent collector is not insensitive to what the museum buys or what it exhibits, or what its 'collectors' are buying." Even in Europe and Asia, the museum had created "a tightly held monopoly on what modern American art is known." Other American museums hesitated to assemble modern exhibitions without Barr's imprimatur. For a 1959 show called "The New Generation" at the Minneapolis Institute of Arts, for example, chief curator Sam Hunter sent Barr a one-page list of the artists he planned to exhibit. In the margin, Barr hastily scribbled his snap opinions: "taste but little originality of form . . . greatly overrated . . . better five years ago . . . too pre-war . . . already celebrated . . . too secondary."

"We all tend to see with the eyes of our own generation," National Gallery director John Walker has observed. He advised the collector over the age of fifty to put his or her faith in a youth who loved art and had a perceptive instinct: "Only the young discern the young," he wrote. Alas, the MOMA senior staff was aging along with the museum itself. The younger people, many of them laden with advanced degrees earned by fussy scrutiny of photos rather than of originals and theses puffing petty detail into dense prose, seldom dared to speak up, so awed were they by Barr's unassailable reputation, influence, and prestige. He claimed to be open-minded, but he sometimes reacted sharply, even paranoically, when he discerned a philistine challenge.

In 1955, Huntington Hartford triggered a flurry of anxiety at the MOMA by announcing that he planned to build a new museum at Columbus Circle in New York. Shortly after he learned this news, Barr wrote to an art critic for United Press International to reveal, in those times of McCarthyist Red-baiting, that Hartford had in his collection "the work of a notorious communist, Gustave Courbet." When Hartford wanted to call his museum the Gallery of Modern Art, Barr rushed to make sure that a dealer who already used that name would not sell it to Hartford. He also wanted the MOMA's lawyers to set up a dummy corporation called Institute of Modern Art so that this alternative would be unavailable to the new museum. The attorneys even asked the New York secretary of state to ban any corporation which used the words *modern art* in its name. When Hartford opened his short-lived Gallery of Modern Art anyway, the MOMA lawyers filed suit, complaining that the name would "dilute the distinctive quality" of the MOMA's name and might "divert goodwill and donations from the established museum."

At the very moment that Barr was so worried about another museum claiming to be modern, he was embarking on a top-secret effort to tap the world's richest, most fabled cache of early modern paintings. Late in 1954, he had been contacted by Marshall McDuffie, a New York lawyer just returned from the Soviet Union, where he seemed to have developed an insider's relationship with important people. Just a year after Stalin's death, McDuffie had obtained a Soviet visa by simply cabling a request to Nikita Khrushchev, whom he had first met during a 1944 relief mission in the Ukraine. During the ensuing ten-thousand-mile tour of the Soviet Union, McDuffie had a three-hour private interview with Khrushchev, and he had recently published four long articles about his odyssey in *Collier's* magazine. As McDuffie was planning another trip to the Soviet Union for the spring of 1955, a counselor at the Soviet embassy in Washington had hinted to him that an "economic reconnaissance" might be possible regarding the sale of some of the hundreds of magnificent early modern works confiscated by the Soviets in 1917. The hoard included some of the finest canvasses by Degas, van Gogh, Gauguin, Cézanne, Monet, Rousseau, Derain, Matisse, and Picasso, many of them bought directly from the artists by two pioneering Russian collectors, Ivan Morosov and Serge Shchukine. The Soviets had confiscated these works soon after the 1917 revolution and had exhibited them briefly before locking them away, even from the eyes of curators, in museum vaults. During Barr's Russian sojourn in 1927 and 1928, he had tried to see these pictures but was refused; the Soviets scorned them as decadent, formalist decorations, devoid of any Marxist message.

When Barr heard McDuffie's news, therefore, he was enormously excited. He recalled that during the 1930s, when the Soviets were desperate for foreign exchange, they had sold a grand collection of Old Masters to Andrew Mellon, works which would form the nucleus of the National Gallery. At that time, Stephen Clark had also obtained four Impressionist paintings from the same source. Only nine months earlier, Barr had written to the American embassy in Moscow to inquire whether the Pushkin Museum was open and what modern paintings were on display. Was it possible that the new rulers of the Kremlin were now ready to sell off some of the Modernist works of which they disapproved?

Barr thought the possibility remote, but he nevertheless sprang into frenzied activity. By the last day of 1954, he had checked out McDuffie's background, getting glowing references from New

York mayor Robert Wagner, governor Herbert Lehman, financier-politico W. Averell Harriman, and even CIA director Allen W. Dulles, and had taken McDuffie to lunch with Nelson Rockefeller. Early in January, he wrote four-page letters to the MOMA's wealthiest supporters, among them William A. M. Burden, John Hay Whitney, and David Rockefeller, about the proposed McDuffie mission. Burden and David Rockefeller noted "a certain instability in McDuffie's character," perhaps because he liked to support liberal politicians, but Nelson Rockefeller was "extremely interested," Barr reported, even to the extent of checking in Washington and learning that the Russians could be paid through French or Belgian banks.

Meanwhile, Barr had combed through the most recent list of the Russian holdings, a crumbling catalog of the long-defunct Moscow Museum of Modern Western Art, which he had brought home from Moscow in 1928. From it, Barr selected the pictures he would want and then arrived at an amount he was willing to bid for each one. Near the end of January 1955, he handed McDuffie a white sheet of plain paper, devoid of date, title, or letterhead. It listed the works only by catalog number, followed by another two-digit number, presumably the amount, in thousands, which would be an appropriate price. Among them were Matisse's magnificent *The Dance*, at $75,000, and *The Red Room*, at $30,000. For one Cézanne, he was willing to go up to $96,000; for a particular Gauguin, to $90,000; and for the most expensive Picasso, to $45,000. He also handed McDuffie photostats of all the works and a memorandum of agreement, on nonmuseum stationery, authorizing him to enter into negotiations with the Russians. He was not to mention "the names of any of the interested collectors or of the institution" he represented. Barr assured him, however, that "it is the intention of the collectors that the institution should benefit from the transaction." Barr did not offer him a precise commission but promised McDuffie that "the collectors whom I represent are fair-minded men." The project might be "a pipe dream," Barr wrote to David Rockefeller, "but the possibility, though remote, was sufficient to make it worth the time and effort."

The pictures Barr lusted for were unquestionably masterpieces, but they were all at least forty years old and some had been painted more than sixty years earlier. By the time they came to the museum, probably many years hence, after the "fair-minded men" died, they could hardly be called modern. Yet, to a man like Barr, who was more than fifty years old himself, they were the masterpieces he had studied in his youth and had hungered to view during his 1928 visit to the Soviet Union. The idea of liberating works of art from an oppressive government's censorship would also have appealed to Barr. The possibility of gathering in such landmark works, even though they were no longer contemporary, proved irresistible to Barr. Although McDuffie's mission failed, Barr continued to spend a great deal of time and effort in pursuing those elusive marvels of his youth.

In the middle fifties, the Soviet Union seemed to be emerging from the decades of gruesome isolation during the Stalin era. The Khrushchev regime was eager for cultural intercourse with the West, and when the long Russian winter thawed in the spring of 1956, Barr decided it was time to pursue seriously possible exchanges of art with the Soviets. Even if the Morosov and Shchukine pictures could not permanently emigrate, perhaps they could come west on a visit. Following friendly explorations with the Soviet cultural attaché in Washington, d'Harnoncourt, Burden, and Barr arrived in Moscow in May and settled into the dusty Victorian red plush of the National Hotel. Barr boasted that he had twelve chairs and a couch in his two-room suite and exulted that "there is a real thaw here. . . . Got into . . . museum storerooms and saw eight Kandinskys and two Malevichs, including the *Black Square!* The staff had never been in there." Shortly before leaving for home, he was also thrilled to obtain a series of rare exhibition catalogs from the twenties and thirties. The Soviets seemed willing to send an exhibition of nineteenth-century Russian painting as well as a selection of the French Modernists in exchange for a show of American nineteenth-century art and the MOMA's famous photo show, "The Family of Man."

Soon after the Americans came home, however, everything fell apart. D'Harnoncourt believed that the exchanges would speedily take place, as soon as a group of Russian museum directors had selected what they wanted from American museums. But the following September, Hungary exploded in revolution and, in retaliation for the Soviet suppression of the revolt, the U.S. government canceled all cultural exchanges. During the frosts of the following winter, Barr also lost the precious catalogs he had gathered in Moscow. In the rush of departure, he had handed them to a Soviet cultural official for mailing. This cautious bureaucrat had checked with the Office of Foreign Relations of the Ministry of Culture, where another cautious bureaucrat decided they could not be sent because they "were all old, dirty, used, selected carelessly or in a slovenly, untidy manner." It was doubtful, wrote Barr's Russian helper, "that the Office of Foreign Relations will be able to bring itself to send such catalogs."

Despite these setbacks, Barr carefully cultivated all the Russian museum people he had met. "One of our stratagems," he wrote to Daniel Catton Rich at the Art Institute of Chicago, "is to be as helpful as we can to the museum personnel, who are, many of them, pathetically starved for contact with the West." Soon after Barr returned, flimsy-looking envelopes with exotic stamps began arriving at the museum, initiating a decades-long tie between the champion of Modernism and his cautious, isolated colleagues behind the Iron Curtain. Invariably handwritten in careful English or French, the Russian letters hid pathetic cries for information behind polite, noncommittal sentiments and uncontroversial trivia. Some wondered about publishing scholarly articles in Western journals, others asked for catalogs and articles published abroad. Like poor but proud relations, they often sent along Soviet catalogs, apologizing for the careless printing and wretched reproductions. Barr graciously acknowledged everything and frequently shipped them books, discreetly addressed to the library of the particular institution rather than to an individual.

With the suavity he had practiced to woo American donors, Barr courted the Russians, always hoping that a sudden thaw might release Modernist paintings for an American tour, if not for purchase. The persistent obstacle, however, had little to do with East-West relations. Having confiscated most of these works following the 1917 revolution, the Russians continued to fear that the previous owners or their heirs could impound the pictures if they came to the West. In 1954, the Soviets had sent a first-rate selection of Picassos to Paris, following a personal appeal from Communist artist Fernand Léger. But the day after the exhibition opened, a cavalcade of embassy Zis limousines pulled up before the exhibition hall and a phalanx of Soviet diplomats marched in, whisked the pictures off the walls, and drove away to the airport, where an Aeroflot jet waited to rush them back to Moscow. The problem was that Irene Shchukine, the daughter of the Russian collector who had bought most of these pictures straight from Picasso's easel, had filed suit for return of her property.

All of Barr's subsequent efforts to obtain loans of the Russian Modernist paintings foundered on the threat of their being impounded by heirs; only in 1986 did the United States government begin to guarantee the safety of Russian pictures, and then exchange exhibitions soon followed. Nevertheless, Barr continued to long for a return visit to the Soviet Union, and in June 1959, after several postponements and complicated negotiations, he arrived again in Moscow as guest of the Union of Soviet Societies for Friendship and Cultural Relations with Foreign Countries.

As a prelude to his visit, Barr had written a cannily worded and stunningly illustrated article for *America*, the State Department's officially sanctioned publication distributed in the Soviet Union. While it was a passionate tract in behalf of modern art, Barr's article was subtly tailored to appeal to Marxist sensibilities. His illustrations emphasized the contributions of radical artists—Shahn, Léger, Picasso—as well as self-taught artists with proletarian backgrounds, such as John Kane, Alton Pickens, and Henri Rousseau. He also featured works by artists from the Third World, such as Clemente Orozco, as well as Max Beckmann's powerful comment on Nazi depravity, *The Departure*. He frankly avoided some of the more bizarre manifestations of Modernism because "even though there might be a latent sympathy for it, if it is presented in too great a quantity and too uncompromisingly, I believe it will play into the hands of the regime."

With the Russians thus educated and humored, the Barrs arrived in Moscow. This time Marga came along, patiently dealing with recalcitrant slide projectors and eager to converse with Russians. During a hectic three-week jaunt, Barr lectured in Moscow, Leningrad, Yerevan, and Tbilisi, engaging everywhere in sharp debate with official museum people, while crowds of gaping young artists jammed the halls. But personal contact with ordinary Russians proved elusive. In a letter home, Marga noted that most of the Russians she met were immensely interested in Western art, but were afraid to say so. All chances to stop and chat with those who spoke English or French were frustrated by their formidable official hostess, "somewhat resembling a bulldog bursting through a tight black suit," rushing them on to the next appointment.

Barr's trip coincided with the American exhibition in Moscow at which Richard Nixon had his famous "kitchen debate" with Nikita Khrushchev. The exhibition featured a large selection of American art, including some abstract works which drew a cross fire of abuse. While conservative Americans complained that some of the paintings were by Communists, a member of the Soviet Academy of Arts lamented that "progressive artists" like Rockwell Kent and William Gropper had been excluded. Conservative American artists hated the exhibition's emphasis on abstraction, and Russian critics heartily agreed. One Russian called them "the works of madmen," while another deplored "enormous canvases covered with spots of dirty paints and fragments of freakish lines." When Khrushchev toured the exhibition, he mumbled "OK," his only English word, in front of each canvas, but when he reached a Robert Motherwell abstraction, he whispered to an aide. Asked what the Soviet premier had said, the aide replied, "He says it looks like bird droppings."

The unnerving mixture of severe ideology and slipshod organization the Barrs encountered during this trip must have been a vivid reminder of his experiences in 1927 and 1928. His lecture in Leningrad, for example, was supposed to be open only to the staff of the Hermitage Museum. The following day, however, he was asked to repeat it for "a hall crowded with persons standing on chairs and spilling over into the corridors." In Tbilisi and Yerevan, he showed a film about Jackson Pollock and an abstract film by Francis Thompson, *NYNY*, receiving tumultuous applause followed by a midnight supper. Then he was brusquely summoned to Moscow, where officials "severely admonished him for the tone of his lectures." The physical arrangements were reminiscent of the ordeals Barr and Jere Abbott had undergone during the twenties.

The MOMA Film Library, founded at Barr's behest in 1935, was the first such institution in the world. Arthur Kleiner provides live musical accompaniment to Lillian Gish in the silent-film classic *The Wind*.

Blanchette Rockefeller views prints with Barr's protégé, William Lieberman, curator of prints and drawings. Mrs. Rockefeller served as MOMA trustee and president for two terms. When Lieberman failed to succeed Barr as director of the museum collections, he moved to the Metropolitan as curator of twentieth-century art.

Elizabeth Shaw headed the MOMA Publicity Department, established by Barr as the first such department in any museum.

(*Left*) Porter McCray, a Rockefeller protégé, assembled dozens of exhibitions to spread the MOMA gospel worldwide. (*Right*) Monroe Wheeler, MOMA's director of publications, cajoled, hassled, and harangued Barr into completing long-overdue manuscripts.

Museum membership has its privileges—lunching amid art in the members' dining room.

Barr persuaded the trustees to start a department of photography in 1940. By 1952, its first director, Beaumont Newhall, had moved on, and the department was headed by Edward Steichen (left).

Barr tracked Picasso's *Three Musicians* for decades before the painting came to the MOMA in 1949, courtesy of Olga Guggenheim. Docent Abe Chanin explains the jazz-inspired work to a crowd.

During a disastrous fire at the museum in 1958, Barr smashed a window in his office and led his staff onto the roof of the adjoining town house. Overriding the objections of the residents' butler, Barr led his people down to safety.

Nelson Rockefeller donned fireman's garb for an interview during the museum's blaze.

David Rockefeller (left), chairman of the MOMA board, and William Paley, president, summarily fired René d'Harnoncourt's successor, Bates Lowry, in 1969, after he was on the job for less than a year.

Barr's successor, William Rubin, proudly poses with a rare Cubist Picasso sculpture, *Guitar*, given to the MOMA by the artist in 1971.

And still they come. More than four decades after Barr
organized Picasso's first one-man exhibition at the MOMA,
crowds line up to enter the artist's giant retrospective in 1980.

After a forty-two-year "visit" at the MOMA, Picasso's *Guernica*
was returned in 1981 to Madrid's Prado museum, the painting's
final home.

HARRY BENSON

Surrounded by beaming MOMA trustees, a frail Alfred Barr acknowledges their tribute in his last public appearance on March 12, 1973. Among those present were: Mrs. Donald B. Straus, Mrs. Bertram Smith, Gianluigi Gabetti, Gustave L. Levy, Monroe Wheeler, William S. Paley, Edward M. M. Warburg, John Hay Whitney, Dr. Henry Allen Moe, Philip Johnson, Mrs. Douglas Auchincloss, Barr, Dr. Mamie Phipps Clark, MOMA director Richard E. Oldenburg, Mrs. Bliss Parkinson, Mrs. Frank Y. Larkin, Mrs. Armand Bartos, Ivan Chermayeff, Mrs. Walter Hochschild, Mrs. John D. Rockefeller III, Gifford Philips, Mrs. Alfred R. Stern, and John L. Loeb.

The pipes in their Moscow hotel room, Marga wrote home, emitted "maddening beats and pulsations, which we called the music of the spheres. Once we kept a couple of plumbers racing around until midnight trying to quiet things down. We could hear them screaming through the vents heaven knows how many floors away." And so, like legions of visitors to the Soviet Union, the Barrs hastened joyously into Vienna when their three weeks were up.

Dealing with the Russians may have been ticklish and frustrating, but it was a tea party compared with the Barrs' infuriating relationship with Picasso. Among the pictures he had tentatively chosen for the 1939 Picasso show, there were four Barr decided to exclude. But Picasso went into "a sudden rage [and] forced these pictures into the exhibition on the threat of cancelling the whole affair." Having scheduled a giant exhibition for May of 1957 to celebrate Picasso's seventy-fifth birthday, Barr contemplated the project with dread. He began scouting out the territory in 1955, with a summer visit to Picasso's sister in Barcelona. The old lady was too ill to see him, Barr reported to Peggy Guggenheim, "but we did see the apartment with the pictures in a most extraordinary state of neglect and dirt . . . a strange, bohemian and rather disquieting atmosphere." Barr then consulted the artist's English friend Roland Penrose as to the best time for a visit with Picasso and learned that summer was "the least propitious. After July 15 he is usually besieged . . . until October." Then Marga consulted another Picasso authority, Douglas Cooper, on what gifts to bring and was told that the artist's mistress, Jacqueline Roque, appreciated records of jazz or Negro spirituals, while the great man "likes trick gadgets—the one in favor at the moment is a musical cigarette lighter and also a comic rubber nose with spectacles!" The Barrs arrived in Cannes late in June 1956, bearing appropriate gifts. For days, they awaited the call to La Californie, the artist's villa in nearby Mougins. Fixed appointments, they well knew, meant nothing to Picasso; indeed, he was famous for keeping visitors cooling their heels, sometimes for more than a week.

The summons came at last and the Barrs ascended the hill to the villa, bearing what Marga called "disgusting loot": records for Jacqueline, and for the great man, a radiometer, socks, pajamas, a sun hat, a dual flashlight, a pair of mirrored blue sunglasses, and another pair with flapping red plastic eyelashes. "All is done on a slapdash basis of just standing around endlessly," Marga wrote home. "The huge place is totally cluttered . . . crates on end [serve] as . . . seats as the few chairs get encumbered with things that He [sic] puts down. When he puts something down, it has to stay there unless he moves it. It is sacred. By now, so much has been put down on the dining room table that they have to eat out if they have guests." Gary Cooper, with his wife and daughter, was also at the villa that day, attempting to select a picture to buy. But Picasso was too busy mugging in his new red eyelash glasses for a *Paris Match* photographer who also was on hand, popping flashbulbs. "All visitations at his villa are so difficult, tiring, and laborious because they last ever so long and there are so many people milling around, a new immense assortment each time," Marga wrote wearily. "He circulates among them and you can hardly ever pin him down or make him stick to a subject. . . . I think that what he likes most is painting."

Despite the ordeal, Barr considered the outcome "highly satisfactory on the surface however frustrating in procedure," he reported to Douglas Cooper. "I *think* all's well and have never known him to be more charming and gay—wonderfully lively and energetic, but wasting hours a day by seeing seven people at once so no one can finish business with him." After three weeks in Cannes and a series of exhausting forays to the villa, Barr thought he had borrowed a considerable group of unknown paintings for the seventy-fifth birthday show, plus seventy-three bronzes and wood constructions that would show the world for the first time the scope of Picasso's genius as a sculptor. All was well until two months before the exhibition's opening, when Picasso refused to send a single one of the promised sculptures.

While Barr was furious, most visitors to the museum were enchanted with the exhibition he had lovingly created. To save wear and tear on his feet, he directed the three-week-long installation effort from a wheelchair, a practical innovation now used by many museum people. "I'm like a middle aged fighter," he jauntily told the *New Yorker*'s reporter, "my legs go first." Even without the sculptures, it was the most comprehensive Picasso exhibition to date, including 328 items borrowed from seventy-three private collections and twenty-two museums. For the third time since its founding, the MOMA had given Picasso a record-size show, and one critic remarked that the museum "owes its existence to the prior existence of Pablo Ruiz Picasso."

Some wondered whether the MOMA was overemphasizing Picasso. In 1952, trustee Philip Goodwin questioned the "exaggerated share of attention" the museum gave to Picasso. He noted that the decor in the members' room and restaurant was exclusively Picasso, that 20 percent of the wall space in the permanent collection was given over to Picasso, and that half of a Picasso-Redon print exhibition on the ground floor also was devoted to Picasso. And one museum curator also believed that Barr was "terribly fixated on Picasso" and suggested that he may have been motivated by the fact that many trustees, especially Rockfellers, had so many Picassos in their collections. Barr, however, had no doubts that Picasso was the century's greatest artist, writing, "He is not only the greatest radical of his generation, but also the greatest traditionalist."

Like the artist, the museum was firmly woven into the American cultural fabric; its exhibitions seldom drew heated criticism, just admiration and sometimes even trenchant analysis. Only behind the Iron Curtain was there still serious debate about the merits of modern art as a whole. In the decade from 1947 to 1957, four times as many articles were published in the United States about modern art as in the previous thirty years. Between 1954 and 1959, the major American art magazines had grown from thin, provincial-looking sheets, carelessly assembled and edited, to slick publications, loaded with color illustrations and articles by well-known authorities. Though still a quarterly, *Art in America* had gone from a drab seventy-six-page magazine with only twelve pages of advertising to a 132-page oversize hardbound book, with fifty pages of advertising. Barr was on its editorial board, along with Dorothy Miller and important museum directors from all over the country. *Arts* magazine doubled in size during these five years, from thirty-four to seventy pages, and tripled its advertising from five and a half to more than sixteen pages. *Art News* had slimmed down from seventy-eight to seventy pages, but its advertising had grown from 17½ to 25 pages and a new, sprightly format promised that improved financial health would soon produce a fatter publication. There was no debate any more about *whether* modern art was acceptable; only discussion of *which kinds* were most appealing and, obliquely, the best investments.

In the spring of 1958, Barr had a heart-stopping lesson in just how much the public adored modern art. Just after noon on April 15, a workman installing air conditioning on the MOMA's second floor started a fire that could have wiped out the museum's entire collection and also dozens of priceless masterpieces in a loan exhibition of Seurat. Barr was in the executive offices on the fifth floor when smoke began to drift out of the newly installed air conditioning ducts. The elevator had stopped and the stairway was like a chimney filled with smoke. He smashed a window with a swivel chair and led the dozen or so staff members who were left on that floor onto the roof next door. This was a brownstone owned by John D. Rockefeller, Jr., and occupied by his sister. When a butler appeared to tell the group, "You cannot come onto the roof of this house," Barr replied in his haughtiest manner: "There will be many more coming. Have the stairs clear so that they can come down out of the fire." The butler meekly said, "Yes, sir," and led the way. Meanwhile, the museum staff was hastily carrying paintings out of the building into the museum garden, where Barr soon joined d'Harnoncourt in supervising the rescue.

Before the firemen were gone, the Art Institute of Chicago's director, Daniel Catton Rich, and his restorer had already flown to the scene to look after Seurat's magnificent, huge *Sunday Afternoon on the Grande Jatte*. The picture had never before left Chicago—and never would again. The fire had been the worst in American museum history, but Seurat's masterpiece was safe, along with almost everything in the MOMA collection. The only pictures totally destroyed were Candido Portinari's *Festival of St. John's Eve*, valued at $20,000, and Monet's 18½-foot-wide *Water Lilies*, then valued at about $100,000. The Monet had a particularly adventuresome history. When the Nazis left Paris in 1944, they passed the artist's home at Giverny and wantonly machine-gunned the studio where Monet had stored many rolled paintings. Monet's son found the ruined works and took them to Paris dealer Katja Granoff, who had them repaired. Soon after the war, Barr had bought three of those works, one for the museum and two for other collectors.

Eight other paintings were damaged by flames or smoke, but all of them were eventually repaired. The museum itself reopened the Seurat show fifteen days after the fire and the rest of the building less than four months later, after extensive remodeling, principally fireproofing. The fire had been a ghastly moment for Barr—he had lost seven pounds that day— but the outpouring of public affection for the museum was a welcome revelation. An emergency committee raised $143,000 for rebuilding in a matter of days. Letters flooded in as though someone had died. Barr's emissary for buying Russian paintings, Marshall McDuffie, suggested that Barr should treasure the destiny that had him "catching women and babies tossed from windows," and Barr replied that he did not want to "diminish your pleasure in knowing a hero, but in truth . . . I didn't catch a single babe, or toss one either!" A self-described "lover of fine painting" from Beverly Hills wanted to buy the charred remains of the Monet, "providing of course prices were reasonable," and one person suggested that the museum sell six-inch squares of charred canvas to raise money. But most of the letters expressed sincere grief and love untainted by greed: "Your loss and heroic battle have brought poignant realization," said one, "that since the Modern Museum was founded, it has been my spiritual home . . . and you have been its High Priest, channelling, energizing."

In many ways, Alfred Barr found it more difficult to deal with the public acceptance of modern art than he had with its rejection; the philistines hammering at the gates engaged him far more intensely than the triumph of the Israelites. On the few occasions when he overcame his aversion to public speaking, his favorite topic was modern art and political oppression. Again and again, his sermonlike talk described the threats to modern art from the evil alliance between conservative artists and politicians and pointed to the arch examples: Soviet commissars and Adolf Hitler, "a bitterly disappointed academic painter and a politician." Barr kept a huge file of attacks on modern art, neatly sorted by the epithets used: foreign, childish, Jewish, communistic, homosexual, a dealers' conspiracy, insane. Perhaps he was wishing that he were still a feisty young man, battling for his beliefs, rather than a middle-aged aesthetic guru, surrounded by millionaires waiting to learn what to buy next.

11

THE DISCIPLES GO FORTH

Alfred Barr was in the stands among the forty thousand guests invited to the inauguration of Pres. John F. Kennedy in 1961. His presence and that of some 155 writers, artists, musicians, scientists, and other cultural figures on that brisk and brilliant January Monday symbolized a profound shift in official American culture. Kennedy's predecessor, Dwight D. Eisenhower, had mouthed a few obligatory words about democratic acceptance of all kinds of art, but he obviously cherished the anecdotal type of art he himself painted. The handsome young president who stood coatless in the cold to symbolize a new frontier would clearly change all that. Not only had he summoned Barr, d'Harnoncourt, and other museum managers to the inaugural festivities, he had also invited twenty-four painters and sculptors to be present. A number of these were traditionalists who had for decades jeered at modern art: Eugene Speicher, Henry R. Shepley, Paul Manship, Ivan Mestrovic. For the first time, however, the White House recognized American Modernists, with invitations to Stuart Davis, Franz Kline, Seymour Lipton, Mark Rothko, Max Weber, and Mark Tobey.

Barr had singled out virtually the identical artists a year earlier as having done the most for modern art in America. But he listed an even greater number of nonartists who had helped to establish modern art among the philistines: Henry McBride, the first critic to write with understanding about Modernism; Holger Cahill, Dorothy Miller's husband, who had been chief of the WPA art programs during the 1930s; Sen. William Fulbright, the patron of thousands of artists who had received scholarships for study abroad; Lloyd Goodrich, creator of the modern Whitney Museum; Grace McCann Morley and Perry C. Rathbone, museum directors who pioneered purchases of modern art in San Francisco and Boston; James Johnson Sweeney and James Thrall Soby, who both had written widely on modern art.

It was evident almost everywhere in the art world that the solitary missionary for modern art had gathered a host of powerful disciples. Serving with Barr on the twenty-two-person editorial board of *Art in America*, for example, were not just Goodrich, Morley, and Soby but also his comrades in many an ancient battle for recognition: architectural historian Henry-Russell Hitchcock, adventuresome collector Duncan Phillips, MOMA curators John McAndrew and Dorothy Miller, critic Alfred Frankenstein, and Buffalo, New York, museum director Gordon Washburn. Edgar Kaufmann, Jr., who had headed the MOMA's design department, was now the magazine's consultant on architecture and design, and Beaumont Newhall, whom Barr had picked to found the MOMA's Department of Photography, was its photography consultant. Having been nominated by Barr, Dorothy Miller in 1960 won the magazine's $1,000 medal award for her contribution to American art. Barr also lent his name to the consultative committee for the European-based *Art Quarterly* and by the middle sixties, after years of solitarily holding the Modernist fort at the College Art Association, he was joined on the board there by artists Robert Motherwell and Grace Hartigan and by art historians Milton W. Brown and Leo Steinberg.

Even though the Association's *Journal* was now publishing a considerable number of scholarly articles dealing with modern art and hefty art magazines were covering the contemporary scene in rich detail, Barr was disappointed. "Commercial publications . . .

have the character of pressure groups devoted to the promotion of a private cause," he wrote. "In prose style and in the nature of their critical concepts, these publications are an embarrassment to American letters." Scholarly publications, on the other hand, he found too cluttered with "academic paraphernalia." To the museum trustees, Barr recommended that the MOMA publish its own journal, a publication applying "professional standards of criticism and scholarship," while remaining "adventurous in ideas." Its articles would supplement the museum's exhibitions and would provide critical guidance to artists, while also explaining why the museum avoided exhibiting certain works. He named seven scholars who might be competent as editors for the quarterly of forty to forty-eight pages. Although Barr's report implied that the publication would turn a profit for the museum, the trustees shied away from the idea, worried perhaps about the effect this loose cannon might have on the already volatile art marketplace.

Nevertheless, Barr's point of view, especially his version of the history of modern art, reached generations of college students through his guidance to the authors of the textbooks they used in art history survey courses. Barr's critique of H. W. Janson's thousand-picture book, *Key Monuments of the History of Art*, was "by far the most helpful I have received," Janson wrote. Barr tartly complained to the art scholar whom he had helped to rescue from Germany during the 1930s that the book contained too many Daumiers, too few Delacroix, too many Henry Moore sculptures and none by Naum Gabo, too much Byzantine art and not enough Russian. While ignoring Barr's critique of *Key Monuments*, Janson's bestselling textbook, *History of Art*, first published in 1962, unquestioningly followed Barr's model of modern art. Janson's bibliography still recommends Barr's two 1936 catalogs and also his Matisse and Picasso books. This extremely influential textbook—in 1976 it was used in 46 percent of college survey courses in art history—also gives short shrift to women artists and to minorities, much as the Museum of Modern Art under Barr did.

Alfred Barr's version of modern art history has also left a heavy imprint on the other standard college text in art history, Helen Gardner's *Art Through the Ages*. Its most recent revision includes a chart showing the interrelations of various twentieth-century art

movements, which bears a striking resemblance to the arrow-
strewn diagram Barr drew up in 1936 to show the origins and
affinities of Cubism and abstract art. Another Barr disciple was
the author of the first bestselling textbook on modern art,
H. Harvard Arnason, who jovially blamed Barr for getting him
involved in the study of modern art at all. In 1936, Arnason had
been "a contented Early Christian archaeologist at Princeton," he
wrote to Barr; then he began "slipping up to New York to look at
some of your shows." His *History of Modern Art*, first published in
1968, also adheres closely to the history Barr developed. Generations of college students in art history courses, therefore, have
imbibed the gospel of modern art according to Alfred H. Barr, Jr.

By 1959, this gospel was rarely questioned. The directors of
other museums, now suddenly interested in acquiring modern art,
closely watched his every move. "What he bought, they bought,"
said Libby Tannenbaum, an art historian who worked with Barr
during this time. The art critics who had been so vicious in their
time were dead or tamed; the few remaining skeptics were
abashed by the astounding acceptance of Barr's version of the
history of modern art, not only by the swarms of academics who
now professed some expertise in the field but also by the marketplace, where the works he had championed virtually alone were
now fetching seven-digit prices. McCarthyism was dying down and
Barr's file of current attacks on modern art was getting thin.

Then in September 1959 John Canaday took over as art editor of
the *New York Times* and soon a vivid debate began to unfold in the
newspaper's good gray art pages. Unlike his predecessors, the new
man was not just a stolid reporter elevated to his critical tasks
because of seniority or proven ability to meet deadlines. Rather, he
was a respected scholar who had taught art history, architecture,
and painting at the University of Virginia; directed the art school
at Tulane University; and headed the education division at the
Philadelphia Museum of Art. He had studied painting at Yale and
for several years at the *Ecole du Louvre* in Paris. He had also
selected the slides and written the breezily informative booklets for
the immensely popular "Metropolitan Seminars on Art," distributed by the Book-of-the-Month Club. As a critic, Canaday wrote
learnedly as well as fluently and, to the dismay of many members

of the modern art establishment, critically. As it had with previous
tenants of this important post, the MOMA cultivated Canaday and
the friendliness seemed to be reciprocated. But Canaday, unlike
the previous tenants, spoke out clearly, cogently, candidly, and
often bitingly about the New York art world.

Canaday wrote frankly about art prices, a subject which continues to be unmentionable (except in gossip) in the museum world.
In early 1960, he told his readers about a West Coast collector who
had wired to the gallery opening a major Abstract Expressionist
show asking to buy "any painting priced at $8,000." Canaday
analyzed the sales from a print show which had visited sixteen
American museums and argued that a market did exist for artists
who pursued their personal visions. "Only the big collectors and the
venal painters will buy or create with an eye to standards imposed
by the tastemakers . . . an artist who creates according to his own
convictions has a good chance of finding a responsive audience
outside the ballyhoo." Canaday also enjoyed puncturing pompous
balloons. Reporting on a MOMA lecture in March 1960, he twitted
art scholar Leo Steinberg for comparing modern art to the biblical
manna. Steinberg had asserted that, like manna, modern art was
food for the soul, to be picked up daily and consumed as needed.
Canaday quoted the relevant Bible passage and pointed out that
Steinberg had failed to mention that if manna were hoarded, it
"bred worms and stank."

Then in September 1960, Canaday called Barr "the most powerful tastemaker in American art today." The critic was merely
stating the obvious: "There is not a dealer in town, nor a collector,
nor yet a painter who hopes to hang in the Museum of Modern Art
who doesn't study each of Mr. Barr's syllables in an effort to deduce
what he should offer for sale, what he should buy, or what he should
paint." Many a museum man might have been overjoyed at such
recognition, but Barr was "more than embarrassed," he wrote to
Canaday. "The artists lead, the museum follows," he maintained.
While conceding the museum's influence in architecture or furniture design, he insisted that the art works it showed or bought
simply reflected what was being done. The effect of the museum's
choices on public taste or on the art market was unavoidable
fallout. "What should museums do?" he asked. "Abandon their

concern with recent art?" He concluded with a fable that might have come straight out of his father's stock of sermon homilies: "Reluctant 'tastemakers' like me and those like you who exaggerate the power of 'tastemakers'" should ponder the two flies who perched upon the axletree of a chariot and "complacently remarked to each other: 'What a dust we do raise!'"

But the dust would not settle. In October 1960 Canaday spoofed Abstract Expressionism by describing a mythical exhibition of works by one Ninguno Denada at the Node Gallery. He illustrated the show's theme, "The Authority of the Accidental," with a vague blot titled *Blue Element* and satirically described the artist's special appeal: "Like it or not, Denada is an artist of our time and a courageous one . . . an ultimate expression of the element of courage that is inherent in the recognition of defeat." This kind of empty wordspinning, he added, "is not much different from the brain-washing that goes on in universities and museums, except that it includes a minimum of jargon." So angry over this gentle parody was Howard Conant, chairman of the New York University art department, that he wrote to *Times* publisher Arthur Hays Sulzberger demanding that he "do something" about this troublesome critic. The letter was signed by sixteen of Conant's colleagues and a carbon went to Alfred Barr. Sulzberger coolly replied that he was surprised that Conant would ask the newspaper to "withdraw our support from Mr. Canaday—that is, to fire him." He wondered "what the reaction would be if Mr. Canaday and sixteen of his colleagues got together and petitioned NYU to fire one of you."

Canaday persistently nipped at the pretensions of aesthetic muckamucks for thinking that they had a monopoly on artistic discourse, and he punctured the illusions that draped art speculators in the costume of artistic patronage. Nor did he always take himself or his critics altogether seriously. Lambasted by Daniel Catton Rich (then director of the Worcester Art Museum) for his reserved view of Abstract Expressionism, Canaday claimed he was most hurt that Rich thought him "uninteresting." In another early column, he wrote that the ideal modern art museum held "a stance with one foot in the grave of the past and the other on the banana peel of the moment."

In February 1961, the *Times* published a letter signed by forty-nine devotees of contemporary art: collectors, artists, critics, writers, and professors. It protested Canaday's references to frauds, freaks, profiteers, and charlatans among contemporary artists, as well as his reference to Barr's extraordinary tastemaking power. The group charged that Canaday was not acting as a critic but as an agitator. Neither Barr nor anyone else connected with the MOMA signed that letter, but a carbon of it ended up in his files. The *Times*'s previously somnolent art department was bombarded with more than six hundred replies to this letter. Edward Hopper called Canaday "the best and most outspoken art critic the *Times* has ever had" and deplored the "strong forces of money and influence against him." Some of those defending the critic were powerful art personalities, like MOMA trustee Ralph Colin. Most were unknown in the art world, including one who wrote that "anyone who can make so many distinguished people so angry must be doing a good job." About 550 letters defended the critic, though Canaday lightheartedly noted, "not all of these . . . for the right reasons."

Meanwhile, the *Times*'s president, Orville Dryfoos, invited Barr to one of the weekly lunches the editors held with various newsmakers. Before going, Barr conferred with Blanchette and David Rockefeller, d'Harnoncourt, MOMA publicity woman Elizabeth Shaw, and Ralph Colin, the trustee whose long letter to the newspaper had complimented Canaday for his courage in being a moderate "in a time when the avant-garde has become more academic than any academy." In the lengthy, much-rewritten account Barr deposited in his files after the lunch, Barr noted that as they sat down to eat, "Dryfoos said immediately that we would not discuss the Canaday matter. . . . Ignoring this, Mr. [Lester] Markel asked me right off what I thought the proportion of letters pro and con Canaday was." Barr had planned to discuss "general ideas which might be advantageous to the museum . . . the greatly increased interest in the arts among the general public and the rapidly growing significance of the arts as factors in national prestige, made acute by the cold war." But he also could not resist a bit of adroit flattery, hoping perhaps to get the *Times* to restrain its outspoken art critic. He told the editors that courses in art history and painting had grown enormously "even in such a philistine college as Princeton, though Princeton, always a poor university, had not been able to catch up with Dartmouth and its magnificent new art center (Dartmouth was Mr. Dryfoos' college)."

After that inconclusive encounter, Barr tried just once more to convert Canaday. In August 1961, Canaday wrote unkindly of a MOMA exhibition of assemblages organized by Barr's protégé, William Seitz. Canaday complained that Seitz's catalog introduction was impenetrable to the average reader; rather, it would "affirm the unhappy impression people now have that the museum is an asylum for intellectual fops." After a bitter phone exchange, Seitz hung up on Canaday and rushed to Barr for balm. As he so often did when threatened or angry, Barr sharpened his pencil, eventually committing to his files four drafts of a four-page defense of Seitz, his catalog, his exhibition, and of the museum in general. Unfortunately, the museum's administrative bureaucracy had so proliferated that by the time it was cleared for submission to the *Times*, three months had gone by, the offending exhibition was long closed, and the newspaper refused to print the letter. Covertly, however, Barr got in a final shot: he vetoed Canaday as the writer for a series of seminars on modern art, to be distributed by the Book-of-the-Month Club. He suggested that Monroe Wheeler not "reduce our rejection of Canadé [sic] to institutional or personal pique" but simply explain that the critic disapproved of too much twentieth-century art.

One reason for Barr's righteous wrath at Canaday was that the critic did not fully adhere to Barr's dogma of modern art, and was proposing a modified alternative gospel. Unlike Barr, Canaday did write a coherent, all-inclusive history of modern art. Published in 1964, Canaday's *Mainstreams of Modern Art* is a handsomely illustrated and blessedly readable volume weaving all of the nineteenth century into a seamless web with the twentieth-century revolutionaries. Canaday was more relaxed than Barr about fitting artists into discrete "schools" and also occasionally referred comfortably to the academic mainstream art of the nineteenth century, showing that the revolutionaries of Modernism had obvious roots in traditionalism. Like Barr, Canaday also had a knack for captivating the average reader with vivid prose and unusually paired illustrations.

Unlike his adversary at the Museum of Modern Art, Canaday luxuriated in the time needed to peruse the New York art scene; indeed, his chief occupation was to do so and to report his findings to the public from the city's most powerful podium. Barr, by contrast, was increasingly handcuffed by petty details. He frequently expressed his frustration at the museum's demands. "I no longer attempt to keep up with my work here at the museum," he wrote in 1961 to German art historian Werner Haftmann, "it's too much and too complicated and I am too distracted." In 1963 he was invited to the reopening of Falling Water, the landmark Frank Lloyd Wright house built by Mr. and Mrs. Edgar Kaufmann in Bear Run, Pennsylvania. It would have been Barr's first chance to see the bronze doors their son, Edgar Kaufmann, Jr., had commissioned from Alberto Giacometti for his parents' crypt. Barr scribbled on the bottom of the invitation: "I don't want to go." To a Dartmouth professor, Barr wrote in 1964 that he was "not *au courant* with the art teaching field." And when an invitation came to speak on contemporary design, in 1965, Barr confessed that "thirty years ago I might have felt competent... but today, no. I've not been able to keep up with design problems. My present work at the museum has made that impossible." He also seemed to find it impossible to fathom that millions of ordinary people yearned for a touch of modern art, no matter how attenuated. When a colleague at the MOMA wanted to bring out a jigsaw puzzle featuring one of the museum's circular paintings, Barr was furious at such trivializing of a work of art. He still saw himself as a proselytizer, the colleague recalled, and "couldn't grasp that the public was now clamoring for this [modern] work."

In some ways, Barr's mother, with her implacable religious faith, seemed to retain more flexibility than her son. In 1957, at the age of eighty-nine, she wrote to Barr that she was pleased to be sleeping without medicines and had taken two car rides, after an operation. "Thank God if I can't walk, he has left me my senses." The Barrs, who were in South America, had sent her a telegram and card and she felt "rich." A week later she wrote to report that she had gained one pound and was up to all of 102 pounds. "My ribs are apparent, my bust nil!" Alert and active, she died four years later at the age of ninety-three.

Barr's mother had a lively interest in family matters and her letters were studded with reports about even distant relatives. By contrast, Barr seemed almost frightened by intimations of intimacy. When his brother, Andrew, asked about how to purchase a sculpture for Grosse Point University, Barr's reply was exceedingly formal and perfunctory, it was signed, "Sincerely." His daughter, Victoria, had grown up in a household where art was an obsession. Her learning disability made academic success difficult and the unsettled times for young people during the late fifties and sixties, not to mention her parents' frequent travels, left her at loose ends. In September 1956, she enrolled in the Parsons School of Design, intending to pursue some kind of artistic career. A year later, she transferred to Yale, where she graduated in fine arts in 1961. She was unsatisfied with the program there and, Barr wrote to a friend, her schooling "ended in exasperation."

Despite her parents' opposition, perhaps even embarrassment, Victoria insisted on becoming a painter. She passed a summer at the MacDowell Colony, a New England retreat for artists, and spent two years in Paris, attempting to find her style. In the summer of 1966, she exhibited her paintings in Rome. Having been courted by aspiring artists throughout his career, Barr felt uncomfortable about Victoria's aspirations. Collector Larry Aldrich, who organized a series of exhibitions for young talent during the late sixties and early seventies, remembered visiting her loft on Fourteenth Street to pick up one of her paintings. When Barr toured the exhibition, he paused before Victoria's work and noted the signature with surprise. "Not bad," he said.

Barr's testiness in his later life was exacerbated by a siege of poor health plaguing him all through the 1960s. The nervousness which kept him awake so often worsened in 1960, and in June he was ordered to avoid excitement and take a cure at Evian. Typically, he talked the doctor who prescribed this treatment into an associate MOMA membership. Sipping the water at the French spa during July, Barr was ill part of the time. The next year, he was ordered to take a three-month rest "since I have reached an unendurable state of exhaustion." In the winter of 1962, Barr again had to take an extended rest. Upon returning to the museum in April, he still felt "exhausted to the point of idiocy," and the

trustees arranged for him to take a six-month sabbatical beginning in June.

The Barrs crossed the Atlantic for a long stay abroad, but their
many hectic odysseys in the past seemed to leave them unable to
savor a more leisurely kind of travel. Along the way, they planned
to visit the Impressionist scholar John Rewald at his summer home
in the south of France. Rewald wanted to pick them up at the
nearest railroad station, but the Barrs adamantly refused. And
then one day Rewald received a typical, memorable telegram from
Marga in Paris: "Arriving Monday Avignon, 4:35. Don't bother." Of
course, Rewald was there and drove them to the neighboring guest
house, where they were to stay for some days. "First thing, we had
to move one of the twin beds out of the sleeping loft," Rewald
recalled, "because they simply did not want to share a bedroom."
Though they worked together harmoniously on Barr's professional
projects and were intellectually compatible, the romance in their
marriage appears to have been cool, if not altogether absent.
Furthermore, Barr's chronic insomnia and consequent restlessness
made it difficult for anyone sharing his sleeping quarters to get a
good night's rest.

The beds duly moved, Marga insisted that she would cook
dinner, even though no groceries were on hand, and Rewald gently
insisted that they join him for dinner. Every evening he had to
insist again. In the mornings, they would swim in Rewald's pool,
Marga counting the strokes in Greek, as she prepared for the next
leg of their journey. But they would never stay for lunch, Rewald
recalled, because they had to nap. In the afternoons, they would
often go for a drive, with the chauffeur under strict instructions to
stop every time they spotted a bird, so that Barr could study it with
binoculars. "For days after they left," Rewald remembered, "the
driver would still slow down for birds."

Traveling on to Greece, the Barrs did not move at a leisurely
sabbatical pace, but rather frenetically; Barr's travel notebooks
indicate that they dashed to Delphi, Olympia, Nauplia, and back to
Athens all in a four-day period, before embarking on a week's
cruise to the Aegean Islands and Istanbul. A *Vogue* article that fall,
based on an interview with Marga, made it all sound romantically
lush and leisured: they had gone to Greece in May "in time to catch

the wildflowers at their wildest color," while at Missolonghi, Barr yearned "to take off my shoes . . . where Byron died." Afterward, "Mr. Barr followed the causeway across the lagoon to the sea, and there at a waterfront cafe tasted the town's great product, the chewy *avgotaraho*, dried fish roe preserved in beeswax."

In the summer the Barrs attended a conference on the arts in Salisbury, Rhodesia, and rushed to East Africa for a week's safari-dash through Mozambique, Kenya, and Tanzania. Always the collector, he reported sighting thirty-one species of animals and almost 140 kinds of birds. On the way to the airport, in the last ten minutes of that hasty junket, they detoured through a game reserve in Nairobi, and Barr was pleased to add a rarity to his "collection," the view of a leopard and three half-grown cubs.

As retirement neared, Barr became even more depressed about his inability to keep up with his self-imposed duties as the apostle of modern art. Asked to cooperate with an exhibition of contemporary Italian painting in 1960, Barr replied, "I am simply not well enough informed on most recent Italian work." To a friend he lamented that "most of my time these days is spent writing apologies for not having written (phoned, called upon) my friends." A colleague who gave him her paper on Henry van de Velde, a Belgian modern architect who had fascinated Barr in the 1920s, received it back with a desperate note: "I simply do not have the eyes or energy to read anything except what is absolutely essential, and that in a superficial manner. Because of my state of exhaustion, of eyes and brain, I haven't read a serious book in several years. Excuse this suggestion of self-pity. . . ."

Work undone, contacts lost, books unread, writing uncompleted—these devils had haunted Barr's career from the beginning. He had always taken on too much and he had always been behind. But now the time to catch up seemed to be sifting all too rapidly through the glass and Barr's Calvinist drive to get things done conflicted painfully with his perennial desire to wander down enticing byways. He still did jury duty almost every year, while complaining loudly of how much time the task stole. He cheerfully answered odd letters, even ones in distinctly childish script: "Dear Sir, I made this picture. Please let me know if you like it. . . . Yours truely [sic], Donald Galler." "Thank you very much for sending me your painting," Barr replied. "I like looking at it and appreciate your thoughtfulness. Please paint some more." When he learned of a new Robert Moses outrage upon Central Park, he wrote with biblical wrath to the *Herald-Tribune*: "The park should begin with woodland, not more building. . . . Birdwatchers with binoculars, mothers with baby carriages have dammed Moses' concrete tide twice in the past five years. *Aux armes*, citizens." To the editor of the *Hartford Courant* Barr objected to the suspension of a high school boy for combing his hair in bangs: "One of the silliest demonstrations of American conformism anywhere."

Perhaps Barr took delight in guerrilla tactics on peripheral issues because his crusade for modern art had become such a rip-snorting success. New York during the 1960s was teeming with new galleries, new dealers, new styles, new artists and it seemed as though new collectors were ready to embrace everything they offered. Abstract Expressionism faded into staid classicism as a wild new group of artists took the city by storm. In a single year, 1962, Roy Lichtenstein unfurled his gaudy blowups of comics at Leo Castelli Gallery, Jim Dine dangled real hammers and saws from a canvas at Martha Jackson Gallery, James Rosenquist sprayed billboard-size collages, while Claes Oldenburg dumped an eleven-foot-long limp fabric ice cream cone on the floor at the Green Gallery, and Andy Warhol signed soup cans and centered a gaudy silkscreen of Marilyn Monroe on a dusky gold canvas at the Stable Gallery. After more than a decade of abstract drips, dabs, and globs, figural art was back, blatantly screaming its commercial origins. "It was hard to get a painting that was despicable enough so that no one would hang it," wrote one observer. Collectors triumphantly were hauling home even a dripping paint rag.

In December of 1962, a distinguished panel of art historians and critics met at the Museum of Modern Art to examine this new phenomenon called Pop Art. While four of the five panelists were dubious about it, a pudgy, nervous, young curator from the Metropolitan vigorously defended this work, arguing that "it is the artist who decides what is art." He was Henry Geldzahler, who had been hired by the Met two years earlier to infuse some life into its American collections. Abandoning a Harvard Ph.D. thesis on the sculpture of Matisse, Geldzahler had thrown himself into the New

York art whirlpool. He was said to visit seven or eight artists' studios every day; he attended every gallery opening and every artists' party and, for some six years, he began and ended each day with a phone call to Andy Warhol.

Geldzahler's articulateness and vigor posed a painful challenge to the MOMA's reputation as the citadel of innovative art. Suddenly, the staid Metropolitan appeared to be leapfrogging into the vanguard of the new. Meanwhile, a great many earlier champions of the avant-garde were mourning the passing of an age. Picasso scholar Douglas Cooper pointed to a "creative outburst" comparable to the Italian Renaissance during the twentieth century but believed it had ended in 1945; since then, he scolded, "no one has worried any more about technical competence, seriousness of purpose or genuine creative effort." A critic in the *Times Literary Supplement* wrote that the very concept of an avant-garde was being questioned, "most keenly by those who most respect its achievements." This writer found it significant that postwar Germany was the most receptive country in Europe to artistic innovation, perhaps to atone for the reactionary barbarism of the Nazis; meanwhile, the Soviet Union's continued intolerance of the new "drove governments and patrons toward the new assumption that avant-gardism might be a symbol of democracy." It was time, he added, "to distinguish between the difficult and the merely unintelligible, the extreme and the merely disgusting, the experimental and the merely affected." After a hundred years of alienation from bourgeois capitalist society, artists were now in league with the commercial system, wrote Donald D. Egbert, a Princeton art historian. "The very conception of the avant-garde is changing."

Clearly, it was a difficult time to be responsible for keeping a modern museum's collection up to date. A respected critic described one exhibition of new MOMA acquisitions as "the last refuge of parrots" and deplored the museum's zealous search for " 'the tradition of the new,' which, as we know, oxidized on the surface of a rusting First World War tank called the avant-garde." Even an insider like William Seitz, whose doctoral thesis on Abstract Expressionism Barr had sponsored, wondered what would become of the museum, now that "scouts . . . are scrambling over each other in search of new talent, jazz, money, and power based in 'avant-garde' art [and] the role of the MOMA has been taken over by a small international army." Barr's old friend and early MOMA trustee Edward M. M. Warburg sadly confessed that he could not appreciate the new art: "Try as I will, nothing comes through to me and I am sorely tempted to cry out, 'The king has no clothes on.' " He worried that works entered the museum's permanent collection not because of their aesthetic quality but "to illustrate a theory, a paper, a lecture or a catalog . . . reduc[ing] the object to secondary interest." Barr was stung that "our tastes have grown so far apart" and suggested that Warburg spend more time reading what artists were saying about their work. The committee on collections often fell into "lively argument" about new works, Barr wrote, and suggested it was time for Warburg to commit his 1905 Picasso *Blue Boy* to the MOMA so that it could be shown in the next exhibition of works given or promised.

Barr tried hard to resist the conservatism that seems to dull the taste of aging connoisseurs. "Collect when you are young," the National Gallery's director John Walker has written. "We all tend to see with the eyes of our own generation . . . after a certain age you will probably fail to perceive the new movement." Barr flailed against such inevitable change in his own aesthetic taste. Indeed, former MOMA administrator Richard Koch remembered a delicious moment when Alfred Barr was trying to persuade the trustees to buy a Warhol triptych featuring Marilyn Monroe. "He waxed marvelously eloquent, giving a long dissertation on Marilyn Monroe as a sex goddess. He compared her to the *hetairae* of ancient Athens." The trustees' jaws dropped, and Koch, who was secretary, scribbled furiously as Barr held forth learnedly and at length on the warm embrace of eroticism and the arts.

Despite such occasional sallies into the contemporary scene, there is no doubt that Barr devoted the bulk of his energies during those last years at the museum to consolidating its collection of older art, to raising funds for buying and displaying time-tested works, and to building up the collections of trustees who might be expected to leave the MOMA important legacies. At the end of 1960, with three exhibitions to direct, Barr was frantic over the extra meetings the MOMA collections committee was scheduling to rule on all the works the museum was being offered. "Our tax

structure is such that we have had to have two and perhaps may
need another . . . meeting," he wrote to a patron, "to cope with end
of the year gifts which are to be counted as deductions."

No collector received more attention and advice from Barr than
Abby Aldrich Rockefeller's second son, Nelson. Abby had gently
steered her youngster toward art from an early age. He had difficulty reading—today he would be called dyslexic—and she believed that he would find in art the satisfactions his handicap
denied him from literature. Nelson was active in the museum
almost from its founding, as a member of the advisory committee
which his mother established as a training ground for future
trustees. He did become a trustee in 1932, at the age of twenty-four
and two years later anonymously gave the museum $1 million, a
sum unheard of in that Depression era. The gift was announced at
a trustees' meeting shortly after $600,000 had been painfully
raised to meet the endowment requirement of the Bliss bequest.
After the meeting, Eliza Bliss Parkinson was sharing a taxi home
with Nelson Rockefeller. As the car approached Central Park she
asked him who could possibly have given the million dollars.
"Nelson turned into a stone statue," Mrs. Parkinson recalled, and
"said not another word" until the taxi exited the park at Seventy-
second Street. At last, he turned to her and explained, "Well, I just
came into my money and . . ." Rockefeller was then, appropriately,
chairman of the MOMA finance committee. Later, he would also
serve on the executive and building committees before becoming
museum president in 1939.

The first work Barr had helped Nelson to buy was an Ahron ben-
Shmuel sculpture, *Pugilist*, which cost the enormous sum of $1,000
in 1934. In the next year, the collecting bug seriously bit and
Rockefeller bought a whole group of sculptures from Gaston
Lachaise's first MOMA exhibition. While guiding Nelson Rockefeller's taste in art, Barr also judged his wife's taste in clothes.
After the gala opening of the museum's fifth-anniversary show,
Barr thanked the first Mrs. Rockefeller, Tod, for her help and
"above all for the magnificent dress which you wore. No wonder
people turned their backs on Matisses when you were in the center
of the room." Barr was not the only bystander seduced into base
flattery by contact with the Rockefeller magic. Some decades later,

Willem de Kooning, a dinner guest at the Rockefeller duplex, was having drinks in the library with Nelson when Tod descended between the Matisse panels flanking the elegant stairway. The artist gazed at her and exclaimed, "Oh, Mrs. Rockefeller, you look like a million dollars!"

Over the years, Nelson Rockefeller accumulated art in great drifts, filling his New York apartment, his weekend retreat in Pocantico, his estate house in Venezuela, the New York governor's mansion in Albany when he moved there in 1958, and the vice-president's residence in Washington, D.C., in 1974. In 1969, when the MOMA sponsored an exhibition of his collection, Rockefeller owned about fifteen hundred modern works. Five years later, a poignant measure of the art boom, *Time* magazine reported that his collection encompassed sixteen thousand items, including an immense hoard of primitive art, and was worth $33.5 million. Just as his father had relied on the Metropolitan's director, James Rorimer, in gathering the treasure of medieval art which became the rich nucleus of the Cloisters, so Nelson Rockefeller relied on his own museum connections. Alfred Barr and his colleagues at the Museum of Modern Art seldom visited a gallery without Nelson's collection in mind. Nor did René d'Harnoncourt object to spending odd afternoons with him hanging pictures; rather, he professed "delight at the exertion and its results." Frequently, Barr would order paintings sent to the MOMA and store them there, sometimes for months, until Nelson had time to decide whether he wanted to buy them. When Nelson's son Michael had to write a paper for a Harvard course in twentieth-century art, Barr advised him about Picasso and read the resulting work "with great interest." On his European trips, Barr always developed recommendations for Nelson's purchases. In 1960, he exulted about Nelson's timely purchase, a few years earlier, of a Pierre Soulages abstraction for some $1,500: "It is worth about nine or ten times as much now. His current show is sold out."

As he did with everything else he tackled, Nelson Rockefeller brought ebullient enthusiasm to his grand accumulation of artistic goods. Like his mother, he bought what he liked and sometimes irritated the museum professionals with his impulsively emotional decisions. While he profited enormously from his shrewd art in-

vestments, Nelson also felt genuine affection for art; he called it
"the greatest recreation ever devised. . . . It goes beyond pleasure, it
is almost an ecstasy." Barr said that of all the collectors he had
known, Nelson had the most insatiable appetite for art and the
purest motives for collecting it. "Status, competition, investment,
pride of possession, pride of taste and even reputation for being a
'patron of the arts' do not interest him. . . . Works of art give him a
deep, almost therapeutic delight and refreshment such as other
men may find in music or alcohol. To see his enthusiasm over a new
painting, or even more, to take off one's coat and help him rehang a
room in his apartment is a pleasure never to be forgotten."

Barr's greatest pleasure, however, was to accept the massive
parade of masterpieces Nelson Rockefeller donated to the museum.
The exact number is difficult to ascertain because the Rockefeller
family often gave the museum art works (and money) anonymously, but two of its greatest treasures were Nelson's gifts:
Rousseau's *The Dream*, which he gave in 1954 after finding that the
picture was too large for the living room in the governor's mansion,
and Matisse's *The Dance*, given in 1963 in honor of Alfred Barr.

By no means all the collectors Barr had pampered and courted
through the years eventually came through. Soby described with
some chagrin how Henry Church had begged Barr to help him buy
a fine Utrillo, *Rue de Crimée*, at a special museum price and
promised to leave it to the museum. After Church died, Barr and
Soby called on his widow in Paris, a woman some thirty years
younger than the deceased collector, to remind her of Church's
promise. "She practically called us liars," Soby wrote, "and had us
ushered abruptly to the door."

Some collectors cut the Museum of Modern Art because they felt
neglected. Columnist Dorothy Norman, for example, gave her
collection of Alfred Stieglitz photographs, many of them never
exhibited in New York, to the Philadelphia Museum. Only after her
bequest was announced did Barr attempt to persuade her to
change her mind, but to no avail; she was furious that "no one at the
Museum of Modern Art has shown the slightest interest" in them.

Other collectors relished the courtship they attracted by keeping
museum people uncertain of their intentions. Peggy Guggenheim
left any number of institutions dangling as she dithered over what

would become of the collection which, it turned out, was the one enduring passion of her life. In 1952 Barr had asked her to consider giving the museum her three first-rate de Chiricos, along with seventy-five out of the 190 items she owned. After pondering for more than two years, Guggenheim replied that she often thought about "what is dearest to your heart" but had still come to no conclusion. "Death," she wrote, "seems very far away." She did not want to be called a collector but rather a patroness, saying that "collectors conjure up images of fat, rich millionaires trying to dodge taxes or be socially in." She also believed that the great art period of the century had fizzled out in the early 1950s and that what came later was "the period of the followers." Nevertheless, she reveled in disclosing that her investment of $250,000 was now worth $30 million. The Barrs paid innumerable calls at Peggy's Venetian palazzo, but in the end, after years of coy correspondence, she determined to leave her collection in Venice, as a branch of the Guggenheim Museum. The Museum of Modern Art did not need everything she owned, she wrote, begging Barr not to "let this alter our friendship."

Also irksome, though hardly unexpected, was Stephen Clark's total disregard of the museum in his will. When he died in 1960 at the age of seventy-eight, not one cent of his $11.5 million estate went to the institution whose efforts had so greatly enhanced the value of his art collection. The Metropolitan, where he had also been chairman of the board, and Yale University, where he had been educated, shared a bounty of Cézannes, Corots, Manets, and Degas, plus works by such Americans as Ryder, Bellows, Blume, Speicher, and Hopper. The Met also received $500,000, while Yale got $1 million cash and van Gogh's *Night Café*, a haunting work which had been on extended loan to the MOMA for many years. The bequests will "keep alive in the long future," intoned the *New York Times*, "the widely ranging influence . . . which [Clark] himself exerted for so many years in the past," but such tribute was small comfort to the busy gleaners at the Modern.

Even more galling, however, was the disaffection of A. Conger Goodyear, the crusty collector from Buffalo who had devoted a decade of his life to launching the Museum of Modern Art as its president from 1929 to 1939. Barr had lavished his energies on buying pictures for the Goodyear collection during this time and later, always with the expectation that they would eventually come home to the MOMA. When Goodyear expressed interest in Giacomo Balla's charming Futurist *Dog on a Leash*, for example, Barr had bargained until Balla gave it away for $600, less than half of his asking price. In 1953, Barr had arranged for Goodyear to have a private tour of Peggy Guggenheim's collection after warning the randy heiress to censor a Marini horseman, whose erect penis was removable when prudish visitors called. "He is inclined to be a bit apoplectic about some of the art after Matisse and Picasso," wrote Barr. Meanwhile, he confided to Goodyear that Guggenheim "might leave us many of the best things she owns. . . . If she speaks of it, please be enthusiastic."

In 1958, however, Goodyear let it be known that he intended to leave most of his collection to the Albright-Knox Gallery in Buffalo, the very institution whose trustees had fired Goodyear in 1928 over his purchase of a mild and pretty early Picasso. When Goodyear announced in 1960 that this legacy would also include an important Matisse, a Léger, a Pascin and, most grievously, the Balla *Dog*, Barr was irate. "Few things in the history of the museum have shocked me more or hurt me as much," he wrote to Goodyear. Less than two months earlier, Goodyear had reaffirmed that he was leaving these pictures to the Museum of Modern Art, so Barr had good reason for "the taste of ashes in my mouth." What had bothered Goodyear for many years was that the MOMA had so many important works in storage that the public hardly every saw. He wanted the museum to sell the older works in order to buy new ones. But the museum's staff and trustees were now so firmly committed to a huge and largely invisible permanent collection that such a suggestion smacked of sacrilege. Furthermore, though the values of even the lesser items in the vaults had risen steeply, the original donors, like Olga Guggenheim, would be alarmed at any sales and future donors likewise would reconsider their bequests. The Albright-Knox Gallery had no such qualms. After receiving Goodyear's legacy in 1964, it held an intermuseum auction and raised more than $1 million for new purchases.

For the MOMA, the decision to form a permanent collection was a straitjacket it could never shake off. Instead of selling or trading older works, the museum was constantly scrambling for space and Barr's time was increasingly occupied with fund-raising for larger facilities. To kick off a drive to raise $25 million in the fall of 1959, Barr arranged a visual propaganda coup. Instead of his usually spare, even monastic, arrangements, he had plastered the walls with pictures, dozens in the space where usually three would hang, and piled in exhibitions of architecture and design, photographs, and prints and drawings. Titled "The Museum Collections—A Bid for Space," the hodgepodge dramatically conveyed the message that the collections were "suffocating for lack of space." A new wing would provide three-and-a-half times the current exhibition space and double the space for storage, wrote Barr for the label on this display, which remained on view for an entire year.

Though a professional fund-raiser ran the campaign, Barr was intimately involved. He tirelessly tracked prospects, keeping in his files, for example, a clipping which listed all contributors of more than $5,000 to the 1956 presidential campaign. He also obtained from collectors, artists, and dealers some fifty works of art to be auctioned for the museum's benefit. The sale at Parke-Bernet on April 27, 1960, was a media event, aired on closed-circuit television to permit bidding at the Chicago Arts Club, the Los Angeles County Museum of Art, and the Dallas Museum of Contemporary Arts. The most valuable picture was Cézanne's *Apples*, contributed by MOMA president William A. M. Burden and sold for around $130,000; the entire sale brought in about $500,000.

"I will be absolutely overwhelmed all this year with fund-raising," Barr grumbled to English critic Douglas Cooper. "I am much too overwhelmed with trying to keep my head above water as a result of half my time being spent on fund-raising," he complained to an NBC producer. "I have been in Paris only five days and in London only four during the past two years. Fund-raising and art seem to be mutually exclusive," Barr fretted to magazine publisher Alex Hillman. But Richard Koch, assistant to d'Harnoncourt, who worked closely with Barr during those years, believes that while Barr called fund-raising "institutional avarice," he also "enjoyed whining about being forced to do things he didn't want to do." He used his fund-raising duties as an excuse to put off more scholarly work. Barr "relished getting gifts of art," says Koch "and the next-best thing was getting money to buy works of art or expanding the space for storing and showing works of art."

The church Barr had built was crammed to the rafters and there was no end in sight to the parade of long-promised gifts pouring in. In 1948, the museum had owned 797 works; a decade later, the holdings had doubled to 1,360; and a decade after that, they had doubled again, to 2,622. But, like the founders of a church, Barr and his colleagues could not conceive that more could ever mean too much. A brochure Barr helped to develop in support of the museum's thirtieth-anniversary campaign in 1960 promised that the new facilities would allow 30 percent of its twelve hundred paintings to be exhibited; of three hundred sculptures, 43 percent would be shown; and of twenty-four hundred posters, which previously were totally inaccessible, 5 percent would be exhibited. All the rest of the museum's holdings would be "conveniently accessible." But the original notion that the museum would remain at the cutting edge was at long last a dead letter: five of the six masterpieces illustrated in the fund-raising brochure were well over fifty years old and the most recent work pictured was John Marin's *Lower Manhattan*, dated 1920.

The planning for the museum's thirtieth-anniversary campaign was immensely more elaborate than the planning that had gone into the museum's opening back in 1929. To prepare every detail of the campaign, the staff and trustees gathered in Northeast Harbor, Maine, during August 1959 for a four-day weekend. So many went that a special car was attached to the Grand Central Railroad's State of Maine Express to carry them to the site and back. In between lunches, dinners, picnics, and cocktail parties at Nelson and David Rockefeller's "cottages" and at Mrs. Edsel Ford's, an elaborate blueprint emerged. The dinner to kick off the campaign was held in the opulent Four Seasons Restaurant in the Seagram Building, Mies van der Rohe's elegant skyscraper on New York's Park Avenue. Along with a detailed description of all those who would sit at his table, complete with the amounts each had pledged to the campaign, Barr also received a split-second timetable of the festivities: 7:45 P.M., soup served; 8:10 P.M., main course served; 8:52 to 9:20 P.M., speech by Governor Rockefeller; 9:22 P.M., dessert and coffee served; 9:45 P.M., lights raised, guests leave.

Alfred Barr's father would have been proud of the draft revisions his son made in the thirtieth-anniversary prospectus (as it was pompously called) and of the speech he wrote for MOMA board chairman Henry Allan Moe, to be delivered at the dinner. "Barrier to full efficiency," was the leaden phrase the brochure's original writer had used; "bursting at the seams," was Barr's revision. For Moe, Barr wrote about how the museum's thirtieth birthday, like an individual's, came "at a time when past and future need to be linked by thought and action . . . it is well for us to ask ourselves . . . Where do we come from? Where are we now? Where are we going?"

On the eve of the dinner, the *New York Times* called the museum Alfred Barr had built "an attraction unique to the city," in a class with the Statue of Liberty, the Empire State Building, and Rockefeller Center. Indeed, Barr had presided over a major revolution not only in the world of art but also in the full spectrum of visual sensibility. In its first thirty years, the museum had exhibited some 70,000 paintings, sculptures, drawings, prints, photographs, architectural models, and objects of daily life in 630 exhibitions attended by nearly 12 million people. The museum also had published 250 titles in a total edition of 3.5 million copies. Fourteen of the museum's publications had gone into foreign editions, translated into nine foreign languages. The publications themselves were exhibited as models of modern bookmaking in thirty-seven cities in Europe, Latin America, Asia, Australia, and New Zealand. The museum had members in every state in the Union and in forty-three foreign countries.

The scope of the collection supervised by Barr was truly staggering—nineteen thousand items, when one counted all the photographs, prints, drawings, book illustrations, architectural models, furniture, and decorative pieces. The film collection was the largest in private hands; the museum owned more Tiffany glass than anyone else; the print collection was the largest in existence, including more Klees than the Klee Foundation in Berne and more School of Paris works than the Bibliothèque Nationale in Paris. As a whole, the museum's collection of modern paintings and sculptures was unquestionably the best in the world, strong in virtually every detail. It owned the best British collection outside London; the best German collection outside, perhaps, Germany; the best Mexican collection outside Mexico City; the best Italian collection anywhere, even in Italy; the best French collection, unmatched even in France; the best Latin American collection anywhere; and, persistent criticism notwithstanding, the best American collection as well. In representing the works of individual artists, too, the Museum of Modern Art had become preeminent. It owned the strongest collections in the world of Beckmann, Blume, Chagall, De Chirico, Ernst, Giacommetti, Graves, Hopper, Lachaise, Lehmbruck, Lipchitz, Maillol, Miró, Mondrian, Henry Moore, Picasso, Pollock, and Ben Shahn and was strong in the works of Matisse, Arp, Boccioni, Brancusi, Braque, Demuth, Derain, Despiau, Gris, Kirchner, Klee, Léger, Malevich, Monet, Orozco, Rivera, and Siqueiros. And on top of all that, seventy-two more outstanding modern works were already partly given to the museum or promised in the wills of their owners.

Along with the explosive growth of the MOMA's collections, however, came a swelling of its staff and consequent bureaucratic sclerosis. The staff now routinely made rough plans for exhibitions five years in advance and firmed them up two or three years ahead. The schedules were top secret to prevent outside dealers or collectors from cashing in on the price rises that inevitably came after an artist's work was shown at the museum, but of course the trustees knew the schedule and benefited accordingly, and so did the dealers and outside collectors positioned to catch the leaks.

In the museum's salad days, its idealism had attracted an idealistic staff, enthusiastic amateurs often informally trained. Among them was Helen Franc, one of Barr's first students at Wellesley, who went on to become a serious art scholar and writer. Another Barr assistant, Olive Bragazzi, started in the MOMA stenographic pool in 1947 and became a sought-after cataloger of private collections, among them that of MOMA president William A. M. Burden. But as the staff grew and the museum aged, formal education weighed far more heavily than enthusiasm or office skills. When Barr needed a secretary in 1961, he chose a young woman who had written a first-rate senior thesis at college on Abstract Expressionism. To prepare for her actual work in Barr's office, he ordered her to take a secretarial course during the summer.

Catalogs also suffered from middle-aged spread, on their way to obesity, and the search for experts to write them sometimes dragged on for years. Now sixty-five years old and on the eve of his retirement, Barr admitted to a Guggenheim Museum curator that he had put off a retrospective exhibition of Kasimir Malevich for six or eight years because "I could not find anyone with adequate discipline as an art historian and at the same time someone who knew Russian and preferably German too."

The arteries hardened also in the circulating system which had sent so many of the museum's exhibitions traveling to the American hinterland. For one thing, works of the fifties and sixties were often too huge for museum loading docks and elevators; for another, insurance had become prohibitive, the major cost of any traveling show. During the thirties Picassos and Matisses had crisscrossed the country in carpentered crates to edify and amaze—and frequently outrage—the visitors to department stores, women's clubs, and college art galleries; now much lesser works could hardly budge. The Ben Heller collection of contemporary paintings never made the rounds, for example, because the rental fees the museum had to charge were so exorbitant that even major museums refused it. During the 1967–1968 season, the museum had fifty-one exhibitions shown in 156 communities in the United States and Canada, hardly more than had crisscrossed the country during 1936.

Like the Frankenstein monster which has fascinated so many mid-twentieth-century artists, the dogma of Modernism Barr had built took on a powerful—and not always beneficent—life of its own. A survey in France during the 1960s found that 66 percent of working class people believed that a museum was most like a church; 45 percent of the middle class and 30.5 percent of the upper class agreed. The art centers proliferating around the world, wrote John Canaday, were expected to "ooze forth . . . a form of enriching plasma that perhaps soaked through the soles of the feet." The public was "so culturally voracious," wrote another critic, "that the avant-garde, far from needing defenders among the critics, is in the public domain." Even a firebrand of Modernism like Julien Levy suggested that the MOMA had gone too far in promoting trendy works of art. The ideal museum, he suggested to Barr, ought to function "a bit like the Federal Reserve, to stimulate in times of depression and to restrain in times of exuberance."

Modernism had inevitably joined the mainstream. Jacqueline Kennedy became an honorary member of the museum's International Council in 1962, soon after the president of the United States himself asked Barr for suggestions on "the possible contributions the national government might make to the arts in America." Even S. Dillon Ripley, secretary of the Smithsonian and a venerable foe of modernism, was spotted one afternoon on the MOMA's third floor, calmly examining works of Pop and Op Art. Nor did one have to set foot in any gallery at all to become aware of the modishness of modern art. Featured in an advertisement for a New York department store was a mohair and nylon sheath dress (twenty-three dollars) for "the Young Cosmopolitan . . . at the Museum of Modern Art."

In such an atmosphere of benign acceptance, the only philistines Barr could reliably count upon for opposition were the Russians. While conducting a tour of the museum for a group of visiting Soviet journalists, Barr patiently defended modern art and when they left, he gave each visitor a copy of *What Is Modern Painting?* He was duly outraged some months later when an article describing the visit appeared in the leading Soviet cultural periodical, *Literaturnaya Gazeta.* "What was one to do," rhetorically asked A. Romanov, "when a polite greyhaired man with whom it was pleasant to argue even if you did not share his views, suddenly backhanded you a ball of rank anti-Soviet propaganda, giving you a book recounting entire paragraphs of insinuations published by the dirtiest American newspapers with regard to the art of Socialism?"

Barr leaped into action upon receiving a copy of this article, along with a mimeographed, unsigned form letter: "The enclosed material is sent to you in the desire to contribute toward a broader mutual knowledge. . . ." To the editor of *Art News* he dispatched a translation, along with his interpretation of it: "Sounds like Dondero . . . in the U. S. House of Representatives. . . ." Barr also telephoned Harrison Salisbury, who had covered the Soviet Union for the *New York Times* for many years, to ask about the author of the article. He was an agit-prop agent, Salisbury told him, "delegated to go along with other Soviet journalists to defend the party and counter-attack whenever feasible."

Beneath the brickbats, however, Barr carried on a cordial correspondence with administrators at the Soviet Union's most important museums. He was asked to contribute to the celebration of the Hermitage Museum director's fortieth anniversary and was immediately notified when the Matisse specialist there died. When poet Yevgeni Yevtushenko visited New York in 1966, he spent four hours in lively conversation with Barr, who appreciated the "candor on the part of both of us." For anyone in the art world who planned to visit the Soviet Union, Barr provided introductions to museum directors—and usually a recommendation to see the magnificent stuffed mammoth in the Moscow Natural History Museum which had so impressed him in 1927 and 1928. Perhaps his greatest sacrifice in behalf of good relations with Russians was that Barr, a man who loved to see his writings in print, withheld from publication until 1978 the diary he had kept during his winter's sojourn in the Soviet Union in 1927 and 1928.

When the *New York Times* art critic Hilton Kramer first visited the Soviet Union in 1967, he learned of the impact of Barr's private diplomacy; Barr was "a venerated name there." Having made an appointment to interview the director of the Hermitage, Kramer arrived with two interpreters only to be told by a secretary that the director was away, lecturing at the university. The ensuing frustrating twenty-minute conversation ended miraculously when Kramer mentioned the magic name. "Ah," said the secretary, smiling and for the first time using her perfect French, "*vous connaissez Monsieur Barr*." In five minutes, the museum director appeared and Kramer began a cordial two-hour interview with him. At the end, the director mysteriously invited Kramer to use the men's room. There, with all faucets running full blast to defeat any listening devices, the director of Russia's greatest museum breathlessly asked the newspaperman about all the museum gossip from the West: "Didn't the Met have a new director?" (Thomas Hoving had replaced James Rorimer four months earlier.) "And what was the new man like? And would he be interested in an exchange exhibition?"

Wherever there still appeared to be a threat to modern art, Barr lent his powerful voice to its defenders. When the city of Los Angeles was threatening to destroy Simon Rodia's playful Watts Towers, Barr rushed to their defense. He had first come upon Rodia's singular masterpiece after traveling through the "flat, forlorn and endless city-scape of Watts," he wrote to the National Council of the Arts. Seeing the towers for the first time, Barr was "deeply moved by . . . their wonder, their beauty, yes, but also by the sense of innocence and of faith that pervades them." Barr compared Rodia with Bartolomeo Vanzetti, "both great-hearted men, a poor tile-setter and a poor fish-peddler, rife with simplicity and noble passion. Their agony was their triumph, the one in death, the other in his Towers, his marvelous evidence of things unseen." The trip to see the Towers, Barr said, was "my pilgrimage."

To the man in the corner office overlooking the sculpture garden, the enemy still appeared to be beating at the gates, even as the museum's public calmly accepted the most bizarre manifestations of contemporary art. On March 17, 1960, at 6:30 P.M., a genial crowd gathered in the garden for the one-time spectacle of a work by Swiss sculptor Jean Tinguely. *Homage to New York* was a gigantic pile of absurd machinery, waggling and jiggling in eccentric spasms, much to the onlookers' delight. Most of the spectators were clutching a two-foot-long handbill on which Barr had written a suitably manic guide to what they were witnessing. "Forty years ago Tinguely's grandadas thumbed their noses at Mona Lisa and Cézanne," it began. The machine in the museum garden that evening would "scribble a moustache on the automatistic Muse of abstract expressionism, and (wipe that smile off your face) . . . [be] an apocalyptic far-out breakthrough which . . . clinks and clanks, tingles and tangles, whirs and buzzes, grinds and creaks, whistles and pops itself into a katabolic Götterdämmerung of junk and scrap. Oh, great brotherhood of Jules Verne, Paul Klee, Sandy Calder, Leonardo da Vinci, Rube Goldberg, Marcel Duchamp, Piranesi, Man Ray, Picabia, Filippo Morghen, are you with it? Tinguely *ex machina/Morituri te salutamos*." Barr's pseudo-dada prose set the tone: within a half hour Tinguely's entire contraption exploded in a fiery auto-da-fé and everyone went serenely home, snug in the conviction that they had witnessed a historic work of art.

Three years later, Barr lent his grave mien and august reputation to an early "Happening," *Hans Hofmann and His Students*, devised by Allan Kaprow. One of the two rooms arranged by the artist resembled van Gogh's bedroom at Arles and at the appropriate moment, Barr stepped in to place a banana inside a pink shoe under the bed. The audience did not seem to know how to react, the *New York Times* reported, being "either too solemn or too giddy to develop the connoisseur's thoughtful and symbolic act." But critic Brian O'Doherty concluded, a shade cryptically, that Barr, "with the chaste banana in the pink shoe has given the lead again."

Whether Barr found these works aesthetically satisfying is difficult to tell, since he seldom wrote about contemporary art any more and confined his few talks to an updating of his stock speech urging freedom for all artists. Nearing the end of his career, he returned to an earlier interest in religion, especially in upgrading the art purveyed by Protestant churches. "Consider the vulgarity and banality of the pictures of Christ now in general use," he had preached in 1957 to the National Council of Churches Commission on Art. " 'Gentle Jesus meek and mild' is translated into art on the level of cosmetic and tonic advertisements . . . these saccharine and effeminate images . . . corrupt the religious feelings of children . . . they call for iconoclasm. . . . When I think of such great Protestant artists as Dürer, Rembrandt, William Blake, I find the feeble drawing and poverty of vision, the petty historicity of our church-sponsored art not simply unendurable, but incredible."

In 1962, Barr became president of the Foundation of the Arts, Religion, and Culture, an offshoot of the National Council of Churches, on the promise that the post was purely honorific. Three years later he resigned, explaining that he had no time or energy for serving as a real president of the organization. He also became a trustee of New College in Sarasota, Florida, an innovative school sponsored by the Christian Congregational Church. He doubted that a picture was worth ten thousand words, Barr puckishly told the college's initial conference on educational objectives; "I think, probably one picture is worth, say, only 150 words." Having leaped into yet another commitment, Barr after this single contribution simply had no time for the college trustees' meetings and repeatedly wrote apologetic letters: "I know I've disappointed you. . . . I cannot do my own job and have consequently and alas! too little time to help others as I should like to. I will have no vacation this summer."

In fact, Barr was spending the summer in Greensboro, working, as usual, in between bird-watching, swimming in the icy lake, and making picnic excursions with Marga. But his health was increasingly frail. Every few months during these last years at the museum, he had to take time away to recuperate from various physical ailments. Even more alarming, however, were the lapses of memory which began to torment him. Larry Aldrich, who had put up a $10,000 annual fund to buy new art for the museum, noticed the problem while the Barrs were luncheon guests at his Connecticut home. "When he couldn't remember a crucial name," Aldrich recalled, "he put his head down on the table in a mighty effort at recalling, but without success." Monroe Wheeler noticed Barr's intense frustration when he forgot the name of an artist. "He would point his finger helplessly and cry out, 'Give me the name!' " Hilton Kramer remembers running into Barr one afternoon when a tour of New York galleries had left him especially depressed. "I greeted him," says Kramer, "and received an answer that chilled my blood. Alfred said, 'I feel very old.' " The idea that Alfred Barr would some day not be at the Museum of Modern Art was inconceivable to Kramer. Sadly, he added, "It was the last thing I ever heard him say."

12

THE ESTABLISHED
CHURCH

O n June 30, 1967, thirty-eight years after he had accepted
the mission of creating the Museum of Modern Art, Alfred
Barr retired. His pension—$25,000 per year—was more
than he had ever received while working full-time. He said he was
looking forward to having the leisure, at last, to revise his books
about Picasso and Matisse and, above all, to write the long-delayed
history of modern art for which publishers clamored. Elected to
the largely honorary post of councilor to the board of trustees, Barr
still maintained an office at the museum and a secretary who
issued no hint that Barr was ailing. Free from the pressures of
managing the museum's swollen collections, he was expected to
quickly wrap up one final MOMA project—a complete catalog of
the painting and sculpture collections.

Partially funded by the Ford Foundation, the unfinished catalog
represented a silent reproach, testimony to Barr's habitual procrastination. When it was still not finished in 1969, the catalog in
progress became an embarrassment to the museum. When a final
desperate push to complete it before Dorothy Miller's retirement in
July of 1972 also failed to produce a publication, the project looked

annoyingly ludicrous. But when Barr's secretary described him nine months later as "deeply engrossed" in the catalog and still nothing emerged, it seemed clear that more than a publication was at stake. As many an artist has shrunk from completing a masterpiece because he fears he will die with the last brush stroke, so Barr stubbornly avoided finishing *Painting and Sculpture in the Museum of Modern Art*. In countless urgent memos, and perhaps in exasperated conversations as well, it became abbreviated as PASITMOMA.

The book that finally emerged in 1977 after more than a decade of dithering and delay was a grand capstone to Barr's career, a richly illustrated tome of 657 oversized pages, weighing more than four pounds. Its hundreds of photographs, their blacks and middle tones velvety on hefty semiglossy paper, illustrated graphically the history of modern art Alfred Barr was not destined to write. Between its first illustration, Rousseau's *Sleeping Gypsy*, and its last, a motorized construction of steel, duraluminum, and plexiglass by Nicolas Schöffer, *Microtemps*, it handsomely illuminates the period of art known as the modern. By the time the catalog appeared, it was already hopelessly out of date and had to be accompanied by a slim 110-page volume edited by Alicia Legg. Its 3,400 entries included 550 works acquired by the museum after Barr's retirement. So the summation of his career was finally in hand, perhaps a grander and more fitting testimony to Barr's extraordinary accomplishments than a written history could have been.

"A fragile wisp of a man," was *Newsweek*'s description of Barr when his retirement was announced. "His tall, lean body, his bespectacled face, gentle voice and abstracted air give him the engaging look of an absent-minded Walt Disney professor." To an art magazine interviewer, Barr said he planned to complete the already "scandalously delayed" catalog and other writing. To a friend, he confided that "retiring from an institution where you've worked for thirty-eight years is an extremely complicated and time-consuming procedure."

A good deal of the complication in completing PASITMOMA resulted from the concurrent retirement of several other key museum figures. Gone was Monroe Wheeler, the feisty, outspoken,

and, some said, Machiavellian director of publications who had for
decades nudged, hassled, and shamed Barr into meeting some kind
of deadline in his writings. Also gone was Barr's unswerving
acolyte, the chairman of the trustees' committee on museum collections, James Thrall Soby. A year later came the most grievous loss:
René d'Harnoncourt retired and shortly afterward, while strolling
near his country home in Long Island, was run over and killed by a
passing motorist.

For almost two decades, René d'Harnoncourt had exercised his
consummate diplomacy for the care and conservation of Alfred
Barr. He replied suavely to Barr's testy memos about this or that
colleague's petty outrage, he mollified trustees who quailed at
some of Barr's more daring acquisitions, he patiently endured
Barr's delays and procrastinations, and, above all, he treated Barr
as the paramount museum asset that he was. D'Harnoncourt's
successor, Bates Lowry, was beset from the beginning by an
unruly band of trustees, a feuding staff, and a host of problems
characteristic of the sixties.

Though ostensibly retired, Barr maneuvered and intrigued and
offered the new director little but prickly snipings. When Lowry,
for example, mildly suggested moving Picasso's *Guernica* to a
different gallery in the museum, Barr mustered his limited energies to fire off a lengthy, magisterial memo reviewing his long
relationship with the artist and the museum's long-standing
guardianship of Picasso's work and reputation. He did not mention
his own frustrating relationship with the artist, but implied that
the MOMA had cordial understandings with the artist to whose
success it had so notably contributed. *Guernica*, Barr informed
Lowry, had been part of the MOMA's first Picasso exhibition in
1939; its sixty associated drawings and paintings, plus thirty-five
other paintings, remained on loan until the closing of the MOMA's
seventy-fifth-anniversary Picasso show in 1959. Then everything
went back to Picasso except the *Guernica* materials. Barr said that
he had persuaded the artist to allow the MOMA to keep the masterpiece until Picasso's death and thus felt responsible for the work.
For twenty years after painting *Guernica*, Picasso had "too generously" lent the picture elsewhere, too often it had been "rolled,
packed, shipped, unrolled, stretched, hung and then unstretched

and rolled." Because of its "vulnerable size and seriously worn condition, Picasso agreed that it should not be shown elsewhere," Barr wrote. The memo put Lowry on notice that Barr would dispute even the smallest changes the new director might propose.

From his perch on the sidelines, Barr wielded perhaps more power in his early retirement years than he had before. For one thing, he was personally an institution, almost an icon; his judgments about art were eagerly sought and rarely contradicted. For another, he was still a compelling suitor for potential donors, a role all the more crucial because the museum was in the midst of yet another fund-raising drive. Once more, the collection had outgrown its space, as the art works so successfully tied up by d'Harnoncourt and Barr arrived at the museum. As Barr was retiring, he complained, as always, of the distractions of fund-raising. He wished to devote himself to scholarship and writing, he told Katharine Kuh. But he found the lure of enlarging and beautifying his church irresistible. While the PASITMOMA languished, he lavished what energies remained to him on the fund-raising drive's steering committee, drawing up lists of potential donors and evaluating how much could be expected from each one.

In addition to his museum writings, magazines begged Barr for articles about such varied artists as Marcel Duchamp, Alexander Calder, and Pablo Picasso. Whether it was simply exhaustion or outrage at the piddling pay they offered—$100 to $200—he invariably declined. Four years before his retirement, Alfred Knopf had asked him for an autobiography, but he had pleaded too much other work which, he hoped, "will fortify me against the folly of autobiography. However," he had added puckishly, "should senility overtake me, I will keep Knopf in mind."

Lightly tossed off at the time, the word senility increasingly shadowed all of Barr's existence. He had been sickly all his life and especially susceptible to vague bugs and pains when deadlines loomed. "He was always ill," recalled Philip Johnson. "There was nothing the matter; it was psychosomatic. I didn't pay much attention to Alfred's complaints because I knew there was nothing to it." But now everyone around Barr noticed his deterioration. Three months before he retired, Soby noted that Barr "sounded exhausted on the phone." Sometimes he would lose his way in the museum itself and colleagues would rush to guide him. Other times he would forget common words and suffer as someone else supplied them.

The term *Alzheimer's disease* was not then current, but Barr himself grievously suffered from his memory lapses. "Writing has become an agony," he wrote to Dominique de Menil in March 1968, "difficult in the past, now almost impossible. The English language evades me: I undertake a paragraph, but the thought fades; I can scarcely write a sentence; words, once friends, seem strange; I cannot even spell them." Three months later, Barr left a dinner party with a napkin in his pocket and afterward confessed to his hostess: "Here is some linen which I discovered in my trouser pocket. I've had it carefully laundered." In October 1968, he wrote to a colleague, "I am not well . . . I have to give all my energy to certain obligations which . . . are more than I can handle."

In June of 1969, the Barrs went to Europe where, he wrote to a friend, "I hope to have a good rest!" In August and September, he underwent a series of treatments at Zurich's Bircher-Benner Clinic. But by the end of the year, Barr could work "only a couple of hours a day." At that rate, there was little he could do that was constructive but much that made mischief. Most serious was Barr's failure to groom a successor; even worse was his vague endorsement of two competing heirs, ironically two Bills, one Lieberman, the other Rubin.

Like Barr, William Lieberman had given his entire career to the museum. The son of a medievalist, he had grown up in Paris, where his parents, he said, knew Matisse, Picasso, and Gertrude Stein. He had made spending money by giving tours of the Louvre and had once been physically struck by Brancusi for touching a polished sculpture. His MOMA tenure began as a summer volunteer in 1943, just after he had graduated from Swarthmore. Two years later, after finishing Paul Sachs's museum course at Harvard, he assisted Barr during his exile in the MOMA library for a dollar per hour. When the Abby Rockefeller Print Room opened in 1949, Barr appointed the twenty-five-year-old Lieberman as curator. In the ninety-odd exhibitions he organized during the following two decades, Lieberman's approach to art remained instinctual, aesthetic, emotional. Finding it difficult to articulate sensitive primal feelings about art, he had little gift for public speaking, but he was socially adept and moved easily among donors and trustees.

Rubin, by contrast, approached art scientifically, historically, analytically. He himself collected art, often works located by his brother, Lawrence, who was an art dealer. As an art history professor, Rubin could be maddeningly didactic. Soby once begged off accompanying him on a visit to Picasso "to wheedle some sculpture out of him," because, Soby confided to Barr, "I just can't take an eight-hour Sarah Lawrence lecture on 'modern' art on the plane." Barr, however, was enormously impressed with Rubin's exhibition of "Dada, Surrealism, and Their Heritage," which opened at the MOMA in March 1968 and would move on to extended, successful stops in Los Angeles and Chicago. The exhibition Rubin had assembled was "really extraordinary," Barr wrote to Soby, "much of it quite unfamiliar to me." Barr also marveled, understandably, at Rubin's fluent speaking style at the exhibition opening and at his feats of memory. Rubin thanked about twenty people, Barr wrote to Soby, "without looking at a list and scarcely stopping for breath."

In style and point of view, the two men vying to succeed Barr represented the two poles of all art since the beginning of time: Lieberman, the sensual, intuitive, impulsive Dionysian; Rubin, the rational, thoughtful, efficient Apollonian. These two men also personified the contradictions in Barr's personality. Like Lieberman, Barr could get carried away by the sheer primitive exuberance of a painting like Matisse's *The Dance* or the shimmering mystery of Rousseau's *Sleeping Gypsy*. But, like Rubin, Barr checked such unbridled impulses by creating coolly rational lists and charts to explain in a coherent manner that most irrational phenomenon, the flow of art.

Barr had given Lieberman the impression that he would inherit the mantle and indeed, he became director of the MOMA Department of Painting and Sculpture two years after Barr retired. But at the same time, Barr brought in Rubin as senior curator of the painting and sculpture collections. Thus the duties encompassed by Barr's title as director of the museum collections were parceled out between two conflicting individuals. But the prestige attached to the person and not to the title. Amid bickering among his successors and among the trustees, the title Barr had so cannily carpentered for himself back in 1947 disappeared forever and with it the singular taste which had shaped the entire MOMA collection.

An adroit museum director who had Barr's unqualified support might have been able to make the new arrangement work. But with the old professional leadership gone, the trustees reasserted their sway, just as they had done in 1943, when Nelson Rockefeller was away. Bates Lowry, a forty-three-year-old art history professor, succeeded d'Harnoncourt, after a hasty talent search by the trustees.

Lowry had not been at his desk long before William Lieberman brought news of an extraordinary hoard of modern pictures for sale in Paris. They had been collected by Gertrude Stein and kept by her companion, Alice B. Toklas, after her death. After Toklas died, they were moved to a vault of the Chase Manhattan Bank in Paris to await settlement of a dispute among Stein's heirs. Now the forty-seven canvases, thirty-eight Picassos and nine by Juan Gris, were available for about $6 million. Lowry and Lieberman hastily assembled a consortium of five of the museum's most affluent patrons to buy them: André Meyer, John Hay Whitney, CBS founder and president William Paley, Nelson Rockefeller, and David Rockefeller, who took two shares. One afternoon in February 1969, they gathered in an office at the Museum of Modern Art and drew lots for first choice of the paintings stacked unframed around the walls. For its "good offices in negotiating the deal," the museum received one picture from each collector.

From his perch on the sidelines, Alfred Barr cantankerously carped about this deal. The collection's quality was not "extraordinarily high," as a museum news release had claimed, but included "a good many minor studies, some of them odds and ends." Furthermore, Stein's Picassos dated from only 1905 to 1907, while the fifty later Picassos bought by Serge Shchukine between 1905 and 1913 was a record never matched. Neither were the Stein pictures in "excellent condition," as the news release had stated. Most of them badly needed cleaning, some were chipped and cracked, and one Gris head had a large stain.

By the time all the pictures were displayed in an exhibition at the museum in 1970, Bates Lowry had been unceremoniously fired by board president William Paley, after only ten months on the job. Then came John Hightower, one of the new breed of "arts executives," who had caught Nelson Rockefeller's eye as executive director of the New York State Council on the Arts. He called himself a "tactful generalist and humanist" but the trustees didn't realize what that meant until he told a reporter that taking a Thanksgiving turkey out of the oven "could be a great artistic experience." Art did not "have to be thought of as connoisseurship," he said. "It's fun."

Beside outraging the trustees with such flip pronouncements, Hightower also was beset from every direction. Around him milled militant artists demanding that the museum pay more attention to art by minorities, women, and heterosexuals; that the board of trustees include one-third patrons, one-third staff, and one-third artists; and that the museum be open for free every evening. Calling themselves the Art Workers Coalition, some three hundred artists issued these demands after a mass meeting at the New York School of Visual Arts in January of 1969. They were emulating artists in France, who were protesting the profits collectors were making on art, and in Brussels, where 250 painters and sculptors occupied the Palace of Fine Arts for two weeks declaring that "art should not be for profit." In America, the Museum of Modern Art was not the only target for radical activists; a dinner meeting of the Metropolitan trustees in the museum's Louis XVI room was disrupted by an invasion of cockroaches, poured onto the table from a jar by members of the Coalition.

From below, Hightower was confronted by the museum's employees, organized as Professional and Administrative Staff Association, its tasty acronym, PASTA, conveying the larky elegance of its members. After seven months of threatening a strike, well-dressed, well-schooled, mostly female members of PASTA walked out, picketing with handsome signs reading "MOMA was built on a ROCKY foundation" and "MOMA is having labor pains." Hightower, whose salary was twice what Alfred Barr had ever gotten, settled after fifteen days by raising the starting annual minimum salary from $4,700 to $5,750.

Finally fatal to the besieged director was a blunt, frontal attack by the oldest, most powerful trustees. William Paley and David

Rockefeller were annoyed by Hightower's efforts to mollify the artists by adding social and political concerns to the museum's traditional role as caretaker and tastemaker of Modernism. They considered him too young, too outspoken, too brash, and too uncertain about the truth of the dogma so long purveyed by Barr. Above all, he was not René d'Harnoncourt: he lacked aristocratic bearing, diplomatic demeanor, or fatherly statesmanship. Early in January 1972, Paley called the museum director and bluntly handed him a letter of resignation to sign. Hightower refused, but in the afternoon of that day he presented his own letter of resignation. To the trustees, Paley and Rockefeller announced that the new acting director would be Richard Oldenburg, who had been director of publications at the museum since 1969. Six months later, the appointment became permanent.

While a great wave of democratization had washed across the United States during the sixties, art museum trustees had remained granitic, invulnerable islands of privilege and wealth. In the most comprehensive survey of the arts ever made, the Twentieth Century Fund showed that 60 percent of museum trustees were at least sixty years old and graduates of Ivy League or Little Ivy League colleges; 38 percent were Episcopalians; 33 percent worked in banking and finance; and 20 percent were lawyers. At the Boston Museum of Fine Arts, more than half of the twenty-seven trustees had attended Harvard or were married to Harvard alumni. The twenty-six-member board of the Art Institute of Chicago included two McCormicks and several scions of the Potter Palmer and Marshall Field families. At the MOMA, the trustees illustrated a particularly tangled web of interlocking affiliations: three Rockefellers and two Paleys, William and his son-in-law, J. Frederick Byers, III; Mrs. C. Douglas Dillon, whose husband was president of the Metropolitan; Mary Lasker, whose stepdaughter Mrs. Leigh B. Block was on the Art Institute of Chicago board and whose other stepdaughter, Mrs. Sidney Brody, was trustee of the Los Angeles County Art Museum; John Hay Whitney, also vice-president of the National Gallery (Washington, D.C.); and John de Menil, also trustee at the Museum of Fine Arts (Houston), the Amon Carter Museum (Fort Worth), and the Museum of Primitive Art (New York).

With his health and strength intact, Barr might have taken a leading role in all the upheavals shaking the museum. But even before his retirement, Barr was fading from the scene. He had refused the most prestigious invitations: a lecture series at Yale, a speech at the banquet celebrating the opening of the Chicago Museum of Contemporary Art, the President's Lectures at Rice University, and the Bollingen Lectures at the National Gallery in Washington, D.C. Even the opportunity to serve as Slade Professor of Art at Cambridge University in any year of his choosing did not tempt him.

However, the chance to preach the gospel of Modernism at his alma mater proved irresistible. Mustering all his reserves of intellect, Barr prepared for the Spencer Trask Lecture to be delivered at Princeton on March 18, 1969. At the school which prided itself on being a pillar of tradition, Barr spoke on "Picasso: Pillar of Tradition." So exhausted that he could not keep a lunch date, Barr prepared his lecture with the aid of research and notes supplied by Marga. Subject matter in painting had been swallowed up in "the magnificent renascence of abstract painting" after the 1950s, he told the distinguished audience. In the light of the complete absence of subject matter from contemporary painting, Barr said, "Picasso, for all his revolutionary reputation, appears at this time to be the last of the great European masters in the grand tradition of Titian, Rubens, Rembrandt, Goya, Delacroix, and Cézanne."

The lecture was Barr's first in nine years and, he believed, would be the last; "at least I hope to be wise enough not to try again," he wrote to the *New York Times* art critic John Russell. The audience agreeably listened to the grand old man of Modernism, even though not everyone in the room yet agreed with his words. Just three days before the event, the secretary to the Princeton faculty committee on public lectures confronted him with an old refrain as she wrote confirming last-minute details: "I just wish I could rid myself of the idea that Picasso is 'pulling my leg,' as it were, or fooling the public."

Even at conservative Princeton, however, Modernism could no longer be mocked. After his retirement Barr served as adviser to the Princeton Art Museum in selecting a series of monumental sculptures to be scattered about the campus as the John B. Putnam

Memorial Collection. For it, Barr chose works by many of the sculptors who had impressed him as he leafed through *The Dial* in the Princeton library almost half a century earlier, as a wide-eyed undergraduate. Picasso's *Head of a Woman* now looms in the place of honor, at the entrance to the Art Museum, and Gaston Lachaise's *Floating Figure* spreads her massive curvilinear arms in the collegiate Gothic courtyard of the Graduate College. Elsewhere on the campus are works by many of Barr's other favorites, people who might be called the Old Masters of Modernism: Reg Butler, Henry Moore, Louise Nevelson, Isamu Noguchi, Jacques Lipchitz, Naum Gabo, Alexander Calder, Antoine Pevsner, and David Smith.

Returning to his second alma mater, Harvard, Barr harshly criticized the art history program. He had been named to the board of overseers in 1965 but took little part until after he retired. Then he studied the same department where he had been a graduate student in the middle twenties and was shocked by the "decline in scholarship." Of 170 applicants to the graduate program in 1968, only twenty-one agreed to attend and then only fifteen actually showed up. Still, the ninety or so students pursuing graduate studies, he said, "are obviously too many for a faculty of a dozen members loaded with other responsibilities." Furthermore, undergraduates were "not effectively taught in courses where they are unequipped and often outnumbered by graduate students." In the art history survey courses during those turbulent times, students were actually hissing and booing. But he was pleased that Harvard was at last interested in pre-Columbian art, photography, and films. Yet he could not help adding sharply that "a number of important films were once given to the Fogg Museum in the hope of initiating a film collection. *That* was in 1927."

While Barr could still be testy with those who strayed from the path he had defined for so many years, his failing memory ambushed him at every turn. He agreed to serve as the director of a new gallery of contemporary art founded by Larry Aldrich, a dress designer who had been a generous donor to the MOMA. In 1971, Aldrich bought a former pizza parlor at 114 Prince Street in New York's lively Soho neighborhood to house the Center for Visual Arts. Barr asked to see the new facility and Aldrich took him to lunch at the nearby Spring Street Café and showed him the gallery space and the free library which included more than one hundred thousand items, including books, files of all important art periodicals, and many exhibition catalogs. Barr was excited and impressed, Aldrich recalled, but three months later, he had forgotten entirely about this visit and asked Aldrich to see it again.

In the summer of 1971, the Barrs traveled to Göttingen, Germany, where Alfred Barr would undergo a series of tests to diagnose his condition. Soby jovially suggested that little was amiss, "except that you knew too many words and once in a while forgot one or two." Earlier, Barr's condition had been described as arteriosclerosis. But Dr. Joachim E. Meyer, who studied his case for some fifteen days as Marga waited anxiously in a nearby hotel, offered a hideous diagnosis: Alzheimer's disease, irreversible senile dementia. "He did not know what it meant," Marga wrote to a friend, "but I, who had a grandmother with it, shivered." In the fall, Barr was asked to contribute to a catalog describing the sculptures he had selected for the Princeton campus. "I cannot possibly deliver enlightened comments," he wrote to the Princeton Art Museum's director. "I find it very hard to speak, considerably harder than two years ago." Uncharacteristically, heartbreakingly, this letter was full of spelling and typing errors.

Some six months later, the Art Dealers Association of America awarded Barr a Calder statuette, nick-named the "Sandy," and $3,000, for his contribution to the understanding of contemporary art. For the dealers, the black-tie dinner at the Metropolitan marked the first time, according to one member, that they could enter the museum's front door. Accepting the award, Barr received awkward applause when he said, "I want to thank you because you've taken so much time."

Although invitations continued to pour into Barr's office, it became increasingly difficult for Barr to attend professional or social events. His pocket diaries for the years 1970 to 1975 reminded him, mostly in Marga's handwriting, of doctors' appointments and other mundane chores. The Barrs still attended a round of museum dinners, cocktail parties, and openings, but with each succeeding occasion friends would notice the tragic change in Barr's behavior. "He would be rational and animated for four or five minutes," one acquaintance recalled, "then he would lapse into silence and detachment." Invited to visit the Baltimore Museum of Art in 1973, Barr replied, "Unfortunately I must now avoid meeting with more than one person at a time, the nervous strain is too much for me." By the fall of 1974, Barr was unable to answer letters himself and Marga wrote to decline an invitation to Washington, D.C., for the gala opening of the Hirshhorn Museum. "It would have been an exciting event for us both, but unfortunately Alfred is now too frail to be able to float gracefully through a splendid though crowded evening."

The ironic tragedy was that while modern art and Alfred Barr's role in legitimizing it were acclaimed all over the world, he was unable to savor the triumph of his lifelong crusade. In 1974, the German Art Dealers Association, which sponsored the busy annual Cologne exhibition and sale of contemporary art, awarded Barr a prize worth $2,500 for his pioneering work in establishing Modernism. But only a clipping announcing the prize entered his files; he was unable to accept it personally. In the winter of 1975, Barr was named by acclamation as an honorary member of the College Art Association. Yet the man who had written the first scholarly articles about modern art and campaigned for decades to make the field a respectable area for scholarly research may not even have been conscious of his final victory.

When the MOMA opened galleries to show its newly installed collections in January of 1973, the trustees dedicated the celebration to Barr. Dwarfed by animated trustees gripping cocktail glasses sat Alfred Barr, a wan and shrunken figure, his hands steepled in a gesture of prayer, his gaunt face blank and inscrutable. When Picasso died the following April, Barr had no statement for the press. Instead, he and Marga brought to the MOMA lobby a bouquet of white flowers, tied with a black ribbon with the artist's name and dates of birth and death printed in gold. Silently, like a ghost, he placed it on a pedestal and departed. His last public appearance was on May 13, 1975, when the MOMA officially renamed its permanent collections galleries in his honor.

A week later, he and Marga were on the way to Switzerland for a final, desperate effort to halt the cruel deterioration of Barr's mind. On May 25, doctors at a private clinic installed a shunt in

Barr's brain, a procedure believed at the time to offer a faint hope of halting the ravages of Alzheimer's disease. It failed totally, destroying whatever intellect remained to Barr. On June 10, he entered a convalescent home, Noble Horizons, in Salisbury, Connecticut. For six interminable years, Marga Barr would make the dolorous journey on the New York Central train and the dial- a-ride to the nursing home. She would bring admiring letters, messages from colleagues and friends, and news of the museum world, as her husband sat unseeing, unknowing. When she brought him the heavy resplendent tome *Painting and Sculpture in the Museum of Modern Art*, completed at last in 1977, she watched, beyond tears, as Barr blindly gazed at its gorgeously illustrated pages, upside down.

On August 15, 1981, Alfred Barr died at Noble Horizons and was buried without fanfare in the country cemetery at Greensboro, Vermont. Marga arranged for, but did not attend, a memorial service at the sanitorium where Barr had spent the last eight years of his life. To their daughter, Victoria, who was living in Jogjakarta, Indonesia, Marga cabled the news, adding, "useless to return, love, Mummy." To Barr's childhood friend Edward King she wrote, "Please do not write to me to sympathize about Alfred's death. It was long drawn out and hideous to witness. I had hoped that—having lost his mind—he would not suffer. It was not so."

In a front-page obituary in the *New York Times*, Grace Glueck called Barr "the soul of the modern . . . possibly the most innovative and influential museum man of the twentieth century." The London *Times* said that the MOMA under his rule "progressed by leaps and bounds to become, by the outbreak of the Second World War, the most famous and progressive museum devoted to contemporary art in the world, and a model for all others to follow." *Art in America* said his career had "an incalculable impact on the public acceptance of modern art." In *Art News*, a Boston University art historian recalled Barr's broad interest in all kinds of art and his dream of holding an exhibition to feature all the forms man had devised to protect his head, from ancient Greek helmets to the headgear of pilots and racing drivers.

From within the museum world, tributes from colleagues and competitors also poured in. J. Carter Brown, director of Washington's National Gallery, said Barr was "the most significant taste-making factor in twentieth century America." Philip de Montebello, director of the Metropolitan, said he was "one of the two greatest twentieth century museum directors in the world." (The other was Wilhelm von Bode, director general of the museums of Prussia before the First World War.) Perry Rathbone, director of the Boston Museum of Fine Art, called Barr "the lodestar of the profession" and described his work at the MOMA and his style in doing it as "a model for all his contemporaries." The MOMA's director, Richard Oldenburg, said Barr's achievements included his "classic writing on modern art" as well as "the very concept of what a modern art museum should be."

Barr's associates at the museum also expressed their sadness at his passing. Curator Alicia Legg placed a memorial exhibition in the MOMA lobby. Arranged around Rousseau's *Sleeping Gypsy* were two works given in Barr's honor—Matisse's 1907 sketch, *Music*, and Picasso's 1906 *Two Nudes*—and two Matisse collages: the cover design for a 1954 Matisse exhibition and the jacket design for Barr's *Matisse: His Art and His Public.* Legg also posted a large photo of Barr taken when he retired in 1967 and a panel of twelve photographs Marga had selected some years earlier for this purpose. MOMA librarian Bernard Karpel wrote to Marga that "the name of the museum and that of Alfred were inextricable. If MOMA was the mother of us all, then surely Alfred was the father." The museum's publicist, Elizabeth Shaw, recalled Barr's devotion to collecting, whether bird sightings or precious art works. "He knew about mushrooms and music, about Freud and wars," she wrote, recalling his warning about beautiful pictures: " 'If it is too pretty, be suspicious,' he would say." Jere Abbott, Barr's travel companion and colleague during the museum's early years, consoled Marga with his belief that "in some minuscule part of that destroyed brain a memory persisted that you were out there, ready to help."

While Victoria's relationship with her father had been ambiguous and relatively distant, his death affected her profoundly. "I saw the art of the modern-day masters every day and it influenced my life," she wrote in the press release for an exhibition of her paintings held the year after Barr died. Sounding faintly like her father, she wrote that she wanted to "develop and extend my ideas in a variety of visual ways. . . . I truly feel the more beautiful, well-designed things you have around you, the more your life is enhanced." Among the tropical landscapes and batik textiles in this exhibition at the Haber Theodore Gallery was a somber group, including *What Is the Color of Death* and an elegy on death, her way of coming to terms with her father's tragic end.

It took more than two months to prepare the effusive memorial tribute held for Alfred Barr at the MOMA. Like the opening of a major exhibition, it was held at the height of the New York art season, on October 21, 1981. And just as he had insisted that there be a first-rate catalog for every exhibition, so the museum prepared a handsome illustrated brochure for the memorial service. The Titus Theater was so packed with notables that most of the museum staff had to stand in the hallway and watch the proceedings on closed-circuit television. A string trio played Bach, a slightly ironic symbol of modern music's indifferent success, as compared with the success of modern art.

Meyer Schapiro, whose career as an art scholar had begun at the same time as Barr's, recalled that during the museum's first ten years "every show was an occasion of delight and of arresting confrontation with challenging works." He reminded the audience, most of whom were not old enough to recall the many bitter battles Barr had fought in behalf of modern art, that Barr had "set a new standard with respect to modernity, in contrast to the museums in which were enshrined a traditional art." The museum's founders had been "generous women," he said, "more farseeing than the men who formed the great collections of Old Masters," but the realization of their dreams rested on Barr, "a providential man." Beaumont Newhall, whose career as a scholar of photography was launched by Barr, was still enchanted by the museum's early days. "We all felt that we were members of a team, a really evangelical team," he said. The joy was in "putting modern art across to the public, but not in a superficial way by any means—in a scholarly way."

Most of the dignitaries in the room saw Barr as an awesome figure, more an icon than a man, and it took Philip Johnson to bring the icon to life. Johnson, whose entire career as a leading

modern architect had been fired by Barr's enthusiasm, described a
man who was "not a convivial type . . . [not] a person who had
crowds around him or chatted in symposia of an evening over
Scotch or anything else." To those who had observed Barr's cool
distance and remote manner, he described three salient aspects of
his character: "Unbridled passion, a torrential passion that I have
never known anyone else in my lifetime to have had . . . stubbornness . . . obdurate bulldog tenacity . . . [and] . . . unbelievable fierce
and flaming loyalty to this institution and to his friends." In the
midst of his many hobbies and interests, military strategy and
tactics and bird-watching, "the passion, the passion was art."
Johnson saw Barr's passion as "narrowly channelled . . . at times a
divine rage, at times a quiet concentration on his goal that was as
inspiring and, yes, as frightening as his rages. Calvin had a true
son."

Among the photographs of Barr displayed during the memorial
tribute was an eloquent picture of his aging, stooped figure
thoughtfully contemplating an Alexander Calder sculpture. His
frail body was almost lost inside the great black overcoat he had
bought for his 1928 visit to the Soviet Union. "No logic, no rhetoric,
no counter-examples," Johnson now said, "could beat down the
passionate logic of his defense of [the overcoat's] beauty and fitness.
To the fact that it was outdated, that it was worn out, that it was
much too heavy for our steam-heated culture, he was oblivious. It
was, he said, functional, the material was no longer obtainable, the
length suitable for winter, though unfashionable to others. He
never gave a fig for others' opinions of his taste. Fashion played no
role. He had his reasons—the rest of the world be damned." Barr
was one of the twentieth century's few great men, Johnson said,
deserving "that most famous of Latin epitaphs *si monumentum
requiris circumspice*. If you seek a monument, look around you."

The sleek building housing the world's greatest collection of
modern art in all its manifestations was, in some ways, the least of
Barr's accomplishments. Far more important was his single-
handed revolution in the very concept of what a museum should
be—not just a storehouse for objects, but an educational institution;
and more, a living, dynamic source for new ideas about all the
visual arts, in the broadest sense. Barr may have resented being

called a tastemaker, but there is no doubt that he formed the taste of a generation of museum professionals and far more than a generation of museum visitors, not only in the United States but all over the world.

In 1929, when he insisted on including architecture, photography, films, graphic design, and commercial design in the museum, even the adventuresome early trustees were dubious. In 1939, when he added a restaurant and bookstore to the building, many thought that the museum's high-minded atmosphere would be compromised. During the early 1940s, when he urged universities and art scholars to engage in serious research into modern art and American art, there were cries of fear that scholarship would be diluted or trivialized. After the Second World War, when he supervised hundreds of exhibitions traveling all over the world, there was anxiety that Americans were engaging in cultural imperialism, attempting to depose the traditional European leadership in the arts. During the 1950s when the Cold War cut off all cultural intercourse with the Soviet Union, Barr quietly and doggedly maintained slender lines of communication with the isolated Russian art scholars. The whole world might mock his beliefs and actions, as it mocked his trusty, ancient overcoat, but Alfred H. Barr, Jr., simply marched resolutely forward, a missionary for a sacred cause.

But like every successful missionary, he seized opportunities provided by history. The world was ready for his message. Culturally, the twentieth century is dominated by science and technology; experiment, innovation, risk taking, daring vaults into the unknown have become the norm. In the arts, quicksilver leaps of fad and fashion come ever faster: this morning's avant-garde is this evening's bore. In his memoirs, retired National Gallery director John Walker found it hard to convey the excitement of the battle for Modernism so fervently fought in Boston while he was a colleague of Alfred Barr in Paul Sachs's Harvard museum course. But forty years later, he wrote, "the innovations of the moment are immediately accepted and novelty produces no shock. Modern art was once a cause; now it is an investment. One wonders who can possibly be behind the avant-garde since everybody is in it."

When the Museum of Modern Art opened in 1929, the publicity

promised the shock of the new, but Alfred Barr was shrewd enough to avoid showing too many contemporary works; instead he featured what were already the Old Masters of Modernism— Gauguin, van Gogh, Seurat, and Cézanne. His first one-man exhibition of Picasso in 1939 highlighted the work of an artist who was then almost sixty years old; it dwelled at great length on his early Blue and Pink Period paintings, convincing demonstrations of Picasso's exquisite draftsmanship and luscious sensibility. When the Abstract Expressionists burst upon the New York art scene during the late 1940s, Barr was extremely cautious in recognizing them. William Rubin, who claims to be Barr's chosen successor at the MOMA, believes that Barr's failure to take these artists seriously was his most glaring professional weakness. By 1986, three out of four Abstract Expressionist works in the museum collection had been purchased by Rubin.

But of course today the Abstract Expressionists' innovations are almost forty years old, a part of history and not much fresher than the Old Masters of Modernism were when Barr featured them in his opening exhibition. The contradiction raised by Gertrude Stein—how can a museum be modern—continues and is unlikely ever to be resolved. Alfred Barr, however, came closest to creating a museum which showed the public a thoughtful cross-section of contemporary visual arts.

In the MOMA's first decade, history provided Barr with several implausible allies. Although he was unaware of it at the time and thought himself beset by misfortune and enemies, the Depression was a key factor assuring the success of his mission. The Depression brought the lost generation home from Europe, a staunch band of allies in the battle against nativism and provincialism. The Depression also spawned the WPA arts programs, which provided financial support for art centers in hundreds of small towns and cities, for art exhibitions, and, most crucially, for artists. For the first time in history, American artists were freed from financial worries and, while most of them were not innovators, the program also supported the few who would become the Abstract Expressionists, the first American art movement to have an impact in the rest of the world. The Depression, with its unprecedented economic misery, triggered a wave of political radicalism in America; an openness to all manner of new ideas. It was widely believed that innovative technology would solve the nation's—and the world's—social problems. Was innovative art not also a boon?

The rise of Fascism and Naziism during the twenties and thirties diverted the European cultural elite from more than a century of creative revolution. Artists and writers squabbled over ideology; patrons and audiences withdrew in bafflement and disgust. The aesthetic upheaval in the first decade of the twentieth century—abstract painting, atonal music, blank verse—reaped its reaction during the thirties as European dictators either co-opted or destroyed the avant-garde in Italy, Spain, and Germany. Those who found refuge in the United States were few in number, but they carried much of contemporary European civilization in their bags. Virtually the entire Bauhaus, which Alfred Barr had admired so extravagantly in 1927, was established in America barely a decade later. In 1932, Barr and Philip Johnson fought the retrograde American architectural organizations in behalf of the International Style. Only five years later, a leading International Style designer, Walter Gropius, headed the school of architecture at Harvard. When Barr was assembling the 1936 exhibition "Dada, Surrealism and Fantastic Art," he and Marga had to scurry all over Europe to gather the items to show. Some seven years later, many of the artists themselves were in New York, wartime refugees from Europe. A good number stayed in the United States.

The Second World War shattered European culture and washed upon the American shore its greatest treasures of modern art. Meanwhile, American artists, primed by the WPA and guided by the many Europeans in their midst, were able to develop new styles with little prompting from overseas. Just as the war ravaged the Europeans economically and politically, leaving America as the dominant force in the postwar world, so did American culture dominate the postwar scene. Before the war, Alfred Barr was canvassing Europe for the latest trends; afterward, he was sending the Europeans catalogs and books to bring them up to date on the latest in modern art.

Postwar prosperity and inflation lured an entirely new cohort of collectors and patrons onto the American art scene and the center of their activity became the Museum of Modern Art. Suddenly, in less than two decades, the museum had moved from being a distant provincial cousin to being the core, the hub of the developing new culture of the Western world. It was at this point, however, that the museum began to move irrevocably from a commitment to the perpetually changing avant-garde to its role as a permanent show-case for the style called modern. With inflation driving the prices of art works through the roof, Barr could not bring himself to dispose of the older works in the collection. Bewitched by the prospect of inheriting so many valuable works promised by a host of wealthy collectors, Barr understandably devoted himself to gathering them in. In the universe of collectors within the museum family, he was, after all, the most knowledgeable and discerning collector of all.

In the end, Barr's mission succeeded beyond his wildest dreams. The little chapel had become a splendid cathedral. The little flock of converts had become a clamoring multitude. The tracts he had written so carefully and pressed upon anyone passing by had become a gospel, preached by numerous disciples. The tenets of his creed, for good or ill, had become a dogma. "But watch thou in all things, endure afflictions, do the work of an evangelist, make full proof of thy ministry."

With his taste for apt brevity, Barr might have added his lifelong description of his own mission: "The conscientious, continuous, resolute distinction of quality from mediocrity."

NOTES

Abbreviations used:
AAA—Alfred H. Barr, Jr., Papers, Archives of American Art, Smithsonian Institution.
Roll refers to the number of the microfilm roll on which the citation occurs.
MOMA Archive—Museum of Modern Art Library.

CHAPTER 2: A LONG LINE OF PREACHERS

Page 5.   **a bottle of Bromo-Seltzer:** Marion E. Warren and Mame Warren, *Baltimore: When She Was What She Used to Be* (Baltimore: Johns Hopkins, 1983), 142.

Page 6.   **an elaborate town house:** Francis F. Beirne, *The Amiable Baltimoreans* (Hatboro, PA: Tradition Press, 1968), 198–99.

Page 6.   **the favorite song:** Beirne, *Amiable Baltimoreans*, 29.

Page 6.   **citizens took great pride:** Warren and Warren, *Baltimore: When She Was What She Used to Be*, 74.

Page 7.   **rejected a proposal:** Robert I. Vexler, *Baltimore: A Chronological and Documentary History* (Dobbs Ferry, NY: Oceana, 1975), 73.

Page 7.   **made it a misdemeanor:** Vexler, *Baltimore: A Chronological and Documentary History*, 73–74.

Page 8.   **A visitor was aghast:** Linda Lee Koenig, *The Vagabonds* (East Brunswick, NJ: Associated University Presses, 1983), 16, 17; Warren and Warren, *Baltimore: When She Was What She Used to Be*, 5, 57.

Page 8.   **petty diversions:** Beirne, *Amiable Baltimoreans*, 267–68.

Page 9.   **The city's elite:** Eleanor Stephens Bruchey, *The Business Elite in Baltimore* (New York: Arno, 1976), 224–25, 299.

Page 9.   **the First Presbyterian Church:** *An Architectural and Historical Guide to the First and Franklin Presbyterian Church*, undated pamphlet, 2–4.

Page 9.   **During the thirty years:** John H. Gardner, Jr., *The First Presbyterian Church of Baltimore* (Baltimore: First Presbyterian Church, 1962), 146–47.

Page 10.   **an impeccably Presbyterian background:** "Rev. Dr. A. H. Barr, Theologian, Dies," *New York Times*, Sept. 4, 1935; Barr, dedication speech for Elbert Weinberg's *Procession*, Jewish Museum, New York, May 10, 1959, Roll 3150, AAA.

Page 10.   **crest of a missionary wave:** Edward M. Deems, compiler, *Holy-Days and Holidays* (New York: Funk & Wagnall's, 1902), 52, 54, 72.

Page 11.   **"relied less upon rhetorical methods":** Gardner, *First Presbyterian Church*, 147–48.

Page 11.   **the Barrs moved from Detroit:** Edward S. King, letter to the author, July 24, 1986; *An Architectural and Historical Guide to the First and Franklin Presbyterian Church*, 2; King to Margaret S. Barr, Aug. 30, 1981, Roll 3145, AAA; interview with King, June 11, 1986.

Page 12.   **an enthusiastic, energetic lady:** Interview with Dorothy Miller, May 31, 1986; interview with Edward S. King, June 11, 1986.

Page 12.   **she tartly reminded him:** Wilbur Frank Dierking to Barr, Oct. 2, 1958, Roll 2183, AAA; interview with Edward S. King, June 11, 1986; interview with Libby Tannenbaum, July 5, 1986.

Page 12.   **prodigy Alfred delighted:** Barr to Olga Guggenheim, Aug. 30, 1965, Roll 2194, AAA; Barr to Emilio del Junco, Mar. 25, 1968, Roll 2195, AAA.

Page 13.   **summers in Greensboro, Vermont:** Barr to James I. Armstrong, Feb. 5, 1968, Roll 2195, AAA; interview with Dorothy Miller, Dec. 16, 1986.

Page 13.   **a gang of young people:** Interview with Edward S. King, June 11, 1986.

Page 13.   **precocious childhood achievements:** Aline B. Louchheim to James J. Doheny, June 1, 1951, Roll 2174, AAA; Priscilla Boughton, "Barr Admits Influence on Art of Youthful Collecting Holiday," *The College News*, Feb. 27, 1946, p. 1, Roll 3265, AAA; Rona Roob, "Alfred H. Barr, Jr.: A Chronicle of the Years 1902–1929," *New Criterion*, Summer 1987, p. 1; interview with Edward S. King, June 11, 1986.

Page 14.   **successful middling entrepreneur:** Interview with Edward S. King, June 11, 1986.

Page 14.   **"not afraid of anything":** Interview with Edward S. King, June 11, 1986.

Page 14.   **Barr's own recollections:** Barr, "Alumnus Narrates Old Life at 'Dunham,' " *The Inkwell*, June 1934, 12, 22.

Page 15.   **Barr also reminisced:** Barr, "Alumnus Narrates," 12, 22.

Page 15.   **"a sincere nut":** Roob, "Chronicle," 2; Barr to Dwight Macdonald, May 12, 1953, Roll 2180, AAA.

Page 16.   **"a terrible sense of agony":** Gardner, *First Presbyterian Church*, 150–52.

Page 16.   **a diligent missionary:** Barr to Henry Luce, III, April 2, 1968, Roll 2196, AAA; Gardner, *First Presbyterian Church*, 149–50.

Page 16.   **fifth-anniversary sermon:** *The Fifth Anniversary of the Pastorate of the Rev. Alfred H. Barr, D. D.* (Baltimore: First Presbyterian Church, 1916), 6–7.

Page 18.   **no new Baltimore building:** G. E. Kidder-Smith, *The Architecture of the United States*, Vol. I (Garden City, NY: Anchor/Doubleday, 1981), 173–79.

Page 18.   **only significant art collection:** Eloise Spaeth, *American Art Museums: An Introduction to Looking* (New York: Harper & Row, 1975), 166–67.

Page 18.   **Housed in crowded annexes:** Koening, *Vagabonds*, 19; Warren and Warren, *Baltimore: When She Was What She Used to Be*, 36–37.

Page 18.   **the Cone sisters:** Beirne, *Amiable Baltimoreans*, 215; Nathaniel Burt, *Palaces for the People: A Social History of the American Art Museum* (Boston: Little, Brown, 1977), 288–89.

Page 19.   **became close friends:** Spaeth, *American Art Museums: An Introduction to Looking*, 165; Burt, *Palaces for the People*, 290.

Page 19.   **the entire collection:** Beirne, *Amiable Baltimoreans*, 216.

Page 20.   **first modern picture:** Edward S. King to the author, July 24, 1986; Barr to James Schuyler, April 12, 1961, Roll 2187, AAA.

Page 20.   **one especially favored:** Bruchey, *Business Elite in Baltimore*, 203.

Page 20.   **examples of every architectural style:** Constance M. Greiff, Mary W. Gibbons, and Elizabeth G. C. Menzies, *Princeton Architecture* (Princeton, NJ: Princeton University, 1967), 78, 84.

Page 21.   **most distinguished buildings:** Greiff, Gibbons, and Menzies, *Princeton Architecture*, 156, 150–53.

Page 21.   **Princeton trustees decreed:** Greiff, Gibbons, and Menzies, *Princeton Architecture*, 169; Alexander Leitch, *A Princeton Companion* (Princeton, NJ: Princeton University, 1978), 502; Thomas J. Wertenbaker, *Princeton 1746–1896* (Princeton, NJ: Princeton University, 1946), 353–54.

Page 22.   **book of Princeton sketches:** Maitland Belknap and Edwin Avery Park, *Princeton Sketches* (Princeton, NJ: Belknap & Park, 1919), unpaged.

Page 22.   **Princeton was a paradise:** Leitch, *Princeton Companion*, 234; Barr to Patrick Kelleher, May 17, 1966, Roll 2197, AAA.

Page 22.   **doctrinal battles:** Lefferts A. Loetscher, *The Broadening Church* (Philadelphia: University of Pennsylvania, 1954), 77, 79.

Page 23.   **"Dome":** Barr to Rev. and Mrs. Alfred Barr and Andrew Barr, undated 1918; "Pome," undated 1918, both Roll 3263, AAA.

Page 24.   **dark tracery of the trees:** J. I. Merritt, *The Trees of Princeton University*, undated, unpaged pamphlet based on articles which appeared in the *Princeton Alumni Weekly*.

Page 24.   **extraordinary amenities:** Gerald Breese, *Princeton University Land 1752–1984* (Princeton, NJ: Princeton University, 1986), 176–77, 16.

Page 24.   **Barr was impressed enough:** Barr to Rev. and Mrs. Barr and Andrew Barr, undated, 1918, Roll 3263, AAA.

Page 25.   **Allan Marquand:** Leitch, *Princeton Companion*, 27, 31, 314.

Page 25.   **Art and archaeology:** Leitch, *Princeton Companion*, 315; "Princeton Alumni Show Advisory Committee," undated 1970, Roll 2197, AAA; Barr, "Modern Art Makes History Too," *College Art Journal*, Nov. 1941, 3.

Page 25.   **"I shall like it":** Rona Roob to William Lieberman, May 30, 1979, Roll 2195, AAA.

Page 26. "confirmed my interest": Barr to Dwight Macdonald, May 12, 1953,
Roll 2180, AAA; Barr to Frank Jewett Mather, June 30, 1949, Roll
2175, AAA.

Page 26. attacked dealers with cynical savagery: Frank Jewett Mather, *The
Collectors* (New York: Holt, 1912), ix, 141–42, 155–57.

Page 27. "Morally considered . . .": Mather, *Collectors*, 177, 181.

Page 27. his views on modern art: Frank Jewett Mather, *Modern Painting*
(Garden City, NY: Garden City Publishing, 1927), 349, 358–61, 366–67.

Page 27. Barr would disagree heartily: Barr to Henry Seidel Canby, Nov. 27,
1931, Roll 2164, AAA.

Page 28. strongly held opinions: Edward S. King to the author, July 6 and
Aug. 21, 1986.

Page 28. enjoyed accumulating: Interview with Edward S. King, June 11,
1986; Barr, notes for a paper on ornament, undated 1922, Roll 3263,
AAA; Barr, "Research and Publication in Art Museums," *Museum
News*, Jan. 1, 1946, 7.

Page 29. "a strong reaction": Barr to Stanton Macdonald-Wright, April 27,
1966, Roll 2198, AAA; Barr, "The 1929 Multidepartmental Plan for
the Museum of Modern Art: Its Origins, Development, and Partial
Realization," undated 1941, Roll 3266, AAA.

Page 29. began spending many hours: Barr to Jane Fiske McCullough, Mar.
1, 1967, Roll 2196, AAA.

Page 30. An anonymous circular: "Artists Rise in Aid of Impressionists," *New
York Times*, Sept. 7, 1921; Henry McBride, "On New York Salons," *The
Dial*, July 1920, 62.

Page 30. "a vision": Interview with Edward S. King, June 11, 1986.

Page 30. "a big splash:" Interview with Edward S. King, June 11, 1986.

Page 31. Oxford's Magdalen Tower: Leitch, *Princeton Companion*, 223.

Page 31. a mock commencement: Willard Thorp, Minor Myers, Jr., and Jere-
miah Stanton Finch, *The Princeton Graduate School: A History*
(Princeton, NJ: Princeton University, 1978), 176.

Page 31. began teaching at Vassar: *Fifty-ninth Annual Catalog of Vassar
College 1923–24*, 56–60, Roll 3263, AAA; Roob, "Chronicle," 5; Katharine Kuh, "Alfred H. Barr," *Saturday Review of Literature*, Sept. 30,
1967, 51–52.

CHAPTER 3: PILGRIMAGE

Page 33. an amibitious itinerary: Interview with Edward S. King, June 11,
1986.

Page 34. the summer's adventure: Interview with Edward S. King, June 11,
1986; Barr, "genoa" sketchbook, Roll 3263, AAA.

Page 35. "When good Americans die . . .": John Bartlett, *Familiar Quotations*
(Boston: Little, Brown, 1980), 675.

Page 35. leading art history textbook: H. W. Janson, *History of Art* (Englewood Cliffs, NJ: Prentice-Hall, 1969).

Page 35. a more casual trip: Interview with Edward S. King, June 11, 1986.

Page 36. "decided suddenly": Roob, "Chronicle," 7.

Page 36. **first course anywhere:** Galley proof of Barr vita, 1932, Roll 2164, AAA; Calvin Tomkins, *Merchants and Masterpieces: The Story of the Metropolitan Museum of Art* (New York: Dutton, 1970), 254–55; Helaine Ruth Messer, *MOMA: Museum in Search of an Image,* Ph.D. thesis at Columbia University, 1979, 31–32.

Page 36. **"He was a kingmaker . . .":** Julien Levy, *Memoir of an Art Gallery* (New York: G. B. Putnam's Sons, 1977), 10–11; Donald Fleming and Bernard Baylin, eds., *The Intellectual Migration* (Cambridge, MA: Harvard University, 1969), 590–91.

Page 37. **slyly told his colleagues:** Barr undated notes, 1925, Roll 3150, AAA; Paul Sachs to Barr, Nov. 3, 1925, Roll 3263, AAA.

Page 37. **"aloof, even haughty":** Interview with Edward S. King, June 11, 1986; Thomas Carr Howe to the author, Sept. 21, 1986.

Page 37. **the motley array:** Messer, *MOMA: Museum in Search of an Image,* 27; Barr to his parents, undated 1926, Roll 3262, AAA.

Page 38. **he wrote to Neumann:** Barr to J. B. Neumann, July 19 and Nov. 15, 1926, Roll NJBN-1, AAA.

Page 38. **his radical views:** Interview with Philip Johnson, Dec. 17, 1986; "Critical Catalog," Spring 1926, Roll 3263, AAA.

Page 39. **"a neat problem":** Levy, *Memoir of an Art Gallery,* 104.

Page 39. **provocative news release:** "Boston Is Modern Art Pauper—Barr," *Harvard Crimson,* Oct. 30, 1926.

Page 39. **devoted a column:** Barr, "The 1929 Multidepartmental Plan for the Museum of Modern Art: Its Origins, Development and Partial Realization," undated 1941, Roll 3266, AAA; Messer, *MOMA: Museum in Search of an Image,* 32–33.

Page 40. **leaped into the fray:** "Great Modern Artists Neglected by Boston," *Boston Evening Globe,* Oct. 20, 1926; "Boston Lack of Interest," *Boston Evening Transcript,* undated clipping 1926; "The Puritan Strain," *Boston Daily Globe,* Nov. 4, 1926; F. W. Coburn, "World of Art," *Boston Herald;* Harley Perkins, "Boston Notes: Harvard Number," and Forbes Watson, Editorial, *Arts,* Dec. 1926, 305–6, 339; Barr to editor, *Art News,* Dec. 18, 1926, all Roll 3263, AAA.

Page 40. **a quiz so provocative:** "A Modern Art Questionnaire," *Vanity Fair,* Aug. 1927, 85, 96, 98.

Page 40. **The answers Barr provided:** *Vanity Fair,* Aug. 1927, 96, 98.

Page 41. **He wrote to J. B. Neumann:** Barr to J. B. Neumann, Oct. 12, 1926, Roll NJBN-1, AAA; interview with Helen Franc, June 6, 1986.

Page 42. **"To keep abreast . . .":** "Wellesley and Modernism," *Boston Transcript,* April 27, 1927, Roll 3263, AAA.

Page 42. **showing lantern slides:** Messer, *MOMA: Museum in Search of an Image,* 30; interview with Helen Franc, June 6, 1986.

Page 42. **held up an egg:** Interview with Edward S. King, June 11, 1986.

Page 42. **bohemian doings were described:** Irving Sandler and Amy Newman, eds., *Defining Modern Art: Selected Writings of Alfred H. Barr* (New York: Abrams, 1968), 54.

Page 43. **Barr was keeping track:** Robert Treat Paine II to Barr, Mar. 2, 1927; Gladys Saltonstall to Barr, undated 1927, both Roll 3262, AAA.

Page 43.   **used the wall labels:** Wall labels for "Progressive Modern Painting: From Daumier and Corot to Post-Cubism," an exhibition at Wellesley College, April 11–30, 1927, Roll 3263, AAA.

Page 43.   **read like a roll call:** "Progressive Modern Painting."

Page 44.   **a series of five lectures:** "A Course of Five Lectures on Modern Art," Department of Art, Wellesley College, April and May 1929, Roll 3150, AAA.

Page 45.   **Harvard Society for Contemporary Art:** Barr, "Contemporary Art at Harvard," *Arts*, April 1929, 267.

Page 45.   **Having invited Alexander Calder:** John Walker, *Self-Portrait with Donors* (Boston: Little, Brown, 1974), 25–27.

Page 45.   **"presupposed a microscopic study":** Forbes Watson, "The Month in the Galleries," *Arts*, May 1928, 292, 306–7.

Page 46.   **a series of book reviews:** Barr, "Review of Frank Rutter, *Evolution in Modern Painting*," *Saturday Review of Literature*, Oct. 30, 1926, 252; Barr (unsigned), "Review of Henrietta Servig, *Five Famous Painters*," *Saturday Review of Literature*, Nov. 20, 1926, 319.

Page 46.   **exquisite reserves of tact:** Barr, "Review of Albert C. Barnes, *The Art in Painting*," *Saturday Review of Literature*, July 24, 1926, 948.

Page 47.   **Sachs had urged him:** Paul Sachs to Barr, Mar. 14, 1926, Roll 3263, AAA; Barr, "Modern Art in London Museums," *Arts*, Oct. 1928, 187–94.

Page 47.   **forego any trips:** Barr to J. B. Neumann, undated 1927 and undated 1928; Edward S. King to the author, Aug. 21, 1986.

Page 47.   **warmly greeted Jere Abbott:** Jere Abbott to Margaret S. Barr, July 10, 1981, Roll 3262, AAA; interview with Edward S. King, June 11, 1986; Henry-Russell Hitchcock to Virgil Thompson, Sept. 27, 1928, Music Collection, Beinecke Library, Yale University.

Page 48.   **"no compromise with dead styles":** Barr, "Dutch Letter," *Arts*, Jan. 1928, 48.

Page 48.   **"indifferent to modern art":** Barr, "Dutch Letter," 49.

Page 48.   **a visit to the Bauhaus:** Barr to Jane Fiske McCullough, Mar. 1, 1967, Roll 2196, AAA; Barr to J. B. Neumann, Sept. 29, and Dec. 12, 1927, both Roll NJBN-1, AAA.

Page 49.   **forty years later:** Barr to Jane Fiske McCullough, Mar. 1, 1967, Roll 2196, AAA.

Page 49.   **called on Paul Klee:** Barr, *Paul Klee* (New York: Museum of Modern Art, 1941), 4–7.

Page 49.   **Lyonel Feininger:** Jane F. McCullough to Barr, Feb. 6, 1967, Roll 2196, AAA; Barr eulogy read at Lyonel Feininger funeral, Jan. 17, 1956, Roll 2182, AAA, and Roll 3150, AAA; Barr, introduction to Dorothy Miller, *Lyonel Feininger, Marsden Hartley* (New York: Museum of Modern Art, 1944), 7.

Page 50.   **a shrine to the middle class:** Raymond J. Sontag, *A Broken World: 1919–1939* (New York: Harper & Row, 1971), 213–14; Philip Johnson to Barr, undated, Roll 3146, AAA.

Page 50.   **"The Jews . . .":** Barr to J. B. Neumann, undated, Roll NJBN-1, AAA; Sandler and Newman, *Defining Modern Art*, 103–4.

Page 51.   **Soviet cultural life:** John E. Bowlt, afterword to Barr, "Russian Diary," *October*, Winter 1978, 53; Barr, "Notes on 1927–28," Roll 3262, AAA.

Page 51. **diary Barr kept:** Barr, "Russian Diary," 11–12.

Page 52. **the LEF:** Barr, "The LEF and Soviet Art," *transition*, Fall 1928, 267–69.

Page 52. **"only the superficials":** Barr, "Notes on Russian Architecture," *Arts*, Feb. 1929, 104–5; Barr, "Russian Diary," 13, 15.

Page 52. **paradox of Soviet life:** Barr, "Russian Diary," 44–45.

Page 53. **noting in his diary:** Barr, "Russian Diary," 44, 45, 50.

Page 53. **wrote in his notebook:** Barr, "Novgorod," Feb. 25, 1928, Roll 3262, AAA.

Page 53. **enthusiasm for Russian icons:** Barr, "Russian Diary," 37–38.

Page 54. **Barr observed dryly:** Sandler and Newman, *Defining Modern Art*, 122.

Page 54. **poking his critical scalpels:** Barr, "Russian Diary," 25, 33, 35–36.

Page 55. **Dom Gertsena:** Sandler and Newman, *Defining Modern Art*, 115; Barr, "Russian Diary," 39–40.

Page 55. **most impressive individual:** Barr to Marie Seton, April 19 and April 10, 1950, both Roll 2172, AAA.

Page 55. **lurking censors:** Barr, "Sergei Michailovich Eisenstein," *Arts*, Dec. 1928, 318–19, 321; Ephraim Katz, *The Film Encyclopedia* (New York: Crowell, 1979), 382.

Page 56. **reel after reel:** Barr, "Russian Diary," 31–32.

Page 56. **diary occasionally exulted:** Barr, "Russian Diary," 50; Jere Abbott, "A Russian Diary," *Hound and Horn*, April–June 1929, 264.

Page 57. **diaries dwell in detail:** Sandler and Newman, *Defining Modern Art*, 134.

Page 57. **black overcoat:** Barr to Marilyn McMullen, Mar. 31, 1961, Roll 2187, AAA; Barr, "Russian Diary," 49–50; Barr to D'Arcy Paul, June 29, 1932, Roll 2164, AAA.

Page 57. **culture of revolution:** James Thrall Soby to Barr, Nov. 26, 1967, Roll 2198, AAA.

Page 58. **"I don't refer . . .":** Barr, undated handwritten notebook, 1928, Roll 3263, AAA.

Page 59. **Abby Aldrich Rockefeller:** Arthur M. Johnson, *Winthrop W. Aldrich: Lawyer, Banker, Diplomat* (Boston: Harvard, 1968), 16; Peter Collier and David Horowitz, *The Rockefellers: An American Dynasty* (New York: Holt, Rinehart & Winston, 1976), 93–94; Joe Alex Morris, *Nelson Rockefeller* (New York: Harper, 1960), 69–70; Mary Ellen Chase, *Abby Aldrich Rockefeller* (New York: Macmillan, 1950), 12–13.

Page 59. **"little else than a roster":** Chase, *Abby Aldrich Rockefeller*, 4–5, 8–9, 11–12.

Page 59. **sternly religious young man:** Joseph E. Persico, *The Imperial Rockefeller* (New York: Simon & Schuster, 1982), 23; Collier and Horowitz, *The Rockefellers*, 94–95; Johnson, *Winthrop W. Aldrich*, 11–12; Alvin Moscow, *The Rockefeller Inheritance* (Garden City, NY: Doubleday, 1977), 26; Chase, *Abby Aldrich Rockefeller*, 27.

Page 60. **"the best thing":** Ferdinand Lundberg, *The Rockefeller Syndrome* (Secaucus, NJ: Lyle Stuart, 1975), 157–58, 198; Chase, *Abby Aldrich Rockefeller*, 112–13.

Page 61. **brownstone town house:** Chase, *Abby Aldrich Rockefeller*, 35; Moscow, *The Rockefeller Inheritance*, 37; "Letters of Abby Aldrich Rockefeller to Her Sister," MOMA Archive.

Page 61.   **suddenly began buying:** Chase, *Abby Aldrich Rockefeller*, 84; William S. Lieberman, *Nelson A. Rockefeller Collection: The Masterpieces of Modern Art* (New York: Hudson Hills Press, 1961), 13; Russell Lynes, *Good Old Modern: An Intimate Portrait of the Museum of Modern Art* (New York: Atheneum, 1973), 152-53, 343; Morris, *Nelson Rockefeller*, 70.

Page 62.   **mature maiden lady:** Interview with Eliza Bliss Parkinson Cobb, Dec. 15, 1986.

Page 62.   **starting a museum:** Dwight Macdonald, "Action on West 53rd Street—II," *New Yorker*, Dec. 19, 1953, 35; Lynes, *Good Old Modern*, 8-9.

Page 62.   **the prevailing attitude:** Lynes, *Good Old Modern*, 3-4, 8-9; Abby Rockefeller to A. Conger Goodyear, Mar. 23, 1936, Roll 3264, AAA; A. Conger Goodyear, *The Museum of Modern Art: The First Ten Years* (New York: A. Conger Goodyear, 1943), 13-14.

Page 63.   **To find a director:** Walker, *Self-Portrait with Donors*, 25; Marianne Hartog to Gertrud A. Mellon, Jan. 23, 1953, Roll 3263, AAA; Goodyear, *Museum of Modern Art*, 17.

Page 64.   **The group was shocked:** Lynes, *Good Old Modern*, 48-49.

Page 64.   **Abby interviewed him:** Lynes, *Good Old Modern*, 19-20; interview with Edward M. M. Warburg, June 3, 1986; Anne Kelly to Barr, Aug. 17, 1929; Barr to Abby Rockefeller, August 1929; Anne Kelly to Barr, Sept. 17, 1929; Abby Rockefeller to Barr, Sept. 18, 1929, all Roll 3264, AAA.

Page 64.   **"I was excited . . .":** Jere Abbott to Margaret S. Barr, July 10, 1981, Roll 3262, AAA.

Page 65.   **"well-known collectors":** A. Philip McMahon, "New Museum of Modern Art," *Parnassus*, Oct. 1929, 31; Albert Sterner, "Art Inventors," *Art Digest*, Oct. 15, 1929, 15-16; Lynes, *Good Old Modern*, 55.

Page 65.   **Forbes Watson predicted:** Forbes Watson, "To Our New Museum," *Arts*, Sept. 1929, 47-48; Lynes, *Good Old Modern*, 33.

CHAPTER 4: A PULPIT FOR MR. BARR

Page 67.   **"Dressed to the nines":** Interview with Helen Franc, June 6, 1986; "New York Season," *Art Digest*, Nov. 15, 1929, 16; Lynes, *Good Old Modern*, 61-62.

Page 68.   **described the chaos:** Edward Alden Jewell, "The New Museum of Modern Art Opens," *New York Times*, Nov. 10, 1929.

Page 68.   **Barr was delighted:** Lynes, *Good Old Modern*, 49-50.

Page 69.   **sparred over the content:** Abby Rockefeller telegram to Barr, Aug. 20, 1929; Abby Rockefeller to Barr, Aug. 23, 1929, both Roll 2164, AAA; Lynes, *Good Old Modern*, 52-53.

Page 69.   **"were respected":** Gerald Reitlinger, *The Economics of Taste: The Rise and Fall of the Picture Market 1760-1960*, Vol. I (New York: Holt, Rinehart & Winston, 1961), 171.

Page 69.   **a syndicate:** Raymonde Moulin, *Le marché de la peinture en France* (Paris: Editions de Minuit, 1967), 35.

Page 70. **provoking angry discussion:** "Tar and Feathers Put on Epstein Statue," *New York Times*, Oct. 10, 1929; "Canvas Hung on Side Wins Academy Prize," *New York Times*, Nov. 10, 1929.

Page 70. **more adventuresome array:** Lynes, *Good Old Modern*, 62; Barr, "Museum of Modern Art," *Art News*, Jan. 4, 1930, 13; Nathaniel Burt, *Palaces for the People* (Boston: Little, Brown, 1977), 337.

Page 70. **a chorus of boosterish hosannas:** "Modern Art Museum Opens," *Art News*, Nov. 9, 1929, 3; Lloyd Goodrich, "Museum of Modern Art," *Nation*, Dec. 4, 1929, 664; Forbes Watson, "In the Galleries," *Arts*, May 1920, 625; Henry McBride, "The Palette Knife," *Creative Art*, Dec. 1929, x–xi, and Jan. 1930, ix–x; "New York Season," *Art Digest*, Nov. 15, 1929, 16.

Page 71. **"several art connoisseurs":** "New Art Museum Visited by Scores," *New York Times*, Nov. 9, 1929; "Throngs View Modern Art," *New York Times*, Nov. 26, 1929; Lynes, *Good Old Modern*, 64–65.

Page 71. **young Italian art historian:** Roob, "Chronicle," 14; Margaret Barr recalls visiting the preview and signing the guest book; she remembers being introduced to Barr a few weeks later, by Vassar professor Agnes Rindge, whom she accompanied on a visit to the exhibition; transcript of an interview by Paul Cummings with Margaret S. Barr, Feb. 22, 1974, AAA; Roob, "Chronicle," 19.

Page 72. **a loner:** Interview with Philip Johnson, Dec. 17, 1986.

Page 72. **strong emotional attachments:** Lynes, *Good Old Modern*, 47; Henry-Russell Hitchcock to Virgil Thompson, Nov. 1, 1929, Music Collection, Beinecke Library, Yale University.

Page 72. **"absolutely a farce":** Transcript of an interview by Paul Cummings with Margaret S. Barr, Feb. 22, 1974, AAA.

Page 72. **excruciatingly shy:** Transcript of an interview by Paul Cummings with Margaret S. Barr, Feb. 22, 1974, AAA.

Page 73. **graduate courses:** Hilton Kramer, "Alfred Barr at MOMA: An Introduction," *New Criterion*, Summer 1987, iii; Roob, "Chronicle," 2; Margaret Scolari Barr, "Our Campaigns," *New Criterion*, Summer 1987, 23.

Page 73. **Barr invited her:** Transcript of an interview by Paul Cummings with Margaret S. Barr, Feb. 22, 1974, AAA.

Page 73. **"a mile a minute":** Lynes, *Good Old Modern*, 68; interview with Helen Franc, June 6, 1986; Margaret S. Barr, "Our Campaigns," 24.

Page 74. **surprise wedding:** Margaret S. Barr, "Our Campaigns," 24; Joseph W. Cochran to Barr, Nov. 24, 1937, Roll 2166, AAA; Sandler and Newman, *Defining Modern Art*, 266–67; interview with Helen Franc, Feb. 8, 1987; Lynes, *Good Old Modern*, 86; Barr to Dwight Macdonald, Dec. 1, 1953, Roll 2180, AAA.

Page 74. **some ambivalence:** Lynes, *Good Old Modern*, 86.

Page 74. **only overt clue:** Barr, unpublished article for *Fashions of the Hour*, Marshall Field, Spring 1930, Roll 3262, AAA.

Page 75. **his own advice:** Lynes, *Good Old Modern*, 93–94; Margaret S. Barr, "Our Campaigns," 25.

Page 75. **she still resented:** Transcript of an interview by Paul Cummings with Margaret S. Barr, April 8, 1974, AAA.

Page 76. **Marga worked late:** Barr to May O'Callaghan, April 20, 1931, Roll 2164, AAA; interview with Edward S. King, June 11, 1986.

Page 76. **As Conger Goodyear remarked:** Goodyear, *Museum of Modern Art*, 19–20; Barr, memorandum on the exhibition of American art, undated 1930, Roll 2164, AAA.

Page 77. **he tried to anticipate criticism:** Barr, *Paintings by Nineteen Living Americans* (New York: Museum of Modern Art, 1930), 9–10.

Page 77. **Now the critics pounced:** Emily Genauer, "The Fur-lined Museum," *Harper's*, July 1944, 133; Edward Alden Jewell, "Contemporary American," *New York Times*, Dec. 22, 1929; McBride, "The Palette Knife," *Creative Art*, Jan, 1930, x.

Page 77. **catalog essay mercilessly shamed:** Barr, *Painting in Paris from American Collections* (New York: Museum of Modern Art, 1930), 18; Burt, *Palaces for the People*, 338; Barr, "The Museum of Modern Art," typed booklet, undated 1936, Roll 3260, AAA.

Page 78. **a steady parade of sensational exhibitions:** Peter Kihss, "These Other Showmen," *New York World-Telegram*, Jan. 6, 1941; Messer, *MOMA: Museum in Search of an Image*, 36.

Page 79. **discussed American painters disdainfully:** Mahonri Sharp Young, "Letter from the U.S.A.," *Apollo*, Mar. 1982, 120; Barr to A. Conger Goodyear, Nov. 21, 1932; Barr to Myrtilla Avery, Nov. 19, 1931, both Roll 2164, AAA.

Page 79. **Barr worried about his ignorance:** Barr to Clifton R. Hall, Jan. 27, 1938, Roll 3262, AAA.

Page 79. **not exactly bereft of ideas:** Barr to Abby Rockefeller, Jan. 25, 1930; Edward L. Bernays, "Modern Museum Membership Campaign," 1930; "Estimated Costs," Jan. 25, 1930, all Roll 3264, AAA; Jere Abbott to Barr, June 2, 1930; Barr to Abby Rockefeller, Jan. 6, 1931, both Roll 2164, AAA.

Page 80. **not a sparrow fell:** Elkin to Barr, Oct. 8, 1930, Roll 2164, AAA; interview with Edward M. M. Warburg, June 3, 1986; Young, "Letter from the U.S.A.," 120; Barr to Abby Rockefeller, June 29, 1933, Roll 3264, AAA; Barr to Abby Rockefeller, April 10, 1931; Anna L. Kelly to Mary Sands, Dec. 26, 1931, both Roll 2164, AAA; Messer, *MOMA: Museum in Search of an Image*, 38; Abby Rockefeller to Barr, Feb. 21, 1931, and Aug. 4, 1932; Barr to Abby Rockefeller, Aug. 6, 1932, all Roll 3264, AAA.

Page 80. **College Art Association's annual meeting:** Program of the nineteenth annual meeting of the College Art Association, Boston, Dec. 26–28, 1929, Roll 3264, AAA; Roob, "Chronicle," 19.

Page 81. **American art critics were mired:** Elizabeth Luther Carey, "Casual Impressions of Modernism," *American Magazine of Art*, Aug. 1930, 424; Barr, "Review of *Modern Architecture*," *Hound and Horn*, April–June 1930, 435, 432.

Page 81. **Barr deplored the low standards:** Barr to Agnes Rindge, Dec. 30, 1930; Barr to J. D. M. Ford, Sept. 12, 1933; Barr to Abby Rockefeller, May 21, 1931; Barr to Simon & Schuster, April 10, 1931; F. A. Whiting to Barr, Mar. 26, 1930; Barr to Whiting, Mar. 29, 1930, all Roll 2164, AAA.

Page 82.   **still smarted from the trauma:** Barr to Mrs. Martin Schuetze, May
           12, 1931; Barr to Audrey McMahon, Jan. 19, 1931, both Roll 2164,
           AAA; Barr, lecture notes, undated 1930; "Application to Borrow
           Slides," Metropolitan Museum of Art, 1930, all Roll 3150, AAA.
Page 83.   **lecture invitations poured onto his desk:** Barr, notes for a lecture,
           undated, Roll 3150, AAA; Barr to William S. Rusk, Sept. 21, 1931;
           Barr to Russell Potter, Sept. 30, 1930, both Roll 2164, AAA.
Page 83.   **Barr's presence was so ubiquitous:** Interview with Eliza Bliss Par-
           kinson Cobb, Dec. 15, 1986; interview with Edward M. M. Warburg,
           June 3, 1986; interview with Helen Franc, June 6, 1986; interview with
           Philip Johnson, Dec. 17, 1986.
Page 84.   **a warm, lifelong friendship:** Interview with Philip Johnson, Dec. 17,
           1986; interview with Eliza Bliss Parkinson Cobb, Dec. 15, 1986.
Page 84.   **"all I had was enthusiasm":** Johnson, "Transcript of Barr Memorial
           Service," Oct. 21, 1981, Roll 3145, AAA.
Page 85.   **Barr and Johnson spent many a night:** Interview with Philip John-
           son, Dec. 17, 1986; Barr, Foreword to *Modern Architecture: Interna-
           tional Exhibition* (New York: Museum of Modern Art, 1932), 13; *Alfred
           H. Barr, Jr.: A Memorial Tribute* (New York: Museum of Modern Art,
           1981).
Page 85.   **long, chatty, opinionated, and affectionate letters:** Johnson to Barr,
           Oct. 16, 1931(?), Roll 2164, AAA; Johnson to Barr, Aug. 23 and Aug.
           26, 1933, Roll 2165, AAA; Barr, "Review of *Modern Architecture*,"
           434.
Page 86.   **a mixture of protest and high jinks:** Sandler and Newman, *Defining
           Modern Art*, 17-18; Barr to Audrey McMahon, April 25, 1931, Roll
           2164, AAA.
Page 86.   **Various versions of it:** Robert A. M. Stern, *George Howe: Toward a
           Modern American Architecture* (New Haven: Yale, 1975), 156.
Page 86.   **alerted many American architects:** *The Public as Artist* (New York:
           Museum of Modern Art, 1932); Roberta Smith, "The Museum of Mod-
           ern Art," *Art in America*, Sept. 1977, 93.
Page 87.   **His persistent propaganda:** Lynes, *Good Old Modern*, 89.
Page 87.   **Contributions for the first year's budget:** Barr to William H.
           Trombley, April 5, 1954, Roll 2183, AAA.
Page 88.   **In a crassly worded moral:** Goodyear, *Museum of Modern Art*, 16;
           Barr, "An Effort to Secure $3,250,000 for the Museum of Modern Art,"
           April 1931, pamphlet, 5-6, 14, 18, 23-24, MOMA Archive.
Page 88.   **Barr asked "for criticism":** Barr to Alfred H. Barr, Sr., Mar. 24,
           1931, Roll 2164, AAA.
Page 88.   **Like an effective sermon:** Barr, "An Effort to Secure $3,250,000," 7.
Page 89.   **Barr yearningly pointed out:** Barr, "An Effort to Secure
           $3,250,000," 13; Barr, undated handwritten notes, early 1930s, Roll
           3261, AAA.
Page 90.   **one Paris dealer also gave:** *Bulletin of the Museum of Modern Art*,
           May 1949, 6; Nico Mazaraki to Barr, Aug. 25, 1931, Roll 2164, AAA.
Page 90.   **the small sums she spent:** Lynes, *Good Old Modern*, 343.
Page 90.   **became more cordial and social:** Barr to Abby Rockefeller, Dec. 5,
           1930, and Sept. 26, 1931, both Roll 2164, AAA; interview with Eliza

Bliss Parkinson Cobb, Dec. 15, 1986; Abby Rockefeller to Barr, Mar. 14, 1931, Roll 2164, AAA.

Page 91.   **Johnson still recalls:** Interview with Philip Johnson, Dec. 17, 1986.

Page 92.   **In the introduction to a catalog:** Barr, *Weber, Klee, Lehmbruck, Maillol* (New York: Museum of Modern Art, 1930), 3.

Page 92.   **"Like everything you do . . .":** Frank Crowninshield to Barr, Feb. 4, 1946, Roll 2171, AAA.

Page 92.   **prompted Barr to write:** Barr to Abby Rockefeller, Feb. 4, 1931, Roll 2164, AAA; Barr, *Modern Painting and Sculpture* (New York: Museum of Modern Art, 1931).

Page 93.   **a five-story limestone town house:** Lynes, *Good Old Modern*, 95.

Page 93.   **Jere Abbott was persuaded:** Lynes, *Good Old Modern*, 94; Jere Abbott to Virgil Thompson, Oct. 2, 1973.

Page 93.   **shocking works to be viewed inside:** Lynes, *Good Old Modern*, 96.

Page 94.   **"all those rich people":** Interview with Eliza Bliss Parkinson Cobb, Dec. 15, 1986.

Page 94.   **trustee Eliza Parkinson recalled:** Interview with Eliza Bliss Parkinson Cobb, Dec. 15, 1986.

Page 94.   **Barr considered persuading:** Barr, unsent draft letter to Hugo Gellert, Spring 1932; Barr to A. Conger Goodyear, April 29, 1932, both Roll 2164, AAA.

Page 95.   **A flurry of fence-mending:** Barr cable to Abby Rockefeller, April 18, 1932, Roll 3264, AAA; Mary Morsell, "The Museum of Modern Art Opens in Its New Home," *Art News*, May 7, 1932, 5.

Page 95.   **reflected the crusading euphoria:** Barr to Abby Rockefeller, May 9, 1930, Roll 3264, AAA; Jere Abbott to Barr, June 25, 1930, and July 31, 1931, both Roll 2164, AAA; interview with Monroe Wheeler, June 18, 1986.

Page 96.   **administration was so casual:** Jere Abbott to Virgil Thompson, Oct. 2, 1973; Lynes, *Good Old Modern*, 117–18; interview with Ione Ulrich Sutton, Dec. 9, 1986.

Page 96.   **collection grew in a sporadic, haphazard fashion:** Gail Levin, *Edward Hopper* (New York: Crown, 1984), 47; Sandler and Newman, *Defining Modern Art*, 148.

Page 97.   **Barr himself later worried:** Jewell, "Museum of Modern Art," *New York Times*, Mar. 29, 1931; Barr to A. Conger Goodyear, Aug. 11, 1941, Roll 3266, AAA.

Page 97.   **motley collection reflected confusion:** Richard Lemon, "The House that Art Built," *Saturday Evening Post*, Jan. 30, 1965, 74; A. Conger Goodyear, "Museum of Modern Art," *Creative Art*, Dec. 1931, 456–57; Barr, draft for radio speech, May 6, 1932, Roll 3150, AAA.

Page 97.   **Barr conveyed his intense ambivalence:** Barr, draft for radio speech, May 6, 1932, Roll 3150, AAA.

Page 98.   **critics complained:** "Purchase Fund," *Art News*, Nov. 12, 1932, 11–12; Forbes Watson, "Gallery Explorations," *Parnassus*, Dec. 1932, 1–2.

Page 98.   **"It is sponsored by wealthy people . . .":** Joan M. Lukach, *Hilla Rebay: In Search of the Spirit of Art* (New York: Braziller, 1983), 135.

Page 98.   **it listed the anniversaries:** Metropolitan Museum of Art, *An Almanac for the Year 1930* (New York: Museum Press, 1930); A. Conger

Goodyear memo to MOMA executive committee, Sept. 1, 1931, Roll 2164, AAA.

Page 99. **Levy crowed:** Julien Levy, *Memoir of an Art Gallery* (New York: G. B. Putnam's Sons, 1977), 137–38.

Page 99. **Goodyear insisted that Barr postpone:** Barr to J. B. Neumann, Sept. 8, 1930, Roll NJBN-1, AAA; Julius Meier-Gräefe to Barr, Nov. 11, 1930, Roll 3145, AAA; Edward Alden Jewell, "Art with a Vengeance," *New York Times*, Mar. 22, 1931.

Page 100. **Barr was put off by prettiness:** Interview with Edward M. M. Warburg, June 3, 1986; interview with Monroe Wheeler, June 18, 1986; "Macdonald Queries," 1953, Roll 2180, AAA.

Page 100. **"even in small towns":** Barr, *Modern Painting and Sculpture* (New York: Museum of Modern Art, 1931), 15–16.

Page 100. **a dose of his customary bile:** Barr, draft of article for *Museum der Gegenwart*, 1931, Roll 3262, AAA.

Page 100. **Dot Sweetness it iss ausgespielt:** Charles Vezin, "Art of the Katzenjammer," *New York Times*, Mar. 29, 1931.

CHAPTER 5: BUILDING THE CONGREGATION

Page 103. **closely typed two-page assessment:** Lena Mayer-Benz, "Handwriting Analysis of '29-year-old American,'" Mar. 14, 1933, Roll 2165, AAA.

Page 104. **increasingly severe bouts of insomnia:** Barr to Abby Rockefeller, June 21, 1932; Barr to A. Conger Goodyear, Dec. 1, 1932, both Roll 2164, AAA.

Page 104. **"a flood of Americana":** Lynes, *Good Old Modern*, 107.

Page 104. **Marga sailed alone:** Margaret S. Barr, "Our Campaigns," 28–30; transcript of interview by Paul Cummings with Margaret S. Barr, April 8, 1974, AAA.

Page 105. **"a natural step in curing insomnia":** Barr to Dwight Macdonald, Dec. 2, 1953, Roll 2180, AAA; Margarethe Garthe to Barr, April 12, 1957, Roll 2184, AAA; Barr to Abby Rockefeller, Feb. 4, 1933; Abby Rockefeller to Barr, Mar. 7, 1933, both Roll 3264, AAA.

Page 105. **"took its revolution very calmly":** Barr, "Art in the Third Reich— Preview, 1933," *Magazine of Art*, Oct. 1945, 212.

Page 106. **Barr reported sadly:** Barr, "Art in the Third Reich," 217–18; William L. Shirer, *The Nightmare Years 1930–1940* (New York: Bantam, 1985), 132.

Page 106. **The paintings were hidden away:** Barr, "Art in the Third Reich," 213–18.

Page 106. **the first Nazi meeting on art:** Richard Grunberger, *The 12-Year Reich: A Social History of Nazi Germany 1933–1945* (New York: Holt, Rinehart & Winston, 1971), 422; Barr, "Art in the Third Reich," 212.

Page 107. **The Barrs listened in horrified fascination:** Barr, "Art in the Third Reich," 213.

Page 107. **Hardly a murmur opposed:** Macdonald, "Action on West 53rd Street—II," 39.

Page 108. **Barr attended a reception:** Barr, "Art in the Third Reich," 218.

Page 108. **Alfred fought his horror and fury:** Barr to Lincoln Kirstein, Oct. 3, 1933, Roll 2164, AAA.

Page 108. **tried desperately to raise the alarm:** Barr to Kirstein, Oct. 3, 1933, Roll 2164, AAA; Barr, "Nationalism in German Films," *Hound and Horn*, March 1934, 278-83.

Page 108. **"wrote the articles in a rage":** Barr to John B. Morse, July 31, 1945, Roll 2174, AAA; Barr to Harper & Bros., Nov. 5, 1948, Roll 2179, AAA.

Page 109. **a terse account:** *Bulletin of the Museum of Modern Art*, June 1933, 4.

Page 109. **"the opportunity to secure":** Barr to Courtauld Institute, May 24, 1933, Roll 2164, AAA.

Page 109. **"persons of this caliber":** Erwin Panofsky to Barr, Oct. 14, 1934, Roll 2165, AAA; H. W. Janson, *History of Art* (New York: Abrams, 1977).

Page 110. **a torrent of desperate appeals:** Justus Bier to Barr, Sept. 1, 1933; Barr to Bier, Oct. 3, 1933, both Roll 2164, AAA.

Page 110. **a flurry of activity at the MOMA:** Edward M. M. Warburg to Barr, Aug. 31, 1933; Philip Johnson to Barr, Summer 1933, both Roll 2164, AAA.

Page 110. **Summing up the MOMA's season:** Edward Alden Jewell, "Very Plump Lean Year," *New York Times*, June 4, 1933.

Page 111. **A stern Presbyterian:** Stanley Weintraub, *Whistler: A Biography* (New York: Weybright & Talley, 1974), 16.

Page 111. **"a returned transatlantic flyer":** Goodyear, *Museum of Modern Art*, 42-43; "Museum of Modern Art," *Fortune*, Dec. 1938, 131.

Page 111. **helped to amplify:** Barr to Dwight Macdonald, Dec. 2, 1953, Roll 2180, AAA; Barr to James A. Farley, May 9, 1934, Roll 3260, AAA; "Museum Protests Whistler Stamp," *New York Times*, May 10, 1934.

Page 112. **"Modern art cannot be defined . . .":** Barr, "The Meaning of 'Modern,'" *New York Times*, May 13, 1934.

Page 112. **would illustrate his view of Modernism:** "Memoranda of next year's exhibitions," undated 1933, Roll 3264, AAA.

Page 112. **sponsored a talk by Gertrude Stein:** "Miss Stein Speaks to Bewildered 500," *New York Times*, Nov. 2, 1934.

Page 113. **"the atmosphere chills":** Forbes Watson, "The Innocent Bystander," *Magazine of Art*, Jan. 1925, 62.

Page 113. **In his catalog essay:** *Modern Works of Art: Fifth Anniversary Exhibition* (New York: Museum of Modern Art, 1924), 17-18.

Page 113. **in an internal memo:** Barr, "Loan Exhibitions," undated 1933, Roll 3266, AAA.

Page 114. **her financial contributions were also modest:** "Mr. Junior's Beneficences: An Audit," *Fortune*, July 1936, 127; William S. Lieberman in *Twentieth Century Art from the Nelson Aldrich Rockefeller Collection* (New York: Graphic Society, 1969), 13; Richard Lemon, "The House that Art Built," 74.

Page 114. **Barr told her biographer:** Barr to Mary Ellen Chase, Feb. 6, 1950; Barr memo to Monroe Wheeler, May 8, 1948, both Roll 2175, AAA.

Page 114. **"his slow meditative analysis":** *Alfred H. Barr, Jr.: A Memorial Tribute*; Barr to Philip Johnson, July 21, 1933, Roll 2165, AAA.

Page 115. **Barr could be curtly arbitrary:** Russell Lynes, "Museum Maker," *Vogue*, May 1973, 199.

Page 115. **trustees' persistent confusion:** Goodyear, "Museum of Modern Art," 456–57; *The Public as Artist* (New York: Museum of Modern Art, 1932); "Museum of Modern Art," *Fortune*, 131.

Page 115. **when Lillie Bliss died:** "Miss Bliss Left Art to Many Museums," *New York Times*, Mar. 20, 1931; press release, Mar. 12, 1934, MOMA Archive; Goodyear, *Museum of Modern Art*, 33.

Page 116. **irrevocably altered the museum's dimensions:** "Modern Museum Receives Bliss Art," *New York Times*, Mar. 13, 1934, 23; Barr to Alfred H. Barr, Sr., Mar. 24, 1931, Roll 2164, AAA.

Page 116. **Barr sketched for the trustees:** Barr, *Painting and Sculpture in the Museum of Modern Art 1929–1967* (New York: Museum of Modern Art, 1977), xiii; *The Museum of Modern Art, New York: The History and the Collection* (New York: Abrams, 1984), 13.

Page 117. **was building a personal collection:** Barr, "The Permanent Collection," Oct. 1933, Roll 3260, AAA.

Page 117. **advising a host of collectors:** F. S. Rollins to Barr, Dec. 21, 1933; Barr to Frank K. M. Rehn, Dec. 22, 1933, both Roll 2164, AAA; *Three Generations of Twentieth Century Art* (Greenwich, CT: Graphic Society, 1972).

Page 118. **not reserved for big donors only:** Barr to T. K. Davis, June 17, 1932, Roll 2164, AAA; *Bulletin of the Museum of Modern Art*, Nov. 1934; Samuel J. Bloomingdale to Barr, Dec. 6, 1933; Barr to Bloomingdale, Dec. 7, 1933, Roll 2164, AAA.

Page 118. **correspondingly detailed advice:** Barr to Walter Gropius, May 28, 1968, Roll 2193, AAA; Undated note in Barr's handwriting, Roll 3262, AAA; Barr to Xanti Schawinsky, Jan. 11, 1950, Roll 2176, AAA; Barr to Abby Rockefeller, May 7, 1931, Roll 2164, AAA.

Page 118. **warned an *Art News* article:** "A Modern Museum," *Art News*, April 30, 1932, 12.

Page 119. **Barr honed his skill:** Barr to Julien Levy, June 29, 1934; Barr to Abby Rockefeller, July 13, 1934, both Roll 2165, AAA.

Page 119. **less than $8,000:** Barr to Abby Rockefeller, July 13, 1934, Roll 2165, AAA.

Page 120. **again he approached Clark:** Barr to Stephen C. Clark, July 13, 1934; Clark to Barr, July 18 and Aug. 8, 1934, all Roll 2165, AAA.

Page 120. **no modern work was too minor:** Barr to Iris Barry, June 22, 1935; A. Conger Goodyear to Barr, Aug. 2, 1935, both Roll 2165, AAA.

Page 120. **the rhetoric of cooperation:** Abby Rockefeller to Barr, Mar. 14, 1931, Roll 2164, AAA; "Two Art Museums Pledge Mutual Aid," *New York Times*, May 10, 1932.

Page 121. **"Luxembourg-Louvre sort of relationship":** Edward Alden Jewell, "Mainly About Our Two Museums," *New York Times*, May 15, 1932.

Page 121. **Coffin tolerantly averred:** Goodyear, *Museum of Modern Art*, 40.

Page 121. **Barr wrote to a jobless friend:** Barr to O. C. O'Callaghan, Feb. 24, 1932, Roll 2164, AAA.

Page 121. **advice came nevertheless:** "A Modern Museum," 12; E. M. Benson, "A New Yorker Looks His Museums in the Face," *American Magazine of Art*, Oct. 1934, 540.

Page 123. **The catalog Barr prepared:** Scrapbook of traveling exhibitions, MOMA Archive.

Page 123. **Packaged in three stout crates:** Scrapbook of traveling exhibitions, MOMA Archive.

Page 123. **museum would send ninety-one exhibitions:** *Public as Artist*; "Accumulative List of Circulating Exhibitions," mimeographed report, 1–4, MOMA Archive.

Page 123. **a deluge of demands:** J. E. Dungan to Barr, Jan. 28, 1932; Earl J. Johnson to Barr, Dec. 14, 1931; Hallie Flanagan to Barr, Feb. 19, 1932; Maxwell Levinson to Barr, Feb. 16, 1932, all Roll 2164, AAA.

Page 123. **Barr declined these requests:** Barr to Bernard Lemann, Jan. 5, 1932, Roll 2164, AAA; Barr to Harmon Tupper, Feb. 3, 1934; W. W. Beardsley to Barr, Oct. 22 and Feb. 9, 1934; Barr to Katrina Van Hook, Dec. 11 and Oct. 10, 1934, all Roll 2165, AAA.

Page 124. **Responding to a casual inquiry:** Barr to Bernhard Scher, Jan. 8, 1935, Roll 2165, AAA.

Page 124. **he could not resist adding:** Barr to Anna H. Clark, May 17, 1932, Roll 2164, AAA.

Page 124. **"so-called collegiate gothic":** Barr to Yandell Henderson, Mar. 16, 1932, Roll 2164, AAA.

Page 125. **Barr vigorously voiced his opinion:** Barr to Hans Lange, Oct. 30, 1935; Barr to Edward M. M. Warburg, Jan. 17, 1935, both Roll 2165, AAA.

Page 125. **informal art history study group:** Meyer Schapiro to Barr, Mar. 8, 1935; Barr to Schapiro, Mar. 11, 1935, both Roll 2165, AAA; Barr to A. Philip McMahon, May 11, 1937, Roll 2166, AAA.

Page 125. **ordinary socializing often tormented him:** Margaret S. Barr, "Our Campaigns," 39.

Page 126. **"never had an intelligent get-together":** Transcript of Paul Cummings interview with Margaret S. Barr, May 13, 1974, AAA.

Page 126. **briskly tackled the minutest detail:** Allan R. Blackburn memo to Abby Rockefeller, Mar. 1, 1932, Roll 2164, AAA; Barr to Blackburn, Aug. 18, 1934, Roll 2165, AAA.

Page 127. **"an extracurricular diversion":** Julien Levy, *Memoir of an Art Gallery*, 11; Barr, "Nationalism in German Films," 279–82.

Page 127. **a 1932 report:** Barr, Notes on the departmental expansion of the museum, June 24, 1932, Roll 3260, AAA; Macdonald, "Action on West 53rd Street—II," 42.

Page 127. **a motion picture committee:** Interview with Monroe Wheeler, June 18, 1986.

Page 128. **"the belle of Bloomsbury":** *Remembering Iris Barry* (New York: Museum of Modern Art, 1980), 3–4.

Page 128. **"By the fall of 1934 . . .":** *Art in Progress* (New York: Museum of Modern Art, 1944), 172–73.

Page 128. **Barr later admitted:** Barr to Mary Ellen Chase, Feb. 6, 1950, Roll 2175, AAA; Iris Barry in *Art in Progress*, 172–73; Lynes, *Good Old Modern*, 111–12; "Museum of Modern Art," *Fortune*, 134.

Page 129. **"we are now getting the films":** Iris Barry to Barr, July 22 and Aug. 27, 1935, both Roll 2165, AAA.

Page 129. **In its first three years:** "Report on the Work and Progress of the Film Library," Dec. 9, 1937; news release, Oct. 24, 1936, both MOMA Archive.

Page 130. **"completely worn out"**: John E. Abbott to Barr, July 10, 1935, Roll 2165, AAA.

Page 130. **a bold bid for the limelight**: Roger Butterfield, "The Museum and the Redhead," *Saturday Evening Post*, April 5, 1947, 108-9.

Page 131. **Newmeyer enthusiastically showered the press**: "Art Museum Is Kept Open an Extra Hour for Einstein," *New York Times*, Jan. 19, 1935; news release and Sarah Newmeyer letter to reporters, Oct. 2, 1935, MOMA Archive.

Page 131. **Barr excitedly reported to Goodyear**: Barr to A. Conger Goodyear, June 28, 1935, Roll 2165, AAA.

Page 132. **Goodyear exulted**: A. Conger Goodyear to Barr, Aug. 2, 1935; Barr to Thomas Mabry, July 31, 1935, both Roll 2165, AAA.

Page 132. **churning out press releases**: News release, July 2, 1935; news release No. 27, undated 1935; news release, Oct. 14, 1935, all MOMA Archive.

Page 132. **further publicity went out**: News releases, Mar. 20 and Sept. 21, 1936, MOMA Archive; "70,000 See Van Gogh Show," *New York Times*, Dec. 20, 1935; Lynes, *Good Old Modern*, 132-36.

Page 133. **a personal triumph for Alfred Barr**: Goodyear, *Museum of Modern Art*, 55; "$1,000,000 Paintings by Van Gogh Here," *New York Times*, Oct. 14, 1935.

Page 133. **Such publicity alienated**: Louis LaBeaume to Henri Marceau, Feb. 6, 1937; Barr to LaBeaume, May 11, 1937; Barr to Meyric Rogers, May 17, 1937; Barr to J. Arthur MacLean, May 17, 1937; MacLean to Barr, May 20, 1937; Barr to LaBeaume, May 29, 1937; Rogers to Barr, May 20, 1937; Barr to LaBeaume, May 29, 1937; Rogers to Barr, June 2, 1937; Barr to MacLean, June 5, 1937, all Roll 2165, AAA; Barr to René d'Harnoncourt, Jan. 23, 1950, Roll 2193, AAA.

Page 134. **van Gogh show had settled a spiritual debt**: "Van Gogh Art Show Visited by 100,000," *New York Times*, Dec. 29, 1935.

CHAPTER 6: CONVERTING THE HEATHEN

Page 137. **"not a traditional museum"**: Interview with Beaumont Newhall, July 27, 1987; Beaumont Newhall, "He Set the Pace and Shaped the Style," *Art News*, Oct. 1979, 134-35.

Page 137. **"a born bookman"**: Paul Vanderbilt to Thomas D. Mabry, July 25, 1935, Roll 2165, AAA.

Page 138. **"a plodder"**: A. Conger Goodyear to Barr, Aug. 2, 1935; Barr to Alice Malette, Aug. 3, 1935, both Roll 2165, AAA; *Alfred H. Barr, Jr.: A Memorial Tribute* (New York: Museum of Modern Art, 1981).

Page 138. **writing to Barr from Europe**: Beaumont Newhall to Barr, Aug. 5, 1935, Roll 2165, AAA.

Page 138. **Barr would stop Newhall**: Newhall, "He Set the Pace," 134-36; Beaumont Newhall to Barr, Aug. 24, 1936, Roll 2165, AAA.

Page 139. **"MOMA was the only place"**: Barr to Dorothy Miller, June 27, 1934, Roll 2165, AAA; interview with Dorothy Miller, Dec. 16, 1986.

Page 140. **thirty-five dollars per week**: Barr memorandum on departmental salaries, Dec. 3, 1935, Roll 3265, AAA; interview with Dorothy Miller, May 31, 1986.

Page 140. **"the eight-day week"**: Joseph Solman in Francis V. O'Connor, ed., *The New Deal Art Projects: An Anthology of Memoirs* (Washington, DC: Smithsonian, 1972), 121.

Page 140. **Miller often stayed**: Interview with Dorothy Miller, Dec. 16, 1986.

Page 141. **"if better ideas present themselves"**: Barr to Thomas Mabry, June 13, 1935, Roll 2165, AAA; interview with Dorothy Miller, Dec. 16, 1986.

Page 141. **"A lot of it was pitiful."**: Interview with Dorothy Miller, May 31, 1986.

Page 141. **"setting and maintaining standards"**: Barr, "Notes for a Reorganization Committee," Feb. 23, 1938, Roll 2166, AAA.

Page 142. **sure it would be "mediocre"**: Barr to Allan Blackburn, Aug. 28, 1933, Roll 2165, AAA; Goodyear, *Museum of Modern Art*, 73.

Page 143. **"problems of personal jealousy"**: Barr to A. Conger Goodyear, Sept. 25, 1934, Roll 2165, AAA.

Page 143. **radio series of lectures**: Holger Cahill and Barr, eds., *Art in America* (New York: Reynal & Hitchcock, 1934); Barr to John Schoon, Mar. 30, 1940, Roll 2170, AAA; Barr to Allan Blackburn, undated 1934, Roll 2165, AAA.

Page 143. **"more expensive than Matisse or Picasso"**: Barr to Robert W. Harshe, Aug. 27, 1936, Roll 2165, AAA; Barr to Lincoln Kirstein, Feb. 4, 1948, Roll 2169, AAA; "Mrs. Rockefeller Gives Modern Art," *New York Times*, May 26, 1935.

Page 144. **491 works by Americans**: Macdonald, "Action on West 53rd Street—II," 60.

Page 144. **this kind of reverse chauvinism**: Interview with Edith Bry, June 12, 1986; Lynes, *Good Old Modern*, 71; American Abstract Artists, *The World of Abstract Art* (New York: Wittenborn, 1957), 133.

Page 145. **"the artist should certainly participate"**: Barr to Robert W. Harshe, Aug. 27, 1936, Roll 2165, AAA; Barr to the editor of *Art Front*, June–July 1937, 5.

Page 145. **reflected his belief**: Richard D. McKinzie, *The New Deal for Artists* (Princeton, NJ: Princeton University, 1973), 80; *New Horizons in American Art* (New York: Museum of Modern Art, 1936), 7.

Page 146. **included some works of Abstractionists**: Rosalind Bengelsdorf Browne in Francis V. O'Connor, ed., *New Deal Art Projects*, 237; Barr, "Surrealists and Neo-Romantics," *Saturday Review of Literature*, Sept. 14, 1935, 6.

Page 146. **"considerable embarrassment"**: Barr to Edward M. M. Warburg, Feb. 27, 1935.

Page 146. **"running with our tongues hanging out"**: Barr, *The Museum of Modern Art, New York*, typed booklet, undated Sept.–Nov. 1936, Roll 3260, AAA; Barr to Paul Sachs, May 12, 1939, Roll 3265, AAA.

Page 147. **Barr often distracted himself**: A. G. Pelikan to Barr, Aug. 25, 1939; Barr to Pelikan, Sept. 21, 1939, both Roll 2166, AAA; Barr to S. John Woods, Dec. 23, 1937, Roll 2195, AAA; "U.S. Widens Levy on Art of Utrillo," *New York Times*, Feb. 10, 1939; Barr to Abby Rockefeller, Jan. 17, 1936, Roll 3264, AAA; interview with Joseph Van Nostrand, Division of Old Records, District Attorney of New York, June 13, 1986; Helen Gardner to Barr, Feb. 9, 1935; Barr to Gardner, Feb. 13, 1935, both Roll 2165, AAA.

Page 147. **he tried to help others:** Transcript of Paul Cummings interview with Margaret S. Barr, April 8, 1974, AAA; Barr to Roberta Fansler, Jan. 13, 1934, and Jan. 15, 1933; Barr to Edward S. King, May 28 and June 27, 1934, all Roll 2165, AAA.

Page 147. **more generalized evangelical do-goodism:** Robert F. Wagner to Barr, May 14, 1936; Barr to Robert Cushman Murphy, Dec. 3, 1937, Roll 2166, AAA.

Page 148. **had to help out donors and trustees:** Barr to Alexander Calder, Oct. 16, 1934, Roll 2165, AAA; Joseph Walker to Barr, Oct. 6, 1936; Barr to Walker, Oct. 14, 1936, both Roll 2166, AAA.

Page 148. **all too mundane activities:** "Notes for the Reorganization Committee," Feb. 23, 1938, Roll 2166, AAA.

Page 148. **trustees had searched diligently:** A. Conger Goodyear to Paul Sachs, Jan. 5, 1935; Goodyear to Gordon Washburn, Nov. 27, 1934; Goodyear to Abby Rockefeller, Nov. 26, 1934, all Roll 3264, AAA; Lynes, *Good Old Modern*, 151–52; "Notes for the Reorganization Committee," Feb. 23, 1938, Roll 2166, AAA.

Page 149. **insistence on rethinking:** Barr to Edward S. King, Oct. 10, 1934, Roll 2165, AAA; interview with Dorothy Miller, May 31, 1986; Barr to Mrs. Barton Hepburn, Mar. 21, 1935, Roll 2165, AAA.

Page 150. **first of these landmark exhibitions:** News release No. 6a, undated 1936, MOMA Archive; "Cubist Art Fails to Pass Customs," *New York Times*, Feb. 22, 1936.

Page 150. **a news story about the opening:** Edward Alden Jewell, *New York Times*, Mar. 8, 1936; Charles G. Poore, "Furiously They Ask Once More: But Is It Art?" *New York Times*, Mar. 8, 1936.

Page 151. **"no longer necessary to pretend":** Thomas Craven, *Modern Art: The Men, the Movements, the Meaning* (New York: Simon & Schuster, 1940), 229–30, 376.

Page 151. **"fatal defect of purity":** Kenneth Clark, "Boredom Blamed," *Art Digest*, Nov. 15, 1935, 13; Clark, *Civilization* (New York: Harper & Row, 1969).

Page 152. **"an example of childish charlatanry":** " 'Abstract' Art," *New York Times*, Mar. 23, 1936.

Page 152. **"the house fell":** Judges 16:21, 25, 27, 29, *King James Bible*.

Page 152. **former student wrote to Barr:** Russell F. Peterson to Barr, Nov. 30, 1937, Roll 2166, AAA.

Page 153. **no less than 386 works:** Press release No. 42324-22, 1942, MOMA Archive.

Page 153. **still struggling to prepare:** Barr to Severin Bourne, Feb. 1, 1936, Roll 2166, AAA; Barr, *Cubism and Abstract Art* (New York: Museum of Modern Art, 1936), cover.

Page 154. **a chaotic nightmare:** "Solid Abstractions," *Time*, Mar. 9, 1936, 50–51; "Schedule for *Cubism and Abstract Art*," undated 1935, Roll 3146, AAA; Rona Roob to Clive Phillpot, Feb. 2, 1981, Roll 3146, AAA.

Page 154. **attracted considerable praise:** Wassily Kandinsky to Barr, June 22, 1936; note to files from Rona Roob, Feb. 2, 1981, both Roll 3146, AAA.

Page 154. **Barr's preface proclaimed:** Barr, *Cubism and Abstract Art*, 2, 9–10.

Page 155. **enhanced the implication:** Barr, *Cubism and Abstract Art*, 11.

Page 155. **anticipated the reader's struggle:** Barr, *Cubism and Abstract Art*, 11–13.

Page 155. **In its 249 pages:** Barr, *Cubism and Abstract Art*, 234–49.

Page 156. **best ever written in English:** Meyer Schapiro, *Modern Art: 19th and 20th Centuries* (New York: Braziller, 1978), 187–88; "Publications," *New York Times*, July 26, 1936.

Page 156. **a 1935 MOMA news release:** News release No. 27, undated 1935; news releases, Jan. 10 and 11, 1935, all MOMA Archive; "Surrealist Revolution Counterclockwise," *Art Front*, Feb. 1935, 1.

Page 157. **Marga supplemented Barr's hasty notes:** Barr travel notebooks, 1930–1962, Roll 3261, AAA; transcript of Paul Cummings interview with Margaret S. Barr, May 13, 1974, AAA.

Page 157. **"sense of absolute conviction":** Barr, "Oelze, 1936 and His *Expectation*," undated, Roll 2197, AAA.

Page 157. **"had to write forty-seven letters":** Barr to A. Conger Goodyear, July 19, 1936, Roll 2166, AAA; Barr to Thomas Mabry, Aug. 1, 1936, Roll 2165, AAA.

Page 158. **such a nightmare world:** Messer, *MOMA: Museum in Search of an Image*, 90–91.

Page 159. **he bought it secretly:** Lynes, "Museum Maker," 196, 199.

Page 159. **"quite pleasantly and painlessly":** Edward Alden Jewell, "Fantasy in Perspective," *New York Times*, Dec. 13, 1936.

Page 159. **"no one could honestly brag":** "Giddy Museum Exhibit," *Newsweek*, Dec. 19, 1936, 26; Milwaukee Art Institute *Bulletin*, scrapbook of traveling exhibitions, MOMA Archive.

Page 159. **news releases about the show:** Book one, scrapbook of traveling exhibitions; "Annual Report to Members," 1938, both MOMA Archive; A. Conger Goodyear to Abby Rockefeller, Dec. 15, 1936, Roll 3264, AAA.

Page 160. **"very large body of writing":** Barr, *Fantastic Art, Dada and Surrealism* (New York: Museum of Modern Art, 1936), 7–8.

Page 160. **a distinctly Dada devil:** Barr, *Fantastic Art, Dada and Surrealism*, 199; clipping from *New York Herald-Tribune*, Dec. 27, 1936, Roll 3265, AAA.

Page 161. **Few men took less interest:** Jane Ritchie to Margaret S. Barr, Aug. 20, 1981, Roll 3145, AAA; James Thrall Soby to Barr, July 6, 1971, Roll 3265, AAA.

Page 161. **had never wanted children:** Interview with Dorothy Miller, Dec. 16, 1986; interview with Helen Franc, June 6, 1986.

Page 161. **Marga resisted the responsibilities:** Transcript of interview by Paul Cummings with Margaret S. Barr, May 13, 1974, AAA; Margaret S. Barr, "Our Campaigns," 23–74.

Page 161. **Victoria disappointed Barr:** Interview with Dorothy Miller, May 31 1986.

Page 162. **mitigating the dire plight:** O'Connor, *New Deal Art Projects*, 43–44; McKinzie, *New Deal for Artists*, 144–45.

Page 162. **he watched impotently:** Messer, *MOMA: Museum in Search of an Image*, 129; Barr to Thomas Mabry, Aug. 1, 1936, Roll 2165, AAA.

Page 163. **he persuaded Goodyear:** Barr to A. Conger Goodyear, Dec. 24, 1959, Roll 2194, AAA.

Page 163. **sums that look ridiculous today:** Barr to Abby Rockefeller, June 21 and July 20, 1935, Roll 3264, AAA; "Notes on the Quotations from Barr," undated 1944; Sally Newmeyer to Emily Genauer, Mar. 24,

1944, both Roll 2173, AAA; Barr to Abby Rockefeller, Dec. 28, 1936, Roll 3264, AAA; Barr to Donald Hall, Jan. 22, 1964, Roll 2186, AAA.

Page 163. **a shy, reclusive lady:** Richard Koch to Ernest Lundell, Mar. 31, 1970, Roll 2194, AAA; Grace Glueck, "Alfred Hamilton Barr, Jr., is Dead," *New York Times*, Aug. 16, 1981.

Page 164. **That broke the ice:** Lynes, *Good Old Modern*, 300; Goodyear, *Museum of Modern Art*, 87.

Page 164. **what America offered in the way of art:** Barr, *Trois Siècles d'Art aux Etats-Unis* (Paris: Editions des Musées Nationaux, 1938), 27.

Page 165. **French bureaucracy had defeated him:** Duncan Phillips to A. Conger Goodyear, Feb. 8, 1933; Abby Rockefeller to Goodyear, Mar. 19, 1936, Roll 3263, AAA.

Page 165. **to educate Parisians:** Edward Alden Jewell, *Have We an American Art?* (New York: Longmans, Green, 1939), 23–25.

Page 165. **catalog essay on architecture:** Barr, *Trois Siècles d'Art aux Etats-Unis*, 72–73.

Page 166. **French were notoriously ethnocentric:** Jewell, *Have We an American Art?* 31–35, 43–44; Serge Guilbaut, *How New York Stole the Idea of Modern Art* (Chicago: University of Chicago, 1983), 42–43.

Page 166. **Barr would later write:** "Exhibition of American Art," undated draft, 1938, Roll 3263, AAA; Goodyear, *Museum of Modern Art*, 73–82; Barr, "Three Centuries of Painting in the United States," for release to European publications, sponsored by the Office of War Information, Sept. 1945, Roll 2175, AAA; Barr to Ernestine Fantl Carter, June 24, 1943, Roll 2169, AAA.

Page 167. **seven parcels adjoining the existing building:** Barr, notes for a talk at a luncheon given by Abby Rockefeller, Nov. 1935, Roll 3262, AAA; Messer, *MOMA: Museum in Search of an Image*, 63; Goodyear, *Museum of Modern Art*, 126.

Page 167. **"volunteer interpreter and general caretaker":** News release, Aug. 20, 1935, MOMA Archive; Barr to Henry-Russell Hitchcock, Nov. 29, 1969, Roll 2186, AAA.

Page 168. **search for an outstanding European:** Richard Hudnut to Barr, May 18 and 19, and Dec. 14, 1936, Roll 2165, AAA; Ernestine Fantl Carter to Barr, May 20, 1936, Roll 2166, AAA.

Page 168. **Rockefeller and Goodyear had already chosen:** Thomas Mabry to Barr, June 18, 1936, Roll 2165, AAA; Abby Rockefeller cable to Nelson Rockefeller, undated, Summer 1936; Nelson Rockefeller to Abby Rockefeller, undated cable, Summer 1936, both Roll 3264, AAA.

Page 168. **Barr was crushed:** Barr to A. Conger Goodyear, July 6, 1936; Barr to Philip Goodwin, July 6, 1936; Barr night letter to Nelson Rockefeller, July 7, 1936, all Roll 2165, AAA.

Page 169. **"I know you will snort . . .":** Messer, *MOMA: Museum in Search of an Image*, 70–72.

Page 169. **he advised another museum director:** Barr to Charles C. Cunningham, Oct. 27, 1964, Roll 2186, AAA.

Page 170. **new MOMA building was a sensational success:** "Museum of Modern Art," *Architectural Forum*, Aug. 1939, 116; interview with G. E. Kidder-Smith, June 10, 1986; Barr to Stephen C. Clark, Mar. 20, 1942, Roll 3265, AAA.

Page 170. **"to smite the host of the Philistines":** II Samuel 5:12, 24.

CHAPTER 7: PREACHING THE GOSPEL

Page 171. **a gala dinner party:** Lynes, *Good Old Modern*, 199–201; *Bulletin of the Museum of Modern Art*, May–June 1939, 6–7.

Page 172. **"a citadel of freedom":** "President Praises U.S. Art Freedom," *New York Times*, May 11, 1939.

Page 172. **" a pretty cheap and unnecessary conniving":** Barr memo to Julian Street, June 12, 1939, Roll 3260, AAA.

Page 172. **an increasing role in managing:** Messer, *MOMA: Museum in Search of an Image*, 40; "Modern Museum Shifts Officials," *New York Times*, May 9, 1939; Collier and Horowitz, *The Rockefellers: An American Dynasty*, 206.

Page 173. **a landmark on New York's cultural scene:** Edward Alden Jewell, "In the Realm of Art," *New York Times*, May 14, 1939; Lynes, *Good Old Modern*, 211.

Page 173. **a generous demonstration of Barr's accomplishments:** Barr, *Art in Our Time* (New York: Museum of Modern Art, 1939), 8–9.

Page 174. **To avoid intimidating:** Edward Alden Jewell, "Museum to Show 'Art in Our Time,' " *New York Times*, May 19, 1939; Barr, *Art in Our Time*, captions for items no. 49 and 50.

Page 174. **functioned in twenty-one cities:** Barr, *Art in Our Time*, 6, 11–12.

Page 174. **catalogs had revolutionized this genre:** Oliver Larkin, "Domesticating Modern Art," *Saturday Review of Literature*, July 15, 1939, 8; Dwight Macdonald, "Action on West 53rd Street—I," *New Yorker*, Dec. 12, 1953, 61; Agnes Mongan, "What Makes a Museum Modern?" *Art News*, Aug. 1944, 12–13; Barr to Leslie Cheek, Jr., May 6, 1942, Roll 2166, AAA.

Page 175. **attendance nevertheless rose by 380 percent:** Museum of Modern Art Annual Report, July 1, 1940, to June 30, 1941, MOMA Archive.

Page 175. **The rest came from donations:** Ione Ulrich to Abby Rockefeller, Mar. 5, 1941, Roll 3265, AAA; Museum of Modern Art Annual Report, 1940–41, MOMA Archive; Ione Ulrich to Abby Rockefeller, Dec. 3, 1943, Roll 3265, AAA.

Page 176. **no reasonable balance in the collection:** Marie Alexander to Michael Middleton, May 17, 1953, Roll 2180, AAA; Messer, *MOMA: Museum in Search of an Image*, 130–31, 145–46.

Page 176. **His ideal painting collection:** Barr, "Ideal Collection," Mar. 6, 1941, Roll 2166, AAA.

Page 177. **part of a monstrous Nazi seizure:** H. H. Pars, *Pictures in Peril* (London: Faber & Faber, 1957), 207–8; Grunberger, *12-Year Reich*, 425.

Page 178. **"more cultivated elements":** "Exiled Reich Art Put on View Here," *New York Times*, Aug. 8, 1939; Edward Alden Jewell, "In the Realm of Art," *New York Times*, Aug. 13, 1939.

Page 178. **the Barrs were in Paris:** Joseph D. Isaacson, "Curt Valentin: Art Dealer of the Forties," unpublished mimeographed essay, May 1967; Barr to Thomas Mabry, July 1, 1939, Roll 2166, AAA; Barr to Whom it may concern, Mar. 18, 1943, Roll 2169, AAA.

Page 178. **uneasiness over the morality:** Barr to Hans Platschek, Dec. 6, 1944, Roll 2175, AAA; Barr to Paul Mocsanyi, Nov. 29, 1954, Roll 2180, AAA; Barr to Kenneth Donahue, Feb. 28, 1956, Roll 2182, AAA.

Page 179. **a price list accompanied:** Scrapbook of traveling exhibitions, MOMA Archive.

Page 179. **trustees reiterated their goal:** Museum of Modern Art Annual Report, 1940–41, MOMA Archive; Barr to Frederick J. Pohl, Nov. 5, 1941, Roll 2168, AAA; Matthew 26:41.

Page 180. **he persuaded Mrs. Guggenheim:** Aline B. Saarinen, *The Proud Possessors* (New York: Vintage, 1968), 236; Edward Alden Jewell, "Museum to Show 'Art in Our Time,' " 27; Barr to Franz Mayer, April 14, 1942, Roll 2167, AAA; Barr to Paul Sachs, Jan. 18, 1955, Roll 2183, AAA.

Page 181. **"one of the great masterpieces:"** "Rousseau Painting Given to Museum," *New York Times*, Jan. 22, 1940, 117; interview with Dorothy Miller, May 31, 1986.

Page 181. **masterpieces would come thick and fast:** Doris Schmidt, "Biography," in Carla Schulz-Hoffmann and Judith C. Weiss, eds., *Max Beckmann Retrospective* (St. Louis Art Museum in association with Prestel Verlag, Munich, 1984), 458, 460.

Page 182. **diverted his pain and isolation:** Doris Schmidt and Stephan Lackner in Schulz-Hoffmann and Weiss, *Max Beckmann*, 153, 461–67; Cynthia Jaffee McCabe, *The Golden Door: Artist-Immigrants of America, 1876–1976* (Washington, DC: Smithsonian, 1976), 40.

Page 182. **the Bauhaus's impact in America:** McCabe, *Golden Door*, 272, 275; Josef Albers to Barr, Mar. 5, 1937; statement by Barr for *P-M* (a magazine published by Albers at Black Mountain College), April 20, 1937, both Roll 2166, AAA.

Page 182. **"I lost all my money . . .":** Alfred Flechtheim to Barr, Aug. 8, 1935, Roll 2165, AAA; interview with Hilton Kramer, June 17, 1986.

Page 183. **Barr tried to help:** Barr to Franklyn Hudgins, Nov. 24, 1936; Barr to Richard Hudnut, May 6, 1937; Barr to James Cochran, Dec. 6, 1937, all Roll 2166, AAA.

Page 183. **"through the harmonious unfolding":** McCabe, *Golden Door*, 309.

Page 184. **"Hitler shook the tree . . .":** Interview with Helen Franc, June 6, 1986.

Page 184. **sent Barr a former film critic:** Meyer Schapiro to Barr, Oct. 7, 1937, Roll 2166, AAA; Siegfried Kracauer, *From Caligari to Hitler* (Princeton, NJ: Princeton University, 1947), v; Barr to Paul Sachs, April 8, 1942; Sachs to Barr, April 13, 1942, both Roll 2167, AAA; interview with John Rewald, June 3, 1986; John Rewald, *The History of Impressionism* (New York: Museum of Modern Art, 1973).

Page 185. **Barr sent them to Dorothy Miller:** Interview with Dorothy Miller, May 31, 1986.

Page 185. **sending out to any agency:** Unsigned letter from Barr's secretary to Maria Heinemann, April 7, 1939, Roll 2166, AAA; Donald Fleming and Bernard Baylin, eds., *The Intellectual Migration* (Cambridge, MA: Harvard University, 1969), 592.

Page 185. **efforts to save them foundered:** Arthur Emptage to Barr, Dec. 11, 1939, Roll 2166, AAA; Kurt Schwitters to Barr, April 12, 1942; Barr to Schwitters, May 14, 1942, both Roll 2168, AAA.

Page 186. **"unbelievably unprofitable and unpleasant":** Wyndham Lewis to Barr, June 7, 1942; Barr to Lewis, June 23, 1942, both Roll 2167, AAA; Wyndham Lewis, *America, I Presume* (New York: Howell, Soskin, 1940), 4.

Page 186. **Barr made Marga responsible:** John Walker to Barr, Mar. 3, 1937, Roll 2166, AAA; Varian Fry to Barr, Oct. 27, 1942; Barr to Whom it may concern, Oct. 29, 1942, both Roll 2167, AAA; Barr to Christian Zervos, Mar. 24, 1941, Roll 2177, AAA; Barr to Nannette Rothschild, April 3, 1968, Roll 2198, AAA.

Page 186. **refused to support a campaign:** Phone message to Barr, Mar. 19, 1942; undated handbills; Louis Bromfield to Barr, Sept. 29, 1942, with penciled notations: "telephoned *yes*" and "card sent," Oct. 2, 1942, all Roll 2167, AAA.

Page 187. **Arensberg described his efforts:** Alice Goldfarb Marquis, *Marcel Duchamp: Eros, c'est la vie* (Troy, NY: Whitston, 1981), 264-65.

Page 187. **now could personally consult:** McCabe, *Golden Door*, 31; Barr to Fernand Léger, June 9, 1942; Barr to Piet Mondrian, April 3, 1942, both Roll 2167, AAA.

Page 187. **"were not entirely friendly":** Barr to Richard A. Brooks, Oct. 21, 1966, Roll 2195, AAA.

Page 188. **outrageous riptide of a woman:** Peggy Guggenheim, *Out of This Century* (New York: Universe, 1979), 237-45.

Page 188. **one work out of every show:** Peggy Guggenheim, *Confessions of an Art Addict* (New York: Macmillan, 1960), 49; *Works from the Peggy Guggenheim Foundation* (New York: Solomon R. Guggenheim Museum, 1969), 9, 14.

Page 188. **"I put myself on a regimen . . .":** *Works from the Peggy Guggenheim Foundation*, 9-10.

Page 189. **she had paid less than $40,000:** *Works from the Peggy Guggenheim Foundation*, 9-11, 46, 68, 122; Guggenheim, *Confessions of an Art Addict*, 75-76.

Page 189. **"had been my Bible for years":** Guggenheim, *Out of This Century*, 259.

Page 189. **invited the Barrs to dinner:** Guggenheim, *Out of This Century*, 260; Barr to Peggy Guggenheim, Oct. 23, 1942, Roll 2167, AAA; Guggenheim, *Confessions of an Art Addict*, 109-10.

Page 190. **threatened tragedy of a different kind:** Barr to J. W. Freshfield, Feb. 25, 1942; Barr to Cornelius N. Bliss, Oct. 19, 1942; Bliss to Barr, Oct. 20, 1942; Dorothy Dudley memo to Removal Squad, Mar. 23, 1942, all Roll 2167, AAA.

Page 190. **still cavalierly dismissed native artists:** G. H. Edgell in Regina Schoolman and Charles Slatkin, eds., *The Enjoyment of Art in America* (New York: Lippincott, 1942), ix; Barr memo to Dorothy Miller, Oct. 10, 1940, Roll 3262, AAA.

Page 190. **"to clean his shoes and speak Spanish":** Messer, *MOMA: Museum in Search of an Image*, 136; interview with Edgar Kaufmann, June 10, 1986.

Page 191. **Kaufmann idolized Barr:** Interview with Edgar Kaufmann, June 10, 1986; Barr travel notebooks, 1930-1962, Roll 3261, AAA; Barr, "Mexican Report," undated 1942, Roll 3264, AAA.

Page 191. **"surrealism alive":** Interview with Edgar Kaufmann, June 10, 1986; Barr, "Mexican Report," undated 1942, Roll 3264, AAA; Barr to Maria Luisa and Mario Carreno, Aug. 10, 1942, Roll 2169, AAA.

Page 192. **"decide how the money is spent"**: Edgar Kaufmann to Barr, Feb. 25, 1943; Barr wire to Kaufmann, undated early 1943; Kaufmann to Barr, undated early 1943, all Roll 2169, AAA.

Page 192. **"should set a standard"**: Barr to Stephen C. Clark, Oct. 21, 1942, Roll 2167, AAA.

Page 192. **could not resist abandoning Modernism:** Minutes of trustees' executive committee meeting, Feb. 14, 1940, Roll 2166, AAA; news release no. 35, undated 1940, MOMA Archive.

Page 193. **a one-day attendance record:** News release, Jan. 16, 1940; news release No. 10, undated 1940; news release, March 11, 1940; news release No. 23, undated 1940, all MOMA Archive; Roger Butterfield, "Museum and the Redhead," *Saturday Evening Post*, 110–11.

Page 193. **"martyrized many of the great innovators"**: Erwin S. Barrie to Barr, Feb. 10 and 28, 1940, both Roll 2166, AAA; Barr, "American Taste in Art," *Think*, May 1940, 16–17.

Page 193. **"stepped into the void"**: Emil Hilb to Barr, Jan. 24, 1942; Barr to Hilb, Feb. 16, 1942, both Roll 2167, AAA; Barr to L. J. Salter, Jan. 30, 1942, Roll 2168, AAA.

Page 194. **a raft of requests for advice:** Dr. Hans Huth to Barr, Feb. 21, 1942, Roll 2167, AAA; Catherine Oglesby to Barr, Feb. 16, 1942; Barr memo to John Abbott, Jan. 15, 1943; Barr to Anna Rutt, Sept. 16, 1942, all Roll 2168, AAA.

Page 194. **"the Museum welcomes you"**: Draft for a handbill, May 19, 1942, Roll 2167, AAA.

Page 195. **"the period in which we are living"**: Alfred Barr, "Modern Art Makes History Too," *College Art Journal*, Nov. 1941, 3.

Page 195. **"the negation of a liberal education"**: Frank Jewett Mather, "Old Art or New," *College Art Journal*, Jan. 1942, 35, 33.

Page 195. **insisted on having the last word:** James Thrall Soby, "In Defense of Modern Art," 63–65, and Lawrence Schmeckebier, "Modern Art First, Not Last," 61–62, both in *College Art Journal*, Mar. 1942; Beaumont Newhall and Robert J. Goldwater, "Modern Art in the College Curriculum," *College Art Journal*, 90–93; Walter W. S. Cook to Barr, Feb. 18, 1943, Roll 2169, AAA.

Page 196. **constantly braced his own troops:** Barr memo to Alice Carson, April 30, 1943, Roll 2169, AAA; Barr memo to Elodie Courter, Oct. 19, 1942, Roll 2167, AAA; Barr memos to Iris Barry, May 1, 1941, May 12, 1941, Feb. 13, 1942, all Roll 2167, AAA; Barr memos to Monroe Wheeler, Dec. 15, 1942, and Oct. 28, 1942, both Roll 2168, AAA.

Page 196. **patiently answered the most trivial letters:** Robert A. Varley to Barr, Nov. 25, 1942; Barr to Varley, Dec. 14, 1942, both Roll 2168, AAA; Barr to Mrs. John W. Becker, April 18, 1943; Barr memo to James Thrall Soby, Nov. 1, 1943, both Roll 2169, AAA.

Page 196. **activities expanded geometrically:** "Weekly Schedule," Jan. 18–24, 1943; Alice Carson memo to Frances Hawkins, Jan. 26, 1943, both Roll 2169, AAA; "News and Comment," *Magazine of Art*, Sept. 1939, 534; Barr to Anna W. Olmsted, June 16, 1942, Roll 2168, AAA.

Page 197. **"might even prove best"**: A. Conger Goodyear to Barr, April 24, 1933; Barr to Frank Crowninshield, Nov. 11, 1933, Roll 2164, AAA.

Page 198. **"we are to specify what his duties are"**: A. Conger Goodyear to Abby Rockefeller, June 30, 1933; Goodyear to Barr, June 30, 1933, both Roll 3264, AAA.

Page 198. **Abby Rockefeller again complained**: Abby Rockefeller to A. Conger Goodyear, undated fragment, Roll 3264, AAA.

Page 198. **"neither physically nor temperamentally fitted"**: Abby Rockefeller to A. Conger Goodyear, Dec. 16, 1936; Goodyear to Abby Rockefeller, Dec. 17, 1936, both Roll 3264, AAA.

Page 199. **a letter to the trustees**: Barr, "Notes for the Reorganization Committee," Feb. 23, 1938, Roll 2166, AAA.

Page 199. **"do not have the strength"**: Barr, draft for a postscript to "Notes for the Reorganization Committee," Roll 2166, AAA; transcript of Paul Cummings interview with Margaret S. Barr, May 13, 1974, AAA.

Page 200. **they replaced him**: Lynes, *Good Old Modern*, 214.

Page 200. **one *unhappy* family"**: Interview with Edgar Kaufmann, June 10, 1986; Lynes, *Good Old Modern*, 225–26; "Modern Art Museum Picks Four Trustees," *New York Times*, Jan. 21, 1940.

Page 200. **began pressuring Barr**: Margaret S. Barr, "Our Campaigns," 62.

Page 201. **the board fell into the grip**: Barr to Abby Rockefeller, Nov. 6, 1933, Roll 3264, AAA.

Page 201. **"it will be better still"**: Lynes, *Good Old Modern*, 16–17; Barr to Stephen C. Clark, Oct. 3, 1942, Roll 3260, AAA.

Page 201. **"as festive as a Christmas tree"**: "A Shoeshine Stand De Luxe," *New York Times*, Dec. 22, 1942; Barr to Dwight Macdonald, Dec. 3, 1953, Roll 2180, AAA.

Page 202. **Clark was livid**: Barr telegram to Monroe Wheeler, Feb. 23, 1943, Roll 2170, AAA; A. Conger Goodyear to Barr, July 9, 1943, Roll 2169, AAA; James Brooks, "Why Fight It?" *New Yorker*, Nov. 12, 1960, 78.

CHAPTER 8: IN THE WILDERNESS

Page 204. **the fable that Dorothy Miller's memory knitted**: Interview with Dorothy Miller, May 31, 1986; Philip Johnson, draft for memorial tribute to Barr, undated 1981, Roll 3145, AAA.

Page 204. **details of Barr's firing**: Margaret S. Barr, "Our Campaigns," 68; transcript of Paul Cummings interview with Margaret S. Barr, May 13, 1974, AAA.

Page 204. **far more interesting story**: Messer, *MOMA: Museum in Search of an Image*, 172–74.

Page 205. **Barr was present**: Barr to John Abbott, undated 1943, Roll 2168, AAA.

Page 205. **"so that you would have plenty of time"**: Barr to Stephen C. Clark, April 22, 1943, Roll 3262, AAA.

Page 205. **"a succinct history"**: Barr to Stephen C. Clark, April 22, 1943, Roll 3262, AAA.

Page 206. **"He was always extraordinarily absorbed . . ."**: Transcript of Paul Cummings interview with Margaret S. Barr, May 13, 1974, AAA.

Page 207. **a crossed-out segment**: Deleted from Barr to John Abbott, undated 1943, Roll 2168, AAA.

Page 207. **one trait particularly enraging:** Interview with Richard Koch, June 17, 1986.

Page 208. **qualities he felt lacking:** Barr to Dwight Macdonald, Dec. 2, 1953, Roll 2180, AAA.

Page 208. **"whisper-voiced . . .":** Emily Genauer, "The Fur-lined Museum," *Harper's*, July 1944, 129, 135, 137; interview with Emily Genauer, June 18, 1986.

Page 209. **politicking and silent maneuvering":** Barr to William H. Trombley, April 5, 1954, Roll 2183, AAA.

Page 209. **get along with Stephen Clark:** Interview with Hilton Kramer, June 17, 1986; Barr to Stephen C. Clark, Nov. 16, 1944, Roll 2172, AAA; Clark to Barr, May 12, 1944; Roll 2170, AAA; Barr to Clark, Sept. 27, 1947, and Mar. 18, 1948, both Roll 2172, AAA.

Page 210. **"Alfred would not leave . . .":** Robert Hughes, "What Alfred Barr Saw: Modernism," *Esquire*, Dec. 1983, 413; I Peter 5:5.

Page 210. **staff wore a pathway:** Interview with Dorothy Miller, May 31, 1986; Barr to Maria Luisa Gomez Mena, Nov. 8, 1943; James Thrall Soby to Barr, Nov. 2, 1943; Barr to Soby, Nov. 6, 1943, all Roll 2169, AAA.

Page 211. **"no one man":** Edward Alden Jewell, "Museum Without a Director," *New York Times*, Jan. 30, 1944.

Page 211. **Barr was indispensable:** Stephen C. Clark to Barr, Nov. 16, 1943; Barr to Clark, Nov. 23, 1943; Clark to Barr, Apr. 18, 1944, all Roll 2170, AAA; Messer, *MOMA: Museum in Search of an Image*, 182; Clark to Barr, Aug. 8, 1945, Roll 3265, AAA.

Page 212. **She felt humiliated:** Transcript of Paul Cummings interview with Margaret S. Barr, May 13, 1974, AAA; Michael Brenson, "Margaret Scolari Barr, a Teacher and Art Historian, Is Dead at 86," *New York Times*, Dec. 31, 1987.

Page 213. **a long letter:** Margaret S. Barr, "Our Campaigns," 71-72.

Page 213. **Barr retracted his salary demands:** Margaret S. Barr, "Our Campaigns," 72-73; interview with Sidney Janis, June 4, 1986; interview with Porter McCray, June 6, 1986; Barr to Betty Chamberlain, Sept. 27, 1943, Roll 2169, AAA; interview with G. E. Kidder-Smith, June 10, 1986.

Page 213. **funeral for Piet Mondrian:** Barr to George Rickey, June 3, 1968, Roll 2198, AAA; Barr, text of eulogy for Piet Mondrian, Feb. 3, 1944, Roll 3150, AAA.

Page 214. **the picture was *Broadway Boogie Woogie*:** Barr to Maria Martins, April 19, 1943, Roll 2199, AAA; Barr to Sheldon Dick, Jan. 28, 1949, Roll 2172, AAA; Les Levine, "A Portrait of Sidney Janis on the Occasion of his 25th Anniversary as an Art Dealer," *Arts*, Nov. 1973, 53; Gerald Reitlinger, *Economics of Taste*, Vol. III, (London: Barrie and Jenkins, 1970), 26.

Page 214. **tempting offers:** Thomas B. Knowles to Barr, Mar. 6, 1944; Barr to Knowles, Mar. 10, 1944; Barr to Paul Sachs, Mar. 15, 1944; Addison Hibbard to Barr, Mar. 23, 1944; Barr to Hibbard, Mar. 30, 1944, all Roll 2170, AAA.

Page 215. **support from art professionals:** Marion R. Becker to Barr, Nov. 11, 1943; Isabel S. Roberts, Nov. 8, 1943; Lawrence Vail Coleman to Barr,

Oct. 29, 1943; Barr to Coleman, Nov. 5, 1943; Coleman to Barr, Nov. 9, 1943, all Roll 2168, AAA; Marianne Moore to Barr, Dec. 18, 1943, Roll 2170, AAA.

Page 215. **"And he said unto them . . .":** Mark 16:5.

Page 215. **"wrote for people who had little experience":** Alfred Barr, *What Is Modern Painting?* (New York: Museum of Modern Art, 1943), 4.

Page 216. **Barr had tested his prose:** Transcript of Paul Cummings interview with Margaret S. Barr, April 8, 1974, AAA; I Corinthians 14:8, 9.

Page 216. **"What is your first impression . . .":** Barr, *What is Modern Painting?* 5, 9, 11, 13, 45.

Page 216. **"an instrument of propaganda":** Barr memo to Monroe Wheeler, Jan. 8, 1953, Roll 3151, AAA.

Page 216. **praise for its simplicity:** Barr memo to Monroe Wheeler, Nov. 23, 1943, Roll 2170, AAA; Julius Mahler to Barr, Apr. 20, 1944; Isabelle W. Holt to Barr, Apr. 11, 1944; Fiske Kimball to Barr, Mar. 29, 1944, all Roll 3151, AAA; H. W. Janson, "Review of *What Is Modern Painting?" College Art Journal,* Mar. 1946, 256–57.

Page 217. **MOMA's scholarship:** Barr, "Research and Publication in Art Museums," *Museum News,* Jan. 1, 1946, 6, 8.

Page 218. **still enraged:** Interview with Monroe Wheeler, June 18, 1986.

Page 218. **It is dedicated to:** Barr, *Picasso: Fifty Years of His Art* (New York: Museum of Modern Art, 1946), 6.

Page 218. **"crowds of bewildered G.I.'s":** Barr, *Picasso: Fifty Years of His Art,* 242–45.

Page 219. **innumerable questions:** Barr, *Picasso: Fifty Years of His Art,* 7.

Page 219. **five-page list:** Barr, *Picasso: Fifty Years of His Art,* 280–84.

Page 219. **Mrs. Guggenheim had inquired:** Barr to Stephen C. Clark, June 26, 1947; Barr to Clark, Sept. 25, 1947, both Roll 2172, AAA.

Page 220. **"Neither the Nazis . . .":** Barr, *Picasso: Fifty Years of His Art,* 11.

Page 220. **completing the Ph.D.:** Barr to Paul Sachs, April 11, 1940; Sachs to Barr, July 25, 1940; Barr, undated abstract of *Picasso: Fifty Years of His Art,* 1946; Dorothy C. Priest to Barr, undated 1946; Barr to Frederick Deknatel, Sept. 19, 1946; all Roll 3263, AAA.

Page 221. **a wide-ranging report:** Barr, "The Museum Collections: A Brief Report," draft of Jan. 15, 1944 (first page revised Mar. 26, 1944), Roll 3149, AAA.

Page 222. **"a relatively elastic term":** Barr, *The Museum of Modern Art, New York,* typed booklet, undated Sept.–Nov. 1936; Barr, notes on Museum of Modern Art purposes and policies, Dec. 1943(?), both Roll 3260, AAA.

Page 222. **tried to reassure:** Barr to Samuel Lewisohn, June 22, 1944, Roll 2170, AAA; Barr to Lewisohn, May 29, 1944, Roll 2179, AAA.

Page 222. **yet another revision:** Barr, "Memorandum E, Range of the Collection," undated 1944, Roll 2170, AAA.

Page 223. **controversial auction sale:** "Museum Will Sell 38 Items on May 11," *New York Times,* April 28, 1944; *Notable Modern Paintings and Sculptures,* catalog of sale, May 11, 1944, Parke-Bernet Galleries, MOMA Archive.

Page 223. **morning of the sale:** Edward Alden Jewell, "Art Auction Sale Listed for Tonight," *New York Times*, May 11, 1944; "Modern Art Museum Gets $64,070 at Sale," *New York Times*, May 12, 1944; "Sale," *Art News*, May 15, 1944, 7; Messer, *MOMA: Museum in Search of an Image*, 188-89, 192-97.

Page 224. **"slaughter...."**: James Thrall Soby to Barr, Dec. 10, 1969, Roll 2198, AAA.

Page 224. **"strictly speaking...."**: Barr, *Art in Progress* (New York: Museum of Modern Art, 1944), 9, 11.

Page 225. **many acute observers**: Wyndham Lewis, "The End of Abstract Art," *New Republic*, April 1, 1940, 439; Samuel Cauman, "Great Moderns: A Reappraisal," *College Art Journal*, May 1943, 107; Clement Greenberg, "Federation of Modern Painters and Sculptors vs. Museum of Modern Art," *Nation*, Feb. 12, 1944, 12; T. S. Eliot, *Notes Toward the Definition of Culture* (New York: Harcourt, Brace, 1949), 17.

Page 225. **"I am not an expert lecturer...."**: Barr to C. A. Ribonson, Jr., June 11, 1946; Barr to Willis F. Woods, Dec. 20, 1951, both Roll 3149, AAA.

Page 225. **six lectures**: "Dogma and Practice in Modern Art," brochure for the Mary Flexner Lectureships at Bryn Mawr, 1946, Roll 3150, AAA.

Page 226. **One of them remembered**: Patricia Hochschild Labalme to Margaret S. Barr, Aug. 19, 1981, Roll 3145, AAA.

Page 226. **"T'ain't what 'cha do ...."**: "T'ain't what 'cha do, it's the way that 'cha do it!" undated clipping from the Bryn Mawr student newspaper, Roll 3265, AAA.

Page 227. **slim resources**: "Bibliography of Modern Art in the Bryn Mawr Library," undated 1942, Roll 3150, AAA.

Page 227. **a chaos of mind**: Barr, "Research and Publication in Art Museums," a paper given at the Art Institute of Chicago, April 1944, Roll 3150, AAA.

Page 228. **a survey**: Macdonald, "Action on West 53rd Street—I," 49; revised notes of an interview between Peter Pollack, public relations counsel at the Art Institute of Chicago, and Alfred H. Barr, Jr., in connection with the 58th American Annual of the Art Institute, Nov. 4, 1947, Roll 2172, AAA; Harry S. Truman to Barr, May 7, 1947, Roll 2199, AAA.

Page 228. **"You know I don't know...."**: Beardsley Ruml to Barr, Nov. 9, 1945, Roll 3154, AAA; Collection, trustee opinions, Jan. 24, 1945, Roll 3265, AAA.

Page 229. **pathetic requests**: "Diplome de Grand Prix, Paris, 1937," Roll 2173, AAA.

Page 229. **The museum filled**: Bernard Karpel memo to Barr, July 25, 1946, Roll 2174, AAA; Karpel memo to Barr, Mar. 3, 1949, Roll 2171, AAA; Louis Carré to James Johnson Sweeney, July 28, 1945; Sweeney to Carré, Aug. 14, 1945; Katherine Dreier to Barr, Sept. 5, 1947, all Roll 2172, AAA.

Page 230. **corresponded with German art historians**: Barr to Hans Hildebrandt, Aug. 7, 1947; Franz Roh to Barr, Mar. 3, 1948; Mimi Catlin to Roh, April 21, 1948; Roh to Catlin, June 16, 1948; Porter McCray memo to Barr, Feb. 13, 1948; "Art materials requested for Dr. Franz Roh," undated 1948, all Roll 2171, AAA.

Page 230. **sought donations**: Barr memo to Edgar Kaufmann, May 15, 1951,

Roll 2174, AAA; Barr to Edward M. M. Warburg, Aug. 7, 1947, Roll 2171, AAA; John Abbott memo to Barr, Dec. 17, 1945, Roll 2174, AAA; Mimi Catlin memo to Bernard Karpel, May 14, 1948; N. E. Graeber to Museum of Modern Art, April 9, 1948; Catlin to Sankt Annen Museum, May 14, 1948, all Roll 2171, AAA.

Page 230. **"the best publications"**: Barr to Rene Huyghe, Nov. 3, 1944; Barr to John Morse, Mar. 22, 1945; Huyghe to Barr, April 10, 1945, all Roll 2174, AAA.

Page 231. **"highly subjective"**: Barr to John D. Morse, Feb. 14, 1947, Roll 2174, AAA.

Page 231. **study of American art**: Olive Bragazzi memo to Dorothy Dudley, Oct. 18, 1948, Roll 2170, AAA; Barr to Alfred Frankenstein, Sept. 6, 1948; Barr to Mildred Steinbach, Feb. 15, 1949; Barr to Frankenstein, May 10, 1952, all Roll 2173, AAA; College Art Association committee on American art history agenda for meeting of Feb. 16, 1945, Roll 2172, AAA; Barr to Stephen C. Clark, April 22, 1943, Roll 3262, AAA.

Page 232. **"characterized by strong nationalism"**: Barr to Philip McMahon, Jan. 30, 1945; McMahon to Barr, Feb. 1, 1945, both Roll 2175, AAA.

Page 232. **the jury**: Guggenheim, *Out of This Century*, 284–85.

Page 232. **busier than ever**: Barr, "Notes on work year ending June 30, 1945," Dec. 12, 1945, Roll 2170, AAA; Barr, "American Art Research Council," *College Art Journal*, Nov. 1944, 41–43; Barr to *Gaceta del Caribe*, July 18, 1944, Roll 2170, AAA.

Page 233. **organized religion**: Barr to George Y. Rusk, April 27, 1944, Roll 2170, AAA; interview with Eloise Spaeth, June 9, 1986.

Page 233. **searching questions**: Barr to George Kibler, Dec. 24, 1946, Roll 2172, AAA.

Page 233. **cries of outrage**: J. Arthur MacLean to Barr, June 13, 1946; Barr to William M. Milliken, June 11, 1946, both Roll 2189, AAA.

Page 234. **American modernists**: Edward Alden Jewell, "Abstraction Lays Siege to Us Anew," *New York Times*, Mar. 29, 1942; "Artists Denounce Modern Museum," *New York Times*, Apr. 17, 1940; "Avant-garde Protest," *New York Times*, Apr. 27, 1940; Messer, *MOMA: Museum in Search of an Image*, 143–44.

Page 235. **"increasingly reactionary policies"**: Clement Greenberg, "Federation of Modern Painters and Sculptors vs. Museum of Modern Art," 12; James Thrall Soby, "Acquisitions Policy," *Museum News*, June 15, 1944, 7; Barr to Lincoln Kirstein, Mar. 13, 1944, Roll 2170, AAA.

Page 236. **"to show how detached"**: Guggenheim, *Out of This Century*, 270–71, 274–76.

Page 236. **"the New York vanguard"**: Guggenheim, *La Collezione Guggenheim* (Venice), 7; Guggenheim, *Out of This Century*, 303–4; *Works from the Peggy Guggenheim Foundation*, 128–29, 144, 163.

Page 237. **stole the idea of modern art**: Guilbaut, *How New York Stole the Idea of Modern Art*, 68.

Page 237. **"as she lay upon the sands"**: "Peggy in Abstract," *Newsweek*, Mar. 25, 1946, 98; "Temptations of Peggy," *Time*, Mar. 25, 1946, 57–58; Guggenheim, *Out of This Century*, 321–22.

Page 238. **Nelson Rockefeller was reelected:** "Heads Modern Museum," *New York Times*, June 7, 1946; "Executive committee recommendation for changes in the organizational structure," July 24, 1946; Barr to James Thrall Soby, undated 1946, both Roll 3260, AAA.

Page 238. **"infidelity":** James Thrall Soby to Barr, Sept. 6, 1946; Barr, "General Administration of the Collections," undated 1946; Barr, "Status of the Director of the Collections," undated handwritten notes, 1946, all Roll 3260, AAA.

Page 239. **trustees gave in:** Nelson Rockefeller to Barr, Jan. 22, 1947, Roll 3263, AAA; Barr to Nelson Rockefeller, Feb. 13, 1947, Roll 2176, AAA; Barr to David M. Robb, July 21, 1947, AAA.

Page 239. **not for money:** Barr, list of 1946 income, undated, Roll 3260, AAA; Monroe Wheeler memo to Barr, Jan. 9, 1953, Roll 3151, AAA; Barr to James Thrall Soby, undated 1946, Roll 3260, AAA.

Page 246. **a different text:** Lynes, *Good Old Modern*, 244; Isaiah 51:7, 8.

CHAPTER 9: DEFENDING THE FAITH

Page 241. **"I give unto you power":** Luke 10:19.

Page 242. **"victims of necromantic systems":** T. H. Robsjohn-Gibbings, *Mona Lisa's Moustache: A Dissection of Modern Art* (New York: Knopf, 1947), 145–46.

Page 242. **called a council of war:** Barr memo to Margaret Miller, Ione Ulrich, Allen Porter, René d'Harnoncourt, Monroe Wheeler, William A. M. Burden, and Nelson Rockefeller, Feb. 4, 1948; Barr to Nelson Rockefeller, Mar. 10, 1948; Barr to Jacques Barzun, Mar. 5, 1948; Barr to William G. Dooley, Feb. 3, 1948; Barr to W. G. Constable, Feb. 3, 1948, all Roll 3157, AAA.

Page 242. **To improve the critical climate:** Barr to Geoffrey Parsons, June 11, 1945, April 15, 1946, and June 13, 1946; Barr to James Thrall Soby, June 13, 1946; E. P. Toms to Barr, June 29, 1945, and July 10, 1946, all Roll 2173, AAA; untitled draft on the state of American art, undated 1948, Roll 2174, AAA.

Page 243. **protested repeatedly:** Barr to the editor, *College Art Journal*, Spring 1948, 77; Henry R. Hope to Barr, Mar. 5, 1948; Barr to Hope, Mar. 10, 1948; marginal note by Millard Meiss to Barr on a letter from Hope to Meiss, Mar. 4, 1948; Barr to Hope, Mar. 1, 1948, all Roll 2192, AAA; Barr to the editor, *Saturday Review of Literature*, July 11, 1950, Roll 2176, AAA; Barr to Gladys B. Ficke, June 6, 1950, Roll 2173, AAA.

Page 243. **he did not appreciate certain paintings:** Emil Oberholzer to Barr, Sept. 16, 1948; Barr to Oberholzer, Sept. 24, 1948, both Roll 3157, AAA.

Page 244. **"brass-bound Philistinism":** Barr to Ralph Pearson, Sept. 18, 1947, Roll 2175, AAA; Boston Institute of Contemporary Art, "Modern Art and the American Public," Feb. 17, 1948, 2, Roll 3263, AAA; Barr, Notes on "Modern Art and the American Public," undated 1948, Roll 2171, AAA; Barr to Dwight Macdonald, Sept. 21, 1953, Roll 2180, AAA.

Page 244. *modern* is deliberately provocative: Barr, Notes on "Modern Art and the American Public," Mar. 3, 1948, Roll 2171, AAA.

Page 245. "that whorehouse on 53rd Street": Calvin Tomkins, *Merchants and Masterpieces* (New York: Dutton, 1970), 30; Francis Henry Taylor, "Art and the Dignity of Man," *Atlantic*, Dec. 1948, 30, 36.

Page 245. agreed heartily to "cooperate": Memorandum of meeting of representatives of Metropolitan Museum of Art and the Modern Museum at the house of Mrs. John D. Rockefeller, Jr., Nov. 28, 1934, Roll 3264, AAA; Burt, *Palaces for the People*, 339; Barr to Stephen C. Clark, June 26, 1947, Roll 2172, AAA; Barr to Nelson Rockefeller, June 26, 1947, Roll 2176, AAA.

Page 245. tri-museum pact was announced: "Museums Start Exchange of Art," *New York Times*, Jan. 22, 1948; Aline B. Louchheim, "Classic or Modern," *New York Times*, Feb. 1, 1948.

Page 246. one of the few modern masterpieces: Barr to Alice B. Toklas, Oct. 17, 1947, Roll 2170, AAA; Barr to Toklas, Feb. 7, 1948; Barr to Thornton Wilder, Feb. 24, 1948; Wilder to Barr, Mar. 3, 1948; Francis Henry Taylor to Barr, Dec. 12, 1949, all Roll 2176, AAA.

Page 246. abandoned the coalition: "Abandons Metropolitan Coalition," *Museum News*, Oct. 15, 1948, 1–2; Calvin Tomkins, *The Scene: Reports on Post-Modern Art* (New York: Viking, 1976), 14; Barr to Nelson Rockefeller, Feb. 8, 1949, Roll 2177, AAA.

Page 247. expressing their "resentful hostility": "Van Gogh," *New York Times*, July 31, 1949; " 'Lonely' Van Gogh Sets Crowd Mark," *New York Times*, Jan. 16, 1950.

Page 247. a competition with $8,500 in prizes: Sanka Knox, "Competition for American Artists Planned by Metropolitan Museum," *New York Times*, Jan. 1, 1950.

Page 248. proclaimed that they would boycott it: "18 Painters Boycott Metropolitan," *New York Times*, May 22, 1950; "75 Painters Deny," *New York Times*, July 4, 1950.

Page 248. glad that the public had a choice: Barr, untitled draft on the state of American art, undated 1948, Roll 2174, AAA; Barr, "From the Museum Collection," notes for an exhibition, Mar. 8, 1949, Roll 2172, AAA; Messer, *MOMA: Museum in Search of an Image*, 216–21.

Page 249. suddenly being ground up: Messer, *MOMA: Museum in Search of an Image*, 241–42, 253–54.

Page 249. artists were taking over more galleries: Samuel Kootz to Barr, Jan. 17, 1949, Roll 2172, AAA; Messer, *MOMA: Museum in Search of an Image*, 255.

Page 250. even steeper rise in the prices: Pars, *Pictures in Peril*, 1; Reitlinger, *Economics of Taste*, Vol. I, 394; Les Levine, "A Portrait of Sidney Janis on the Occasion of His 25th Anniversary as an Art Dealer," *Arts*, Nov. 1973, 51; Buchholz Gallery invoice to Barr, Dec. 23, 1948, Roll 2171, AAA; Daniel-Henry Kahnweiler to Barr, Aug. 2, 1949, Roll 2174, AAA; Reitlinger, *Economics of Taste*, Vol. III, 234.

Page 250. he had been able to buy: Barr to Olga Guggenheim, July 2, 1949, Roll 2194, AAA; Barr to Henry Hope, June 30, 1949, Roll 2173, AAA; Barr to James Thrall Soby, April 17, 1953, Roll 2181, AAA; "The Art Market's Prime Commodities," *Fortune*, Dec. 1955, 130.

Page 251. an overheated bazaar: Geraldine Keen, *Money and Art* (New York:

G. B. Putnam's Sons, 1971), 29; Raymonde Moulin, *Le marché de la peinture en France* (Paris: Editions de minuit, 1967), 219.

Page 252. **had no trouble in persuading her:** Barr to Helen Resor, Nov. 30, 1954, Roll 2180, AAA.

Page 252. **"an important change of policy":** *Bulletin of the Museum of Modern Art,* Summer 1953, 3; Macdonald, "Action on West 53rd Street—I," 56; "New Permanence and Changes at the Modern," *Art News,* Mar. 1953, 7; Sanka Knox, "New Policy on Art Set Up by Museum," *New York Times,* Feb. 15, 1953.

Page 253. **considerable acquisitions funds:** "Information requested by Acquisitions Committee," June 12, 1950, Roll 2199, AAA; Barr to Peyton Boswell, June 2, 1950, Roll 2170, AAA; *Bulletin of the Museum of Modern Art,* Vol. VII, No. 2 (1949); Barr to Abby Rockefeller, May 12, 1936; Barr wire to Walter P. Chrysler, July 6, 1936, both Roll 2166, AAA; Howard Devree, "Museum Acquires Work by Picasso," *New York Times,* July 26, 1949; Howard Devree, "A Picasso Landmark," *New York Times,* July 21, 1949.

Page 253. **had complained of overcrowding:** Barr to Antonio R. Morey, Jan. 4, 1948, Roll 2171, AAA.

Page 253. **Barr bought wholesale:** "Works by Italian Artists Acquired by the Museum of Modern Art Since Sept. 9, 1949"; "Museum Purchases," undated news release, Sept. 1949, both Roll 2172, AAA; "Modern Art Museum Buys Italians' Works," *New York Times,* Sept. 14, 1949; Barr to Romeo Toninelli, Sept. 15, 1949, Roll 2181, AAA; Barr to Gio Ponti, April 13, 1950, Roll 2172, AAA; Barr to James Thrall Soby, Dec. 20, 1950, Roll 2176, AAA; Bar to Toninelli, Dec. 11, 1952, Roll 2181, AAA; Margaret S. Barr, handwritten note, undated, with draft of news release on Futurist acquisitions, Sept. 1949, Roll 3260, AAA; Betsy Jones memo to Barr, Dec. 7, 1961, Roll 2194, AAA.

Page 254. **had traveled to Italy:** Monroe Wheeler memo to Barr and James Thrall Soby, April 17, 1946; Nelson Rockefeller to James C. Dunn, April 21, 1948; Wheeler to Leroy Davidson, Feb. 24, 1947; Frances Keech memo to Ione Ulrich, Nov. 1, 1949; Wheeler memo to Barr and Soby, July 1, 1949; "Selling Prices—Italian Show—Tentative List," July 15, 1949, all Roll 3153, AAA.

Page 254. **Barr began to guide them carefully:** Barr to Henri-Pierre Roché, April 13, 1949; Barr to Nelson Rockefeller, April 22, 1949, both Roll 2176, AAA; Barr to Mrs. Paul Moore, Dec. 12, 1950, Roll 3149, AAA.

Page 254. **difficult to draw any line:** Barr to Samuel Lewisohn, Oct. 27, 1949, Roll 2179, AAA; Barr to Philip Goodwin, Sept. 19, 1949; Goodwin to Barr, Sept. 22, 1949; Barr to Earl H. Stendahl, Jan. 12, 1950; Barr memo to Philip Johnson, April 19, 1950, all Roll 2173, AAA.

Page 255. **"a unique situation":** Dorothy Miller memo to Barr, July 26, 1957; Miller to Barr, July 26, 1957, both Roll 2189, AAA.

Page 255. **a MOMA trustee since 1943:** "Museum Names Burden," *New York Times,* June 29, 1953; Barr to William A. M. Burden, Aug. 17, 1952, and Mar. 17, 1952, both Roll 2178, AAA.

Page 256. **"big, important early Tanguy":** Barr to Roland Penrose, Aug. 25, 1952, Roll 2197, AAA; William A. M. Burden to Olive Bragazzi, Mar. 27, 1952; William F. Pedersen to Barr, Mar. 15, 1952, both Roll 2178, AAA.

Page 256. "most unconventional and effectual patron": Chase, *Abby Aldrich Rockefeller*, 140; Collier and Horowitz, *The Rockefellers: An American Dynasty*, 513; Lynes, *Good Old Modern*, 242–43.

Page 256. a twinkling mischievousness: Chase, *Abby Aldrich Rockefeller*, 33; Persico, *The Imperial Rockefeller*, 176–77.

Page 257. another veteran of the amateur era: Saarinen, *Proud Possessors*, 238–40.

Page 257. claimed to have founded: Marquis, *Marcel Duchamp*, 244–46.

Page 258. may have had some guilt: Katherine Dreier to Barr, Feb. 19, 1927, Roll 2164, AAA; Dreier to Barr, Mar. 4 and Mar. 14, 1927, Roll 3263, AAA; Nicolas and Elena Calas, *The Peggy Guggenheim Collection of Modern Art* (New York: Abrams, 1966), 15.

Page 258. "a very muddled book": Barr to Henry Seidel Canby, Mar. 4, 1930, Roll 2164, AAA.

Page 258. Barr's acquisitive ardor: Katherine Dreier to Nelson Rockefeller, Jan. 7, 1948; Barr to Ranald H. MacDonald, Nov. 23, 1948; Barr to Dreier, Nov. 4, 1949; Barr, text for "Gauguin, Malevich, and Boccioni," *Collection of the Société Anonyme: Museum of Modern Art* (New Haven, CT: Associates in Fine Arts at Yale University, 1950); Nelson Rockefeller to Dreier, April 30, 1950; Dreier to Barr, May 5, 1950; Monroe Wheeler to Susan Cable, Jan. 16, 1948, all Roll 2172, AAA; Barr to Nelson Rockefeller, April 25, 1950, Roll 2175, AAA.

Page 259. it was hung upside down: Katherine Dreier to Barr, June 7, 1949, Roll 2172, AAA; *Bulletin of the Museum of Modern Art*, Vol. VII, No. 2–3, 1949 and Summer 1950; Dreier to Philip Goodwin, June 26, 1950, Roll 2171, AAA.

Page 259. "She was extraordinarily stingy . . .": Barr memo to Monroe Wheeler, Aug. 11, 1950, Roll 2177, AAA; Katherine Dreier to Barr, Mar. 2, 1951, Roll 2172, AAA.

Page 259. "I grew fond of her": Barr to Robert Faeth, Nov. 9, 1948; Barr to Katherine Dreier, Mar. 9 and Aug. 13, 1951, all Roll 2172, AAA; Barr to James Thrall Soby, June 25, 1952, Roll 2181, AAA.

Page 260. began a delicate negotiation: Barr to Henry Allen Moe, May 21, 1953, Roll 2180, AAA; Barr to Benjamin Sonnenberg, June 5, 1953, Roll 2181, AAA; Aline B. Saarinen, "Museum Showing Rousseau 'Dream,'" *New York Times*, Sept. 12, 1954.

Page 260. an endless sideshow of diversions: "Agreement Between the Institute for Sex Research at Indiana University and the Museum of Modern Art," Jan. 21, 1949; Alfred Kinsey to Barr, Oct. 15, 1949, both Roll 2174, AAA; Barr to the editors of *Life*, Oct. 20, 1953, Roll 2179, AAA; Barr to Kevin McCarthy, July 16, 1953; McCarthy to Barr, July 17, 1953; Dorothy Miller to McCarthy, Aug. 14, 1953; Barr to McCarthy, Oct. 20, 1953; McCarthy to Barr, Oct. 22, 1953, all Roll 2179, AAA; Barr to editor of *New York Times*, Jan. 8, 1954, Roll 2178, AAA.

Page 261. "you serve your greatness shamefully": Barr to Frank Lloyd Wright, June 3, 1953, Roll 2181, AAA.

Page 261. one foot in the world of scholarship: Richard H. Parke, "Princeton Honors Franks and Bonnet," *New York Times*, June 15, 1949; Barr to E. Baldwin Smith, Nov. 27, 1959; William Seitz to Barr, Sept. 2, 1951, both Roll 2180, AAA.

Page 262. **meant a great deal to him:** Interview with Irma Seitz, Dec. 13, 1986; interview with Larry Aldrich, June 5, 1986.

Page 262. **"originality, energy, and vitality":** Barr, Recommendation of William Seitz for a fellowship from the American Council of Learned Societies, undated Mar. 1952; Barr to Grace McCann Morley, Mar. 20, 1947, both Roll 2180, AAA; interview with John Rewald, June 3, 1986.

Page 263. **they found the French resentful:** James Thrall Soby, "Bulletin, Paris," April 20 to May 5, 1948, Roll 3153, AAA; Barr memo to Monroe Wheeler, Feb. 29, 1952, Roll 3153, AAA.

Page 263. **arranged to sell any of its books wholesale:** "Libraries and Institutions Receiving Museum Publications," undated May 1948, Roll 2171, AAA; Monroe Wheeler to "Dear Friend," June 17, 1949; Barr to Carl Kjersmeier, Dec. 30, 1948, both Roll 2173, AAA; Aline B. Louchheim, "Museum Reports on Tour Program," *New York Times*, Dec. 16, 1953.

Page 263. **abstract art hardly counted:** Jean Clay, "Interview with Denise René," *Studio*, April 1968, 192; Mimi Catlin to Barr, Nov. 25, 1948; Barr to Catlin, Dec. 6, 1948, both Roll 2172, AAA.

Page 264. **he drew up a list of works:** Barr, "Notes from Paris," July 20, 1952; "Paris Exhibition," undated Spring 1953; Jean Cassou to Barr, Feb. 26, 1953; Andrew C. Ritchie to Margaret S. Barr, May 24, 1953, all Roll 2171, AAA.

Page 264. **"a bad record for fires":** Barr to William A. M. Burden, Dec. 27, 1954, Roll 2180, AAA.

Page 264. **"greatly admired and envied":** Janet Flanner to Barr, Feb. 5, 1955, Roll 2182, AAA.

Page 265. **an inordinately painful gestation:** Monroe Wheeler memo to Barr, April 11, 1946, Roll 3265, AAA; interview with John Rewald, June 3, 1986; Barr to Carl O. Schniewind, July 30, 1953, Roll 2178, AAA; Barr to Grace McCann Morley, Mar. 10, 1952, Roll 2180, AAA; Barr to Dwight Macdonald, Mar. 15, 1954, Roll 2190, AAA; Barr memo to René d'Harnoncourt, Roll 2176, AAA.

Page 265. **lack of "facility in writing":** Olive Bragazzi and Jean Stepanian memo to Barr, Aug. 10, 1950, Roll 2176, AAA; interview with John Rewald, June 3, 1986; Barr, *Matisse: His Work and His Public* (New York: Museum of Modern Art, 1951), 4.

Page 266. **"curious and heretofore unknown data":** Katharine Kuh, "Review of *Matisse: His Art and His Public*," *College Art Journal*, Fall 1951, 309; Benedict Nicholson, "Review of *Matisse: His Art and His Public*," *Art Bulletin*, Sept. 1952, 247; Franz Roh to Barr, Oct. 10, 1953, Roll 2180, AAA.

Page 266. **"cover the history of abstract art":** Draft of Fulbright proposal, undated 1950, Roll 2170, AAA.

Page 267. **dickered over the fellowship:** Barr to Howard B. Backus, Oct. 27, 1950; Barr to committee on international exchange of persons, Nov. 1, 1950; Barr to Gordon T. Bowles, Dec. 9, 1950; Bowles to Barr, Nov. 22, 1950; Barr to Bowles, Dec. 6, 1950; Francis R. Young to Barr, Jan. 24, 1951; Barr to Young, Jan. 30, 1951; Barr to Bowles, April 19, 1951; Young to Barr, Feb. 6, 1951; Barr to Young, May 1, 1951; Young to Barr, May 17, 1951; George T. Moody, May 18, 1951; Barr to Bowles, June 13, 1951; Barr to Moody, June 13, 1951, all Roll 2170, AAA;

Louise Goldwater to Barr, April 9, 1951; Robert B. Goldwater to Barr, April 21, 1951; Barr to Goldwater, May 23, 1951, all Roll 2173, AAA.

Page 267. **mid-life search for alternatives:** Barr to William Eisendrath, June 5, 1950; Barr to Richard Lindabury, Mar. 6, 1947; Barr to Harriet Bailey, Jan. 30, 1950; Barr cable to George Downing, Oct. 3, 1948; Barr to Thomas Munro, May 14, 1947, all Roll 2171, AAA; James Thrall Soby memo to Barr, Feb. 5, 1948; Nikolaus Pevsner to Soby, Mar. 11, 1948; Soby to Pevsner, April 2, 1948, all Roll 2176, AAA.

Page 268. **"some days here I go crazy":** Barr to Irita Van Doren, May 25, 1951, Roll 2173, AAA; Barr to Selden Rodman, Nov. 6, 1954, Roll 2180, AAA.

Page 268. **he could "never catch up":** Barr to William A. M. Burden, Aug. 3, 1953, Roll 2178, AAA; interview with Alicia Legg, June 16, 1986; interview with John Rewald, June 3, 1986; interview with G. E. Kidder-Smith, June 10, 1986.

Page 268. **taste tended "toward a certain severity":** Barr to Paul Mocsanyi, Nov. 29, 1954, Roll 2180, AAA; Barr to Ernest DeWald, Nov. 24, 1953, Roll 2178, AAA; interview with John Rewald, June 3, 1986; interview with Porter McCray, June 6, 1986; interview with Alicia Legg, June 16, 1986.

Page 269. **"he was amusing and interesting":** Interview with Sidney Janis, June 4, 1986; Barr to Mrs. Roland Penrose, Jan. 15, 1953, Roll 2179, AAA; interview with Mildred Constantine, June 19, 1986.

Page 269. **Barr was a classic workaholic:** Transcript of Paul Cummings interview with Margaret S. Barr, May 13, 1974, AAA; John Russell to the author, May 3, 1987.

Page 269. **A disappointment to her father:** Interview with Libby Tannenbaum, June 2, 1986; Barr to Herman W. Williams, Feb. 13, 1948, Roll 2171, AAA; Barr to Francis Henry Taylor, Sept. 20, 1948, Roll 2175, AAA.

Page 269. **"not very much men either":** Interview with Steven Watson, July 9, 1987.

Page 270. **"you are not susceptible to magnetism":** Margaret S. Barr to Alfred Barr, July 1 and July 15, 1954, both Roll 2178, AAA; Gregory Hesselberg to the author, Aug. 3, 1988.

Page 270. **"supervising tadpole catching":** Carver Roundebush to Margaret S. Barr, Aug. 26, 1981, Roll 3145, AAA.

Page 271. **Barr felt constrained to answer:** Barr to Eleanor Roosevelt, June 29, 1949, Roll 2176, AAA; Barr, "Graduate School Alumni Letter," Jan. 1950, Roll 2180, AAA.

Page 272. **Barr leaped into action:** Interview with Helen Franc, June 6, 1986; Barr to Mrs. Frederick Kiesler, Jan. 22, 1951; Barr to Lawrence M. C. Smith, Jan. 19, 1951; Betty Chamberlain memo to Barr, Jan. 9, 1951; Barr memo to John Hay Whitney, Nelson Rockefeller, René d'Harnoncourt, Jan. 15, 1951; Barr day letters to Thomas E. Dewey, William J. Wallin, John P. Meyers, Jan. 15, 1951, all Roll 2174, AAA; Barr to Christopher Gerould, Feb. 14 and 20, 1951, both Roll 2175, AAA; Chamberlain cable to Barr, undated 1952, Roll 2174, AAA.

Page 272. **his impassioned defense:** Barr, "Is Modern Art Communistic?" *New York Times Magazine,* Dec. 14, 1952, 30; John Cunning, "People's Art,"

New York Times Magazine, Dec. 28, 1952, 2; Rockwell Kent, "Surrender," *New York Times Magazine*, Jan. 18, 1953, Sec. VI, 6.

Page 273. **impressed with Barr's passion:** Macdonald, "Action on West 53rd Street—I, 49, 71-72, 76.

Page 273. **he provided him with a list:** "Macdonald Queries," undated 1953, Roll 2180, AAA.

Page 273. **insisted on reviewing the drafts:** Barr to Dwight Macdonald, Nov. 30, 1953; Dwight Macdonald, "Profile of Alfred H. Barr, Jr.," manuscript for *New Yorker* article, undated 1953; Macdonald to Barr, Dec. 1 and 8, 1953, all Roll 2180, AAA.

Page 274. **"I wish I had never got involved . . .":** Macdonald, "Profile of Alfred H. Barr, Jr."; Barr memo to René d'Harnoncourt, Dec. 16, 1953; Barr to William A. M. Burden, Dec. 9, 1953. Roll 2180, AAA.

Page 274. **"modern art is fashionable":** Macdonald, "Action on West 53rd Street—II," 51; Macdonald, "Action on West 53rd Street—I," 59-60.

Page 274. **"record of rewarding speculation":** "The Big Gamble: 33 Blue Chips at the Museum of Modern Art," *Vogue*, Nov. 1, 1954, 106-9.

Page 275. **a sumptuous picture volume:** Barr memo to Elizabeth Shaw, Oct. 22, 1954, Roll 3151, AAA; Aline B. Saarinen, "Of Tombs, Temples, and Museums," *New York Times*, Sept. 12, 1954; "Modern Art on 53rd St.," *New York Times*, Oct. 19, 1954.

Page 275. **Enthusiastic reviews:** Barr to Peggy Guggenheim, Nov. 30, 1954, Roll 2194, AAA; S. Lane Faison, Jr., "25th Anniversary," *Nation*, Nov. 20, 1954, 449; Philip Johnson to Barr, Oct. 20, 1954, Roll 2182, AAA; Horace Shipp, "Review of *Masters of Modern Art*," *Apollo*, Nov. 1955, 152-53.

Page 276. **list would prove "valuable and interesting":** Barr memo to Philip Johnson, July 29, 1953; Barr memo to Richard Griffiths, Feb. 18, 1953, both Roll 3153, AAA.

Page 276. **disturbing flickerings of doubt:** Henry McBride, "How Modern the Collection of the Modern Museum?" *Art News*, Nov. 1954, 79; "Aging Modern," *Time*, Oct. 25, 1954, 68; interview with Edgar Kaufmann, June 10, 1986; Address by William A. M. Burden, Oct. 19, 1954, Roll 2178, AAA.

CHAPTER 10: EXPANDING THE CANON

Page 279. **"I have no leisure time at all":** Barr to Frederick Kiesler, Oct. 18, 1956, Roll 2182, AAA; Barr to Janice Levitt, Nov. 18, 1957, Roll 2184, AAA; Barr to Kenneth Campbell, Dec. 1, 1955; Campbell to Barr, undated Dec. 1955, both Roll 2189, AAA.

Page 280. **"lowered our standard of living":** Stephen C. Clarke to Barr, May 7, 1945, Roll 3264, AAA; Barr to Nelson Rockefeller, July 18, 1947, Roll 2176, AAA.

Page 280. **"we are quite broke":** Paul Sachs to Barr, Oct. 6, 1954; Margaret S. Barr to Alfred Barr, July 5, 1954, both Roll 2178; Lynes, *Good Old Modern*, 407; transcript of Paul Cummings interview with Margaret S. Barr, April 8, 1974, AAA.

Page 280. **health problems afflicted Barr:** Barr to Mrs. Leigh Block, June 26,

402   BARR/MISSIONARY FOR THE MODERN

1953, Roll 2178, AAA; Barr to Antoni Ribera, Oct. 26, 1955, Roll 2182, AAA; Barr to David Sarnoff, April 26, 1954, Roll 2180, AAA; interview with Alicia Legg, June 16, 1986.

Page 281. **time-consuming byways:** Barr to Edgar Kaufmann, June 6, 1957, Roll 2182, AAA; Barr to Charles James, Mar. 24, 1958, Roll 2184, AAA; Barr to Marie Alexander, undated, Roll 2181, AAA.

Page 281. **a remarkably counterproductive working style:** Barr to Tourneau Watches, undated draft, 1955, Roll 2183, AAA; Barr to S. Dillon Ripley, Sept. 24, 1956, Roll 2182, AAA; Michele Hief to Barr, Feb. 4, 1958; Barr to Hief, Feb. 12, 1958, both Roll 2184, AAA; Barbara Fill and class to Barr, April 28, 1955; Barr to Miss Fill and members of the eighth grade art class, June 3, 1955, both Roll 2182, AAA.

Page 282. **exchanged literally dozens of letters:** John Cournos to Barr, Oct. 19, 1957; Ethel Chase to Barr, Jan. 25, 1958; Barr to Cournos, Feb. 5, 1958; Barr to Chase, Mar. 24, 1958; Cournos to Barr, April 13, 1958; Barr to Chase, Nov. 20, 1959, Barr to Cournos, Nov. 20, 1959, all Roll 2183, AAA.

Page 282. **Barr sent her a book:** Frank Edwards, *Strange Worlds* (New York: Lyle Stuart, 1964); Ivan T. Sanderson, *Abominable Snowmen: Legend Come to Life* (New York: Chilton, 1961); Barr to Irma Seitz, handwritten note, undated, author's files.

Page 283. **"he should snub them all":** Barr to the editor, *New York Herald-Tribune*, Jan. 31, 1957, Roll 2182, AAA.

Page 283. **a protracted epistolary campaign:** "Irate Rambler" to the editor, *New York Times*, Jan. 28, 1957; Barr to Charles Mers, Jan. 28, 1957; Barr to John B. Oaks, Jan. 28, 1957, all Roll 2178, AAA; Marie Alexander to the editor, *New York Times*, Feb. 11, 1957.

Page 283. **a running skirmish:** Barr to Milton Fox, April 4 and Dec. 9, 1957, Roll 2183, AAA; Barr to Douglas Cooper, May 29, 1959, Roll 2193, AAA; Barr to Amos Vogel, Feb. 24, 1956, Roll 2181, AAA.

Page 284. **persistently volunteered for jury duty:** Barr to Roland Penrose, Jan. 22, 1958, Roll 2195, AAA; Barr to G. E. Kidder-Smith, May 27, 1960, Roll 2192, AAA; Barr to Herbert Weinstock, Nov. 6, 1958, Roll 2184, AAA.

Page 284. **competent hands of René d'Harnoncourt:** "Promoted to Director of Modern Art Museum," *New York Times*, Oct. 19, 1949; "New Director," *New Yorker*, Dec. 3, 1949, 27–8.

Page 284. **on condition that Barr stay:** Interview with Eliza Bliss Parkinson Cobb, Dec. 15, 1986; interview with Richard Koch, June 17, 1986; René d'Harnoncourt to Barr, July 29, 1949, Roll 2172, AAA.

Page 285. **a study in contrasts:** Interview with G. E. Kidder-Smith, June 10, 1986; interview with Richard Koch, June 17, 1986; "d'Hoodles," undated, Roll 2194, AAA; interview with Porter McCray, June 6, 1986.

Page 285. **genuine mutual respect and admiration:** Interview with Philip Johnson, Dec. 17, 1986; draft of Barr tribute at René d'Harnoncourt memorial service, undated 1968, Roll 2194, AAA.

Page 286. **"made no gesture toward it":** Barr to Dwight Macdonald, Dec. 2, 1953, Roll 2180, AAA.

Page 286. **"a master escape artist":** Walker, *Self-Portrait with Donors*, 30; interview with Richard Koch, June 17, 1986.

Page 287. **donors craved intimate contact:** Interview with Dorothy Miller, May 31, 1986; interview with Hilton Kramer, June 17, 1986; interview with Irma Seitz, Dec. 12, 1986.

Page 287. **this practice stopped abruptly:** Barr to David Rockefeller, Feb. 7, 1957; David Rockefeller to Barr, Feb. 13, 1957, both Roll 2198, AAA; interview with Dorothy Miller, Dec. 16, 1986.

Page 288. **Barr would be acceptable:** Marie Alexander memo to Barr, Oct. 2, 1956, Roll 2184, AAA.

Page 288. **"The successful curator ...":** Walker, *Self-Portrait with Donors*, 30; Stanley Marcus to Barr, May 3, 1956; Barr to Marcus, May 14, 1956, both Roll 2182, AAA; Dorothy Miller memo to William Lieberman, June 21, 1956, Roll 2183, AAA; program of luncheon for American Committee for Israel's Tenth Anniversary Celebration, Feb. 27, 1958; Barr to John Hay Whitney, Oct. 18, 1956; Barr to Nelson Rockefeller, Oct. 23, 1956, all Roll 2182, AAA.

Page 289. **it was auctioned:** "Christie's to Sell a Van Gogh in London," *New York Times*, May 1, 1987.

Page 289. **supplied background information:** Barr to Peggy Burden, Nov. 28, 1955, and Sept. 30, 1958, both Roll 2192, AAA.

Page 289. **museum also responded eagerly:** William A. M. Burden to Barr, Nov. 30, 1955; Olive Bragazzi to Barr, Mar. 30, 1956; Burden to Barr, Nov. 19, 1959; Olive Bragazzi to Dorothy M. Dudley, Dec. 5, 1959, all Roll 2192, AAA.

Page 290. **"a collaborative effort":** Barr memo to Elizabeth Shaw, July 25, 1957, Roll 2189, AAA.

Page 290. **"one of the principal joys":** Walker, *Self-Portrait with Donors*, 49; Barr to Mary Lasker, Dec. 10, 1957, Roll 2184, AAA; Barr to John Hay Whitney, Jan. 9, 1957, Roll 2183, AAA; Barr to William A. M. Burden, Dec. 2, 1955, Nov. 5, 1955, Sept. 8, 1955, and Jan. 17, 1958, all Roll 2192, AAA.

Page 291. **Barr found other favors:** Guggenheim, *Out of This Century*, 354; Elizabeth Shaw to Barr, undated Summer 1957, Roll 2183, AAA; Peggy Guggenheim to Barr, Oct. 22, 1957; Barr memo to Porter McCray, Nov. 15, 1957, both Roll 2194, AAA.

Page 291. **world's most extensive files:** Barr travel notebooks, 1930–1962, Roll 3261, AAA; Frances Keppel telegram to Francis Brennan, undated 1955, Roll 2182, AAA.

Page 291. **cast bread upon the waters:** Barr memo to files, Jan. 21, 1959, Roll 3146, AAA; Barr telegram to Mrs. Lovis Corinth, May 23, 1955; Barr cable to Mrs. Eugenie Kupka, July 20, 1957, both Roll 2182, AAA; Barr to Mr. and Mrs. Harry L. Winston, Mar. 29, 1955, Roll 2183, AAA; interview with Dorothy Miller, May 31, 1986.

Page 292. **Barr became exceedingly defensive:** Thomas B. Hess, "Editorial," *Art News*, Summer 1957, 27; Barr, "Editor's Letters," *Art News*, Sept. 1957, 6, 56–57.

Page 292. **wrote in righteous anger:** Barr memo to René d'Harnoncourt, Jan. 20, 1960, Roll 2184, AAA.

Page 293. **"protective vocabulary":** Walker, *Self-Portrait with Donors*, 40.

Page 293. **a relatively slight motivation:** Eric Hodgins and Parker Lesley, "The Great International Art Market—I," *Fortune*, Dec. 1955, 158; "The

Museum and the Private Collector," seminar at the Brooklyn Museum, April 4, 1958, Roll 3150, AAA; Tomkins, *Merchants and Masterpieces*, 73.

Page 293. **the excitement of the chase:** Walker, *Self-Portrait with Donors*, xvii; Maurice Rheims, *The Strange Life of Objects* (New York: Atheneum, 1961), 28, 31.

Page 294. **honors rained upon him:** Barr to Robert S. Hutchins, Mar. 21, 1955, Roll 2181, AAA; Eric Hodgins to Barr, Oct. 4, Oct. 12, and Nov. 8, 1955, all Roll 2182, AAA; Barr to Porter McCray, Aug. 27, 1957, Roll 2198, AAA; Barr to Robert W. Weise, Mar. 24, 1959, Roll 3158, AAA; American Federation of the Arts, citation read April 24, 1955, Roll 2189, AAA; *Art Newsletter*, Summer 1959, 1-2; "Germans Cite Museum Aide," *New York Times*, Oct. 17, 1959, Joseph P. Hazen to Barr, Dec. 16, 1959, Roll 2184, AAA.

Page 295. **art market is "boiling":** Hodgins and Lesley, "International Art Market—I," 119; Hodgins and Lesley, "International Art Market—II," 122-23.

Page 295. **signaled a radical change:** Reitlinger, *Economics of Taste*, Vol. I, 231; Bonnie Burnham, *The Art Crisis* (New York: St. Martin's, 1975), 192; Richard H. Rush, *Art as an Investment* (Englewood Cliffs, NJ: Prentice-Hall, 1961), 1-2.

Page 296. **heralded a spectacular price rise:** John Parker, *Great Art Sales of the Century* (New York: Watson-Guptill, 1975), 41-42; Burnham, *Art Crisis*, 192-93; Reitlinger, *Economics of Taste*, Vol. I, 231-34.

Page 296. **"framed money":** Elaine Cannell, *Good Taste: How to Have it; How to Buy It* (New York: David McKay, 1978), 89; Reitlinger, *Economics of Taste*, Vol. I, 230.

Page 297. **began to look more attractive:** Hodgins and Lesley, "International Art Market—I," 119, 152; Levine, "Portrait of Sidney Janis," 53.

Page 297. **excited rapt attention:** Dorothy Miller to Barr, May 29, 1956, Roll 2181, AAA; interview with Dorothy Miller, May 31, 1986; Guggenheim, *Confessions of an Art Addict*, 171-73.

Page 298. **"not the result of indifference":** Barr, "Editor's Letters," *Art News*, Sept. 1957, 6, 56-57.

Page 298. **Andy Warhol brought his portfolio:** Interview with Irma Seitz, Dec. 12, 1986.

Page 298. **Barr became cautious:** Leonid Massine cable to Rose Fried, Feb. 13, 1957; Fried to Massine, Feb. 14, 1957; Massine to Fried, Nov. 15, 1957; Fried bill to Museum of Modern Art, Feb. 14, 1958, all Rose Fried Papers, AAA; Messer, *MOMA: Museum in Search of an Image*, 292-93; Leo Castelli, speech at the La Jolla (CA) Museum of Contemporary Art, Feb. 6, 1980.

Page 299. **Barr relied on the prestige:** Castelli speech at La Jolla Museum of Contemporary Art; Rose Fried to Barr, Sept. 2, 1959; Barr to Fried, Oct. 5, 1959; Fried to Barr, Oct. 8, 1959; Museum of Modern Art to Fried, March 26, 1965, all Rose Fried Papers, AAA.

Page 299. **he tended to become curt:** Aline B. Saarinen, "Success Story of Modern Art," *New York Times Magazine*, Oct. 5, 1958, 83; Sam Hunter to Barr, Feb. 11, 1959; Barr to Hunter, Mar. 16, 1959, both Roll 2184, AAA.

Page 300. **"with the eyes of our own generation"**: Walker, *Self-Portrait with Donors*, xviii, 27.

Page 300. **a flurry of anxiety**: Barr to Paul McSanyi, June 2, 1955; Barr memo to René d'Harnoncourt, May 10, 1956; James W. Husted to New York Secretary of State, Dept. of Corporations, Nov. 18, 1957; "Summary of Press Comments," Feb. 9, 1959, all Roll 2194, AAA.

Page 300. **a top-secret effort**: Stephen C. Clark to Barr, Jan. 13, 1955, Roll 3158, AAA; Martin Manhoff to Barr, April 17, 1954, Roll 3160, AAA.

Page 301. **sprang into frenzied activity**: Barr to William A. M. Burden, Jan. 4, 1955; Barr to John Hay Whitney, Jan. 6, 1955, both Roll 3158, AAA.

Page 302. **a white sheet of plain paper**: Untitled, undated sheet, Roll 3159, AAA; Barr to Marshall McDuffie, undated draft; Barr to William A. M. Burden, Jan. 21, 1955; Barr to David Rockefeller, Jan. 21, 1955, all Roll 3158, AAA.

Page 303. **"a real thaw here"**: Barr, excerpt from a letter in memo to Porter McCray, June 4, 1956, Roll 3159, AAA.

Page 303. **everything fell apart**: René d'Harnoncourt to Nelson Rockefeller, June 7, 1956; G. A. Orvid to William A. M. Burden, undated 1956, both Roll 3158, AAA; "U.S. Halts Soviet Cultural Trade," *New York Times*, Sept. 4, 1956; Nicolai V. Tchorny to Barr, Jan. 25, 1957, Roll 3158, AAA.

Page 304. **"to be as helpful as we can"**: Barr to Daniel Catton Rich, June 19, 1956; letters from Soviet museum officials to Barr, all Roll 3158, AAA.

Page 304. **Barr courted the Russians**: Barr to William A. M. Burden, Nov. 29, 1954, Roll 3158, AAA; interview with Porter McCray, June 6, 1986; "The Hermitage Treasures: II," *Time*, Feb. 11, 1957, 79.

Page 305. **foundered on the threat**: Museum of Modern Art, International Council invitation, Dec. 4, 1959, Roll 3149, AAA; Monroe Wheeler memo to René d'Harnoncourt, Mar. 9, 1966, Roll 2193, AAA.

Page 305. **stunningly illustrated article**: Barr to Virginia Evans, Mar. 9, 1959; Marie Alexander memo to Barr, undated 1959; Barr to Ruth Adams, Feb. 11, 1959; U.S. Information Agency purchase order, Jan. 30, 1959, all Roll 3261, AAA.

Page 305. **the Barrs arrived in Moscow**: "U.S. Abstract Art Arouses Russians," *New York Times*, June 11, 1959; Barr to Leslie Brady, May 21, 1959; Margaret Barr to Victoria Barr, June 22, 1959.

Page 306. **American exhibition in Moscow**: "Books Back at U.S. Fair in Moscow," clipping from *International Herald-Tribune*, Aug. 6, 1959; William V. Shannon, "The Blue Period," *New York Post*, undated clipping 1959, both Roll 3158, AAA; translation of article from *Soviet Culture*, Aug. 11, 1959, Roll 3159, AAA; "U.S. Abstract Art Arouses Russians", *New York Times*, June 11, 1959; John E. Bowlt, "Russian Paintings at the Met," *Art in America*, May–June 1957, 76.

Page 306. **unnerving mixture**: Elizabeth Jones in Barr, "Russian Diary," 55–56; Margaret S. Barr to Victoria Barr, June 22, 1959, Roll 3158, AAA.

Page 307. **infuriating relationship with Picasso**: Barr to Roland Penrose, April 20, 1956; Barr to Peggy Guggenheim, Sept. 13, 1955, Roll 2194, AAA; Penrose to Barr, Mar. 28 and May 11, 1956; Barr to Penrose, July 7, 1956, all Roll 2197, AAA; Douglas Cooper to Margaret S. Barr,

May 24, 1956, Roll 2193, AAA; Carl Nesjar to Patrick Kelleher, Oct. 3, 1969, Roll 2197, AAA.

Page 307. **summons came at last:** Margaret S. Barr to Barr, June 8, 1956; Museum of Modern Art purchase order No. 9408, July 5, 1956; Margaret S. Barr to Victoria Barr, undated July 1956, all Roll 2181, AAA.

Page 308. **"highly satisfactory":** Barr to Douglas Cooper, July 6, 1956, Roll 2193, AAA; "Picassos," *New Yorker*, June 15, 1957, 23.

Page 309. **most comprehensive Picasso exhibition:** "Picassos," 23–24; Frank Getlein, "Picasso at 75," *New Republic*, July 29, 1957, 18.

Page 309. **"exaggerated share of attention":** Philip Goodwin to Barr, Dec. 4, 1952, Roll 2179, AAA; interview with Libby Tannenbaum, June 2, 1986; Barr, "Portraits by Picasso," *New York Times Magazine*, May 19, 1957, 28.

Page 310. **started a fire:** Interview with Helen Franc, June 6, 1986; Russell Lynes, "When the MOMA Suffered a Fire," *Smithsonian*, May 1973, 60; "Museum with Bounce," *Newsweek*, April 28, 1958, 84–85.

Page 310. **fire had been the worst:** Interview with Helen Franc, June 6, 1986; interview with Larry Aldrich, June 5, 1986.

Page 311. **reopened the Seurat show:** "MOMA Re-opens All Galleries," *Museum News*, Oct. 15, 1958, 1–2; Lynes, *Good Old Modern*, 371; Marshall McDuffie to Barr, May 9, 1958; Barr to McDuffie, May 19, 1958; W. Barclay to Barr, April 16, 1958, all Roll 2183, AAA; Barbara Morgan to Barr, undated 1958, Roll 2184, AAA.

Page 311. **his favorite topic:** Charles McCurdy, proposal to compile a chronology of modern art 1850–1950, July 30, 1958, Roll 2184, AAA; "Painting and Politics, I and II," speeches at Sarasota Art Symposium, April 3 and 4, 1955, Roll 3149, AAA; untitled, undated notes, Roll 3155, AAA.

CHAPTER 11: THE DISCIPLES GO FORTH

Page 313. **symbolized a profound shift:** "News, Inaugural Committee 1961," release I-174; Barr cable to Kay Halle, Jan. 16, 1961; John L. Saltonstall to Barr, Nov. 4, 1960, all Roll 2199, AAA.

Page 314. **greater number of nonartists:** Barr to Sir Alfred Bossom, Dec. 1959, Roll 2183, AAA.

Page 314. **a host of powerful disciples:** Jean Lipman to Barr, May 12, 1958; Barr, "Nominations for *Art in America* Annual Award," Sept. 1958; Dorothy Miller to Antony Bower, Oct. 16, 1959; Jean Lipman to Barr, Sept. 1, 1959; E. P. Richardson to Barr, June 29, 1956; Paul Grigaut to Barr, June 29, 1956, and Nov. 4, 1959, all Roll 2183, AAA; College Art Association to all members, Nov. 1, 1967, Roll 2192, AAA.

Page 315. **"the character of pressure groups":** Subcommittee Report on the Proposed Journal of the Museum of Modern Art, undated 1959, Roll 3153, AAA.

Page 315. **Barr's point of view:** Barr to H. W. Janson, Mar. 10, 1959; Janson to Barr, Mar. 15, 1959, both Roll 2184, AAA; H. W. Janson, *History of Art* (Englewood Cliffs, NJ: Prentice-Hall, 1969), 601; Patricia Hills, "Art History Textbooks: The Hidden Persuaders," *Artforum*, June 1976, 61.

Page 315. **left a heavy imprint**: Horst de la Croix and Richard G. Tansey, *Gardner's Art Through the Ages* (New York: Harcourt, Brace, Jovanovich, 1975), 770; Barr, *Cubism and Abstract Art*, 2; H. H. Arnason, *History of Modern Art* (Englewood Cliffs, NJ: Prentice-Hall and New York: Abrams, 1968).

Page 316. **"What he bought . . ."**: Interview with Libby Tannenbaum, June 2, 1986.

Page 317. **wrote frankly about art prices**: John Canaday, "A Quiet Market," *New York Times*, Feb. 28, 1960; John Canaday, "It Talks Good," *New York Times*, Mar. 6, 1960.

Page 317. **"more than embarrassed"**: Barr to John Canaday, Sept. 15, 1960, Roll 2192, AAA.

Page 318. **dust would not settle**: John Canaday, "Odd Forms of Modern Criticism," *New York Times*, Oct. 23, 1960; Howard Conant to Arthur Hays Sulzberger, Nov. 23, 1960; Sulzberger to Conant, Nov. 30, 1960, both Roll 2192, AAA.

Page 318. **"one foot in the grave"**: John Canaday, *Embattled Critic* (New York: Noonday, 1962), 3, 34–35.

Page 319. **Canaday lightheartedly noted**: Canaday, *Embattled Critic*, 219–38.

Page 319. **one of the weekly lunches**: Orville Dryfoos to Barr, Mar. 1, 1961; Barr to files, Mar. 3, 1961, both Roll 2192, AAA.

Page 320. **Barr tried just once more**: Barr to John Canaday, fourth draft, undated 1951; William Seitz to Barr, Aug. 16, 1961; Canaday to Barr, Nov. 24, 1961; Barr to Canaday, Nov. 30, 1961, all Roll 2192, AAA; Barr memo to Betsy Jones, Aug. 23, 1961, Roll 3151, AAA.

Page 320. **a modified alternative gospel**: John Canaday, *Mainstreams of Modern Art* (New York: Holt, Rinehart & Winston, 1964).

Page 321. **increasingly handcuffed by petty details**: Barr to Werner Haftmann, Feb. 20, 1961, Roll 2186, AAA; Betsy Jones memo to Barr, Oct. 21, 1963, Roll 2195, AAA; Barr to John B. Scotford, Jr., June 9, 1964; Barr to Allen F. Hurlburt, Aug. 24, 1965, both Roll 2186, AAA; interview with Michael J. Gladstone, June 16, 1986.

Page 321. **"he has left me my senses"**: Mrs. Alfred H. Barr, Sr., to Barr, Sept. 4 and 11, 1957, both Roll 2183, AAA.

Page 322. **exceedingly formal and perfunctory**: Barr to Andrew W. Barr, June 1, 1957; Barr to Mrs. Julius Ochs Adler, Sept. 19, 1956, both Roll 2181, AAA; Barr to Robert Osborn, April 1, 1968, Roll 2197, AAA.

Page 322. **insisted on becoming a painter**: Mily Staempfli to Barr, undated May 1965, Roll 2188, AAA; Betsy Jones to Christian Sorenson, July 12, 1966, Roll 2193, AAA; James T. Soby to Margaret S. Barr, July 5, 1966, Roll 2198, AAA; interview with Larry Aldrich, June 5, 1986.

Page 322. **a siege of poor health**: Barr to Roland Penrose, June 7, 1960, Roll 2197, AAA; Betsy Jones memo to Mrs. Woodruff, July 18, 1960, Roll 2188, AAA; Barr to E. P. Richardson, May 12, 1961, Roll 2195, AAA; Barr to Edward M. M. Warburg, Feb. 1, 1962, Roll 2188, AAA; Barr to Douglas Cooper, May 1, 1962, Roll 2193, AAA.

Page 323. **"did not want to share a bedroom"**: Interview with John Rewald, June 3, 1986.

Page 323. **he had to insist again:** Interview with John Rewald, June 3, 1986.

Page 323. **romantically lush and leisured:** Barr, handwritten calendar for trip in May, June, July 1962, Roll 3260, AAA; Barr, "What I Want to See on My First Visit to Greece," *Vogue*, Sept. 1, 1962, 211.

Page 324. **thirty-one species:** Barr to Blanchette Rockefeller, Aug. 23, 1962, Roll 3259, AAA.

Page 324. **became even more depressed:** Barr to Carlo L. Ragghianti, April 7, 1960, Roll 2187, AAA; Barr to Earle Ludgin, Jan. 30, 1961, Roll 2189, AAA; Barr to Libby Tannenbaum, April 12, 1967, Roll 2198, AAA.

Page 324. **devils had haunted:** Barr to Truman B. Douglass, Dec. 21, 1964, Roll 3148, AAA; Donald Galler to Barr, undated Aug. 1961; Barr to Galler, Sept. 19, 1961, both Roll 2186, AAA; Barr to the editor, *New York Herald-Tribune*, July 11, 1960, Roll 2194, AAA; Barr to the editor, *Hartford Courant*, Dec. 18, 1964, Roll 2187, AAA.

Page 325. **a wild new group of artists:** Tomkins, *The Scene: Reports on Postmodern Art* (New York: Viking, 1976), 18; David Sylvester, "Comment," *Studio International*, Sept. 1967, 79.

Page 325. **"the artist who decides what is art":** Tomkins, *The Scene*, 16–17, 19.

Page 326. **mourned the passing of an age:** Douglas Cooper, "Establishment and Avant-Garde," *Times Literary Supplement*, Sept. 3, 1964, 823–24; "The Changing Guard," *Times Literary Supplement*, Aug. 6, 1964, 675–76; Donald D. Egbert, "The Idea of the Avant-Garde in Art and Politics," *American Historical Review*, Dec. 1967, 365.

Page 326. **it was a difficult time:** Sidney Tillim, "Month in Review," *Arts*, Feb. 1962, 37; William Seitz to Barr, Sept. 2, 1962, Roll 2187, AAA; Edward M. M. Warburg to Barr, Jan. 22, 1962; Barr to Warburg, Feb. 1, 1962, both Roll 2188, AAA.

Page 327. **tried hard to resist the conservatism:** Walker, *Self-Portrait with Donors*, xviii; interview with Richard Koch, June 17, 1986.

Page 328. **"structure is such that":** Barr to Mrs. Heyward Isham, Dec. 6, 1960, Roll 2186, AAA.

Page 328. **"turned into a stone statue":** Interview with Eliza Bliss Parkinson Cobb, Dec. 15, 1986.

Page 328. **Barr had helped Nelson to buy:** Nelson Rockefeller to Barr, Mar. 3, 1934; Barr to Nelson Rockefeller, Mar. 8, and 13, 1934; Nelson Rockefeller to Barr, Mar. 14, 1934, all Roll 2165, AAA; Douglas Cooper, ed., *Great Private Collections* (London: Weidenfeld & Nicolson, 1965), 273; Barr to Tod Rockefeller, Nov. 22, 1934, Roll 2165, AAA; interview with Edgar Kaufmann, June 2, 1986.

Page 329. **accumulated art in great drifts:** MOMA, *Twentieth Century Art from the Nelson Aldrich Rockefeller Collection* (New York: New York Graphic Society, 1969), 6; "Capitalizing on a Collection," *Time*, Nov. 13, 1978, 101; Burt, *Palaces for the People*, 5; "René d'Harnoncourt Dead at 67," *New York Times*, Aug. 14, 1968; interview with Libby Tannenbaum, June 2, 1986; Barr to Kazuo Nakamura, Nov. 21, 1961, Roll 2188, AAA; Michael Rockefeller to Barr, Jan. 1, 1958; Barr to Michael Rockefeller, Feb. 18, 1958, both Roll 2198, AAA; Barr to Marie Alexander, June or July 1960, Roll 2181, AAA.

Page 330. **"the greatest recreation":** Lieberman, *Nelson A. Rockefeller Collection*, 47; *Twentieth Century Art from the Nelson Aldrich Rockefeller*

Collection, 9; Barr, untitled draft for *Art in America*, undated 1965, Roll 2189, AAA; Francine du Plessix, "Anatomy of a Collector: Nelson A. Rockefeller," *Art in America*, April 1965, 27.

Page 330. **massive parade of masterpieces:** Lieberman, *Nelson A. Rockefeller Collection*, 23–24, 37–38.

Page 330. **"practically called us liars":** James Thrall Soby to William Paley, Mar. 9, 1962, Roll 2198, AAA; Soby to A. Conger Goodyear, April 6, 1962, Roll 2194, AAA.

Page 330. **she was furious:** Dorothy Norman to Barr, Nov. 28, 1967, Roll 2197, AAA.

Page 330. **relished the courtship:** Barr to James Thrall Soby, July 18, 1952, Roll 2181, AAA; Peggy Guggenheim to Barr, Aug. 23, 1954, Roll 2194, AAA; "Venerable Bohemian of Venice," *Life*, June 18, 1965, 101–4; John H. Davis, *The Guggenheims: An American Epic* (New York: Morrow, 1978), 461; Barr to Peggy Guggenheim, Dec. 27, 1961; Guggenheim to Barr, Jan. 8, 1962, both Roll 2194, AAA.

Page 331. **Clark's total disregard:** "Charity and Art Willed Millions," *New York Times*, Sept. 30, 1960; "Extended Loans," *Annual Report 1941–42*, Museum of Modern Art, Roll 2199, AAA; "Mr. Clark's Bequests," *New York Times*, Oct. 1, 1960.

Page 331. **Even more galling:** Barr to A. Conger Goodyear, June 6, 1960; Barr to Peggy Guggenheim, July 1, 1953, both Roll 2194, AAA; Barr to Goodyear, June 30, 1960, Roll 2179, AAA.

Page 332. **Barr was irate:** Barr to A. Conger Goodyear, June 6, 1960; Goodyear to Barr, June 10 and July 7, 1960; Goodyear to Blanchette Rockefeller, Jan. 9, 1962; James Thrall Soby to Goodyear, Mar. 18, 1962; Soby to Blanchette Rockefeller and René d'Harnoncourt, Mar. 26, 1962; Gordon M. Smith to d'Harnoncourt, Jan. 15, 1964; Barr to Smith, Feb. 14, 1964; Smith to Barr, Feb. 29, 1964; Smith to d'Harnoncourt, Nov. 20, 1964, all Roll 2194, AAA.

Page 333. **a visual propaganda coup:** Barr, "The Museum Collections—A Bid for Space," copy for wall label, Nov. 16, 1959, Roll 2181, AAA; Museum of Modern Art, *Annual Report*, 1960–61, MOMA Archive.

Page 333. **a media event:** "List of Contributors," *New York Times*, Feb. 3, 1956; "Benefit Sales," *Arts*, April 1960, 11.

Page 333. **"absolutely overwhelmed all this year":** Barr to Douglas Cooper, Jan. 15, 1960, Roll 2193, AAA; Barr to Eugene S. Jones, April 4, 1960, Roll 2187, AAA; Barr to Alex Hillman, Nov. 7, 1960, Roll 2186, AAA; interview with Richard Koch, June 17, 1986.

Page 334. **crammed to the rafters:** Barr, *Painting and Sculpture in the Museum of Modern Art 1929–1967*, xiii; *Toward the New Museum of Modern Art*, pamphlet, 1960, 19–21.

Page 334. **an elaborate blueprint emerged:** "Agenda for Weekend at Sea Change," Aug. 1959; Ellen McKethan memo to Barr, July 14, 1959; Elizabeth Shaw memo to Barr, Aug. 3, 1959, all Roll 3260, AAA; Museum of Modern Art thirtieth-anniversary dinner guest list and time schedule, undated 1959, Roll 3259, AAA.

Page 335. **"bursting at the seams":** Draft of prospectus, Oct. 15, 1959, and revision, Oct. 26, 1959; Barr, text for speech by Henry Allan Moe, Nov. 16, 1959, all Roll 3259, AAA.

Page 335. **"an attraction unique to the city"**: *Toward the New Museum of Modern Art* (New York: Museum of Modern Art, 1959), 10-11, 30-31, 37.

Page 335. **truly staggering**: Barr, "A Presentation to the Rockefeller Foundation," Oct. 21, 1960, 8, 19-21, 26-27, 39, 46, Roll 3259, AAA.

Page 336. **an idealistic staff**: Dorothy Miller to Joseph Cantor, Jan. 25, 1962, Roll 2193, AAA; Barr to Linda Dubinsky, July 20, 1961, Roll 2168, AAA.

Page 337. **"anyone with adequate discipline"**: Barr to Edward Fry, Feb. 14, 1967, Roll 3146, AAA.

Page 337. **The arteries hardened**: Porter McCray to Ben Heller, Mar. 27, 1961, Roll 2195, AAA; Bates Lowry, untitled handbill, Mar. 30, 1969, Roll 2196, AAA; Barr, *The Museum of Modern Art, New York*, typed booklet, Sept.-Nov. 1936, Roll 3260, AAA.

Page 337. **"a form of enriching plasma"**: Kenneth Hudson, *A Social History of Museums* (Atlantic Highlands, NJ: Humanities Press, 1975), 113-14; John Canaday, *Culture Gulch: Notes on Art and Its Public in the 1960's* (New York: Farrar, Straus & Giroux, 1969), 164; Tim Yohn, "Cultural Contradictions of Capitalism," *Artforum*, Dec. 1976, 61; Julien Levy to Barr, Nov. 17, 1962, Roll 2187, AAA.

Page 338. **inevitably joined the mainstream**: Jacqueline Kennedy to René d'Harnoncourt, Feb. 5, 1962; John F. Kennedy to Barr, Sept. 8, 1961, both Roll 2199, AAA; Barr to S. Dillon Ripley, Feb. 21, 1961, Roll 2193, AAA; clipping from *New York Times*, undated 1961, Roll 2197, AAA.

Page 338. **"What was one to do . . .?"**: A. Romanov, "Mr. Barr's Souvenir," *Art News*, Jan. 1962, 30-31, 51.

Page 338. **Barr leaped into action**: Barr to Thomas B. Hess, Jan. 31, 1962; Edward Saratov to Barr, Aug. 23, 1961; Barr to Jay Leyda, Aug. 23, 1961; Barr, Notes from a conversation with Harrison Salisbury, Sept. 25, 1961, all Roll 3261, AAA.

Page 339. **a cordial correspondence**: Celebration committee to Barr, undated 1961; Barr to Dr. Levinson-Lessing, Dec. 26, 1961; Dimitri Orbeli to Barr, Mar. 24, 1969; Barr to Yevgeni Yevtushenko, Nov. 12, 1966; Perry Rathbone to Barr, June 2, 1966; Barr to Rathbone, June 10, 1966; Rathbone to Barr, June 17, 1966; Barr to Mary Hochschild, April 27, 1965, all Roll 2186, AAA.

Page 339. **"a venerated name there"**: Interview with Hilton Kramer, June 17, 1986.

Page 340. **Barr lent his powerful voice**: Barr, Statement to the National Council of the Arts, undated April 1968; Barr to Kate Steinitz, July 20, 1965, both Roll 3261, AAA.

Page 340. **"scribble a mustache"**: Barr, "Homage to New York," handbill, Mar. 17, 1960, MOMA Archive.

Page 341. **"either too solemn or too giddy"**: Brian O'Doherty, "Art: Furniture Comedy," *New York Times*, April 19, 1963.

Page 341. **"the vulgarity and banality"**: Barr, draft of remarks for National Council of Churches Commission on Art, Nov. 9, 1957, Roll 2184, AAA.

Page 341. **he had no time or energy**: Barr to Martin Halverson, May 8, 1962;

Foundation for the Arts, Religion, and Culture, Inc., minutes of organizational board meeting, May 10, 1962; Barr to Truman B. Douglass, May 9, 1965, all Roll 3148, AAA; Barr to Philip H. Hiss, April 28, 1962; "Statement by Barr," Conference on Educational Objectives, New College, Sarasota, FL, Apr. 5-6, 1962; Barr to John W. Gustad, Aug. 18, 1963, all Roll 2197, AAA.

Page 342. **his health was increasingly frail**: Barr to John Richardson, Mar. 20, 1963, Roll 2186, AAA; Bryan Robertson to Barr, Feb. 11, 1964; Barr to Lawrence M. C. Smith, Feb. 14, 1964, both Roll 2187, AAA; Barr to E. H. Fletcher, Feb. 24, 1964; Barr to Scott Hodes, July 15, 1964, both Roll 2186, AAA; Dorothy Miller to Jean Lipman, Sept. 3, 1965; Barr to Mr. and Mrs. Joseph Akston, Jan. 18, 1966, both Roll 2189, AAA; interview with Larry Aldrich, June 5, 1986; interview with Monroe Wheeler, June 18, 1986; interview with Hilton Kramer, June 17, 1986.

CHAPTER 12: THE ESTABLISHED CHURCH

Page 343. **more than he had ever received**: Interview with Larry Aldrich, June 5, 1986.

Page 343. **project looked annoyingly ludicrous**: Bates Lowry to Joseph H. McDaniel, Jan. 14, 1969, Roll 2196, AAA; Dorothy Miller to Perry Rathbone, July 8, 1972, Roll 3159, AAA; Rona K. Roob to Warren Schmidt, Mar. 7, 1973, Roll 2198, AAA.

Page 344. **a grand capstone to Barr's career**: Monawee Richards memo to Dorothy Miller, July 25, 1977, Roll 2196, AAA.

Page 344. **description of Barr**: "Mr. Barr," *Newsweek*, July 31, 1967, 77; Katharine Kuh, "Alfred Barr: Modern Art's Durable Crusader," *Saturday Review*, Sept. 00, 1967, 53; Barr to Margo Plass, June 30, 1967, Roll 2197, AAA.

Page 346. **"it should not be shown elsewhere"**: Barr memo to Bates Lowry, Jan. 31, 1969, Roll 2196, AAA.

Page 346. **yet another fund-raising drive**: "Toward the New Museum of Modern Art," undated pamphlet, MOMA Archive; Kuh, "Alfred Barr"; "Steering Committee Report," April 21, 1970; Walter N. Thayer memo to Barr, Dec. 22, 1969, Roll 2196, AAA.

Page 346. **begged Barr for articles**: Cleve Gray to Barr, Nov. 27, 1968, Roll 2193, AAA; Jean Lipman to Barr, May 21, 1970; Barr to Lipman, June 3, 1970; Creighton Gilbert to Barr, Oct. 7, 1973; Barr to Gilbert, Oct. 17, 1973, all Roll 2189, AAA; Barr to Judith B. Jones, April 30, 1963, Roll 2187, AAA.

Page 346. **noticed his deterioration**: Interview with Philip Johnson, Dec. 17, 1986; James Thrall Soby to Margaret S. Barr, Mar. 15, 1967, Roll 2198, AAA; interview with Alicia Legg, June 16, 1986; interview with Helen Franc, June 6, 1986.

Page 347. **suffered from his memory lapses**: Barr to Dominique de Menil, Mar. 1, 1968, Roll 2196, AAA; Barr to Mrs. Eleanore Saidenberg, June 7, 1968, Roll 2198, AAA; Barr to John Bauer, Oct. 8, 1968, Roll 2189, AAA.

Page 347. **"hope to have a good rest":** Barr to Larry Aldrich, May 27, 1969, Roll 2189, AAA; David Rockefeller to Barr, Aug. 4, 1969, Roll 2192, AAA; Barr to Dwight Berry, Dec. 5, 1969, Roll 2189, AAA.

Page 347. **had given his entire career:** W. S. Lieberman, Statement for work, Jan. 26, 1948, Roll 3150, AAA.

Page 348. **"really extraordinary":** James Thrall Soby to Barr, July 15, 1969; Barr to Soby, Mar. 29, 1968, both Roll 2198, AAA.

Page 349. **an extraordinary hoard of modern pictures:** Margaret Potter, *Four Americans in Paris* (New York: Museum of Modern Art, 1970), 10; E. J. Kahn, Jr., *Jock: The Life and Times of John Hay Whitney* (New York: Doubleday, 1981), 127–28; "Gertrude Stein's Pictures to MOMA," *Art News*, Feb. 1969, 10.

Page 349. **Barr cantankerously carped:** Barr, Notes on the release about the Stein Collection, Jan. 9, 1969, Roll 2196, AAA.

Page 350. **"tactful generalist and humanist":** Lynes, *Good Old Modern*, 421.

Page 350. **beset from every direction:** Therese Schwartz, "Politicalization of the Avant-Garde," *Art in America*, Nov. 1971, 103; Grace Glueck, "Power and Aesthetics," *Art in America*, July 1971, 78.

Page 350. **Hightower was confronted:** Lynes, *Good Old Modern*, 420, 422–25.

Page 350. **a blunt, frontal attack:** Lynes, *Good Old Modern*, 427–30.

Page 351. **islands of privilege and wealth:** Grace Glueck, "Power and Aesthetics," *Art in America*, July 1971, 78, 81–82.

Page 352. **Barr was fading from the scene:** Jack Tworkov to Barr, Nov. 21, 1967; Jan van der Marck to Barr, July 28, 1967; J. L. Franklin to Barr, June 2, 1967; undated note of a telephone conversation with John Walker, 1964, all Roll 2195, AAA.

Page 352. **the last of the great European masters:** Barr to John Russell, April 21, 1969, Roll 2198, AAA; Introduction, "Picasso: Pillar of Tradition," Spencer Trask Lecture, Princeton, Mar. 18, 1969, Roll 3149, AAA.

Page 352. **"I hope to be wise enough":** Lemma J. Endersby to Barr, Mar. 12, 1969, Roll 3149, AAA; Barr to John Russell, April 21, 1969, Roll 2198, AAA.

Page 352. **a series of monumental sculptures:** Patrick J. Kelleher, *The Sculpture of Princeton University: The John B. Putnam, Jr., Memorial Collection* (Princeton, NJ: Communications/Publications, Stanhope Hall, 1982).

Page 353. **Barr harshly criticized:** Barr, "Informal Oral Report to Overseers on *Fine Arts*," Mar. 10, 1968, Roll 3150, AAA.

Page 354. **Barr was excited and impressed:** Interview with Larry Aldrich, June 5, 1986.

Page 354. **a hideous diagnosis:** James Thrall Soby to Barr, June 12, 1971, Roll 3265, AAA; penciled note by Rona Roob at the foot of Ruth and Joachim E. Meyer to Margaret S. Barr, Oct. 10, 1985; Margaret S. Barr to Edward S. King, Aug. 22, 1981, both Roll 3145, AAA; Barr to Patrick J. Kelleher, Sept. 21, 1971, Roll 2197, AAA.

Page 354. **"you've taken so much time":** Grace Glueck, "Barr Gets Sandy Award," *New York Times*, April 21, 1972.

Page 354. **tragic change in Barr's behavior:** Barr pocket diaries, 1970–1975, Roll 3260, AAA; interview with Eloise Spaeth, June 6, 1986; Barr to

Tom L. Freudenheim, undated 1973, Roll 2189, AAA; Margaret S. Barr to Hirshhorn Museum, Aug. 26, 1974, Roll 2195, AAA.

Page 355. **unable to savor the triumph:** "Kunstpreis an U.S. Professor," *Muenstersche Zeitung*, Oct. 24, 1974, clipping in MOMA Archive; Albert Elsen to Barr, Feb. 4, 1975, Roll 2192, AAA.

Page 355. **a wan and shrunken figure:** Sam Hunter, intro., *The Museum of Modern Art* (New York: Abrams, 1984), 34; Sandler and Newman, *Defining Modern Art*, 273.

Page 355. **a final desperate effort:** Rona Roob memo to files, June 23, 1984, Roll 3260, AAA; interview with John Rewald, June 3, 1986.

Page 356. **buried without fanfare:** Interview with Helen Franc, Oct. 10, 1988; Rev. Frank O. Reed to Margaret S. Barr, Aug. 29, 1981; Margaret S. Barr mailgram to Victoria Barr, Aug. 16, 1981; Margaret S. Barr to Edward S. King, Aug. 22, 1981, all Roll 3145, AAA.

Page 356. **"the soul of the modern":** Grace Glueck, "Alfred Hamilton Barr, Jr., Is Dead," *New York Times*, Aug. 16, 1981; "Mr. Alfred Barr," London *Times*, Sept. 4, 1981; "Art World," *Art in America*, Oct. 1981, 218; "Alfred H. Barr, Jr.," *Art News*, Nov. 1981, 166–67.

Page 357. **"the lodestar of the profession":** Calvin Tomkins, "Alfred Barr," *New Yorker*, Nov. 16, 1981, 184–85; interview with Philip Johnson, Dec. 17, 1986; Perry Rathbone to Margaret S. Barr, Oct. 5, 1981, Roll 3145, AAA; M. Sharp Young, "Alfred H. Barr, Jr.," *Apollo*, Feb. 1982, 120–21.

Page 357. **also expressed their sadness:** Alicia Legg to Margaret S. Barr, Aug. 25, 1981; Bernard Karpel to Margaret S. Barr, Oct. 21, 1981; Elizabeth Shaw, date missing but probably 1981; Jere Abbott to Margaret S. Barr, Aug. 17, 1981, all Roll 3145, AAA.

Page 357. **"it influenced my life":** Press release, Haber Theodore Gallery, undated 1982, MOMA Archive.

Page 358. **a handsome illustrated brochure:** *Alfred H. Barr, Jr.: A Memorial Tribute* (New York: Museum of Modern Art, 1981); text of memorial tribute to Barr by Beaumont Newhall, undated 1981, Roll 3145, AAA.

Page 358. **more an icon than a man:** *Alfred H. Barr, Jr.: A Memorial Tribute*; Philip Johnson, draft of memorial tribute to Barr, undated 1981, Roll 3145, AAA.

Page 359. **"the passionate logic of his defense":** Johnson, memorial tribute to Barr.

Page 360. **"now it is an investment":** Walker, *Self-Portrait with Donors*, 25.

Page 361. **his most glaring professional weakness:** Interview with William Rubin, June 4, 1986.

Page 363. **"do the work of an evangelist":** II Timothy 4:5.

Page 363. **"distinction of quality from mediocrity":** Interview with Philip Johnson, Dec. 17, 1986; Calvin Tomkins, "Alfred Barr," *New Yorker*, Nov. 16, 1981, 184–85.

INDEX